POLITICAL
ANALYSIS

D0220716

Series Editors:
B.Guy Peters, Jon Pierre
and Gerry Stoker

Political science today is a dynamic discipline. Its substance, theory and methods have all changed radically in recent decades. It is much expanded in range and scope and in the variety of new perspectives – and new variants of old ones – that it encompasses. The sheer volume of work being published and the increasing degree of its specialization, however, make it difficult for political scientists to maintain a clear grasp of the state of debate beyond their own particular sub-disciplines.

The Political Analysis series is intended to provide a channel for different parts of the discipline to talk to one another and to new generations of students. Our aim is to publish books that provide introductions to, and exemplars of, the best work in various areas of the discipline. Written in an accessible style, they will provide a 'launching-pad' for students and others seeking a clear grasp of the key methodological, theoretical and empirical issues, and the main areas of debate, in the complex and fragmented world of political science.

A particular priority will be to facilitate intellectual exchange between academic communities in different parts of the world. Although frequently addressing the same intellectual issues, research agendas and literatures in North America, Europe and elsewhere have often tended to develop in relative isolation from one another. This series is designed to provide a framework for dialogue and debate which, rather than advocacy of one regional approach or another, is the key to progress.

The series will reflect our view that the core values of political science should be coherent and logically constructed theory, matched by carefully constructed and exhaustive empirical investigation. The key challenge is to ensure quality and integrity in what is produced rather than to constrain diversity in methods and approaches. The series will provide a showcase for the best of political science in all its variety, and demonstrate how nurturing that variety can further improve the discipline.

POLITICAL
ANALYSIS

Series Editors:
B.Guy Peters, Jon Pierre
and Gerry Stoker

Published

Colin Hay
Political Analysis

Jon Pierre and B. Guy Peters
Governance, Politics and the State

Cees van der Eijk and Mark N. Franklin
Elections and Voters

Forthcoming

Peter Burnham, Wyn Grant, Zig Layton-Henry and Peter John
Research Methods in Politics

Vivien Lowndes
Why Institutions Matter

David Marsh
Political Behaviour

David Marsh and Gerry Stoker
Theory and Methods in Political Science (2nd edn)

Martin Smith
Power, Politics and the State

Political Analysis Series
Series Standing Order
ISBN 0–333–78694–7 hardback
ISBN 0–333–94506–9 paperback
(**outside North America only**)

You can receive future titles in this series as they are published by placing a standing order. Please contact your bookseller or, in case of difficulty, write to us at the address below with your name and address, the title of the series and one of the ISBNs quoted above.

Customer Services Department, Macmillan Distribution Ltd, Houndmills, Basingstoke, Hampshire RG21 6XS, England

Elections and Voters

Cees van der Eijk
and
Mark N. Franklin

palgrave
macmillan

© Cees van der Eijk and Mark N. Franklin 2009

First published 2009 by
PALGRAVE MACMILLAN

Palgrave Macmillan in the UK is an imprint of Macmillan Publishers Limited,
registered in England, company number 785998, of Houndmills, Basingstoke,
Hampshire RG21 6XS.

Palgrave Macmillan in the US is a division of St Martin's Press LLC,
175 Fifth Avenue, New York, NY 10010.

Palgrave Macmillan is the global academic imprint of the above companies
and has companies and representatives throughout the world.

Palgrave® and Macmillan® are registered trademarks in the United States,
the United Kingdom, Europe and other countries.

ISBN 978–1–4039–4127–5   hardback
ISBN 978–1–4039–4128–2   paperback

This book is printed on paper suitable for recycling and made from fully
managed and sustained forest sources. Logging, pulping and manufacturing
processes are expected to conform to the environmental regulations of the
country of origin.

A catalogue record for this book is available from the British Library.

A catalog record for this book is available from the Library of Congress.

10 9 8 7 6 5 4 3 2 1
18 17 16 15 14 13 12 11 10 09

Printed in Great Britain by CIP Antony Rowe, Chippenham and Eastbourne

Contents

List of Figures, Tables and Boxes

Figures

Tables

Boxes

Preface and Acknowledgements

This is a book about elections and voters. It is intended as a textbook for those who want a general introduction to the topic; but it is not first and foremost concerned with imparting exhaustive factual knowledge about the nuts and bolts of electoral systems, voting arrangements, party systems and policy differences. Such a book would necessarily focus on only part of what we want to cover, and such books (each one dealing with only a part of our agenda) already exist. This is primarily a book about the logic of representative democracy and about the role of the electoral process within this logic. We see elections as opportunities for strategic action on the part of voters and politicians, and we try to explain how election outcomes should be understood as resulting from the interplay of preferences and strategies, which in turn are constrained and channelled by institutional arrangements and communication structures. We hope to provide a picture of how electoral democracy works, together with an assessment of how well it works, using a complete (though not exhaustive) set of tools and theories as employed at the cutting edge of political science research. This is a book about what has been called 'the wider agenda of electoral research' (Thomassen 2000), and we will attempt to integrate theories about specific aspects of the electoral process, including theories about electoral systems, coalition formation, voter motivation and mobilization, political communication, and so on. We try to relate all these theories to one another in an encompassing view of electoral democracy.

We also try to clarify some important reasons as to why politics in different countries has a different flavour: not because voters are different in different countries, and seldom because of differences in political leadership, but more usually because institutions and party systems are different. Though there are of course differences in individual values – and historical differences with a contemporary resonance in terms of social structure – we see systemic characteristics as being fundamental in explaining why party systems differ from country to country, why political leaders approach elections differently, and why voters make their choices in different terms. Because the characters of electoral and other institutions are so fundamental, and because these institutions differ primarily between countries (and only secondarily over time), in our view elections and voters can only be understood comparatively. That is what we try to do.

The countries that we study are mainly established democracies, where the electorates of today have only democratic life experiences. However, from time to time we do refer to democracies that are not yet established, and in Chapter 7 we devote an entire section to the analysis of voting behavior in the countries of Central Europe that recently became members of the European Union.

The knowledge base on which we build this story is incomplete, but still we try to give a complete and coherent picture, filling in gaps by extrapolating from cognate knowledge and sometimes even by speculation (though we try to be absolutely clear about the basis in political science research for the claims that we make). As such, this book is an invitation to readers to think along with us and bring to our framework specific information that they may have about political systems and periods that we cannot provide in a volume of this compass. Thus we provide a skeleton that can be fleshed out by the reader – or by an instructor using this book as a classroom text. For such usage additional materials are available on the website that accompanies this book (http://www.palgrave.com/politics/votersandelections).

The authors and publishers would like to thank Cambridge University Press for permission to use Figures 3.2 and 3.3, originally published in *Voter Turnout and the Dynamics of Electoral Competition in Established Democracies since 1945* by Mark N. Franklin, with Cees van der Eijk, Diana Evans, Michael Fotos, Wolfgang Hirczy de Mino, Michael Marsh and Bernard Wessels, Copyright © 2004 Mark N. Franklin; and Blackwell Wiley for permission to use Figure 4.4 originally published in *Party Identification and Beyond* by I. Budge *et al.*, 1976. Every effort has been made to contact all the copyright-holders, but if any have been inadvertently omitted the publishers will be pleased to make the appropriate arrangement at the earliest opportunity.

Because we have had to stretch so widely for findings on which to base our story, we owe debts of gratitude to many individuals and groups. Intellectually our greatest debts are to: Eric Schattschneider, who most eloquently pointed out that politics is a strategic game played simultaneously on several boards; David Easton and Karl Deutsch, who stressed the fruitfulness of a systems perspective on social and political affairs; Arend Lijphart and Bingham Powell, upon whose comparative findings about elections and voting this book leans heavily; and James Stimson and Christopher Wlezien, whose insights about long term change are fundamental to our own insights into dynamic processes.

In practical terms, our first debt of gratitude is to members of the European Elections Study research group with whom we have worked for over 20 years, amassing empirical data about the electoral process in highly comparable terms across the ever-widening group of countries that are members of what is now called the European Union. These data, though ostensibly concerned with elections to the European Parliament, have been shown to be exceedingly helpful in revealing features of national elections that had previously been obscure. Among members of the EES research group we are particularly indebted to Wouter van der Brug, Michael Marsh, Hermann Schmitt and Jacques Thomassen for sharing with us their insights and expertise.

The book originated as a set of lectures (each one following an hour-long transatlantic telephone conversation, and given to students at Trinity College Connecticut); the responses by three different classes of these students were important in helping to hone our approach. A little later, Sam Abrams helped prepare the dataset from which US cohort analyses were generated. More recently the entire manuscript was read by PhD students at the European University Institute and the University of Nottingham – Jessica Andersson, Elias Dinas, Carolien van Ham, Jonathan Rose and Till Weber – who meticulously pointed out errors and (some major) omissions, and suggested organizational changes. We are grateful for Allison Pearson's help with bibliographical information and assistance in preparing the book in its final form. We should not fail to mention our publisher, Steven Kennedy, who – apart from his considerable diplomatic skills (not to mention patience) in the face of repeated delays – also read the book several times and made insightful comments.

Our greatest debts, as always, are to our spouses Kitty and Diane, for their support and encouragement.

CEES VAN DER EIJK
MARK N. FRANKLIN

Other books by Cees van der Eijk:

The Multilevel Electoral System of the EU (with Hermann Schmitt) (Mannheim: Connex) 2008

European Elections and Domestic Politics: Lessons from the Past and Scenarios for the Future (with Wouter van der Brug) (Notre Dame, IN: University of Notre Dame Press) 2007

The Economy and the Vote – Economic Conditions and Elections in Fifteen Countries (with Wouter van der Brug and Mark N. Franklin) (Cambridge: Cambridge University Press) 2007

Een politieke aardverschuiving; een kritische blik op de verkiezingen van 2002 en 2003 [A political Landslide – The elections of 2002 and 2003] (with Robbert Coops a.o.) (Alphen a.d. Rijn: Kluwer) 2003

De Kern van de Politiek [The Essence of Politics] (Amsterdam: Het Spinhuis) 2001

Citizen Participation in European Politics (with Hans Agné a.o.) (Stockholm: Statens Offentliga Utredningar) 2000

In Search of Structure. Essays in Methodology and Social Science (with Meindert Fennema and Huibert Schijf) (Amsterdam: Het Spinhuis) 1998

Choosing Europe? The European Electorate and National Politics in the Face of Union (with Mark N. Franklin) (Ann Arbor: University of Michigan Press)1996

Verkiezingen zonder Mandaat - Politieke Communicatie en Provinciale Verkiezingen, [Absent Mandate: Political Communication and Regional Elections] (with Ingrid van der Geest a.o.) (Den Haag: Sdu) 1992

De Nederlandse Kiezer '86 [The Dutch Voter in 1986] (with Joop van Holsteyn a.o.) (Amsterdam: Swidoc) 1987

De Strijd om de Meerderheid. De Verkiezingen van 1986 [In Search of a Majority. The National Elections of 1986] (with Philip van Praag Jr) (Amsterdam: CT Press) 1987

Electoral Change in the Netherlands. Empirical Results and Methods of Measurement (with Kees Niemöller) (Amsterdam: CT Press) 1983

In het Spoor van de Kiezer. Aspecten van 10 Jaar Kiezersgedrag [Tracking the Voters. A Decade of Electoral Behavior] (with Kees Niemöller a.o.) (Meppel: Boom) 1983

Kiezen in Nederland. 26 mei 1981: Wat de Kiezers Deden en Waarom [Voting in the Netherlands] (with Harry Eggen and Kees Niemöller) (Zoetermeer: Actaboek) 1981

Other books by Mark N. Franklin:

The Economy and the Vote: Economic Conditions and Elections in 15 Countries (with Wouter van der Brug and Cees van der Eijk) (New York: Cambridge University Press) 2007

Voter Turnout and the Dynamics of Electoral Competition in Established Democracies Since 1945 (New York: Cambridge University Press) 2004

The Future of Election Studies (edited with Christopher Wlezien) (Oxford: Pergamon) 2002

Choosing Europe? The European Electorate and National Politics in the Face of Union (with Cees van der Eijk *et al.*) (Ann Arbor: University of Michigan Press) 1996

Parliamentary Questions (edited with Philip Norton for the Study of Parliament Group) (Oxford: Oxford University Press) 1993

Electoral Change: Responses to Evolving Social and Attitudinal Structures in Western Nations (with Thomas T. Mackie *et al.*) (Cambridge: Cambridge University Press) 1992 *Electoral Change* will be re-issued as a 'Classic in Political Science' by the ECPR Press in 2009

The Community of Science in Europe: Preconditions for Research Effectiveness in European Community Countries (Aldershot: Gower) 1988

New Directions in Coalition Research (edited with Eric C. Browne) (Special Issue of *Legislative Studies Quarterly*) 1986

The Decline of Class Voting in Britain: Changes in the Basis of Electoral Choice 1964–1983 (Oxford: Oxford University Press) 1985

Chapter 1

Why Elections?

Elections are everyday events in the modern world. In representative democracies, their purpose is to allow voters to express their political preferences by making choices – between parties and/or between candidates – choices with implications (sometimes clear consequences) for the conduct of government and the policies that a government will pursue. Elections are opportunities for citizens to render a verdict on the past performance of their government and to establish guidelines for future government actions. Yet as soon as we refer to citizens we raise an enormous question mark over the electoral process in democratic countries. How well do ordinary men and women perform in making the sorts of judgements and choices that these lofty goals imply? Many critics of democracy have denied that members of the public have either the knowledge or the perspicacity required for rendering such verdicts or establishing such guidelines. And political scientists who have studied the behavior of voters at election time have sometimes expressed exactly the same doubts. This book is centered on the question of how citizens in democracies go about making the choices that elections call upon them to make. It also tries to assess the extent to which these choices turn out in practice to be good ones, and whether there are institutional arrangements that make it more or less easy for citizens to exercise their democratic judgment.

Before we start on this major task, we need to introduce a number of concepts and concerns that will be encountered frequently in later chapters. We begin by focusing on what it is that voters choose between when they vote in a national election.

Political parties

In some elections – elections for the President of the United States, for example – voters might be thought of as choosing primarily between different individual contenders for the *office* concerned. In other elections – elections for the British or French Parliaments, for example – voters might be thought of as choosing primarily between different *political parties*. Even in the United States, however, it is impossible to ignore the fact that the candidates are running on behalf of political parties, and many voters focus on the party that a presidential candidate belongs to as well as on her or his individual characteristics. When discussing elections, it is thus almost unavoidable to speak of political parties. But what we mean by the term 'party' is very different in different parts of the world; and the critical role that parties play in electoral politics makes it important for us at the very outset of this book to confront a major difference between types of parties. At one extreme we have parties that are loosely organized coalitions of *political elites* (*politicians* and other politically influential individuals) who may even switch between parties as it suits them. Such parties usually do not have formal *mass memberships* and have only weak organizations. Politicians operating under the banner of such parties may have widely different views on important policy issues without being sanctioned by their parties. At the other extreme, we find parties that are highly *disciplined*, which means that politicians are active on behalf of the party and are therefore expected to follow the party's program. Failing to do so can lead to serious sanctions, including expulsion from the party. Such parties are often based around organized mass support, where individual citizens can be formal members of the party and play a role in determining its policy stances and choosing its candidates. Moreover, these parties are characterized by strong organizations that in principle represent the members and keep politicians in line.

Within any particular political system we often find different sorts of party with characteristics that vary between these extremes. However, there are often even greater differences between systems, with all the parties in a particular country sharing characteristics that are different from those of parties in other countries. Among established democracies the United States is most often seen as the epitome of the first extreme, having loosely organized, relatively undisciplined political parties. Politicians, rather than parties, are at the center of the political stage. This is why we often refer to politics in the United States as *candidate-centered*. The countries of Western Europe fall closer to the other extreme, and established parliamentary systems generally have more disciplined parties and more *party-centered* politics than does the United States. We will explain in Chapter 2 why it is, in party-centered countries, that parties tend to be *policy centered*.

In countries with party-centered politics, a further distinction needs to be made between *top-down* and *bottom-up* politics (Esaiasson and Holmberg 1996). Top-down politics occurs when politicians make promises and try to fashion policies that will appeal to voters, with the primary objective of getting elected, along the lines first suggested by Joseph Schumpeter (1942) that we now associate with the term *vote-seeking*. Bottom-up politics occurs when grass-roots movements (like the Socialist Movement or the Ecology Movement) organize themselves as political parties that incorporate into their platform the objectives of the original movement. Such parties exist to 'sell' a set of policies and are thus *policy-seeking*. Parties that can be characterized as mass membership parties (like the socialists and communists) tend to have their origins in bottom-up political movements and contain many *activists* who play important roles in governing the party and mobilizing its electoral support. Such parties often have their origins in *social cleavages* (for instance distinctions between religions or between social classes). We will have more to say about social cleavages in Chapter 4. Top-down parties, by contrast, tend to be dominated by their founding elites and tend not to have mass memberships (Duverger 1967). They are thus often referred to as *elite parties*.

Between these extremes, policy-centered party systems can contain a number of other party types, most notably the *cadre party* – identified by Duverger (1967) as a party with its origins in a mass movement but whose leadership has divorced itself from the control of that mass movement (we are thinking here of classic Marxist–Leninist-style Communist parties) – and the *catch-all party*, identified by Kirchheimer (1966) as an elite party that has become successful in garnering support beyond its personalistic clientele or even a mass movement party that has become successful in appealing to voters beyond the bounds of those that it was originally founded to represent. More recently a new party type, the *cartel party* (Katz and Mair 1995), has been identified as a party so strongly entwined with government power as to be able to take advantage of government finance in electioneering. Such parties often have reputations for effectiveness honed by decades of participation in government that give them enormous advantages at election times. Of course, these various categories are not distinct, and parties of one type can easily evolve into parties of a different type.

Historically, a different kind of mass party has also had enormous importance. The *anti-system party* implicitly or explicitly sought votes in order to attain a position of power from which to change the existing political order. One form that this could take (epitomized by fascist parties in the 1920s and 1930s, and communist parties up until 1989) was by aspiring to abolish the liberal-democratic character of the country. Significant electoral support for such parties endangered democratic political systems not just by providing an electoral threat that, if realized, would result in the demise of democratic politics, but also by removing often large numbers of legislative seats from the pool of those that might support a coalition government (because anti-system parties won those seats). This made it hard to achieve alternation in office by pro-democratic parties (see Box 3.4 on p. 73, on electoral reform in Italy) and tended to throw the democratic political system into disrepute, in turn increasing the danger of electoral victory by anti-democratic forces. With the defeat of fascism in 1945 and the collapse of communism 44 years later, these anti-system parties lost most of their power to disrupt political life, and today's anti-system parties (generally left-libertarian, anti-immigrant and/or anti-EU parties of the far left and far right) often present themselves as wanting to abolish the cartelized form of political power that characterizes some contemporary democratic polities or to change existing definitions of citizenship and legal residence (Katz 1997). Some of them claim to be more rather than less democratic than the parties they seek to supplant (Meny and Surel 2002) – though such claims (at least from right-wing anti-party-system parties) need to be treated with skepticism given the often poor democratic credentials of the parties concerned.

Different types of parties behave differently in electoral processes. Some – in particular catch-all parties and anti-system parties – can easily adapt their policy positions in the hope of attracting more voters, while others – mass membership parties and cadre parties – find this more difficult. For some parties elections are a plausible way to government power, for others – anti-system parties in particular – this is not the case. So elections serve different functions for parties of different types.

Functions of elections

The specific functions that elections fulfill, and the way in which they do this, are not only different for different political parties but also for different individuals, as we will see. Moreover, they are not the same at all times or in all places. These differences even cause problems with the very terms that we employ in discussing the topic: not only the term 'party' can be confusing, as we have just seen. Likewise, what it is that is elected can be different at different elections – sometimes it is a single office (like a president), sometimes a set of offices (like a legislature). Sometimes these offices have fundamental roles in government, and sometimes not. Even abstract notions such as 'representation' carry quite different meanings in different systems. Because of all of this it is impossible to talk of elections and voters in the abstract. We have to pay attention to these differences by speaking of both elections and voters in terms of specific instances. That is what we do in the early chapters of this book.

Even non-democratic countries sometimes hold elections. Understanding why they do this helps us to understand some of the functions that elections have. In the first place, elections serve a *legitimating function*. The very fact that citizens troop to the polls in large numbers to cast a ballot, even if that ballot serves no function in terms of choice, provides legitimation for a regime. Moreover, people are likely to rationalize their behavior in terms of regime acceptance roughly in the same way that, after making an impulsive purchase, they might later rationalize their behavior in terms of their need for the item purchased. Moreover, even if the election was not a democratic one, and involved no choice, the apparently willing ratification of a regime's bona fides in this way can influence world opinion and international agencies such as the World Bank. Legitimation can also shade into nation-building, as the experience of performing a common act helps to generate a sense of community. Certainly, many despots seem to believe that conducting elections, even if they are neither free nor fair, helps to cement their power.

Elections that provide no real choice between candidates and policies can still provide a safety valve if they include the opportunity to vote against the available options. Electoral rules in the old Soviet Union provided the somewhat unlikely option of casting a 'vote against all'. This was a genuine (though not explicit) option, invoked by scoring out the names of all candidates, and in the later days of the regime this option was increasingly actually used by voters and responded to by the Communist Party which was genuinely embarrassed on those occasions when a majority cast their ballots for no candidate.

Turning to democratic elections, these perform a number of additional functions (and of course also provide better legitimation than do non-democratic elections). Most importantly, democratic elections *allocate power to office-holders*, generally by providing voters with a choice between different contenders for the offices concerned. Sometimes the contenders are individual candidates, such as those who contest a presidential election. But often the contenders are not individuals but political parties, which present the voter with alternative slates of individuals to be elected in greater or smaller numbers depending on the number of votes cast for each party list. When the election is for representatives to a decision-making body such as a national legislature, the election also determines the relative strengths of the parties to which those representatives belong: parties that receive more votes will generally receive more *seats* in the legislature (the mechanics of translating votes into seats in legislative elections will be explained in Chapter 3).

Since some of the candidates in any democratic election will generally be incumbent office-holders, elections also serve the function of *holding those office-holders accountable* for the manner in which they have used their power since the previous election, recording popular approval for their actions or 'kicking the rascals out' (a classic phrase meaning that voters inflict an electoral defeat on the government). In the process voters may also have the opportunity to make a choice between the policies proposed by government parties and those proposed by parties that would like to replace them. If the winning parties or candidates are chosen on the basis of voters' policy preferences, a *mandate* may be said to exist for those particular policies. However, politicians are often quicker than they should be to claim a mandate as a result of an election outcome.

To the extent that governments are responsive to the choices manifested in election outcomes, elections serve as a guidance mechanism that may help to bring the course of public policy closer to what voters want. Moreover, the sight of candidates submitting to the popular will presumably provides voters with at least some sense of empowerment. Research in the Netherlands has shown that support for democracy is greater after elections have been held – and not just among those whose parties gained seats and might thus be considered to have 'won' (van der Eijk 2000). Even when voters are disappointed or even disgusted with the way elections were conducted, as was the case for many US citizens after the 2000 election with its taint of voter intimidation and even fraud, such elections almost certainly still play a positive role in bestowing legitimacy on the eventual winner.

The turnout paradox

Elections for nationwide office (the elections studied in this book) marshal thousands, generally millions, of votes in order to elect a candidate or party. The chances of any one vote being decisive in such a contest are thus vanishingly small. Voting is generally not difficult. It involves a few minutes of minor inconvenience and a rather minimal amount of prior thought. However, it is not cost-free. A question often asked by scholars is why would anyone at all engage in an act that is not cost-free when the chances of that act having any effect whatsoever are vanishingly small (Downs 1957; Riker and Ordeshook 1968). The fact that people do vote in large numbers in national elections gives rise to the so-called 'impossibility' result – positive turnout in the face of a theoretical expectation of none.

Yet the ubiquity of a form of behavior often characterized by theorists as not rational tells us something important about the voting act. The act of voting is not done in the expectation of any sort of benefit that would not have been received otherwise (no individual stands to gain anything from her or his individual vote). It is rather a social act that people perform because it is expected of them as members of a group that collectively benefits from as many as possible of its members voting. The group concerned apparently differs from one individual to the next. For some it is their fellow citizens who expect them to vote as a social duty, for others it is their colleagues at work or their fellow union or church members whose expectations they do not wish to disappoint. For some it is the other supporters of the same political party who need the votes of all of that party's supporters if the party is to have a chance of winning (Franklin 2004, ch. 2).

This view of the voting act is not universally shared by scholars, since many political scientists still believe that the only reason to vote is in order to be a good citizen (Riker and Ordeshook 1968) or to affirm a political belief or identity (Schuessler 2000). However, these alternative ways of thinking about the voting act do not explain why the same people are more likely to vote in elections they view as important than in less important elections; or why countries in which elections play a more critical role see a higher turnout. Ideas about duty and expressive behavior also utterly fail to explain why people would vote for a party or candidate that is not their first choice, which is common.

We will come across each of these behavior patterns throughout this book, and we will find that elections are all about group behavior. If we do not see voters as social beings who act as members of various kinds of social groups we will not understand very much about the voting act.

Limitations of elections

Having millions of people express their preferences in such a way as to yield an intelligible outcome from which a mandate to govern can be derived requires organization, discipline and sophistication. Different political systems over the course of time have found their own solutions to these challenges, making democracy in each country unique in important respects. As a consequence, democratic elections differ from one another in the ways in which they permit voters to influence the course of public policy. Indeed, elections can be seen primarily to vary along two dimensions: meaningfulness of choices and conclusiveness of outcomes. By meaningful choice we refer particularly to the number of options between which a voter can choose. The more options the more likely it is that each voter will find one that is attractive to her or him. By conclusive outcome we mean an outcome whose policy implications are clearly defined – something that generally requires one option to receive an outright majority of the votes cast. Both are desirable features of an election: ideally one would want elections at which citizens were able to select their most desired policies in the knowledge that, if enough other citizens agreed with them, those policies would be enacted. In practice the two dimensions constitute something of a trade-off. To be more meaningful, elections must allow voters to choose from a larger set of alternatives. But when voters are presented with a large number of choices their votes rarely produce a majority in favor of any one of those choices. When choices are framed in terms of political parties, the failure of elections to generate a majority for any one of those parties brings about the need for compromise and negotiation as the parties try to overcome the inconclusive result, meaning that voters cannot be sure ahead of time how their vote will influence policy. On the other hand, simplifying the choices to the point where an unambiguous winner can emerge generally requires pre-election mechanisms (of which the most obvious are American primary elections) that simplify the alternatives on offer by removing some of them.

The trade-off is illustrated in the graph in Figure 1.1, which shows the conclusiveness of the outcome falling as the number of parties contesting an election increases. By allowing for more choice we reduce the policy implications of the outcome because the likelihood increases that no single candidate or party will get a mandate to govern. Choice is good, and some lack of conclusiveness has to be tolerated in return; but conclusiveness drops off more rapidly as the number of options increases beyond two. At some point, it is clear, additional options result in less reduction in definitiveness (15 parties make things quite complicated, but five more do not make things much worse). Still, too much choice can reduce the definitiveness of the outcome virtually to zero, making it impossible for voters to anticipate the policy consequences of their votes and vitiating a primary purpose of elections.

How far do options need to be limited in order for elections to have meaningful policy consequences? The exact extent to which options need to be limited cannot simply be read off from Figure 1.1. The pictured curve only illustrates the principles at work, not the detailed nature of the trade-off (which itself is also affected by a variety of institutional factors that differ from country to country). The way in which options are limited has to do primarily with the electoral system that is employed in different countries, but also with other 'rules of the game', including the system of nominations and even the system of party formation. These rules provide mechanisms for channeling and stylizing the options available to voters.

Figure 1.1   *Suggested trade-off between choice and conclusiveness*

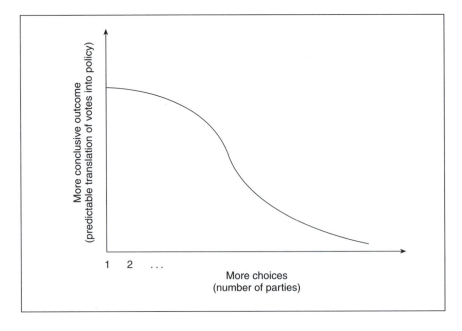

Different electoral systems and other political arrangements place countries at different points in terms of the trade-off illustrated in Figure 1.1. These differences will be explored in later chapters, along with other trade-offs that have to be made in designing the institutions of electoral democracy: for instance how disciplined the parties are and the ways in which political power can be either concentrated or dispersed. In particular there always has to be some mechanism for translating votes into outcomes, and the mechanisms adopted to arrive at an election outcome may have unintended side-effects. For instance the rules used in the United States to translate votes into outcomes in presidential races may lead to the victory of the candidate who did not win the most votes (as happened in the 2000 presidential election there – see Box 1.1).

So far we have talked as though there is some absolute standard according to which elections matter or not, but different people can have different views about this. The American political parties, for example, choose their candidates via a process of caucuses and primary elections. The 2008 race for the Democratic Party's nomination between Barack Obama and Hillary Clinton could have been won by either of these two candidates. A different

Box 1.1 The American Electoral College and the 2000 American election

In November 2000 the election for President of the United States, contested by George Bush and Al Gore, ended in a very messy legal dispute regarding contested votes in the state of Florida (words like 'hanging chads' and 'butterfly ballots' entered the general vocabulary at that time). The case went to the US Supreme Court which ruled that a recount was unnecessary and upheld the existing count that gave the Electoral College votes for the state of Florida to George Bush. The consequence was that Bush won more Electoral College votes than Gore and was declared the winner, despite Gore having won a greater number of votes nationwide (even without a recount). The case was important for a number of reasons. In the first place, it marked a milestone in US judicial politics as the first time the Supreme Court had decided a contested election for President. In the second place, the outcome was the first in over a hundred years to give victory to a candidate who had not won the popular vote. The US constitution provides for an arcane electoral process (more appropriate to an era when it took weeks to travel by horse across even the 13 original states) in which votes for President are cumulated in each state and determine the composition of an Electoral College with the duty of actually selecting a president. These days (and since almost the earliest presidential elections) the Electoral College delegates from each state cast their votes in a predetermined fashion, generally giving them all to the candidate who won in the state concerned. This usually gives victory to the candidate with the most votes, but is not bound to do so.

winner would have changed the nature of the ensuing election for certain people. Not only was there the question as to whether there would be a female or a black person as a first-ever major party nominee, but for some Clinton did not sufficiently represent 'change', while for others Obama was as yet insufficiently tested in the arena of national and international politics. So different choice options turn the election into a different contest, and different voters are motivated differently by the different contests they see as taking place.

Recurring themes

This book is arranged in terms of topics which are the subjects of different chapters. As we investigate these topics we will come across a number of themes that will recur in chapter after chapter. There are seven of them:

1. Elections can be looked at individually but, in our view, they can only be understood comparatively (seen in contrast to earlier elections in the same country or to elections elsewhere).
2. What is at stake in an election is not the same for all contenders. Challengers view the opportunity to win very differently from incumbents who view the possibility of losing; moreover, some contenders have no serious expectation of winning but participate in order to publicize their views, in order to lay down a marker for future elections, or just for fun.
3. Elections can be understood in terms of a relationship between the rulers and the ruled. Effective elections permit voters to select among alternative 'teams' of potential rulers – what are referred to as 'elites' – or to pass judgment on how ruling elites have used their time in office. Elections can thus be seen as channels of communication, with elites making their views known by way of party *manifestos* or *programs* and voters communicating their own views by way of their electoral choices.
4. The character of the choices presented to voters determines the extent to which they can choose an outcome that makes sense in terms of their ideals, interests and values; but quite often voters support a party or candidate other than the one that is closest to these ideals, interests and values. Voters engage in so-called *strategic* or *tactical* behavior if they believe that the vote they would otherwise have cast would be ineffective, as we will explain in Chapter 4 (pp. 103–13). So choices are not always simple expressions of voters' sincere preferences.
5. In particular, both candidates and voters often find themselves having to anticipate the behavior of others and condition their own behavior on that basis. This fifth theme stresses that elections constitute a strategic

game in which many players are looking over their shoulders to see what other players are doing or might do. It also stresses that not just candidates but also many voters behave quite instrumentally in considering the practical implications of voting one way rather than another, given the likely behavior of candidates and other voters.

6. The nature of the electoral contest at any particular election is largely set by the extent and nature of electoral competition between parties (or candidates). If each party has a set clientele of voters who will support that party under all circumstances then there is no real electoral competition. For competition to occur there has to be some doubt about the choices that will be made by at least some of a country's voters. The more voters there are who hesitate between different parties, the greater the extent of electoral competition. The extent and nature of this competition is a major topic to which we return repeatedly in different ways.

7. Voters have to be distinguished in terms of the periods and conditions under which they acquired their political orientations and habits. Differences between generations, and thus also generational replacement, are crucial for understanding electoral change (see Box 1.2).

Box 1.2 The study of generational replacement in electoral research

In this book we give special attention to a mechanism that, while prominent in early electoral research (e.g. Campbell *et al.* 1960, 1966; Nie *et al.* 1979), has hardly figured in recent electoral scholarship. Miller and Shanks (1996: 34–5) speculated on the reasons why the study of *political generations* has been largely ignored in contemporary electoral research and unequivocally demonstrated its importance. However, the lack of attention given to this topic continues to this day and a recent work on electoral realignment (Stonecash 2006) does not even mention generational replacement. Recent trends in political research stress the importance of *heterogeneity* (which is to say differentiation) in the electorate, distinguishing educated from less educated voters, for example, or the politically engaged from those who are unengaged; but it is still not common to focus on heterogeneity in terms of generational differences. In this book we follow the lead of Miller and Shanks in giving considerable attention to this neglected theme.

The implication that flows from these themes is that no single unequivocal answer can be given to common questions such as whether elections matter, whether voters act responsibly or whether elites compete. The answers to such questions depend on features of particular elections in relation to their social and political environment. So elections can only be studied in their proper contexts.

Voters, electorates, parties and party systems

A fundamental feature of elections is that they can be examined from a number of different *levels of analysis*. Voters are individuals, best examined at the *individual level*, but (since an election involving only a single person makes no sense) elections must intrinsically be investigated at a higher level of analysis. In this book we generally concern ourselves with elections at the *country level*. When we view voters at the country level of analysis we call them collectively an *electorate*, but an electorate does not take its characteristics uniquely from the voters of which it is composed. It has *aggregate* characteristics that could not be applied to any of its individual members (an average age, for instance, or a bulge in the number of its middle-aged members deriving from a baby boom long past). An electorate can be small or large, which generally depends on the population of the country in which it is found; but note that an electorate is not the same as a population, some of whose members at any time will be under voting age, not citizens, or otherwise disqualified from voting.

When they vote, voters choose between the parties that vie for their support. This implies that voters have *preferences* for different parties such that, at any time, parties can be arrayed for each voter in order of preference and that the strengths of these preferences can be compared. We measure these preferences in terms of voters' *propensity to vote* for different parties (see Box 1.3).

When we consider the various preferences in the minds of individual voters, we are thinking in terms of a level of analysis *below* that of the individual, since each individual voter has multiple parties in her or his preference structure. When we come to study voters' preferences, in Chapter 7, that will be the level of analysis that we employ.

Just like individual voters, parties can be viewed at different levels of analysis. They can be viewed at the level of voters' preferences for each of them, as just explained. More usually though they are viewed at the *party level*, which is the level at which one would examine such things as their organizational structure or the number of their members or the policies they propose; but they can also be viewed at the country level, as a competitive *party system*. A party system is to a party as an electorate is to a voter: the aggregate counterpart of a lower-level phenomenon. But just as electorates have characteristics that voters cannot have, so party systems have characteristics that parties cannot have: above all, the number of parties. Much has been written about party systems, which have been defined in all sorts of ways (e.g. Mair 1997; Sartori 2005). For us a party system is simply the structure of competitive and collaborative relationships between parties. These relationships provide considerations that voters will need to bear in mind when deciding how to vote.

Box 1.3   *Studying preferences for political parties*

A second way in which this book differs from much of contemporary scholarship, in addition to its focus on generational replacement as a mechanism of change (Box 1.2), is in its focus on voters' preferences for parties in addition to the more widespread focus on their choices between parties. In Chapter 2 we expand on some of the implications of this distinction. The strength of voters' electoral preferences for political parties is measured by a survey question that asks voters about the likelihood that they would ever vote for each of the available parties. We refer to these measures as the 'propensity to vote' for each party. The theoretical expectation, that voters choose the party they prefer the most, is reflected empirically in their tendency to choose the party for which they hold the highest vote propensity (van der Eijk *et al.* 2006; see also Further Reading). This is the observational equivalent of Downs's (1957) theoretical proposition that voters choose the party that yields them most 'utility', a proposition that implies the need to conceive the voting act in two stages: the stage at which preferences ('utilities' in Downs's terminology) are formed or updated and the stage at which a choice is made. In past research it has been customary to focus exclusively on the second of these stages, all but ignoring the first, despite various more or less strident reminders (e.g. Powell 2000) that knowledge of preferences is needed in order to understand voter motivations. In this book we are thus concerned with voters' party preferences, as well as the vote choices that derive from those preferences, and how both of these are shaped by institutional arrangements and other country characteristics.

Akin to the distinction between electorate and population, a distinction needs to be made between *parties in the legislature* and *parties in the electorate* (this is short for 'party system in the legislature' and 'party system in the electorate'). There will generally be more parties competing for votes (parties in the electorate) than parties that actually win enough votes to gain seats in the legislature. For the most part in this book we will be talking about parties in the legislature, but the distinction between these two views of the party system will occasionally be relevant.

The axis of political competition and the median voter

In any political system, it is often found convenient to differentiate politicians and political parties along a political continuum, providing a short-cut means of identifying differences between parties and politicians. The most common continuum or 'axis' along which parties are distinguished is the so-called *left–right* axis, which derives its name from the physical positions where members of different parties sat in the first French Assembly elected after the French Revolution. In the United States, the equivalent dimension is known as the *Liberal–Conservative* axis, and politicians are often characterized in terms of their alleged positions on this axis (more or less liberal than other politicians, for example). In the political vocabulary of left and right, parties of the left generally propose what Americans would call 'liberal' policies (though this word is used differently in Europe), while parties of the right are oriented towards conservatism.

In countries where the party system is in flux, with parties being frequently dissolved and re-established under different names, it may be very difficult for voters to learn their way around the system, and a common vocabulary such as that provided by the concepts of left and right may be hard to establish. If such a vocabulary is already in use, however, it can prove quite useful for navigating a complex political system, with parties being identified in the minds of voters rather in terms of their left–right locations than in terms of the plethora of their proposals and activities, providing the opportunity for *ideological identification* of voters with a position on the political spectrum, as will be discussed in Chapter 2. We will defer until Chapter 6 the question of how adequate a single dimension really is for encapsulating the differences seen between the parties in a party system.

Not only parties and politicians but also voters can be arrayed on the same axis, from what Americans would think of as most liberal to most conservative or from what Europeans would think of as most left to most right, providing the opportunity to think of representation in terms of how closely the orientation of individual political parties matches the equivalent orientation of the voters who support those parties. Moreover, the ranking of voters from left to right gives rise to a concept often used in political science (and referred to repeatedly in later chapters of this book) of the *median voter* – the voter who stands in the exact center of the political spectrum, with as many voters to her or his left as to her or his right. When we come to talk about the adequacy of political representation in a country, the question of how well the median voter is represented looms large – especially if the median position in the issue space is occupied by large numbers of voters. The assumption that the median voter is indeed representative of large numbers of voters is a common one, which we will consider carefully in this book.

Representation

In a democracy, political decisions are supposed ultimately to reflect the wishes of a country's citizens. If this is the case then the government of a country should to some extent reflect popular sentiments. In which sorts of ways might governments reflect the concerns of the governed? And, given that in most democracies political parties are the vehicles for achieving *representative government*, how *responsive* are political parties to what voters want? These and similar questions motivate much research and theorizing about the electoral process.

The general concept of political representation contains a number of related yet somewhat different aspects which can best be distinguished by distinctive adjectives. *Social representation* considers the similarity between citizens and representatives in terms of their social characteristics, specific forms of which are 'women's representation' (Norris and Inglehart 2003), 'minority representation' and 'ethnic representation', all of which focus on whether elected representatives (and governments) 'look like' the people they are supposed to represent. Implicit in the notion of social representation is that such similarity is required for politicians to represent the interests of the group involved in an authentic fashion. Linked to these ideas is *ideological representation* – the idea that representatives and governments should 'look like' or be 'close to' their supporters in ideological terms. This idea is at the heart of the *proximity* (sometimes known as the *smallest distance*) theory of party choice, a theory we will discuss in Chapter 6. *Output representation* or *policy representation* is more concrete and focuses on the substance of what governments bring about. Do the policies that governments enact match the needs and demands of their supporters or of the society as a whole?

A related question is what motivates parties and their leaders. Politicians might be *policy-seeking* (see p. 3), in which case they would primarily be concerned to win votes for the policies they believe in. Alternatively they might be *office-seeking* (also known as *vote-seeking*, see p. 2), in which case they might craft policies that would appeal to as many voters as possible. Or they might be motivated by a combination of objectives, having certain policy objectives on which they hoped for voter support while crafting other policies so as to create a maximally attractive package.

In this book we do not attempt to unravel the motivations of politicians, but assume that both types of motivations exist, perhaps even in the same individuals. This assumption allows us to focus our attention on ideological and policy representation, and to concern ourselves mainly with whether governments, for whatever reason, actually provide the policies that voters want.

Electoral change

A major preoccupation of this book is to understand how change occurs. How and why do party systems evolve? Why do ruling politicians lose elections, to be replaced by new faces? Why do parties gain or lose support and hence find their political influence enhanced or reduced? Why are there sometimes big discontinuities in the pattern of election outcomes (often referred to as 'realignments') while for much of the time change appears rather to take the form of trendless fluctuation?

To understand electoral change one must understand some basic concepts and distinctions used by political scientists to talk about change. The most important of these is the distinction between change on the part of an individual voter and change on the part of an electorate. Aggregate entities, such as electorates, can remain the same even if many or all of their members change. For example, in the case of only two parties, many voters can switch in their choice of party but, if the same number change in one direction as in the other direction, then the aggregate (or 'net') change is zero: individual changes can cancel each other out. On the other hand, electorates can change even if no single individual voter does. This is because they can change their *composition* as individuals leave or die and are replaced by new voters with different characteristics and/or preferences.

Indeed, there are three ways in which change can affect an aggregate entity such as an electorate. First, and most obviously, its members can change their minds and/or their behavior. Something can happen – a war, a nuclear accident, generally something dramatic – that is felt by large numbers of individuals, and the behavior of many of those individuals may change in a similar way as a consequence. This also gives rise to a change in the behavior of the entity of which those individuals are part. Because change of this kind is generally associated with a particular event (sometimes a series of linked events like the Great Depression of the 1930s) we refer to it as a *period effect*. This is the sort of change that is the easiest to understand, because the aggregate entity is behaving just like the individuals of which it is composed. This type of change is rare, however.

A second type of change, an *age effect,* is much more common. It occurs as individuals grow older and learn new behaviors and attitudes. Voters in particular learn their way around the political world by experiencing it. They learn what parties stand for, which party to support, and generally they learn the habit of voting for that party. As they learn, they change (cf. C. Franklin 1992; Franklin and Jackson 1983). At the other end of the life cycle, voters grow infirm and find it hard to get to the voting booth; they suffer loss of function and find it hard to make decisions, and so on. Indeed, it can be seen that an electorate – like many other aggregate entities – is in constant flux as its members age and evolve. But the important thing about this sort of change is that, in itself, it need not affect the character of the aggregate entity. Voters individually age and change, but so long as those who leave the electorate are replaced, one for one, by new voters who have the same characteristics as the departing voters had when they were young, the aggregate character of the electorate is unchanging. It evinces what is known as a *steady state*.

It is of course possible to get aggregate change from the aging process if the rate of replacement of the electorate changes. A baby boom will evidently lead to an electorate with many more young members, later to one with many more middle-aged members, and finally to one with many more old members. At each stage in this process the electorate as a whole will change to reflect the character of the age the baby-boom generation has reached. This is known as a *composition effect* because it arises from a change in the composition of the electorate – the proportion of the electorate with certain characteristics becomes greater or smaller. A war that kills a great many young men or a medical breakthrough that extends the lifespan of older people can similarly bring about a change for compositional reasons. Composition effects are ubiquitous, but are usually very small in the short run (cf. Franklin 2004). Continuing change in the same direction could have large cumulative effects, but some mechanism is required to produce continuing change in the size of a particular group of people. One such mechanism is long-term social evolution that is sometimes referred to as 'development' or 'modernization' and that has generated during the 20th century increasing proportions of the population in established democracies that are literate, educated, urbanized and who enjoy minimum levels of material security. The third way in which an aggregate, such as an electorate, can change is by *generational replacement*.

As we will see in later chapters, the group of citizens who became eligible to vote at a particular election often acquires a particular character that the group retains during the rest of its lifetime. Such groups are known to political scientists as *electoral cohorts*. Their unique character is caused by the particular social, economic and political circumstances that existed at the time that their members entered the electorate and that constituted formative experiences. A particular electoral cohort may, for example, have a lower propensity to turn out and vote than other cohorts because of the political circumstances they encountered at the time when they were first eligible to vote. Obviously, the next cohort may experience quite different circumstances by which it, in turn, will be formed. These enduring differences between cohorts are known as *cohort effects*; and, if successive cohort differences are idiosyncratic or random, are still compatible with a steady state. However, it sometimes happens that some development gives rise to an effect that is not restricted to a single cohort but characterizes a series of successive cohorts or even all cohorts after a given point in time. If successive cohorts continue to evince the same distinctiveness then the changing cohort-composition of the electorate does not yield a steady state. In such circumstances the electorate can show a progressive change as a larger and larger proportion of the aggregate entity comes to be made up of individuals who are distinctively different from members of earlier cohorts when they were the same age. We call this a *progressive cohort effect* and will explore it in some detail in

Chapters 4 and 7. A progressive cohort effect starts almost imperceptibly as only a tiny fraction of the electorate is initially distinctive. But this tiny fraction expands inexorably as older voters leave the electorate, taking their characteristics with them, to be replaced by a continuing influx of new voters with different characteristics. Because of the inexorable nature of generational replacement, progressive cohort effects end up being very powerful – often the most powerful of the processes involved in electoral change.

Topics

This book covers a lot of ground. As illustrated in Figure 1.2 the contents of the book can be seen in terms of two organizing principles. From left to right we differentiate topics according to where they fall in causal sequence: the things that happen first – the prime causes – are represented towards the left of the page, while the election itself and things about the election are pictured at the right of the page. In technical terms, the concepts at the right of the page are *dependent variables*, so called because their character depends on the factors to their left, the *independent variables*. Up and down the page we differentiate topics according to the level of analysis at which they fall. Higher-level topics provide the context within which lower-level topics operate. At the top are topics having to do with electoral institutions and other features of the country as a whole. The middle row of topics has to do with political parties. At the bottom we place topics that have to do with individual voters. Elections are inherently about multiple levels of analysis which need to be considered all at the same time. One cannot understand the choices made by individuals unless one also understands the choices on offer: the *menu* (if you like) from which the choices are made. But to understand the menu one has to understand political parties and the factors that lead those parties to propose the particular policies that they put on offer. The behavior of political parties in turn is constrained by the electoral and party systems in which they operate. The upward-pointing arrows towards the right of Figure 1.2 indicate the way in which contextual characteristics are created by aggregating lower-level concepts: the votes that are cast by individuals determine the sizes of parties, and these in turn, taking all parties together, constitute an *election outcome*.

Elections can be thought about in terms of which party won (the top row) but parties need also to be thought of in terms of their relative performance (the middle row). Did they do better than another party or better than they did at the previous election? And the performance of parties cannot be understood unless we study why individuals choose to support each party, or choose not to (the bottom row). Moreover, the outcome of an election has generally to be thought of at every level in terms of turnout as well as in

Figure 1.2   *Topics covered and their causal priorities*

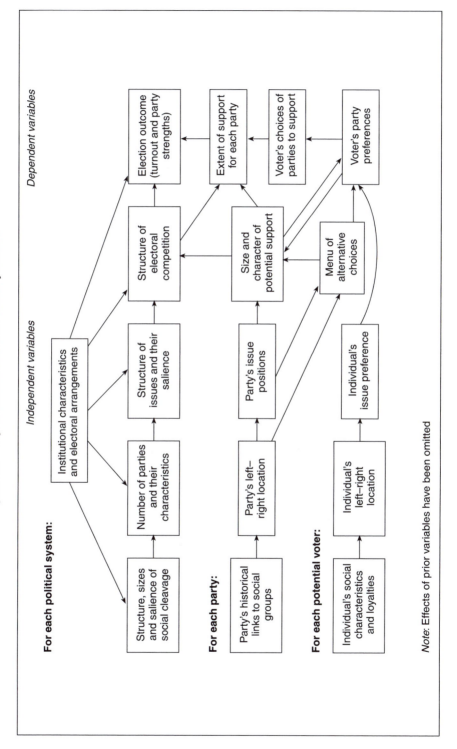

Note: Effects of prior variables have been omitted

terms of choices between parties. This is because, except in countries with compulsory voting, one of the choices that is always available is the choice not to vote at all. Indeed, for many people at most elections the choice is not one between parties but between voting or not voting for the party they normally support.

The arrows drawn onto the diagram indicate the general direction of causal flow, but the diagram should not be interpreted as exhaustive. Causes do not flow only along each arrow. All considerations depicted to the left of the diagram have the opportunity to influence, directly or indirectly, considerations depicted to the right, though arrows that would have passed around rather than through subsequent boxes have generally been suppressed so as to improve legibility. Just as importantly, the diagram generally ignores *reciprocal causes*: effects felt on topics to the left of the diagram that are consequential on topics to the right. The picture is a static snapshot of what is in reality a *dynamic system*. If time is allowed to flow, all sorts of reciprocal effects become evident as parties change their stances in the light of election outcomes and individuals change their preferences in the light of government performance and changes in the menu of alternatives on offer. But those reciprocal effects take, in general, more time to materialize than the ones pictured. This implies that, in the short run, causality flows along the arrows pictured, while only over a longer time scale do processes in the reverse direction manifest themselves.

Despite our wish to avoid reciprocal links, one of the boxes in the diagram does have an arrow entering from its right: the 'size and character of potential support' of political parties. This box represents the party-level counterpart of the 'structure of electoral competition' in a political system (the box above in the diagram, which is indirectly affected by the same reciprocal link). This box in turn corresponds to the sixth of the general themes listed earlier as being central to this book. The reciprocal arrow influencing this concept in Figure 1.2 emphasizes the centrality of this theme, which is intimately tied to the structure of party preferences in the minds of each voter and to the resulting choices that each voter makes to support a particular party with her or his vote.

The topics in Figure 1.2 do not map cleanly into different chapters of this book. Indeed, some topics are dealt with multiple times from different perspectives in different chapters, while others are only touched on in passing. Still, Figure 1.2 displays the structure of our subject matter in semicausal terms, and readers may find it useful to look back at it from time to time in order to remind themselves of where different topics fit within that causal structure. From this perspective the figure can be treated as a conceptual map illustrating the way in which different topics are connected (close or far, directly or indirectly), just like cities on a geographic map, and we will ourselves have reason to refer to it repeatedly in later chapters.

Countries

This is a book about elections and voting in established democracies. Though we take our examples from any available source, our focus is on countries for which we have good data and understanding – generally countries that have held elections continuously for 60 years or more. These examples are an important part of the text, since they are intended to illustrate how the mechanisms we discuss work out in practice.

The reason we focus on countries that have held elections for a considerable period is because, as we shall see, understanding the current election in any country requires an understanding of all the different influences acting on citizens who might participate in that election. Several of the most important of these influences are those that were felt by citizens at the time of their first electoral experiences which could have occurred as long as 60 years earlier. By focusing on countries that were holding free and fair elections 60 years ago – what we call *established democracies* – we avoid our findings being affected by pre-democratic experiences. Nevertheless, in order to extend the number of presidential systems we do include some examples from Mexico, even though that country only recently qualified as a democratic country by virtue of the previously ruling party losing power in 2000 for the first time since 1929. This was the outcome of a variety of reforms which had generally been viewed as creating free and fair elections there from about 1994 onwards.

Despite the book's focus in terms of countries, our objective is to provide an understanding of the forces at work in any electoral democracy. Though we mainly deal with established democracies, what we have to say about them should increasingly come to be true of other democracies as well, as they become established in terms of our usage. In Chapter 7 we do deal explicitly with one particular set of quite new democracies: those ex-communist countries that became members in 2004 of the European Union. Our examination of electoral behavior in those countries suggests that individuals in new democracies rapidly acquire behavior patterns very similar to those in more established democracies. What we are unable to do is talk about the evolution of party systems and election outcomes in new democracies, because in those countries such developments are idiosyncratic in ways that are not yet well understood.

Institutional arrangements

In some countries the executive is directly elected by the people, while in others it is appointed by an elected legislature. This major constitutional difference colors many aspects of the electoral connection between voters and their governments, and we will deal with this in Chapter 2. The United States is in many ways a quite exceptional country – not least in terms of its political system – and the fact that we can explain electoral behavior there in the same terms as in other countries serves to validate many of the conclusions reached in this book. Taking the Unites States as an explicit case enables us to better understand elections and voting in other countries; and comparing the United States with those other countries enables us to better understand elections and voting in the United States. American readers may find parliamentary systems hard to understand, and readers outside the United States may find the American system equally perplexing, but the effort it takes to understand the other type of system will pay off handsomely in a greater understanding of the electoral processes in systems of both types.

Other constitutional differences are less important for this book than the difference between parliamentary and presidential systems, but we occasionally refer to the fact that some countries are unitary, while others are built out of largely self-governing components. We call the latter federal or confederal countries. Most countries also have elections to fill executive or legislative positions at subnational levels (states in the US, Länder in Germany, regions or provinces in most other countries). If elections at these subnational levels are contested by the same parties as at the national level, they are often referred to as *second order* national elections because the national character of the parties and their concerns overshadows whatever concerns might be different in these elections from those at *first order* elections (the national elections we focus on in this book). Moreover, many countries have forms of functional government where the relevant authorities are elected (for instance school boards in the United States or water boards in the Netherlands). In this volume we will not deal with subnational or functional governments but will concentrate on elections for executive and legislative offices at the national level. We can do this because governments at the national level determine the boundaries of autonomy and self-governance at all levels of government, except to the extent that this is prevented by explicit constitutional prohibition.

In addition to specifically constitutional arrangements, there are additional institutional differences between countries that are important to us in this book. The most important of these are *electoral institutions* (sometimes these are specified in a country's constitution, but often they are not). Electoral institutions determine the rules under which elections are held. Here the most important distinction is between elections that yield *proportional representation* (PR) and other systems which are variously known as *majoritarian, plurality* or *first past the post* (FPTP). This bifurcation constitutes the other primary organizing feature (besides the difference between presidential and parliamentary systems) around which this book is organized. Because of the importance of these institutional differences we devote Chapter 3 to discussing them.

A third set of distinctions that need to be made are those that characterize different *party systems*. Such differences are often regarded as quasi-institutional since they are often relatively stable: the number of parties, their characteristics and the distribution of electoral support that they enjoy determines the nature of electoral competition in different countries. Electoral competition is central to our concerns, as mentioned earlier, so the nature of the party system is also central and is discussed at various points (mainly in Chapters 2 and 3).

The distinction between different types of party system overlaps with and partly leads to a final distinction between the types of government that are customarily formed in different countries. Presidential systems and certain parliamentary democracies have what are called *single-party* or *unitary* governments in which the *executive* (the President in presidential systems, *cabinet members* elsewhere) all belong to the same political party and gain their executive positions as a straightforward consequence of the fact that their party 'won' the election. Having a single winner is natural in countries where two major parties are the only real contenders for government office. In other parliamentary systems the larger number of political parties makes it unlikely that any one party will win an outright majority of the votes in an election (or seats in the legislature). If such countries have parliamentary systems, then the governments that are formed generally consist of *coalitions* of two or more parties that divide up the responsibilities of government between them, so that cabinet members are drawn from different parties. Indeed, many countries have traditions of governing either with single-party or coalition governments and these traditions sometimes supersede the actual strengths of parties that result from particular elections. Whether the government that will be formed following an election is expected to be a unitary or a coalition government has enormous importance for the nature of the electoral contest, and this difference is explored mainly in Chapters 2 and 3.

These four sets of institutional and quasi-institutional differences between countries can be seen as more or less fixed features that distinguish countries from each other. Constitutional arrangements are the most fixed (most difficult to change) and sometimes endure for centuries. Electoral systems are generally fixed over considerable periods of time but are not as immune to change as are the more strictly constitutional arrangements. Few have lasted unchanged for as long as a century and in some countries they are changed quite frequently. Party systems can endure for considerable periods but are not regarded as being fixed in the way that electoral and constitutional arrangements are fixed. This is because the objective of many political leaders is to change the party system of their countries by founding a new party or ousting an existing party from its dominant position.

Many of the countries that we study are members of the European Union and for these countries there is an additional layer of institutions above the national level that we have been considering. Most of these institutions have no relevance to the concerns of this book, but the European Parliament is relevant because of the regular five-yearly occurrence of elections to that Parliament in EU member countries. These elections are of a type that we have just described as 'second order' elections; but, because they are second order *national* elections, what we observe are national electoral forces at work, and because these elections are conducted simultaneously in a large number of countries they provide unparalleled insight into the role and importance of institutional differences between countries.

Voters and the puzzle of the ignorant electorate

This is a book about elections and voters, yet we have hardly mentioned voters so far. Voters only occupy the bottom row in Figure 1.2. Nevertheless, they are actors of central importance. Elections in a democracy provide a primary link between rulers and the ruled, and they are often seen as justification for referring to the system as democratic. The extent to which voters succeed in guiding a political system towards the policies they favor is critical to assessing the performance of democratic institutions.

Because parties and elections are policy centered in some systems but candidate centered in others, we have a major distinction to make repeatedly throughout this book. Nevertheless, it turns out that much of voting behavior can be described in general terms that do not need to take account of this distinction. This is just as well, or we would not be able to take the comparative approach that we have already said is needed in order to understand anything much about elections and voting. But readers should note that when we use the words 'party choice' we mean 'party or candidate choice' unless we explicitly differentiate between the two.

A major puzzle, often referred to as the 'puzzle of the ignorant electorate', confronts anyone who would study elections and voters. Once every four or five years (depending on the country concerned) parties and political elites submit themselves to the judgment of voters who are expected to rule on the adequacy of past government and on the relative merits of the competing claims of those who would participate in future governments. Unavoidably, these voters will often be uninformed about many details of government performance and about the credentials of those who wish to become future office-holders. Most of them are also unavoidably incapable of discerning which of myriad alternative policies will most likely lead to their desired objectives (a problem shared, it must be said, by political elites as well). Despite the fact that individual voters are so lacking in information, collectively they appear to make quite sensible decisions. Viewed at the country level of analysis, election outcomes do make sense. So the puzzle of the ignorant voter is also the puzzle of how electoral democracy works. That is one of the principal puzzles that we address in this book.

Plan of the book

The book consists of seven more chapters, four that mainly focus on the institutions that govern the conduct of elections and their implications for the voting act, and three that evaluate how elections work in practice. The reason why we start with institutions is because voting behavior can only be understood in the context of the institutional and party structures in which it takes place and so we need to spell out how the behavior of voters is channeled by the institutional contexts in which those voters find themselves. In Chapter 2 we lay the groundwork by setting out how elections should be studied. The chapter describes how political power is allocated by elections in three very different kinds of political system: presidential systems, two-party parliamentary systems and multiparty parliamentary systems. We ask what decides elections and what elections decide in each type of system. In Chapter 3 we further differentiate between the different contexts in which elections occur by describing the different sorts of electoral systems that are employed in established democracies, focusing on what Bingham Powell (2000) refers to as the 'two great visions' of electoral democracy: the proportional and majoritarian visions. In Chapter 4 we turn to the various ways in which parties serve as linkage mechanisms between voters and governments, and the way in which parties provide a focus for electoral contests. In Chapter 5 we complete our survey of the nuts and bolts of how elections are conducted, and what voters do when they go to the polls, by focusing on election outcomes, discussing the ways in which outcomes are different in proportional than in majoritarian systems. In Chapter 6 we turn to public opinion, along with the news media that play such an important role in informing the public, and explore the interplay between public opinion and electoral behavior, while in Chapter 7 we focus on the individual voter, seeking to understand how voters' party preferences are shaped by the forces that were investigated in earlier chapters. Here we take advantage of a linked set of public opinion surveys covering both established and emerging democracies in order to consider the question: how does the nature of electoral democracy evolve over time? In Chapter 8 we sum up, first by asking to what extent the policies promised by winning parties correspond to the policies wanted by the voters who elect them, and then by considering the adequacy of electoral democracy and ways in which it could be or is being improved.

The book ends with a guide to further reading in which we provide detailed suggestions for those who want to extend their understanding beyond the material contained in this book. To document our assertions, chapters do contain traditional references to sources, but these are generally kept to a minimum. Additional sources are listed in the guide to further reading. When actual research findings are reproduced in our text, the sources are documented in notes to the tables and figures concerned.

Chapter 2

Studying Elections, Parties and Voters

This is a book about voters, politicians, parties (sometimes referred to as 'actors') and electoral politics (sometimes seen as the 'stage' upon which these actors perform). In it we see elections as providing a sort of ritualized encounter in which voters engage politicians and parties. In order to understand the nature of these encounters, we need to describe how they fit into the wider political system – by which we mean both the institutions of government and the party system (electoral systems are described in Chapter 3). So first we will distinguish three fundamental types of institutional context on the basis of the differences in these characteristics. Subsequently we will argue that these wider contexts and the largely institutionalized ways in which elections are conducted provide the opportunity for learning to take place and habits to form, both for voters and for parties.

The political context: party systems

Elections are about choice, but in different countries voters have more or less choice depending on the nature of the party system. The US has a two-party system. Those parties have changed in character over the course of history, and other parties have competed successfully in American elections; but since 1912 there has been no presidential candidate with a realistic chance of winning who was neither a Democrat nor a Republican, and no minor party has won seats in the Congress since the 1920s (occasionally a seat is won by an 'independent'). Today, and for most of the past century, at American elections voters have had a choice between just two parties. So, at each election, if one party does not win the presidency then the other one must. The same applies to each of the houses of Congress.

However, the US is just about the only established democracy with a party system that can reasonably be characterized as a two-party system. In other established democracies voters almost invariably have more choice. Even in countries such as Britain and Canada, which are sometimes thought of as two-party systems because one or other of only two parties generally forms a majority one-party government, voters do have additional parties to choose from. These might be called 'effectively two party' systems. Sometimes they are known as two-and-a-half party systems (Blondel 1972; cf. Sartori 2005), but this is misleading. In Britain, for example, there are currently 11 parties represented in Parliament, and most voters have a choice between four or five parties running candidates in their *constituency* (what Americans would call a *district*). The system is effectively a two-party system because the minor parties receive very few votes (and very few seats), not because there are few minor parties.

Then there are genuinely multiparty systems, which exist in most other established democracies. In multiparty systems it is not common for any one party to win a majority of the seats in the legislature, so parties have to cooperate in forming coalition governments – though in some countries, such as Sweden and Spain, the largest party is frequently large enough to govern alone, sometimes as a minority government with tacit support from other parties. In multiparty systems voters have the choice between more than two genuine contenders for government power. Sometimes as many as five or more parties are potential members of a governing coalition, depending on the outcome of an election.

The concept generally employed to distinguish between these different types of multiparty system is the concept of *fractionalization* or the *effective number of parties*.[1] In an effectively two-party system fractionalization is low because most people are voting for just two parties. As the effective number of parties increases so fractionalization increases because more votes are going to the smaller parties. Even in genuinely multiparty systems the extent of fractionalization is of interest in distinguishing systems with relatively few true contenders for government power (like the Netherlands or today's Poland) from countries like Poland during the early 1990s or France during the Fourth Republic (1946–58) when most parties were very small.

Party systems are shaped by political entrepreneurs (politicians, especially party leaders) who react to the opportunities provided by different electoral systems in the context of different historical traditions and social settings. Generally, where there is demand for a particular type of party such a party will be provided; but whether that party will be successful electorally depends not only on the number of people voting for it but also on the rules of the electoral game. On the whole, countries that have few successful parties do so because the system penalizes additional parties by means of what we will see are effectively high costs of entry.

So established democracies can be divided into three types. These are distinguished, first, according to whether they are presidential or parliamentary (with the US presidential system constituting a type of its own) and, second, among parliamentary systems, whether they are essentially two-party systems or genuinely multiparty systems. We will first explore the difference between presidential and parliamentary regimes.

The institutional context: presidential versus parliamentary

In presidential systems the Chief Executive is directly elected. In parliamentary democracies the executive – which is not a single person but the entire cabinet – is elected indirectly. Among established democracies there is only one true presidential system: the US. Exploring the difference between parliamentary and presidential systems is therefore also to explore the differences between the US and other established democracies. We have already in the previous chapter introduced one fundamental respect in which the US differs from other countries – that of the lack of party discipline and the corresponding failure of US elections to be as policy-oriented as they are elsewhere. What we have to say here about the differences between parliamentary and presidential systems of government helps to explain that distinction but also adds additional detail that helps to explain American idiosyncrasies.

The easiest way to picture the difference between a presidential and a parliamentary system is in terms of two diagrams. The presidential system is very straightforward in democratic terms. As shown in Figure 2.1, candidates for each office are elected directly by the people. Leaving aside minor complications such as that provided by the US Electoral College (see Box 1.1), one can picture the electorate as a body of people with direct links to the President (the executive) as well as to the legislature, which is generally referred to as the Congress (House of Representatives and Senate).[2] One component of the government is not linked directly to the electorate: this is the cabinet (and the bureaucracy that is directed by it), which is appointed by the President and is answerable to him. The picture is complicated mainly because there are so many elected institutions. Thus, the diagram shows arrows from the electorate to the House, to the Senate, and to the President.

Figure 2.1   *Electoral and other linkages in a presidential system (the United States)*

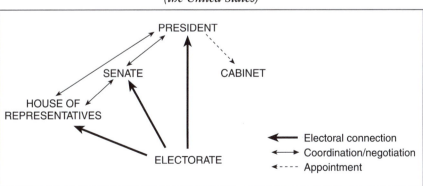

In addition to these arrows that show the electoral connection to each office, a number of double-headed arrows represent coordination activities – the negotiations that need to be conducted between President and Senate, between President and House of Representatives, and between House of Representatives and Senate, in order to produce a bill that can be passed by both houses of Congress and signed by the President. Though the concepts are really simple, there are a lot of arrows. Each arrow represents a relationship that has to be studied and understood in order to understand how the government functions and what role is played by elections in such a system.

If we turn to the parliamentary system we see a picture (Figure 2.2) that is conceptually more difficult to understand, but organizationally much simpler. As in the case of the US we start with an electorate and this electorate elects a legislative body – the Parliament. Some parliamentary systems are unicameral, which means they only have one house containing directly elected representatives (these individuals are known by various names in different countries but in this book we will refer to them all as elected representatives – or representatives for short). Just as the US has a bicameral legislature, so do certain parliamentary systems; but in contrast to the US the 'upper' house in parliamentary systems generally has significantly fewer powers than the lower house (and, more importantly, it is subject to discipline by the same political parties). Moreover, the electorate does not generally elect the upper house directly in parliamentary systems. Therefore only the lower house needs to be pictured here. The executive (the government) is chosen by parliament, not by the people. So when the people elect a parliament they are indirectly electing an executive also. Sometimes this is a completely automatic process. If one party wins a majority of the seats in the Parliament that party will form the executive and the party's leader will become the head of the government, the Prime Minister (at such times parliaments act just like the American electoral college – see Box 1.1 – translating the will of the voters automatically into a choice of executive). When no single party wins a majority of the seats in the Parliament, the mechanism by which the Parliament chooses an executive is more complicated, but we will come back to that later.

Here we have to stress another fundamental difference between presidential and parliamentary systems. In a presidential system the people elect a president and he or she appoints a cabinet to direct the executive. In a parliamentary system, by contrast, it is the Parliament that plays the primary role in 'appointing' the Prime Minister –indeed it 'appoints' not only the Prime Minister but the whole cabinet. 'Prime Minister' just means 'first minister'. This is a member of the cabinet who is more important than other members but not fundamentally different in terms of how he or she is recruited or in terms of who he or she is answerable to. Prime ministers are not just indirectly elected presidents.

Figure 2.2   *Electoral and other linkages in a parliamentary system*

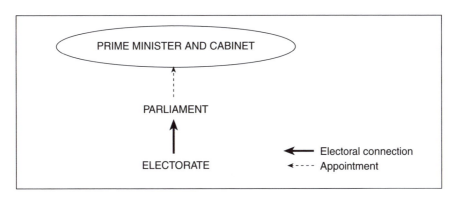

So the diagram shows the Parliament appointing a cabinet which is led by the Prime Minister. The Prime Minister is thus an integral part of the cabinet but plays a major role in choosing its other members. In practice the Prime Minister and cabinet are selected as a team. In the case of a one-party cabinet, the Prime Minister will be the leader of the party and will generally have been so long before an election took place. So, when voters place a parliamentary majority in the hands of one party, they know who their Prime Minister will be – though the exact identity of the other members of the cabinet may not be known and will to some extent be a matter for negotiation between the Prime Minister and other Members of Parliament.

In a parliamentary system, once a government has been chosen, the coordination problems which make up such a big part of politics in America do not exist as such (there are no double-headed arrows in Figure 2.2). Another way of saying this is that the American system has a dual chain of command rather than a single one (Strøm 2000). As long as a cabinet has the confidence of the Parliament, the Parliament will support that cabinet, its policies and its legislative proposals. Should there be a serious difference of opinion one of two things will normally happen. Either some accommodation will be reached or the cabinet will resign and a new one will be appointed (perhaps after new elections) that does have the confidence of the Parliament. Because of this, no arrow is required in the diagram to represent coordination between parliament and cabinet.

This is the primary consequence of a system in which the cabinet is appointed by the Parliament: the executive and legislative branches of government (cabinet and parliament, respectively) will generally agree on policy. However, the primary role of the Parliament is to oversee the operations of the government, acting as a sort of stand-in for the electorate. It is as though, in the period between elections, the electorate had delegated its legitimating powers to the Parliament. In the unlikely case of serious disagreement between parliament and government, parliament withdraws its support thus forcing a change in the composition of the government (and thus of its policies) or new elections, after which the new parliament appoints a new cabinet.[3]

This brings us to a final contrast between parliamentary and presidential systems. Though the presidential system provides no way of resolving an impasse between President and Congress other than by holding elections, elections in the US are held on a fixed timetable established in the constitution: the Congress every two years, the President every four. So, in the event of an insoluble disagreement between the President and Congress the country will experience real gridlock – not just the minor inconvenience of an inability to agree on some legislative proposal – and might have to wait until the next election for an opportunity to resolve it. In the American system, an impasse of this kind cannot be resolved by replacing the cabinet (because the President cannot be replaced between elections) or by calling an early election (because the system does not allow for such an eventuality).

Of course, even in parliamentary systems, because the circumstances that would bring about an early election are well known, and because the likely outcome of an election is also generally knowable (from opinion polls), it is quite rare in practice that insoluble conflicts arise between government and parliament. A famous book by a retired British cabinet minister (Morrison 1954) contains a chapter entitled 'How Government and Parliament Live Together Or Die'. Early elections are nevertheless quite common and often originate from insoluble conflicts within the government itself (Gallagher *et al.* 2005). The government generally proposes policies that it hopes will in due course bring support from voters, and the Parliament goes along with these proposals on the same basis. Only in the event of grave lack of judgment on someone's part (Prime Minister or Members of Parliament) does the scenario sketched out above play out, with the government being defeated in parliament on a crucial issue or a vote of no confidence, leading to a new government or new elections being called. But because this is the ultimate resort that keeps the system running without coordination problems, the voter has an importance in parliamentary systems that is ordinarily lacking in the US. This is actually somewhat paradoxical since it has been shown that election outcomes have a stronger impact in terms of changing the executive in presidential systems (Maravall 2008). But the problem in presidential systems is that replacing the executive does not, on its own, necessarily result in the implementation of policies that the voters want. A new president still has to deal with a congress whose political complexion is often unchanged (see Box 2.3 on Mexican politics).

The fact that in most parliamentary systems new elections can be called at short notice has a number of other consequences, some of them quite surprising. A primary consequence is that parties must hold themselves ready for the possibility that an early election will be called. This means that every party must to some extent keep its party platform and lists of candidates updated. Early elections do not provide parties with sufficient time to hold a party conference (what Americans would call a 'convention') in which a platform of campaign promises can be put together. For this reason it is normal for parties in parliamentary regimes to hold party conferences annually (some hold them every six months) so as to ensure that they are constantly ready for the possibility of an early election. The frequency of party conferences also means that various party offices have to be constantly manned. Party organizations in parliamentary regimes cannot be allowed to fall into disarray, as frequently happens in the US during the four years that pass between party conventions.

Indeed, the leaders of the various parties in a parliamentary system find it quite easy to stay in the public eye, since they all have roles in parliament. Moreover, the frequency of party conferences also ensures that parties have regular opportunities to present publicly their policies, which is one of the reasons why elections in these countries are more policy oriented than in the US. Because policies are better known there is also a larger premium on continuity. A party dare not make an unprepared major change to its program for fear of losing credibility and/or confusing its voters. Keeping roughly the same program and only incrementally adapting it, convention after convention, election after election, ensures that, even though the voters are not paying any more attention to politics than they do in the US, there is not the same need for a long campaign to bring a party's policies and candidates to the attention of voters. In the US, the long gap between party conventions, together with the fact that a party can adopt as candidate for high office someone that most voters have never heard of, allows American parties much more flexibility in coming up with candidates and election platforms that break with past tradition (and thereby try to avoid blame for past failures); but this adaptability is one reason why American voters are less aware of what these platforms contain.

On the other hand, the very fact that European voters do know (and are attached to) their parties' policy positions makes it hard for policy-oriented parties to change drastically their existing policies or to take new policies on board, since they can lose support in the process. In multiparty systems this rigidity of policy-oriented parties is largely balanced by the ease with which new parties can arise to propose policies that established parties are ignoring, but in two-party (or quasi-two-party) parliamentary systems like the British it is also difficult for new parties to gain support, so the political system can prove quite resistant to new ideas. Environmental policies, for example, were more slowly adopted in Britain than in the US or Germany. And the change that led the British Labour Party to start referring to itself as 'New Labour' in the 1997 parliamentary elections in Britain actually took more than 20 years to accomplish (and a major split in the party in the early 1980s).

The fact that US parties can quite easily change their policy orientations also makes it easier for new issues to come onto the policy agenda and provides one reason why new parties find it hard to get a foothold. New political parties are generally founded on an issue that existing parties are neglecting (as happened in Germany with the foundation of the Green Party). This does happen in the US, but if newcomers have some degree of success it is easy for the major parties to simply adopt the policy that was proving successful, thus pulling the rug out from under any new party that was founded to promote that policy. In the US, three-party battles over policy have been relatively rare, though one such battle occurred in 1992 when Ross Perot ran for President as a third-party candidate, opposing the North American Free Trade Agreement and promoting a balanced budget.

Another mechanism by which new policies enter the agenda of American politics is through individual candidates trying out new ideas on an individual basis in their election campaigns. This entrepreneurship on the part of individual candidates ironically contributes to the difficulty of having policy-centered elections in a country where a party's candidates for different offices do not speak with the same voice. In the US each individual candidate has to make himself or herself known to potential voters, incidentally giving enormous advantages to politicians who already hold elected office (incumbent politicians); each individual candidate is generally considered to be the best judge of what message to put before his or her prospective voters. In parliamentary systems it is the party that is responsible for getting out its message, and there is less room for individual candidates to define their own policy platforms. The primary expectation in a parliamentary system is that candidates associate themselves with the program of their party and promise to work hard for its implementation.

Problems of parliamentary government: single-party versus coalition governments

From all of the above the parliamentary system of government may sound like a pretty good system; and, broadly speaking, so it is. It is not by accident that the US is the only presidential system among the 22 countries that have held elections continuously since World War II (though the important role given to voters is not the only reason successful democracies have preferred the parliamentary system). One of the most renowned American analysts of democracy, Robert Dahl, has repeatedly listed a large number of arguments against the adoption of an American-style presidential system by countries involved in a transformation of their systems to representative democracy (Dahl 2002).

The parliamentary system does, however, have a major complication. What happens when, after an election, no single party commands a majority of seats in the Parliament (called a 'hung parliament)? The answer is different in different countries; and some parliamentary systems handle the problem more gracefully than others. Nevertheless, every parliamentary regime is threatened with the possibility that parliament cannot agree on a cabinet, and new elections do not solve the problem. For a variety of reasons the potential for such a crisis is seldom realized in practice.

Some countries minimize the possibility of a hung parliament by employing an electoral system that magnifies the winner's margin to the point of manufacturing an absolute majority of parliamentary seats for the leading party even should that party fail to win a majority of the votes cast. This electoral system (generally referred to as the 'first past the post' or FPTP electoral system and which is used mainly in Anglo-Saxon countries) has the disadvantage, however, of frequently producing governments that do not represent the majority of voters (see Box 2.1 on the British election of 2005). And even though an advantage is given to the winning party in such systems,

Box 2.1   The British general election of 2005

In the British general election of 2005 the Labour party won an historic third consecutive term in office. The party acquired 35.2 per cent of the valid votes cast, which gave it 356 seats in the House of Commons, that is 55.1 per cent of the total of 646 seats. Here is a summary of the election results:

	Votes (%)	Seats (no.)	Seats (%)
Labour	35.2	356	55.1
Conservatives	32.4	198	30.7
Liberal Democrats	22.0	62	9.6
All other parties combined	10.4	30	4.6

Turnout was 61.3 per cent, which implies that the Labour vote amounted to no more than 21.5 per cent of the population of voting age, a record low for British general elections since World War II. During the 1950s the winning party represented approximately 38 per cent of the voting age population, a share that declined to somewhat over 30 per cent in the subsequent period up until 1997, but then fell further to 24 per cent in 2001 and 21.5 per cent in 2005 (cf. Rallings and Thrasher 2007). The FPTP electoral system gives the largest party a larger share of seats than its proportion of votes. Combined with the lower turnout that is a feature of FPTP countries (Franklin 2004), this results in the proportion of the population supporting the winning party falling far below 50 per cent.

this advantage is not guaranteed to be enough to give that party a majority of seats in the Parliament. A hung parliament is still possible even with FPTP elections, and such an outcome generally (three times during the 20th century in Britain) gives rise to a minority government – a government supported by less than a majority of the seats in the Parliament – that exists on the sufferance of other parties and which usually has to call early elections when that sufferance wears thin. In such circumstances the existence of a viable government rests in the hands of parties who are not part of the government and who must show restraint if any government at all is to be carried on. This is not a satisfactory state of affairs, though it is one that Britain and several of its former colonies managed fairly gracefully on those few occasions when it became necessary.

In countries where the electoral system attempts to allocate seats to parties in proportion to the votes cast for each party (so called 'proportional' or PR systems used in many continental European countries) it is rare for an election to result in one party gaining a majority of seats in the Parliament. In those countries it is usual for the parliamentary election to be followed by a period of uncertainty as parties court each other as potential partners in a *coalition government*. After a good deal of bargaining a deal is generally struck and a government is formed consisting of two or more parties which have been able to agree on a program of government activity and which between them control a majority of the seats in the Parliament. This system also relies on restraint. Parties must be willing to give up some of their campaign promises and to compromise with other parties on a program of legislation in which all of them find only some of their desired policies included. The process is complicated by the need to make the compromise palatable, which takes time, both at the level of party members and at the mass level of voters who supported the parties in question. A party that too easily compromises on its campaign promises will be seen as 'selling out', risking punishment at the next election. But a party can also be seen as too intransigent, also risking loss of support if it is seen as squandering its chances of government participation and of getting at least some of its desired policies enacted – let alone if it is seen as endangering the governability of the country (see Box 2.2).

The process of coalition formation is often a messy one as parties seek the delicate balance between giving way too easily and standing too long on principle. And the outcome of the process can be quite disappointing to voters who supported a party on account of a particular policy that is dropped in the coalition bargaining process.

The often lengthy periods of time between an election and the inauguration of a new government, and the fact that the policies of such a government are indeterminate at the time of an election, is the basis for critiques of PR from supporters and opponents alike. On the other hand, even opponents

Box 2.2   Government formation in the Netherlands

In the Netherlands parties usually keep their cards close to their chest when it comes to the parties with whom they would be willing to form a coalition. As a consequence, the construction of a coalition only starts after the results of a parliamentary election are known. Because parliamentary power is rather fragmented there are – at least in numerical terms – usually multiple possibilities for constructing a majority. Even when taking into account considerations of ideological homogeneity and a desire to keep the number of participating parties to a minimum, there are commonly still several different possibilities. The largest party in parliament is allowed the first try at putting together a workable coalition. This involves several rounds of interparty consultation. Even if this first attempt is successful, it commonly takes up to three months to hammer out a programmatic policy agreement and to recruit a team that is willing to implement it and of which the members are not at each others' throats. There is no guarantee, however, that the first try will be successful, and additional iterations may well be required. Until a new coalition government has been sworn in, the old government acts as a caretaker but is expected not to take major new policy initiatives.

Since World War II, the average period involved in coalition formation was 85 days (excluding caretaker governments), with a range from 31 days in 1948 to 208 days in 1977 (Andeweg and Irwin 2009).

concede one desirable property of PR elections: far more than in FPTP elections every vote counts and does so equally. In FPTP elections, a district in which one candidate wins by a landslide is a district in which many of the votes were unnecessary. Knowing that one of the candidates in an FPTP election is far ahead in the polls discourages both supporters and opponents from voting, giving rise to the so-called 'wasted vote syndrome'. And even if a district is closely fought, the votes for the losing parties are effectively wasted. In PR elections this does not happen. Every vote goes towards electing a candidate from one party or another, and every vote above the number needed to elect one candidate for a party goes towards electing another candidate for the same party. PR systems usually see higher turnouts than FPTP systems, and it is generally assumed that the fact that every vote counts in PR systems is the reason for this. Moreover, most PR systems manage successfully to produce effective governments election after election, often with the help of elaborate procedures that have evolved over the years to guide politicians to an acceptable compromise in a reasonable length of time. We will describe some of these procedures in the next chapter.

Though PR systems are often criticized for the indeterminacy that results from the coalition bargaining phase of the process, as with other aspects of parliamentary democracy parties have it in their power to mitigate this problem. Indeed, the entire coalition bargaining process can be virtually eliminated if groups of parties make pre-election pacts or alliances, agreeing with each other beforehand to form a coalition government should they receive sufficient seats in the legislature, and agreeing beforehand on the policies that such a coalition government would pursue. When this is done, the electoral process resembles that in countries where single-party governments are the norm. Voters are able to cast their votes for particular parties knowing what policies would be pursued if those parties (together with their announced coalition allies) were to win the majority of seats in the Parliament. In such elections the uncertainties that result from the coalition bargaining stage in PR elections are considerably reduced. Such situations have occasionally occurred in countries where a successful coalition government asks the voters for a continued lease on life as a team. It has also occasionally happened that a non-incumbent coalition has proposed itself to the voters, as happened in Italy in 2008, in Germany in 1998, in the Netherlands in 1972, and regularly in Norway.

Problems of presidential systems

Aside from the US, there are seven or eight new democracies (or new semi-democracies like Russia) that are presidential, and several more in Latin America. A number of countries in Africa and Asia that started out as parliamentary systems rewrote their constitutions to become presidential systems.

Presidential systems are actually quite common among new democracies, transitional democracies and shaky democracies. This is because properly functioning parliamentary systems depend on many people observing rather intricate *rules of the game.* Countries without considerable experience of self-government in one form or another are often thought to be better off with a presidential system, not least because such countries often have fluid and fragmented party systems which defy the prerequisites of parliamentary government. A presidential system virtually guarantees that there will always be a government because the President is directly elected by the people and there does not have to be a legislative majority in support of any one set of policies in order for the government to be carried on. Unfortunately, these governments are often not very functional. Because the legislature does not have to get its act together in order to appoint the executive, there is no guarantee that it will ever get its act together; yet this is required for the enactment of legislation. As a consequence, it may be exceedingly difficult for a president to get any legislation enacted at all.

So presidential systems are liable to gridlock, and even at the best of times are quite unresponsive to public opinion. The separation of powers in a presidential system means that the will of a regular majority in the legislature can easily be blocked, as happens in the US. Moreover, the advantage enjoyed by incumbent politicians means that when political change takes place it is quite likely to take place in one branch of the government (House, Senate or President) but not in more than one of the other branches. So a newly constituted majority can find it very hard to get its policies enacted (as was the case for Vicente Fox in Mexico – see Box 2.3). Only when change results in the presidency and both houses of congress coming under the control of the same political party is it at all easy for electoral change to result in policy change – something that only happened eight times during the entire 20th century in the US, a period during which there were no fewer than 20 occasions when political power moved from one party to another in at least one house of Congress or the presidency.

Box 2.3　Mexican politics after the election of Vicente Fox

In Mexico in 1999 a candidate for president was elected who, for the first time in the history of the republic, was not a member of the previously ruling PRI (Institutional Revolutionary Party). Vicente Fox was the candidate for the PAN (National Action Party), and he won a comfortable victory in the presidential election. However, his party did not have any chance of gaining a majority in the Mexican House of Deputies, so he found himself facing a legislature that was still dominated by the PRI – the party that had governed Mexico for over 70 years. In this situation it was virtually impossible for him to carry out his legislative program and voters who had supported him hoping for a new dawn in Mexican politics were quite disappointed.

Government formation

We have already noted the fact that, whereas parliamentary elections decide – directly or indirectly – who will run the government and also what policies the government will be able to pursue, presidential elections in the US decide only who will run the government. Who runs the government does of course influence the nature of the policies made by that government, but not in any definitive fashion, as we will see later in this chapter.

Talking about the differences between the two sorts of system is complicated by a difference in vocabulary. Americans use the word 'government' to talk about the full complement of people who man both houses of Congress (and their aides) as well as the whole executive branch. They use the word 'administration' to talk about the members of the executive who get their jobs as a consequence of a new president taking office, and the bureaucracy that is directed by those appointees. In parliamentary systems, on the other hand, the word 'government' refers to what Americans would call 'administration': the cabinet together with the bureaucracy directed by that cabinet (including many who held the same jobs under the previous government). There is no easy way to overcome this disjunction since the government in a parliamentary system includes the whole of the bureaucracy and also extends to cabinet members who are elected members of the Parliament. But since we have no need to refer to the entire apparatus of government in any country we will use the words 'administration' and 'government' interchangeably to refer to the executive branch of government in both types of system. A similar linguistic confusion attends the name given to a member of a governing cabinet who in parliamentary systems is referred to as a 'minister' but in the US is referred to as a 'secretary'. We will refer to such individuals as 'cabinet members' in both types of system.

In the US, the number of people who will change jobs with a change of administration is vastly greater than the number who will change jobs with a change of government in other countries. In the US literally thousands of individuals lose their jobs when there is a change of administration following a presidential election.[4] These large numbers start with the cabinet members themselves, who are not generally recruited from the Congress (which in any case would require them to resign their seats) and so retain no role in the government of the country when they cease to be cabinet members. But the numbers of individuals who lose their jobs following a change of government in the US – individuals who in other countries would be civil servants – is vastly greater than this, since each new cabinet member expects to appoint every member of his or her department with any responsibility for policy-making: some 4,000 in all. Indirectly, the election decides who all these people are. But the election does not decide policy. Policy only starts to be decided as all these thousands of new faces find their offices, make their connections, pick up the work of their departments and start to build the relationships with Congress and with congressional lobbyists that will be needed in order for legislation to be enacted.

In parliamentary regimes things are different. There a new government takes office with a flurry of movement that looks a bit like a game of musical chairs, as members of parliament who were cabinet members in the old government lose their plush offices and chauffeur-driven limousines to return to their roles as simple members of parliament, giving way to a different set of cabinet members in the new government. In some of these countries a small number of ministerial aides may also lose their jobs to be replaced by aides to the newly appointed cabinet members, but we are talking of a few dozen individuals at most –not thousands. Where one party wins a majority it takes office immediately, often within 24 hours (see Box 2.4). Much the same is true in cases where victory goes to a preannounced coalition of parties with preannounced policies. In these cases the new cabinet is often in place within weeks and policy starts to be made immediately as veteran civil servants are briefed on the policies of the new government. In such cases the impact of the election on policy is palpable and virtually instantaneous. In cases where one party (or a preannounced coalition) does not win a majority of the seats in the legislature there will often be a significant delay between the election and its policy consequences, as parties bargain with each other and try to find a combination of parties and policies that will yield a majority in the legislature, together with a program of legislation acceptable to all coalition members (see Box 2.2 on government formation in the Netherlands). But still it is rare for this to take as long as the nine months that regularly elapses in the US between the announcement of a presidential election outcome and the date when a new administration is fully in place.

Box 2.4   A transfer of power in Britain

On 2 May 1997 Labour came to power after a prolonged period of Conservative rule under Prime Ministers Thatcher and Major. The results became known early in the night, and the Prime Minister – Conservative John Major – conceded defeat. The next morning Major offered his resignation to the Queen, who subsequently asked the Labour leader – Tony Blair – to form a new government. At 1 p.m. that day, Blair moved into the official Prime Minister's residence at 10 Downing Street and started his first term in office. The 'dead tide' between the outgoing and incoming governments, between Major conceding defeat and Blair being entrusted with the reins of government, lasted little more than 12 hours.

The work done during the period of delay is also very different. In contrast to the US, in a parliamentary regime policy is at the centre of what happens when a new government takes office, even when coalition bargaining is needed. In such countries the election outcome sets the parameters within which bargaining can take place by determining which combinations of parties would be able to control a majority of the seats.

How elections condition coalition bargaining

Political scientists have long been fascinated by the coalition bargaining process, seeing it as an opportunity for testing a variety of theories about political decision-making. In Chapter 3 we will discuss the formation of coalitions in some detail, but for the moment we want to focus on the way in which elections condition that process. Table 2.1 sets out the implications of an imaginary election outcome for coalition formation. The parties are named at the top of the table according to their policy preferences represented in left–right terms, from left through centre-left and centre-right to right (see pp. 13–14 for a discussion of this political spectrum). The number of seats each party controls in the legislature – a number established in the imaginary election just past – is listed immediately below. These numbers determine which possible coalitions will control more than half the seats in the imaginary 100-seat legislature. We suppose that the cabinet will contain 20 members, and the cells in each subsequent row of the table give the number of cabinet members that each party would expect to have if they joined in a coalition with the other party(ies) with entries in that row. The reason we can be unequivocal about this is that one of the best-established regularities in political science is that parties that are members of a coalition government gain cabinet members pretty much in proportion to the seat shares they contribute to the coalition (Browne and Franklin 1973).

The table tells us that there are a number of ways in which to build a coalition that would command a majority in the Parliament (seven different possible cabinets are listed, named A to G). Which of these is formed will depend on the criteria that parties apply in choosing coalition partners and on their skills in the bargaining process, as we will explain in the next chapter. However, it can be seen immediately from the table that the number of cabinet positions (ministries) received by each party is greatest in the cabinet that controls fewest seats in the Parliament (Cabinet A) and that, for each party, this number declines progressively as the number of seats that the coalition controls increases beyond that minimum needed for control of the legislature. Other things being equal, therefore, parties will prefer to be members of a coalition towards the top of the table (where they would

Table 2.1 *Seats contributed and cabinet members received with various coalitions arising from a 100-seat legislature and 20-member cabinet*

	Parties			
	Left	*Centre-left*	*Centre-right*	*Right*
Seat shares (out of 100)	15/100	23/100	34/100	28/100
Cabinet A (51 seats) ministries		9/20		11/20
Cabinet B (57 seats) ministries		8/20	12/20	
Cabinet C (62 seats) ministries			11/20	9/20
Cabinet D (66 seats) ministries	5/20	7/20		8/20
Cabinet E (72 seats) ministries	4/20	6/20	10/20	
Cabinet F (77 seats) ministries	4/20		9/20	7/20
Cabinet G (85 seats) ministries		5/20	8/20	7/20

control policy-making in more government departments) rather than one towards the bottom of the table where they would have less influence. Other things are not always equal, of course, and the other factors involved in coalition negotiations will be discussed in Chapter 3.

In some ways the hand that is dealt by elections in multiparty systems is analogous to the hand that is dealt by elections in the US. There, too, coalitions have to be built in order to pass legislation – coalitions that combine legislators from one party with those from the other as necessary to compensate for the lack of party discipline in the US Congress. But the hand that is dealt by elections in the US does not play out until after the government has already taken office, as the President and his administration try to build coalitions in Congress to pass legislation. Indeed, it happens bill by bill in an extraordinarily protracted fashion, with different coalitions forming on different issues to get different pieces of legislation passed. And in the American case elections have much less influence because the coalition-forming process is much less affected by the hand dealt at election time. Because it is so protracted, it continues long after the election itself has been forgotten, opening the way for interest groups to dominate the process of coalition bargaining (see Box 2.5 on US health care reform).

Box 2.5   **President Clinton's attempt to enact health care reform**

In the 1992 presidential election in the US, the candidate for the Democratic Party, Bill Clinton, made a number of promises that helped him to defeat the elder George Bush who was the incumbent President and Republican Party candidate. One was the famous promise to bring better economic times ('It's the economy, stupid!'), a promise he redeemed with flying colors. The other promise that is still remembered was that of enacting health care reform and introducing a system of insurance for more than 40 million Americans who lacked health care insurance and hence access to any but emergency health care. Opinion polls showed this to be a popular promise and, once elected, Bill Clinton (now President Clinton) set about trying to redeem it. He established a high profile commission, headed by his wife Hillary (later Senator for New York and then Secretary of State), who eventually brought forward a plan of legislation to establish a universal health insurance system. However, the proposal was not passed by the Congress – even though this was a Congress in which a majority of both houses were Democrats and thus of the same political party as the President. The reasons are too numerous to list here, but an important role was played by interest groups defending the interests of wealthy insurance companies. The important point for now is that the President was unable to redeem a major campaign promise because he could not get members of his own political party to support the resulting proposals.

Coming back to coalitions in parliamentary democracies with a proportionally elected parliament, the deals and compromises needed to reach agreement on a legislative program happen before a cabinet takes office. Therefore, when the cabinet does take office it does so with a set of proposals that it is committed to carry into law and for which it has the support of parliament. Because coalition negotiations happen behind closed doors, what emerges is based on the best deal that each party can get for the policies it espouses – interest groups have very little role in the process.

Institutional influences on the structure of political life

This repositioning of political bargaining, depending on institutional features, is an excellent example of how institutions affect politics. Politics is all about compromise. Compromises have to be made within parties as well as between them. The same things happen in all democratic polities, but they happen at different times and may involve different groups and different people depending on institutional arrangements, the number of parties and the manner in which elections are fought (the number of parties is also partly a function of institutional arrangements, but we will not go into that here). Different institutions change the whole appearance of political life in a country and give elections a greater or a lesser role in determining policy outcomes. That is what makes institutions so important.

The more issues that elections decide, the more important the election will appear to voters. Additionally, the more influence that voters have, the more important the election will appear to them. In the US, in normal times, elections are doubly eviscerated. Their importance is weakened firstly because they are candidate-centered and do not solve coordination problems between President and Congress or between the two houses of Congress, as they do in policy-centered parliamentary systems. And their importance is weakened secondly because election outcomes, especially for House elections, seem to be more determined by the advantages of incumbency than by agreement of voters with the policy positions of candidates (Fiorina 1989). So elections are generally less competitive and settle fewer fundamental questions in the US than elsewhere, which is one reason why turnout in American elections is so low compared to most other established democracies (Powell 1986; Franklin 2004). In parliamentary systems much more is at stake, and turnout is generally much higher.

However, elections in the US are not invariably eviscerated. Occasionally – once or twice in a century – America has seen elections in which a presidential candidate with radically different policies has won an election at which so many congressional seats changed hands that the checks and balances normally standing in the way of palpable policy change are ineffective (Brady and Stewart 1991). But such elections are infrequent.

Coming back to the normal run of American elections, the main difference from parliamentary systems is that the party in government is often not in a position to fulfill its most important campaign promises, whereas the opposite is true in parliamentary systems. Americans might well ask 'Why would we expect politicians to fulfill their promises?'. Evidently it is quite common in the US for politicians to promise some policy and then fail to enact that policy – see Box 2.5 about President Clinton's attempt to enact health care reform. Not only was President Clinton not able to enact this reform, he also was not punished for his failure when the time came to re-elect him in 1996. Indeed he won this election with a bigger majority than in 1992. The reason for this is that voters generally understood that it was not Clinton's fault that health care reform was not enacted. He simply could not get the Congress to vote for it. So the 1996 election was fought on other grounds (a balanced budget, for example).

Such a scenario, so common in the US as to arouse no anger on the part of voters, would be most unlikely to occur in a parliamentary democracy. There, a cabinet that formed with the intention of introducing a reform as extensive and high profile as the Clinton health care reform would already have the necessary parliamentary majority in support of that reform. Once a cabinet has been formed and appointed by a parliament, it effectively has a 'contract' with that parliament to bring forward certain policies and submit relevant legislation on the expectation that there is a majority in parliament to enact those policies. In such circumstances, if the government did not bring forward the promised policies it might be held accountable at the next election for its failure to do so – if the parliament had not replaced it long before the next election on account of the same failure. Of course, not many policies have the salience in any country that health care reform had in the US in 1992, and it is only on highly salient policies that voters could be expected to be sufficiently aware of government failure as to hold that government to account. But they seldom if ever have the chance to actually do so, even in parliamentary regimes, precisely because governments in those systems generally do deliver on high profile policies of this kind. Much more frequent is the sight of a parliament holding a government to account for failing to enact some promised policy.

Something else we seldom if ever see are elections called to decide an issue that comes up during the term of a parliament – during the period between elections – that was not on the agenda at the time of the previous election. In the modern world it is hard to think of a single occasion when such an election has actually been called, both because parliamentary majorities seldom disagree with the governments they support regarding new policies (giving the voters no role as adjudicators) and because parties have opinion polls to help them decide what the outcome of such an election would be (providing the opportunity for 'rational anticipation', discussed in Chapter 5, p. 125). But in principle the Parliament could object to any policy proposed by a government that had not been included among the policies put before the voters at the previous election, and it would do so if it feared that a future election would cost a lot of members their seats as a result of the policy concerned. In such circumstances they would not have to wait for the next election to roll around on a fixed timetable. Most parliamentary democracies can call an election at a few months' notice. And the fact that this can happen keeps the politicians focused on what would happen in such an election. In a sense, the politicians in a parliamentary democracy are always looking over their shoulders at the electorate because the electorate is the final arbiter of any dispute between government and parliament.

We should also note in passing that in some parliamentary regimes it is normal for the Prime Minister to be allowed a degree of latitude in calling for an election at the end of a parliamentary term. In Britain, for example, the law stipulates that new elections must be held within five years, but in practice elections are usually called any time within the final year of the parliamentary term (if an election was not held earlier for other reasons). This latitude allows the Prime Minister to take advantage of fluctuations in economic conditions or other developments that might provide his or her party with a marginal advantage in an election. In principle there is nothing to stop a Prime Minister from calling an election at any earlier point to take advantage of a favorable economy or other advantageous factors, but in practice he or she would be restrained by the knowledge that voters really dislike unnecessary elections and would penalize a party that was seen as having called an election merely for partisan advantage (as happened in France in 1997 – see Box 2.6).

Habits and routines

The stability provided by relatively slow-changing institutions gives rise to opportunities for learning on the part of voters and parties. Learning gives rise to habits and habits are necessary for the functioning of the electoral process. Without an important role for habit, everyone would be required to start from scratch at each election and spend inordinate amounts of time acquiring an orientation that allowed them to make sensible choices. This is one reason why elections in newly democratizing countries show great instability. Once systems have become stable, however, voters and parties can act on the basis of existing knowledge and experience in a cost-effective manner. The repeated reiteration of a pattern of behavior or choice constitutes a learning process leading to choices being made increasingly on the basis of habit rather than on the basis of conscious reflection.

Box 2.6   An early French election

The constitution of the French Fifth Republic was written with a built-in possibility of what the French call 'cohabitation' (which has the same meaning in English). France is a semi-presidential system where executive power is divided between the (directly elected) President and a cabinet, which, as in parliamentary systems, can only function if it is supported by a parliamentary majority. The problem arises when the President is of one party while the legislature, and thus the Prime Minister and cabinet, are from a different party. Because the presidential term was originally set at seven years but the Assembly's term at five years, cohabitation was possible towards the end of the term of a president whose popularity was declining (as often happens towards the end of a government's tenure in office). By 1997 this had happened only twice in the history of the Fifth Republic, but Jacques Chirac (President since 1995 and faced with declining popularity) decided to call parliamentary elections after only two years in office, hoping to take advantage of unpreparedness by the opposition socialists and gain a mandate for his party in the Assembly which would then last the remaining five years of his presidency. Unfortunately, the French voters were quite aware of this strategy and what remained of his party's popularity evaporated in the face of what the voters regarded as an unnecessary election called for party political purposes. The conservative majority the President had enjoyed in parliament was voted out and replaced with a socialist majority with which he then had to cohabit unhappily for the remaining five years of his term. Eventually, the prospect of repeated cohabitations for the final years of a presidential term led to an amendment to the constitution establishing five-year terms for the President, so that a new mandate could be found both at the parliamentary and at the presidential level at about the same time. Though the elections were not made simultaneous, the expectation is that parliamentary elections will normally occur within a year of presidential elections, all but eliminating the periods of cohabitation that had proved so irritating to previous presidents.

One of the things that voters need to learn is the habit of voting. In countries where everyone (or virtually everyone) votes, the learning process leading to that habit is evidently short and obstacles are readily overcome. In countries where turnout is lower, those who fail to learn the habit of voting are those who fail to overcome various obstacles that are not necessarily greater in those countries. As far as we know it is rather that the motivation to overcome those obstacles is lower.

Motivation is lowest among voters who have only recently reached voting age, especially so after the lowering of the voting age in many countries has resulted in the enfranchisement of individuals whose educations are not complete and who are, many of them, following courses of study away from home (Franklin 2004). It seems that learning to vote is principally facilitated by membership in social networks and by contact with people who deem it important that someone newly of voting age votes (Plutzer 2002). Such networks are harder to come by for individuals who are at college or who are in the process of establishing themselves in a new career and social circumstances: precisely the situation of many in the 18–22 age group. In Chapter 1 we referred, in the context of electoral participation, to a general tendency to find retrospectively reasons for our own behavior, even if that behavior came about by chance. Once having 'found' such reasons, these stay in force unless the experience was utterly unrewarding (Fiorina 1981). This applies not only to the habit of voting. Just as importantly, each time someone fails to vote at an election it is more likely that they will fail to vote at the following election also. So a lot depends on the situation people find themselves in during the first elections at which they are old enough to vote. Those who are finding it hard to make ends meet, who are working in multiple jobs or who have young children at home are less likely to learn the habit of voting than those in more fortunate circumstances. The result is a link between poverty and non-voting, especially in countries where motivations to vote are low to start out with.

The fact that voting involves a learning process has consequences in all countries for the age structure of the voting electorate: older people are more likely to be voters than younger people. Partly this is what social scientists call an age effect (see p. 16 for a discussion of this type of change): older people have had the time in which to learn their way around their political systems and to acquire the habit of voting, so they vote at higher rates than younger people. But partly it is also what social scientists call a period effect. Learning to vote was easier before the voting age was lowered, because the first election at which most people were eligible to vote came later in life when circumstances for acquiring the habit were more propitious. It is ironic that the well-intentioned extension of the franchise to 18-year-olds in many countries after the mid-1960s (previously the voting age was generally 21 or higher) had the unanticipated consequence of a lifetime of non-voting for many of the intended beneficiaries (Franklin 2004).

We have already mentioned that election outcomes can be affected by who actually does vote and who not. More importantly, who does vote reflects how inclusive the political system is. If large numbers of people regularly fail to participate in elections in some country that puts into question the democratic nature of those elections, especially if those who fail to vote can be expected to hold different political preferences than those who do vote (Piven and Cloward 2000). The most important force that determines whether individuals will vote or not is party loyalty, often known as 'party identification'. We will focus on this in Chapter 4, but now is a good time to introduce the basic concepts involved.

Socialization, immunization and party identification

About half a century ago, a landmark book called *The American Voter* (Campbell *et al.* 1960) was published that established the nature of party loyalty and the manner in which it was acquired in the US. Nine years later, one of the co-authors of this book co-authored *Political Change in Britain* (Butler and Stokes 1969, 1974). These two books detail the mechanisms involved and the fact that essentially the same mechanisms operate in a policy-centered as in a candidate-centered democracy. The critical concepts are socialization and immunization, which are different aspects of the same phenomenon.

Socialization is the mechanism by which most norms and values are acquired. The process happens during a person's 'formative years' which stretch – as far as political norms and values are concerned – from childhood into early adulthood. Socialized behavior is habitual behavior not founded in explicit deliberation. It thus provides stability in behavior, unless it is unlearned in later life, which would require severe and persistent dissatisfaction with the outcomes of the socialized habits. This is how we learn most of our behavior patterns, and it seems that this is how many of us learn to identify with politically relevant objects (often parties or ideologies, sometimes labor unions or other political reference groups). The main source of partisanship is, of course, the home; but other powerful socializing agents are neighbors, friends, fellow students and, ultimately, colleagues at work. Important socializing institutions include schools and churches. If these influences reinforce each other, then young adults are virtually certain to enter the electorate with a partisanship consistent with those influences. If the influences are absent or cross-cutting, however (far more likely in the modern world than used to be the case), then initial partisanship is less certain and may be altogether absent.

Partisan influences are most likely to be coherent for children brought up in a homogeneous ethnic or religious environment in which similarity of values and interests has bred uniformity of party preference. So specific religious or ethnic environments have historically been fertile breeding grounds for strong partisanship. Such influences are synonymous with membership in a self-conscious social or ethnic group, and group memberships are commonly regarded as the prime cause of partisanship, since they generate mostly uniform socializing pressures for members of that group.

Once a person reaches voting age a new force comes into play: what Butler and Stokes (1974) called 'immunization'. This arises from the act of voting itself – or perhaps rather the act of choosing, which precedes the actual vote. By supporting a particular party at the ballot, voters affirm socialized identification with that party, and repeated affirmations of support for the same party eventually lead to a psychological identification with that party which will then override most normal efforts to pry the voter away. This process of immunization works also in the absence of any socialized party identifications, by way of peer-group influence, careful consideration of choice options, *ex post* rationalization of an impulsive choice or other mechanisms. After supporting the same party for at least three times in successive elections, according to Butler and Stokes, a voter has become virtually immunized against change. One or two affirmations do not do it, however. Even after voting the same way twice, Butler and Stokes found that it was possible for a voter to choose a different party on the third occasion. Such a choice would effectively break the immunization mechanism and, though voters who had defected from an initial partisanship were likely to return to their initial partisanship, still they would need to vote for that party multiple times before becoming immunized against further change. As a result it is possible for some voters never to become immunized, and Butler and Stokes found some such voters in their samples. But most people in most countries do become immunized – generally during the course of their first three elections, and the proportion of committed partisans in the electorate increases steadily with increasing age – especially during the period before a young adult's third electoral experience (Miller and Shanks 1996: 131). It follows that swing voters are generally young voters, something often overlooked by politicians and commentators who are likely to confuse malleable young adults with a much larger category of voters who report being 'undecided', though people can be undecided for all kinds of reasons, while not being malleable in their preferences.

In order to assess how individuals' orientations towards their party system evolve as they age, we may look at the proportion expressing tied preferences for more than just one party. Starting in the early 1980s, Dutch election studies have questioned respondents about the likelihood that they would ever vote for specific parties. Each voter was questioned about all parties represented in the Dutch Parliament and responses were found to reflect their strength of preference for each of the political parties (van der Eijk and Niemöller 1983, 1984), sometimes referred to as the 'propensity to vote' for each party (see Box 1.3).

From these vote propensities it is possible to calculate for each voter how many parties are tied at the highest rating and how many other parties are given an almost equally high rating. Table 2.2 shows – for the Netherlands in 2004 – that younger voters, on average, have more parties tied or nearly tied at their highest rating. Moreover, the difference in preference between the top-scoring party and the average of the scores for all other parties increases steadily from 5.3 among the youngest members of the electorate to 7.2 among the oldest.

From Table 2.2 it can be easily seen that older voters in the Netherlands are less likely to be cross-pressured between different parties and that they

Table 2.2 *Differences in propensity to vote by cohort, Netherlands 2004*

Age in 2004	Per cent tied for first place	Per cent within one point of being tied for first place	Difference between top ranked and mean of other scores
18–22	33	58	5.3
23–27	39	58	5.8
28–32	27	55	5.9
33–37	27	53	5.6
38–42	25	50	5.9
43–47	29	53	5.9
48–53	20	43	6.2
54–57	19	41	6.0
58–63	17	45	6.1
64–67	21	39	6.3
68–73	10	31	6.4
74–77	18	33	6.6
78 and older	10	21	7.2

Source: European Election Study (2004).

are more unambiguous in their support of a single party than younger voters are. The same is true in other countries for which we have relevant data (cf. Kroh *et al.* 2007).

The extent to which socialization and immunization result in strong preferences for a single party also differs between countries. The percentage of members of an electorate having more than a single party tied or nearly tied for highest preference is shown in Figure 2.3.[5] Italy has close to 60 per cent of its voters strongly cross-pressured between at least two parties, more than twice the number of apparently unimmunized individuals as in Greece – but there are good reasons for that (see Box 3.4 about electoral reform in Italy). In other countries the proportions range from 35 per cent to 50 per cent, implying quite a large number of unimmunized voters. Some of these will doubtless have stable affinities with a small number of parties (see Box 2.7) – a situation that seems to be characteristic of contemporary Italy, France, the Netherlands and Finland. But even if less than 30 per cent of an electorate finds at least two parties equally attractive (as in Greece), this implies ample scope for aggregate electoral change, even among older voters (Mair 1997). On the other hand, except in Italy, we find majorities of people in all these countries with a clear preference for just a single party, which attests to the importance of the various processes that generate stable partisan preferences, amongst which socialization and immunization rank high in importance.

The extent to which socialization and immunization restrict the scope for electoral change (except among young adults) also varies considerably between historical periods. Really strong socializing forces require a perva-

Figure 2.3   *Percentage of electorate with more than one party closely tied (within one point) for first place, West European countries*

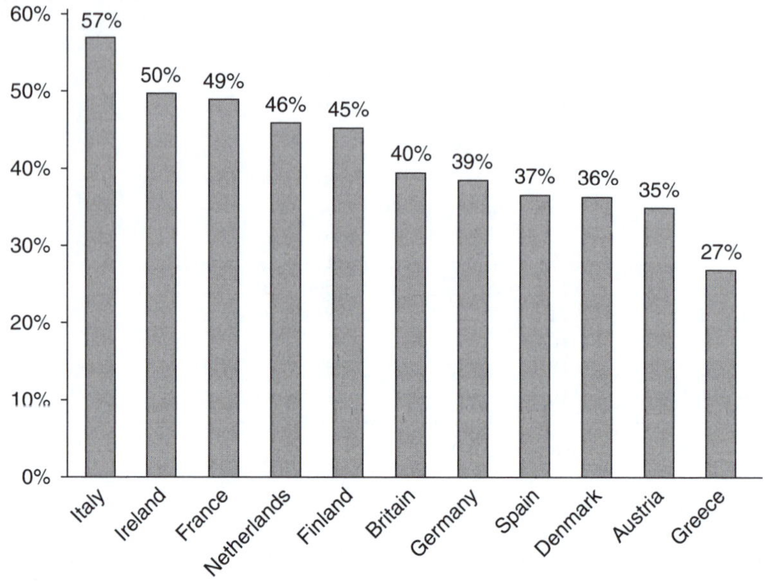

Source: European Election Study (2004).

siveness of self-conscious social groups, each of which is linked to a specific political party. In established European democracies, such groups – traditionally mainly defined in terms of religion and class – seem to have declined considerably in size and importance since the 1960s. This is the so-called 'decline of cleavage politics' (M. Franklin 1992) that will be described in Chapter 4 (pp. 95–8).

It seems clear that having a single party at the pinnacle of a citizen's party preferences rapidly leads to (if it does not already start with) a degree of partisan loyalty 'that merits the shorthand of habit' (Fiorina 1981). The mechanism that gives such consistency to habitual party supporters is not the ability to ignore evidence of failure by the party they support, but the ability to reinterpret everything they learn about that party and others in the light of their party identification. Partisanship serves as a filter that gives a partisan tint to virtually any political information. Moreover, it gives rise to various ways in which people relate selectively to information that contradicts cherished beliefs: *selective exposure* (avoiding such information), *selective acceptance* (discounting the veracity of such information) and *selective retention* (the tendency to forget such information). Additionally, partisanship serves as a cue that helps people to 'fill in the blanks' in their political knowledge. How is the economy doing? If their preferred party is in charge then the economy must be doing well. Where do they stand on stem cell research? If their party is against it then so are they. Are civil liberties being invaded by the government? Not if the government is being run by the party they support. And so on. In this way partisanship, though itself often the result of socializing influences predating voting age and of early adult decisions, in turn colors almost everything else that relates to the voting act. We will return to partisanship in Chapter 4 (pp. 87–9).

Preferences and choice

In the case of very strong and unique party identifications, voting for a party is a simple reaffirmation of that partisanship. But many voters do not (yet) have a strong party identification, or they identify with an ideology or social group that can be represented by several political parties (see Box 2.7). In all those cases it is likely that voters have preferences for more than just one

---

Box 2.7   Ideological identification

Party identification has traditionally been assessed by way of surveys in which respondents are asked how they generally think of themselves in relation to the political parties. In the US the question invites people to state whether they think of themselves as Democrats, as Republicans, or as neither. In multiparty systems this has to be phrased differently, usually in the form of two questions: the first asking whether the respondent sees him/herself as an adherent of any political party; the second – if the answer to the first question is yes – asking which party that is. Initially it was assumed that such identification would only exist in relation to a single party, and this assumption could not be challenged so long as only these questions were asked. However, in the 1981 Dutch National Election Study the traditional question was followed up by subsequent questions that probed for additional parties to which the respondent might adhere. It turned out that approximately half of those who had answered 'yes' to the original question saw themselves as adherents of more than just one party. Inspection of the combinations of parties mentioned by respondents revealed that these combinations involved political parties that were close together in left–right terms, reason for van der Eijk and Niemöller (1983) to interpret the responses as not reflecting *party* identification but *ideological* identification. Similar results were later found in other countries as well, where they are occasionally referred to as 'multiple party identification' (Niemi *et al.* 1987; Schmitt 2000; Garry 2007).

party, and we need to study those preferences in addition to the choice that they make at the end of the day (see Box 1.3). Knowing which party was voted for only gives us information about which party stood first in the voter's preference order, not which party was second or lower, and certainly not by how far those parties lagged behind the first preference party.

In Table 2.3 we illustrate these ideas and the consequences of changing circumstances for preferences and choice in a fictitious example relating preference to votes. In the top panel we look at the consequences of an increase in preferences for one of the two available parties. At the left side of this panel we report for each of five imaginary voters their preferences for each of two parties, and the choice that they make on the basis of these preferences. At the right side we report the preferences and choices of the same five voters after changing circumstances have led to an increase by two units in their preferences for Party A while their preferences for Party B remain unchanged. The division between light and shaded cells separates those voting for Party A from those voting for Party B. As can be seen, the change in preferences between the two time points $t = 1$ and $t = 2$ has no consequences at all for the choices made by any voter in the top panel. Among those who were already voting for Party A at t_1, their increased preferences for this party at t_2 only makes them more inclined towards that party, and for those who voted for Party B at t_1, the increase in their preferences for Party A was not sufficiently large to make them alter their choice. Although the distribution of choices is the same at t_1 and t_2 it would nevertheless be incorrect to conclude that nothing had changed. At the very least, Party A has acquired a much stronger position which might help it to weather the effects of adverse developments without actual loss of votes.

In the lower panel we see the consequences of changing circumstances leading to a decrease in preferences for Party A, again by two points, between t_1 and t_2. In this example, again, most people's choices are unchanged despite the change in their preferences. But this time one voter does switch parties as a result of the change in his or her preferences. For Voter 3, the reduction in preference for Party A was enough to change the order in which he or she ranked the two parties, as highlighted by the shift in the shaded area encompassing the cells involved in a choice of Party B.

The example illustrates two asymmetries in the consequences of political events and developments that impinge on voters' preferences. First, a given change in preferences for a particular party may or may not lead to a change in party choice. Second, increases in preferences for a particular party do not necessarily have consequences for choices that are the mirror image of decreases of the same magnitude. What the consequences are of events and developments on changes in party choice is therefore dependent on the existing structure of preferences, which cannot be deduced from the choices made but which must be observed empirically at each election.

Table 2.3   *Preferences and choices for parties in the light of changing preferences*

	Preferences and choices t=1			Preferences and choices t=2		
	Preference for A	*Preference for B*	*Vote choice*	*Preference for A*	*Preference for B*	*Vote choice*
Voter 1	8	1	A	10	1	A
Voter 2	7	2	A	9	2	A
Voter 3	6	5	A	8	5	A
Voter 4	3	6	B	5	6	B
Voter 5	2	7	B	4	7	B

	Preferences and choices t=1			Preferences and choices t=2		
	Preference for A	*Preference for B*	*Vote choice*	*Preference for A*	*Preference for B*	*Vote choice*
Voter 1	8	1	A	6	1	A
Voter 2	7	2	A	5	2	A
Voter 3	6	5	A	4	5	B
Voter 4	3	6	B	1	6	B
Voter 5	2	7	B	0	7	B

This apparent indeterminacy of consequences is responsible for a lot of puzzlement in the face of seemingly inconsistent findings regarding the effects of various sorts of circumstances on election outcomes in different countries and at different moments in time. It might seem plausible, for example, to suppose that economic developments should have the same consequences for the vote shares of incumbent parties in Britain in 1992 as in the US in the same or any other year. Yet, on the basis of the asymmetries seen in Table 2.3, it should be obvious why any such expectations are naïve (for worked examples see van der Brug *et al.* 2007a, App. B).[6]

We will discover that preferences derive from a multitude of factors that voters can take into account, such as any party loyalties that they may have developed, their proximity to each party in terms of ideology and particular policies, their assessment of party performance as a steward of government, and so on. The result may well be that a voter's preferences for several parties are tied or nearly so. On election day, the choice of such voters will go to the party which then stands highest in their preference ranking. Still, during the run-up to an election, if the difference between the highest-ranking parties is small, we can imagine this order being changed as a consequence of all kinds of factors. For such voters the election provides a real decision – sometimes perhaps a challenge – as they need to find a basis upon which to break this tie, which may involve factors that, when not seen as 'tie breakers', would be considered minor, irrelevant or even frivolous. This is often overlooked by analysts who try to understand the bases of voter behavior from answers to the obvious question: 'why did you choose the party you voted for?'. Invariably, such questions yield high proportions of answers that have little or no connection with political matters, such as the personal charm of the candidate, or how cute his children are, or even professions of ignorance such as 'I could not say'. Yet, such answers cannot be interpreted at face value. Voters whose top preferences are tied or nearly tied tend to interpret the question as referring to what broke the tie between equally attractive alternative options. That is obviously something entirely different from the factors that caused them to have high preferences for these parties in the first place (which is what the analyst really wants to know).

When we speak about electoral competition (as we will repeatedly in coming chapters), we refer to the rivaling efforts of political parties to win the votes of this pool of tied or nearly tied voters.

Our discussion so far has focused on what can happen in a particular election. This focus constrains us to consider only changes in preferences that can plausibly occur within a short period of time (e.g. the run-up to an election) during which positions of parties and voters are relatively stable and only limited changes can occur. Seen in a longer-term perspective, however, these constraints are greatly reduced. Over a longer period, all sorts of things can change, thereby establishing new baseline structures of electoral competition within which short-term developments have their consequences – an idea that will be developed further in Chapter 4.

Institutional change

Any electorate will always contain voters who are not immunized, and who therefore provide possibilities for (aggregate) electoral change. Partly this is because there is a constant influx of new voters providing a constant source of potential change. In addition, institutions themselves are not unchanging. They do change, if infrequently, and when they do so they throw everyone back a couple of steps in their processes of habituation. Everyone has to adapt to new rules of the game and figure out how to achieve their goals within the new rules. One institution that has changed repeatedly during the history of virtually all established democracies has been the *franchise* – the right to vote.

At the start of the democratic age only certain adult males were eligible to vote: generally those who owned their own homes or other property and paid taxes. Through the course of the 19th century these eligibility rules were successively liberalized in many Western countries, so that by the early 20th century all adult males enjoyed the right to vote in most countries that are now established democracies. These successive enlargements of the electorate were responsible for political tidal waves in many countries that brought new political parties into being in response to the policy demands of the newly enfranchised, and these new parties often quickly became major players, replacing existing parties in some countries and adding to the number of parties in others. In the US since 1860, candidate-centered elections enabled the existing two parties to absorb the demands of newly enfranchised voters, but even in that country the growing electorate was responsible for several major political realignments. In the 20th century, further enlargements of the electorate resulted from the enfranchisement of women, the lowering of the voting age and (in the US) the removal of voting rights restrictions that were based on race in certain states. These further extensions of the franchise have not had the same repercussions for party systems as earlier ones, however. Still, party systems have continued to evolve and, whether as a result of the enfranchisement of new segments of a population or for other reasons, the emergence, disappearance, merging, splitting or other transformations of political parties all shake the foundations on which voters' habits were built, so that these habits need to be rebuilt under new circumstances. All such changes increase the likelihood that voters will behave as though unimmunized, and this will increase their responsiveness to short-term political forces.

Yet other forms of fundamental change involve reform of electoral systems, as took effect at the end of the 20th century in Italy, New Zealand and Japan, or in the definition of what offices are to be filled (directly or indirectly) by election. An example of the latter that we will discuss in Chapter 4 (pp. 108–9) is the reform in Israel in the 1990s that instituted direct election to the office of Prime Minister, a reform that was abandoned again only a few years later. Another example that we will discuss in Chapter 7 (pp. 191–3) is the reform in Switzerland that instituted a governmental cartel after World War II. These sorts of changes provide evidence for some of the assertions we have made in this chapter regarding the ways in which the behavior of parties and voters, and the outcomes of elections, are constrained by institutional factors. We will see repeatedly that election outcomes and the electoral behavior of individuals cannot be understood without taking into account the wider institutional context within which they take place.

These changes in the constraints that voters experience are, of course, themselves the result of – deliberate or inadvertent – decisions by voters and party leaders. The institutional context, though usually stable in regard to its major characteristics, is in minor ways constantly in flux, and voters are constantly being forced to adapt in minor ways (even if less often in major ways) to such changes.

Chapter 3

Electoral Institutions

This chapter and the next describe a number of basic elements that define the character of an election. These can be divided into institutional and behavioral factors. This chapter focuses on electoral institutions. Our objective is not to give a complete account of the differences in election laws amongst the countries that we study, but only to provide a picture basic enough for an understanding of the differences that condition the behavior of voters.

Free and fair elections

What does it take for a country to hold free and fair elections? The overriding requirement is that office-holders, and particularly those who control the power of the state, should be willing and ready to give up their offices should they lose the election. A closely related requirement is that such power-holders should refrain from taking actions that might affect the outcome in unscrupulous ways – by intimidating voters, by making it hard or impossible for some of them to vote, or by interfering with the vote count. Of course, challengers too have to refrain from such practices, but it is generally the existing government authorities that have the greatest ability to affect election outcomes, just as these same authorities may be able simply to set aside an election outcome that does not suit them. Such practices are not uncommon in developing countries and countries governed by dictators of one kind or another. Yet electoral irregularities do occasionally also occur in established democracies where elections are normally free and fair. The US is exceptional among established democracies in having decentralized election laws that give considerable power to local officials and make it hard to enforce uniform impartial standards across the country.

Whether an election is fair depends to some extent on who has the right to vote. As mentioned at the end of the last chapter, in all countries rules of enfranchisement have changed greatly over time, and currently there are still important differences between countries in this respect. In the early days of democracy only a minority of property-owning white males had the vote, but over the course of 200 years the idea that all adults should have the vote, regardless of race, gender, property or education, was gradually enshrined into law in established democracies. The US was among the last democracies to remove de facto inequalities based on race, with the passage of the Civil Rights Act in 1965. Switzerland was the last to remove restrictions on female suffrage when, in 1971, it granted women the vote in federal elections. Several other countries granted women the vote only following the end of World War II.

Until quite recently there were still important differences between countries regarding citizenship. Some countries effectively enfranchised all those residing in the country who met other eligibility rules, such as age. Other countries have only ever given the vote to their citizens, and some have had very stringent requirements for citizenship that effectively created large unenfranchised populations. Citizenship is now virtually everywhere a requirement for the right to vote in national elections. Germany was perhaps the last established democracy to change its citizenship rules to allow citizenship to anyone born in the country – but this can still leave large groups of unenfranchised non-citizens, especially in an age of global migration.

Extensions of the franchise can have important implications for voting behavior, since those who did not learn the habit of voting in their formative years will not necessarily begin to vote just because the franchise has been extended to them. The initial turnout rate among previously disenfranchised groups is generally lower than in the general population, and it can take 50 years or more for the disparity to work its way out of the electorate, as we will elaborate on pp. 190–2. The story regarding the granting of voting rights to 18-year-olds – the last great franchise extension of the 20th century – is different, as has already been explained (see pp. 47–8).

Votes and outcomes

Votes have to be translated into an 'election outcome' – the consequences of the election in terms of winners and losers. The outcome of an election is different depending on whether the chief executive is being elected directly (in a presidential system) or indirectly (in a parliamentary system). The outcome is also different depending on whether we are thinking about the consequences of an election for policy-making or just in terms of which individual candidates are elected. We will use the term 'electoral outcome' to refer to the parties and people who win political office, irrespective of whether this is a direct or an indirect result of an election. When thinking about policy, we refer to the policy consequences of an election.

The translation of votes into election outcomes involves two sets of rules: rules for converting votes into office-holders and, in the case of parliamentary systems, rules for converting office-holders into governments. The first set of rules is embodied in a country's electoral system. The second set of rules is more disparate, frequently involving conventions rather than laws, and which are often referred to as 'rules of the game'. Presidential systems evidently do not need separate rules for converting parliamentary seats into governments. In the US, a presidential election happens at the same time as a congressional election, though they are separate elections. People cast separate votes for a congressional candidate and for a presidential candidate (they also cast a multitude of additional votes for senator, governor, state representative, and so on). But each of these elections uses much the same set of rules.

Both sets of rules are important (where both sets exist) because the behavior of voters is influenced by them both. As already suggested, voters want to affect election outcomes. The outcomes that they focus on may be different for different voters. Some want to elect a party or candidate of a particular stripe (a Catholic, or a woman, for instance). Others want to promote a particular policy (for example environmental protection). Yet others may have still different objectives in mind, like throwing the rascals out. The problem voters have to solve is how to get the outcomes that they want.

But there is another game going on, involving another set of actors: those who want to be politicians and, within that group, those that want to run the government. They are affected by the same electoral rules but in different ways than the voters because they have different concerns. The problem these actors have to solve is how to get elected and, when elected, how to form a government. The fact that elections are about these two different sets of actors accounts for the bottom two rows of Figure 1.2: the two rows headed 'for each party' and 'for each potential voter'. In most political systems politicians are elected as members of parties, and elections are seen as awarding offices to parties. In America the objects are candidates rather than parties; but still, even there, candidates generally belong to parties which gain advantages when more of their candidates win.

A number of factors help to account for the importance of candidates in the American system (and, in principle, in all presidential systems). One of these is that a presidential system tends to force a choice between two viable alternatives, which promotes the development of two major parties in each of which people who differ enormously from each other have nevertheless to find ways to coexist. This results in parties with less policy coherence than in parliamentary systems and consequently a stronger focus on candidates. The need to come up with only one candidate in each of the two dominant parties in the US eventually led to a system of primary elections (some states use caucuses, which are intended to achieve the same results). These are preliminary elections in which those who want a role in deciding who will be a party's official candidate make their choices among the available contenders. Primary elections focus attention on candidates rather than parties, precisely because the choices on offer are within-party choices. If these candidates differ from each other in policy terms, the policy platform of the party is largely determined by the winner, which further reinforces the importance of candidates over party.

The candidate centeredness of American politics is further enhanced by the plurality or first past the post (FPTP) system for electing members of Congress: a separate election in each district, with only one winner in each. In such a system there is no need for the policy views of the winner in one district to be the same (or even to be consistent with) those of the winner in another district – not even if they are from the same party. In such a system one would need strong central coordination in order to avoid incoherent campaign promises by elected representatives from the same party, and such coordination is lacking in the US.

Moreover, in a system where the survival of the government does not require the support of the legislature, there is no strong incentive for party discipline. And without party discipline party leaders cannot ensure that a party's program is enacted, so the party as such has nothing to 'sell' to the electorate, much in contrast to parliamentary systems where enough votes translate into enough seats to permit a party to carry out its program, provided those who fill its seats behave in a disciplined manner. Parties may have to compromise in parliamentary systems, but only because voters did not give them sufficient power to enact their full programs, and in general the more support a party gets the more of its promises it will be able to keep. In the US, by contrast, in normal times no party can promise with any real credibility to deliver any specific policy because voters cannot give them the power to deliver on such a promise. Irrespective of the margin by which a president is elected, he still cannot impose his policies on Congress. Similarly, the majority party in Congress can generally not impose its will on the President. Without a pay-off of this kind from party discipline, candidate-centered elections follow naturally.

There are more reasons for the lack of party discipline, and more reasons for candidate-centered elections in the US, but the reasons given are enough, and they come straight from the differences in the rules of the game for presidential and parliamentary systems. The degree of discipline (or the lack thereof) of American parties is not always the same, and developments since 1994 (for example in centralized campaign funding) have led to greater discipline, especially for the Republican party, than used to be found in earlier decades in either party. However, it is most unlikely that party discipline in the US will ever reach levels routinely found in parliamentary systems because the incentives for such a level of discipline are lacking.

When we move beyond America, the question of how the executive is chosen looms large. France has a semi-presidential system in which the President is directly elected by the voters, as in the US (though not simultaneously with elections to the legislature – see Box 2.6), but the French

President is not the sole embodiment of the executive. He shares executive power with a prime minister who depends on a majority in parliament, as in other parliamentary systems. Finland, Portugal and some other countries have similar systems in which the President has reserved powers that give to her or him a coequal (or even superior) position to the Prime Minister in at least some aspects of executive decision-making (generally foreign policy and defence). Even so, for most purposes semi-presidential systems can be treated as variants of the parliamentary model because governing the country requires majority support in the Parliament. The primary distinction in parliamentary systems is between single-party governments and coalition (or multiparty) governments. As can be seen in Figure 3.1, countries normally ruled by single party governments are generally countries with some form of FPTP electoral system, as is used in the US and Britain. Other countries tend to have coalition governments.

The US always has a single party controlling the executive, though the same party often fails to have a majority in both houses of Congress. In a typical parliamentary system, with or without proportional representation (PR), the absence of a presidency provides less pressure for a two-party system, and thus less reason to force alternative political orientations into a two-party mold. To the extent that we find effectively two-party systems (see pp. 27–8) this is a consequence of the electoral system. On the other

Figure 3.1   *Direct and indirect elections of the chief executive in established democracies*

Proportionality of electoral system (type of government)	Source of executive power	
	Direct elections for executive	Executive power derives from the legislature
Majoritarian electoral systems and disproportional PR systems (generally single-party governments)	USA France (directly elected president with reserved powers and appointed prime minister)	United Kingdom, Canada, Australia, Greece
PR, mixed and STV electoral systems (generally multiparty governments)	Finland, Portugal (directly elected presidents with reserved powers and appointed prime ministers) Briefly in Israel	Other west European countries, Iceland, New Zealand, Japan and generally Israel

Note: The table cannot reflect the fact that certain countries sometimes have single-party governments and sometimes multiparty governments. Countries that straddle this divide are located on the basis of their electoral systems.

hand, the fact that the executive requires the support of the legislature implies the need for disciplined parties. Thus, when a candidate is selected by a party, this signals to voters the candidate's commitment to support that party's preferred policies so that, even when voters ostensibly vote for a candidate, they in fact choose between one or another of a set of policy-oriented parties.

Electoral rules

The rules pertaining to the translation of votes into seats are collectively referred to as a country's electoral system. Systems for electing legislatures can be *majoritarian* (where the contest gives rise to a single winner in each district or constituency) or *proportional* (where *legislative seats* are allocated to parties in proportion to the votes they received). The single transferable vote system (STV), though based on different ideas as we shall see, generally gives rise to proportional outcomes.

FPTP elections are usually plurality elections in which each voter marks just one name on a ballot and the legislative seat goes to the candidate who wins the most votes, which may be considerably less than a majority of the votes if more than two candidates were running in the *district* concerned (sometimes called a *constituency*). Some electoral systems provide for run-off elections between the leading vote-getters if no candidate wins an outright majority of the votes – an example is the electoral system used in France. These are the only truly majoritarian electoral systems, but plurality electoral systems generally yield an outcome that puts a legislative majority into the hands of one party, and they are generally referred to as majoritarian for this reason (see also Box 2.1).

The List PR system is also very simple. The country is divided into a small number of districts (sometimes only a single district), each of which is allocated a number of seats in the legislature (not necessarily the same number in each district, and not necessarily in proportion to the size of each district's electorate). In each district each party puts forward a list of candidates and voters pick just one of those lists by marking it on their ballots. The election gives to each party a proportion of the total number of seats for the district that is as close as possible to the proportion of the votes it received, allocating these seats to candidates in the order they are named on the party list.[1] If the number of legislators is large enough, the resulting allocation of seats to parties will closely reflect the proportions of votes cast for the various parties. This is why it is known as a proportional representation (PR) system. However, in districts that elect only a few representatives, proportionality will suffer because of the fact that a party cannot receive some fraction of a seat in the legislature.

STV systems are based on a different view of how to reach a proportional outcome. Instead of voters being allowed to express only a single preference on their ballots, they are encouraged to rank the candidates in order of preference. Second preferences (and sometimes third and even lower preferences) are taken into account when deciding how many seats have been won by each party. The method of counting votes is very complex in STV systems, and before the advent of computers it could take a week or more to determine the election result for an entire country. Essentially this electoral system works by initially counting the first preference votes for each candidate and if, on this basis, any candidate reaches the necessary number of votes to receive a seat, that candidate is elected. But the surplus of the votes that were not needed to elect that candidate are redistributed among the other candidates on the basis of voters' second preferences; votes for those candidates are then counted again as though the transferred votes were first choices. If none of the other candidates receives the required number of votes to be elected, the candidate with the fewest votes is eliminated and her or his votes are redistributed according to the second preferences on the ballots involved. This is repeated until a candidate has been elected to fill each of the available seats. How many seats are available in a district (the so-called 'district magnitude') is very important for STV, as we shall see. Usually STV will yield roughly the same result as a list proportional system. However, if there is a party that a great many people rank second – far more proportionately than rank that party first – such a party can benefit from an STV election (see Table 3.1).

STV elections are also distinguished by a relatively strong emphasis on candidates rather than parties, and they can sometimes appear almost as candidate centered as are elections in the US. However, as long as countries that use STV have disciplined parties, the election ends up in practice deciding the degree of support for the policy platforms of those parties, even if some of the voters did not focus on this aspect of the election (Marsh *et al.* 2008).

The way these systems work is most readily explained in terms of a hypothetical example. Table 3.1 shows the different ways in which a small legislature, comprising only six seats, might be filled under different systems. The first column shows 18 voters (numbered 1–18) and their preference rankings for three parties, A, B and C (but keep in mind that these preference orders are not observed in FPTP and list PR systems, as in those systems voters may only indicate their first preference). The second column shows how the three parties would receive votes from these individuals if the contests were organized in six FPTP single-member districts with three voters each (the cell entries in this column show which party wins in each district). The next two columns each combine all districts into a single district that elects six candidates. The first of these two columns shows the result for list PR and the

Table 3.1   *Consequence of different electoral systems for election outcomes*

Voters and their party preference rankings	Winners under FPTP	Winners under list PR	Winners under STV
1: A-B-C 2: B-C-A 3: A-C-B	Party A	Party A (10 votes out of 18: 3 seats)	Party A (3 seats)
4: C-B-A 5: A-C-B 6: A-C-B	Party A		
7: B-C-A 8: B-C-A 9: C-A-B	Party B	Party B (5 votes out of 18: 2 seats)	Party B (1 seat)
10: C-A-B 11: A-C-B 12: A-C-B	Party A		Party C (2 seats)
13: B-C-A 14: A-C-B 15: A-C-B	Party A	Party C (3 votes out of 18: 1 seat)	
16: A-B-C 17: A-C-B 18: B-C-A	Party A		
Overall result:	A 5, B 1, C 0	A 3, B 2, C1	A 3, B 1, C 2

second for STV. The bottom row of the table summarizes the results in terms of the number of seats going to each party.

As can be seen, FPTP strongly advantages the party with most votes and strongly disadvantages the party with least votes – a normal pattern in FPTP systems. The party coming second is moderately disadvantaged by this electoral system, getting in this example one fewer seat than it would have expected on a proportional basis. The other two systems both result in the largest party getting no added advantage from its position, but they differ in how they allocate the seats not given to that party. Party C does better under STV than Party B, because the example was contrived so that this was the party most people placed second in their preference order, if they did not place it first. It is this feature of STV that makes it attractive to its promoters – it gives people a chance to express second and subsequent preferences which may play a role if first preferences do not. The result is a system in which every vote counts, just as in PR systems.

It is difficult to envisage STV elections except where a small number of votes are cast for each representative, because of the number of times each ballot may have to be counted. Computerized voting might overcome this problem, though at some potential cost in transparency (a system that is only possible because a computer did the work might cause considerable misgivings). At all events, STV elections only occur in a very few small countries (Malta, Ireland) or parts of countries (Scotland, Northern Ireland), or in a small number of local communities in various Anglo-Saxon countries.

One can think of numerous other electoral systems in addition to FPTP, list PR and STV, but most of these are not currently used in national elections, with one important exception. The mixed member proportional (MMP) system combines features of majoritarian and proportional systems by having some portion of the legislature filled by FPTP elections in single member districts and the remainder filled from national party lists. All voters are given two votes in such systems, one to cast in the districts where they live and one to cast for a national party list. The second vote determines the balance of party forces in the legislature, because every party has the district seats it won 'topped up' from its party list in order to achieve total representation proportional to votes cast for the party list. Even if it does not come first in any district, and thus wins no district seats, it can still get seats from its party list if it receives sufficient party votes. Mixed systems exist in Germany and New Zealand and did exist briefly in Italy. For most of our purposes we do not need to distinguish these from other PR systems. Both yield outcomes in which seats in the legislature are apportioned in close relationship to votes cast at an election, though there are other types of mixed systems which do not yield such proportional results (for example in Japan).

Finally, we should mention the so-called 'reinforced' proportional system (which actually is misnamed because it is the largest party that is reinforced, not proportionality). Such a system used to exist only in Greece, but in 2006 it was introduced in Italy as well, in a blatant bid for partisan advantage by Silvio Berlusconi, the leader of the largest party there. In these two countries the largest party or electoral coalition is given additional seats in order to improve its ability to form and maintain a government. A typology of countries showing their different electoral systems will be developed below (see Table 3.2).

Electoral systems differ from one another also in a number of ways that are somewhat more technical (see Further Reading). However, it is important to know about malapportionment and the related concept of gerrymandering (see Box 3.1). Malapportionment violates the ideal of political equality, as it leads to the votes of some groups being given more 'weight' than others, though this might be thought desirable in order to protect minorities whose voice would otherwise hardly be heard (citizens of small states in the US, for example, or of the inhabitants of Wales in Britain). Sometimes malappor-

Box 3.1   Malapportionment and gerrymandering

Malapportionment relates only to systems that comprise multiple districts. A well-apportioned system is one in which the number of voters per representative is roughly equal across districts. Any electoral system (whether it be majoritarian or proportional) that breaks the country up into districts has the possibility of malapportionment – which might be the accidental result of drawing districts to match historical boundaries, such as those that define the Spanish provinces (see Box 3.5 on the 2008 Spanish election). Malapportionment can also result in the underrepresentation of certain classes or ethnic groups if district boundaries are defined in such a way that larger districts are populated by particular groups.

A related concept is gerrymandering, named after a certain Governor Gerry of Massachusetts who, in 1812, was responsible for drawing a district shaped like a salamander in order to benefit his party by grouping together voters who would not have constituted a majority in any of the more compact constituencies of which they might have been members. Among established democracies this practice continues to the present day in the US where (except in Arizona and Iowa) state legislatures regularly draw the boundaries of congressional districts in such a way as to benefit electorally the party with the power to do this – the party that controls a majority of the seats in the state legislature. In most other established democracies, district boundaries are drawn by independent and non-partisan commissions, who often must satisfy multiple criteria designed to make it impossible to draw the boundaries in such a way as to benefit a particular political party.

tionment takes the form of specifically reserving seats in the legislature for ethnic or linguistic minorities (Maoris in New Zealand, for instance, or a Swedish-speaking region in Finland). Gerrymandering, by contrast, generally implies a deliberate attempt to gain partisan advantage at the expense of the minority party or parties.

Malapportionment and gerrymandering apply only to district-based electoral systems. Proportional systems have additional special terms that need to be understood. One is district magnitude, which refers to the number of seats that are to be divided proportionally amongst the contending parties, and another is the associated concept of an electoral threshold (see Box 3.2). In FPTP systems the district magnitude is almost always 1 (one seat per district): so district magnitude is not of much interest in such systems. FPTP systems also have an implied threshold – which is the number of votes needed to win one seat. How high this threshold stands in practice will not be the same for all parties, as it depends on how evenly spread a party's votes are across

Box 3.2   District magnitude and electoral thresholds

There are no fractional seats in a legislature, so 'proportional' means at best 'as proportional as possible given the number of seats in play'. The larger the number of seats to be elected from a district, the more closely the result will approximate perfect proportionality. The most proportional results that could possibly be achieved in a given country would arise from having the whole country as one district and all the candidates running for office competing in that one district. That is the system used in Israel and the Netherlands, which are both countries with quite small legislatures where, if the countries were to be broken up into districts, the results would not be very proportional.

District magnitude (the number of seats per district) comes with an implied 'electoral threshold', which is the percentage of votes needed by a party in order to be awarded one seat. This percentage is called the 'electoral quotient'. The number of seats a party gets is found by dividing its number of votes by the electoral quotient, and rounding down. Any remainders have to be shared out in some fashion, and this can be done in a variety of ways that we will not go into here. But such an implicit threshold is not the only sort of threshold a country can have. Thresholds can also explicitly state the proportion of votes a party must receive in order to have any representatives elected. In Germany, for example, there is a high threshold of 5 per cent of the party votes. A party must receive at least that many votes to receive any seats; though, because Germany has a mixed system, a party can also receive a district seat simply by winning more district votes in some district than any other party (if a party wins three seats in this way the 5 per cent threshold for party seats is waived). If there is no explicit threshold, then there is still an implicit one, determined by the district magnitude.

districts. A party with votes that are quite evenly spread may require a great many votes in order to win a single seat in the legislature. A party with regional concentrations of support can have an easier time receiving enough votes to get at least a few legislators elected. Thresholds are far more relevant in PR systems, since they determine the ease of entry for new parties.

In STV systems there are only implicit thresholds, deriving from district magnitude. District magnitude works differently with STV than in PR systems, however, because there is a cost to having too many candidates of the same party running in the same district. If districts are too large, then candidates from the same party will find themselves competing against each other, which could make it hard for such candidates to later work together in the Parliament if several of them are elected (it could also give rise to policy differences within a party if candidates differentiate themselves by proposing different policies, as in US primary elections). So in STV systems parties are restrained from fielding more candidates than they can plausibly expect to see elected, which may well limit the responsiveness of such systems.

Like all other kinds of institutions, electoral systems tend to be extremely stable over time. Among established democracies, few countries have repeatedly adjusted their electoral system in recent years (only Greece and, more recently, Italy). Frequent changes in electoral system undermine the predictability needed if parties and voters are to behave purposefully. Yet, occasionally the rules governing parliamentary elections are rewritten, for example after the restoration of democracy following an interruption by dictatorship, or, very occasionally, when functioning democracies feel that their electoral systems do not (any longer) fulfil a number of widely subscribed goals. At such times, constitution writers have the opportunity to learn from accumulated experience and institute rules that 'improve' the functioning of democratic systems (see Boxes 3.3 and 3.4 and Further Reading).

Trade-offs in designing an electoral system

There is no perfect electoral system, just systems in which the trade-offs that have been made are thought to be appropriate for particular countries, their culture and their people's expectations about what an election should be.

A major trade-off is between party representation and individual representation. In a proportional system voters effectively choose between parties by marking the name of a particular party or its list leader. As a consequence of these votes a whole group of representatives are elected to the legislature, proportional to the number of votes cast for that party list. But, for particular voters, who is their representative? There is no such person, as all those elected (i.e. the entire Parliament) are everyone's representatives. In other words, there is no close, let alone unique, link between a voter and a particular representative in a list proportional system. That is viewed as not very satisfactory by proponents of majoritarian elections. A feature of FPTP countries is that voters have a single representative whom they can consider to be 'their own' (though shared, of course, with other voters in the same electoral district or constituency). A particular voter may not have voted for that representative but the representative is duty bound to represent every voter in her or his district. So if we want good constituency service we probably want an FPTP or MMP system. On the other hand, if we want representation in terms of policy platforms rather than constituency service, then we definitely want a proportional system (a mixed system provides good proportionality as we have already explained).

A second trade-off arises from the types of governments that tend to result from different electoral systems in parliamentary regimes. FPTP elections tend to exaggerate the national winner's margin (see Box 2.1) and generate a single party government, which also discourages the proliferation of parties because voters hesitate to cast their vote for a party that 'cannot win'. PR tends to lead to more parties and hence to the need for coalition governments, thought by many to blur the electoral connection between voters and governments by introducing uncertainty into the translation of votes into governments.

There is a third trade-off, which comes when we have chosen a proportional system, between district magnitude and proportionality. We can have a shortlist of representatives who live somewhat close to the voter by making the districts quite small in terms of number of representatives. If geography is important in generating a bond between voters and representatives, as it is in the US and some other countries, this can still be obtained to some extent in a proportional system with small districts. But small district magnitudes lead to larger deviations from proportionality. The smaller the number of seats to be elected in a given district, the more 'lumpy' the translation of votes into seats becomes and the more likely it is that some voters' party preferences will not be represented at all because they were not sufficiently numerous in their districts to elect even one representative (see Box 3.5). This is where mixed (MMP) systems score strongly, by providing the smallest possible districts, each containing only a single representative, while maximizing the degree of proportionality over the country as a whole.

It should be evident that these different types of representation bring with them different ideas about what a member of a legislature should do and different roles for elected representatives. Individual representation implies concern on the part of the representative for 'her' or 'his' geographically defined constituents: a representative does *constituency service* which often includes dealing with the relations between individual voters and the national political system. No such concerns need animate representatives in a list PR system, nor do voters in such systems expect such 'service' from their representatives.

So three overlapping trade-offs encapsulate virtually everything that is important to know about electoral systems: (1) party representation versus individual representation; (2) single-party governments versus coalition governments; and (3) geographical representation versus proportionality. There are things almost everyone wants. Everyone wants some degree of proportionality, everyone wants some say in policy-making, everyone wants representatives to whom they can relate (made easier if they are close to home). Everyone values all of these things but no electoral system provides all of them. Countries have to choose, and different countries have made different choices, which is why they have different electoral systems. Therefore in all countries by necessity there will always be those who criticize the existing electoral system because it does not provide something that they want, and there will always be more or less potent proposals for electoral reform.

One more consideration needs to be mentioned concerning the viability of different electoral systems, which is achieving an adequate supply of parties. The desired number of parties for a political system may seem largely a matter of opinion. We have mentioned the trade-off between numbers of choices (parties) and conclusiveness of outcomes (see Figure 1.1): generally speaking, fewer parties make it more likely that there will be single-party governments; and proponents of FPTP elections tend to favor small numbers of parties. Indeed, there is no question that FPTP elections tend to produce fewer parties. Among list PR systems, higher thresholds also serve to reduce the number of parties. Indeed, the German system, with a relatively high threshold, has fewer different parties in its parliament than the British system with FPTP elections. Many political scientists believe that too many parties are bad for democracy because they make it hard for voters to keep track of them all, and because the low threshold that encourages large numbers of parties would also tend to promote a large turnover of short-lived parties replacing each other election after election. Yet, the empirical basis for these beliefs is thin and contested. Moreover, it is not clear whether it is the *number* of parties or the extent of *fragmentation* of parliamentary power that would be bad for democracy (see p. 28).

The number of parties required is to some extent a function of the diversity of political ideals in a population. However, over the course of time the institutions of a country – such as its party and electoral systems – become 'natural' to the people living in that country, and help to shape their expectations and their notions of what is 'fair'. The number of parties in, for example, the Danish Parliament (which is frequently in excess of ten), may appear bewildering to Canadians, yet it is perfectly normal to Danes who have grown up in that context and who would find preposterous any proposal to reduce artificially this number. At the same time, the small variety of choices on offer in Canada would be unpalatable to many Danes, while being accepted as perfectly normal by Canadians. So there is no easy answer to the questions what is too many and what is too few. Empirically, however, it is possible to assess the proportion of an electorate that persistently has no affinity at all with any of the established parties, and if that proportion were to be non-negligible then that would certainly suggest an undersupply of relevant choice options.

Electoral reform

The problems we have just listed might well prompt citizens to think about the desirability of reforming their electoral systems. For a country to change its electoral system, or the way in which it translates election outcomes into government coalitions, is difficult and very uncommon, but it is happening more frequently these days. Since the 1990s Italy, New Zealand and Japan have all changed their electoral systems. Israel changed the way its prime minister was chosen – and then changed back again. These are countries that had kept the same institutions for many years before finally deciding on a change. So there is a sort of movement, if not very extensive as yet, towards reform and experimentation. Moreover, the three countries that have changed their electoral systems in recent years have all changed to the same thing. They all adopted mixed systems, either coming from list PR, in the case of Italy (though Italy reverted to list PR in 2006), or from a majoritarian system, in the case of New Zealand (see Box 3.3), or from a home-grown quasi-majoritarian system, in the case of Japan. It would not be surprising in this atmosphere if more countries were to change to mixed systems, and there is active debate in Britain and elsewhere about the advantages and disadvantages of different electoral systems. However, reform is always difficult. The main reason is that the legislators who have to institute the reform became legislators by winning their seats under the old rules. And, inevitably, many will be afraid –particularly those that were advantaged by the old system – that new rules may be disadvantageous to them.

A prototypical case is found with the regularly recurring movements for campaign finance reform in the US. The legislators who have to vote on this

Box 3.3   Electoral reform in New Zealand

In two successive elections, in 1978 and 1981, the New Zealand Labour Party failed to win a majority of seats in the Parliament even though it had won a plurality of the votes. Even worse, in both cases the National Party did win enough seats to form a government even though that party had lost the popular vote. Such a result is possible in parliamentary elections using an FPTP system, but nowhere else has it happened in two successive elections. The result in New Zealand caused considerable disquiet and an unprecedented awareness of the possibilities for undemocratic outcomes when such a system is employed. In 1985 a Royal Commission on Electoral Reform was established to suggest alternative electoral systems for the New Zealand House of Representatives and in December 1986 it recommended the adoption of the MMP system, adapted from the additional member system employed in Germany. After several years of hesitation by major parties unsure of how they would fare under such a system, a binding referendum was finally held in 1993 and the proposal was carried by 54 per cent on a turnout of over 85 per cent. Supporters of the unlucky Labour party were the most strongly in favor.

reform are the very legislators who are really good at using the existing system for raising money to pay for their campaigns. If they change things so that somebody can win who is not as good as themselves at raising money, then they increase the likelihood of being defeated because they eliminate an advantage that helped them to win. So campaign finance laws that are actually passed regularly fail to fulfil the goals of many of their proponents.

It is very difficult to get people to change the very rules that benefited them. And this is true not only for campaign finance reform in the US. It is equally hard to achieve reform in countries that are considering a move to a new electoral system. Those who have to bring in the new system are those who won office under the old system. Often such a move requires that the old system be so discredited as to be considered beyond repair (as happened in Italy in 1993 – see Box 3.4).

Box 3.4   Electoral reform in Italy

Nineteenth-century Italian democratic elections were held under the rules that France uses today: single-member districts in which a candidate had to win an absolute majority with run-off elections, as needed, to ensure this. In 1919 the system was changed to a list PR system until the takeover of the Italian state by Mussolini's Fascists in 1922. The First Republic, established in 1946, duplicated the 1919 electoral system. It also included a secret ballot in legislative decision-making, which made it hard to ensure party discipline in the legislature and contributed to a succession of short-lived governments (more than 50 of them by 1992), all of which contained the large Christian Democratic Party in coalition with one or more small parties – an arrangement made necessary time and time again as a means of keeping the large Communist Party from gaining government power. Only after the Cold War did the ostracism of the Italian Communist Party end, which made major changes possible in Italian politics. The opening up of new coalition possibilities coincided with the discrediting of the Christian Democrats and its allies in the old system on grounds of widespread corruption. The electoral system that had resulted in the same parties holding office for so long was also discredited. Most of the proportional elements of the electoral system were replaced by FPTP elections in single member districts. PR was, however, retained to 'top up' the legislature on the basis of a second vote for party lists (on the German model, but with only a quarter of the seats elected by PR instead of half). Only 12 years later, however, in the run-up to the 2006 parliamentary elections, Berlusconi's right-wing government changed the electoral system back to one based on PR – apparently believing that parties of the right could more easily maintain their power in such a system and suggesting that Italy was moving in a direction long taken by Greece, where the electoral system has regularly been revised by governments trying to adapt the system to their own advantage.

The institutions of representative democracy are a work in progress. Political representation has evolved in the course of an 800-year process that started with the calling of the first British Parliament in the 13th century. Parliaments as first invented in Britain had virtually no power, other than as a sort of advisory group for the king that would give some legitimacy to his attempts to raise taxes. And they have been constantly evolving ever since then. The recent reforms in New Zealand and Japan are steps that these countries have taken to try and improve their versions of electoral democracy. Even in the US, in spite of the inflexibility of its constitution and the major hurdles in the way of amending it, improvements have been made by reinterpreting the meaning of the written texts and by occasional constitutional amendments.

As people gain experience some problems are solved. New constitutions, as they are written, have the advantage of building upon accumulated experience that permit a certain degree of 'engineering' to promote good government. In the meantime, technological evolution and changes in social and economic relations generate new challenges for the functioning of electoral democracy, some of which may require change in institutional arrangements.

Rules of the game for government formation

After the election is over in many countries there is still the question of how a government is to be formed. In the US the government is formed by the candidate winning the most votes in the presidential Electoral College. Generally speaking that is the same as winning the most popular votes in the election for president, though not invariably (see Box 1.1). In a parliamentary system it is more complicated. When a parliamentary election is complete, it is necessary for the Parliament to convene and appoint a government (the usual word is 'invest'). A government is invested by receiving support of a majority of the Parliament – sometimes in an explicit 'vote of confidence' or 'vote of investiture'. But how is that government chosen?

If one party holds a majority of the seats in the Parliament then, provided its members vote in a disciplined fashion, it can form a government alone. This commonly happens in majoritarian parliamentary systems, in not very proportional PR systems, such as the reinforced PR system in Greece (see p. 66), or in the rather malapportioned system in Spain (see Box 3.5), whose electoral system magnifies the advantage of the largest party. Only occasionally in FPTP systems does no party hold a majority of the seats, and in those cases the largest party forms a minority single-party government (see pp. 79–80). Single-party governments also happen occasionally even in highly proportional systems, either because one party wins a majority of the votes (and hence a majority of the seats) or because putting a coalition together

Box 3.5   The Spanish general elections of 2008

General elections of the Spanish Parliament took place on 9 March 2008. The 350 members of the lower house of the Cortes are elected proportionally in each of 52 electoral districts. A few of these are quite large, so that a reasonable degree of proportionality is achieved, but most districts elect just a handful of representatives. Proportionality in such small districts is low, as the small number of seats to be elected gives rise to a large implicit threshold, in most districts exceeding 10 per cent. The extreme cases are two districts that elect just a single representative, one that elects two MPs, and eight that elect no more than three MPs. Parties that fail to pass these very high district thresholds remain unrepresented in the districts concerned.

The nationwide winner of the election was the social democratic PSOE, which won 169 seats, while the center-right Popular Party (PP) won 154 seats. If PR had been applied to the nationwide distribution of votes in 2008, rather than district by district, then these two large parties would have obtained fewer seats (nine and six respectively), while the IU (United Left) would have gained 14 seats rather than the two it actually obtained. Some other minor parties would even have acquired parliamentary representation (which they failed to under the existing system). In all likelihood, the advantage of the major parties is considerably larger, as the existing system discourages voters from 'wasting' their votes on minor parties. (*El Pais* 10 March 2008)

proved so difficult that some party or parties decide to provide a minority government with ad hoc support rather than to become fully fledged members of a coalition government. In some countries (for example Denmark and Sweden) such minority single-party governments are not uncommon at all. Understanding why some parties might prefer not to be members of a government will help us to understand the problems of coalition formation, as we shall see in the next section. But first we need to review and extend our understanding of how coalition governments are formed.

We have already touched on coalition governments in the previous chapter, when we discussed the ways in which elections condition coalition formation. A coalition government is a government in which two or more parties share the reins of office. Government posts (cabinet positions with responsibility for defence, finance, education, and so on) are allocated roughly in proportion to the sizes of the parties that are members of the coalition (see Table 2.1). In such a government the Prime Minister is almost invariably the leader of the largest of the coalition's parties.

Forming a coalition government requires finding two or more parties that can agree on a joint program of legislation. Such a program will certainly not include all the measures promised by each party at the election just past. So forming a coalition requires each party to decide on its priorities – often a strain on party unity in the immediate aftermath of an election. Moreover those decisions have to be acceptable to their voters if the parties want to gain as much or more electoral support at the next election. This is often a tricky judgement call, but a party may well decide that it is better off in opposition, making strident calls for the policies its voters want, than yoked to a government (and pledged to support a government) with a different agenda.

If only a few of the items wanted by the party's supporters will be included in a coalition accord, one way to alleviate the problem would be by providing it with opportunities to get credit for the general aspects of administration that governments are expected to carry out but which are not often prominent planks in party platforms. To get credit for contributing to good government, a party needs to control as many ministries as possible. That way its leaders get to make news and will be seen in the media taking credit for achievements of various kinds. One should not forget that most politicians actively aspire to run their country (or some aspect of it) and that government responsibility is therefore a major 'perk' for any politician – the big payoff for a lifetime of long hours and hard work.

It follows that most governing coalitions have two characteristics in common: they tend to contain like-minded parties – parties that have compatible or similar preferences for policy – because such parties will be able to maximize the number of preferred policies that can be included in a coalition's programmatic agreement, and they tend to be as small as possible while controlling a majority of seats in the legislature. By 'small' we do not mean only the smallest number of parties (technically these are known as 'minimal winning' coalitions), though coalitions with more parties than necessary do land themselves with additional coordination problems. 'Small' refers primarily to the number of seats that the coalition controls in parliament, since this will maximize the number of cabinet ministries each partner gets (as is obvious from Table 2.1).

A third feature of coalition governments also deserves mention. Parties that have joined together in a previous coalition tend to propose continuing their partnership, at least if they themselves considered the previous coalition partnership to have been successful, and if the coalition partners have between them retained a majority in the Parliament. This is not just because of policy compatibility, but because coordination problems are reduced when there are positive personal relationships across parties that developed with the experience of working together. Such experiences can transcend other considerations when it comes to forming a new coalition government (Franklin and Mackie 1983). The reverse can also be true. Working together can sour relationships. There seems to be something like an 'expiration date' on the relationships between cabinet members, even within single-party governments.

These three features of coalition governments – small size, ideological compatibility and the experience of working together – explain between them about half of the variation in the outcomes of coalition formation (ibid.). Still, one must be aware that these frequently observed characteristics of forming coalitions are by no means ubiquitous, as half the variation in outcomes is *not* explained by these factors. But coalitions that conform to these criteria do tend to last longer than coalitions that do not, so most of the coalition governments in existence at any given point in time are small, ideologically compatible and/or based on personal compatibility.

The logic of these criteria also explains why we very seldom see a 'grand coalition'. Such a coalition is formed when the big parties put together a coalition that is supported by much more than 50 per cent of the seats in the Parliament. It very seldom happens because each of those big parties can manifestly do better (i.e. have more influence and more ministries) by governing with a smaller partner. And even if one of these large parties was willing to give up ministries in order to join with the other, the chances that both of them would be willing to do this are really slim. Still, grand coalitions do occur, mostly in wartime in order to project an image of national unity (but see Box 3.6 on coalition formation in Germany).

An election determines the seat shares of the parties in parliament and provides the foundations on which parties try to come to an agreement about forming a coalition that can run the country. In a parliament with relatively few parties, as in Germany for many years when there were only three parties, it is not so hard to find a coalition that the necessary parties can agree on – and in Germany it has almost always been possible to found a coalition of not more than two parties. Those coalitions never had any spare parties and were generally of minimum size. The only times the Germans did not have minimum size coalitions was when they created a grand coalition in the period 1966–69 and again after the 2005 election. In Ireland, where two large parties – Fianna Fáil and Fine Gael – are almost indistinguishable in left–right terms, the same pattern pertains, although these parties would presumably find it easier to make policy in a grand coalition together than either of them finds it to make policy with a different, more ideologically distinctive, party. The division between these two parties has its origin in the Irish civil war of the 1920s, often thought to overshadow their commonality in contemporary policy terms. Even though first-hand memories of that war are rapidly fading, each of these large parties is better off in terms of number of cabinet positions when it joins a coalition with smaller but ideologically more distant parties than it would be in an ideologically more homogeneous grand coalition. This consideration has so far evidently been of overriding importance as a grand coalition has never emerged, nor was it ever seen as a plausible outcome of an Irish election.

Box 3.6   Coalition formation in Germany after the 2005 elections

In July 2005 German Chancellor (Prime Minister) Gerhard Schröder purposefully engineered a loss in a confidence vote in the German Parliament (by asking MPs from his own party to abstain) in order to bring about early elections. The background of this little charade was the losing (by government parties) of a recent election in one of the German Länder (provinces), which caused the government to lose the support of the upper house of the Parliament (the Bundesrat, which represents the governments of the Länder). The resulting different majorities in the lower and upper houses would in all probability have led to legislative gridlock for the remainder of the national government's term. Rather than enduring that, the Chancellor hoped that this bold move would muster sufficient support to get a new electoral mandate – bold indeed in view of the commanding lead of the opposition in opinion polls. The early elections were held on 18 September, and the result was a virtual tie between the previously ruling Socialist Party (SPD) and the previously largest main opposition party, the conservative CDU/CSU. The latter won a slight plurality with 35.2 per cent while the SPD won 34.3 per cent. Neither party obtained a majority of seats in parliament, not even in combination with their most likely coalition part- ners (the Greens for the SPD and the FDP for the CDU/CSU). The only majority coalitions that could be formed would either have included the (now renamed) successor to the Communist Party that once ruled the eastern part of Germany (which neither the SPD nor the CDU/CSU was comfortable with) or been a 'grand coalition' of socialists and conservatives. This grand coalition therefore came into being, with Angela Merkel, the leader of the larger CDU/CSU, as chancellor, the first woman in that posi- tion in Germany. Very soon after the election result became final, an accord for a grand coalition was concluded, but it still took about six weeks before all the minutiae of that accord were negotiated and new cabinet members were recruited. The new coalition was invested on 22 November.

The role of the voters

Why do parties who do not themselves command a majority of seats in the legislature willingly compromise their policy proposals in order to come up with a platform that is acceptable to enough additional legislators to secure a majority? One reason, mentioned earlier, is the lure that government power has for politicians. A complementary reason, however, relates to voters. Voters want two things. They want their preferred policies to be enacted, but they also want a government. Of course, there always is a government, even when a new coalition has not yet been formed after an election. The old cabinet remains in place as a caretaker government; but, without a fresh investiture, the caretaker role precludes it from taking new policy initiatives. Moreover, as a result of the election it may very well have lost its former parliamentary majority. We have already mentioned that parties have to tread a fine line between compromising away too many of their policies too easily and being too recalcitrant in insisting on including their cherished policies in the program of any coalition government. The balance between the two is established by the voters' tolerance for the uncertainties of a coalition forming situation. If the situation goes on for what seems to the voters an unreasonable time, they will blame one or several parties, and parties that are accused of being unduly recalcitrant will lose public support. Moreover, although voters (and politicians) do not want too easily to give up preferred policies in order to become part of a government coalition, they are also loath to miss out on opportunities to implement at least some policies on their wish list.

So parties will do their best to be seen as statesmanlike and accommodating – to the extent that they think their voters will stand for it. Parties are generally quite skilled at treading this narrow line. See Box 3.6 which demonstrates the complications that can arise in a 'hung' parliament when the distribution of seats prevents any of the 'simple' and straightforward coalitions of minimum size that would be based on policy affinity between parties. The Box also illustrates the fact that the possibility of gridlock is not limited to presidential systems: it can occur also in parliamentary systems with a strong upper house of parliament which is (or becomes) controlled by a politically different majority than the lower house.

If no majority coalition can be constructed a minority government takes office. Minority governments – which themselves can be coalitions – survive on the sufferance of other parties, as already mentioned, and those parties must evidently refrain from voting that government out of office. Particularly when the non-government parties are ideologically divided (e.g. some to the left of the minority government and others to the right of it), it is unlikely that the opposition will unite to dispose of the minority cabinet which can thus govern for quite some time with the support of ad hoc and alternating majorities. In majoritarian systems minority cabinets are usually less viable, although the chances are good that such a minority government will, in fact, stagger on, perhaps for a considerable period and perhaps even manage to pass some of its preferred policies into law before calling the inevitable early election.

A minority government can play an interesting game with the opposition parties. It can bring in legislative proposals and challenge the Parliament to vote them down at the risk of early elections. Some non-government parties may in this way be 'coerced' into supporting a government of which they are not part – particularly when they are not really opposed to the legislation in question and do not want to be blamed for an early election. It must be borne in mind that voters do not like unnecessary elections and will not reward parties that vote just to spite the government while legislation is at stake that they do not substantively oppose. Particularly in situations of minority governments, the common juxtaposition made by commentators of government versus opposition is too simplistic, as it would suggest all non-government parties were of the same mind. Stark differences between opposition parties about the direction of public policy may lead to a sort of equilibrium where the government can introduce legislation as long as that legislation has support beyond the (minority) government, but not when the legislation is only supported by the government party or parties. A prime minister who plays the game well can probably after a couple of years gain enough credit for walking this tight rope that she or he may actually win the next election.

The same situation can arise for a majority coalition government faced with a policy choice that was not part of the negotiations that led to the formation of that government. Such choices can cause disagreements among coalition partners. Still, much the same game can be played as would have been played by the leader of a minority government. As long as the opposition is ideologically divided, such a government can often survive lapses of party discipline or minor rebellions in the ranks of one or several coalition partners, so long as its proposed policies gain some support from parties outside the coalition. Still, one might have thought that coalition governments would more frequently fall into disarray and that opposition parties would more frequently take the opportunity to bring down a government in such a state, and it is an interesting question as to why coalitions do not fall apart more frequently.

The answer emerges logically from various points already made in this and the previous chapter. When parties join a coalition, they do so in the knowledge that they will have to stay yoked together for a certain amount of time. If a party pulled out too quickly, and this led to an early election, that party would be blamed. All coalition members have to be prepared to demonstrate that they did all they could to make the coalition a success before they can make a good case to the voters that the coalition has run out of steam (or unity). This takes time, in general at least one to two years, during which laws have been passed, reputations have been made or lost and opinions have had a chance to change. Those changes may make it reasonable to ask the voters for a fresh verdict. Even at that point, parties must present the voters with good reasons for pulling out, lest they risk being punished for bringing the government down unnecessarily. A political saying in the Netherlands – a country that can only be ruled by coalition governments – is that 'if you break it, you pay for it', which refers to the common political wisdom that the party seen as the cause of government failure will be punished electorally. Yet, a coalition may break down if it fails to deliver an agreed-upon policy that is of central importance to one of its members. If one of the coalition partners reneges on the coalition accord, or obstructs its implementation, and the coalition falls apart as a consequence leading to an early election, the voters know exactly whom to blame.

This game goes on continuously with the voters acting as the implicit arbiters. An early election may never be called because all sides know what game is being played. So any party that feels short changed can (often implicitly) threaten to pull out while having a plausible justification for doing so. Rather than see that happen, the other parties may choose to neutralize the threat by giving in to some of the desires of the party that otherwise would be short changed. Such rational and self-interested processes of anticipated reactions help maintain a coalition. Coalitions are actually quite stable so long as everybody understands the game (Laver and Schofield 1990; Powell 2000). However, if one of the partners in government does not understand these implicit rules, or does not abide by them, the government is likely to fall.

Coalition governments can be hard to establish or can break down once established, leaving only a caretaker administration to run the country. That is the Achilles heel of coalition governments. Moreover, since any parliamentary system can find itself in the position of having no party with a majority in parliament, it is also, more generally, the Achilles heel of parliamentary systems. Indeed, it is possible in a parliamentary system to reach a condition of gridlock in which politicians cannot agree on any line of action at all. The Fourth Republic of France (1946–58) and the First Republic of Italy (1946–93) seemed at times to reach such a condition. But this is different only in form from what can happen in the US where gridlock can also result from politicians failing to make necessary compromises. In both cases the gridlock can have severe consequences if it is not resolved in a reasonable length of time (for example in time to pass the budget). Since 1865 the American system has generally appeared relatively bullet proof while several parliamentary systems have collapsed in the face of crises that could not be resolved (as occurred in a number of European countries in the 1920s and 1930s). However, several innovative reforms in parliamentary systems have reduced the likelihood of these systems breaking down. Parliamentary systems have actually proved themselves quite robust over the past 60 years or so; and it should not be forgotten that American history does contain one famous episode when failure to compromise led to the American Civil War of 1860–65.

The majoritarian and proportional visions

We have seen that the world of democratic politics is effectively divided into two groups of countries: a first group that is generally ruled by single-party governments and which is also characterized by majoritarian electoral systems (or very disproportional PR systems), and a second group that is generally ruled by coalition governments and is characterized by proportional electoral systems of one kind or another. Bingham Powell (2000) has pointed out that the division of the world into these two groups is not accidental (see also Lijphart 1999). The different arrangements for government formation in different countries correspond to different visions of how democracy should work.

Supporters of majoritarian parliamentary systems with single-party governments stress the fact that such governments are easier to hold accountable because it is clear who is in charge, making it easy to identify and replace a party that proves inept or corrupt. The party in government controls a majority in the Parliament and is easily punished for bad policies by reducing its seat share at the next election. Given the mechanics of parliamentary government formation, this should result in a different government taking office. The US, however, constitutes something of an anomaly among majoritarian systems because, not being a parliamentary system, it has a government that cannot readily be held to account at election time (see pp. 43–5).

Supporters of proportional systems with coalition governments stress the fact that such governments are more likely than majoritarian systems to produce policies that are supported by a majority of the electorate. We would add the fact that countries with a proportional vision tend to provide voters with a larger number of viable choices between parties that might realistically be able to get their policies enacted. The downside of the proportional vision is a lack of clarity in holding governments accountable. Who is responsible when things go wrong? All members of the coalition? The party that controlled the offending ministry? The party of the Prime Minister? Or who? The same problem occurs, of course, if government policy is very successful: who then is to be credited? Given that voters do not spend a lot of time following the details of political life, many may find it difficult to answer these questions and thus come to base their choices on parties' past performances.

Proponents of each vision have important values to defend – values that proponents of the other vision tend to downplay or ignore. In practice the two visions are to a large extent incompatible. It is hard or impossible to design a democratic system that will provide both for clear accountability (what we have called 'definitive outcomes') and also for a sufficient variety of choice options to satisfy a majority of voters (see p. 8). Unfortunately, proponents of each of these two visions of democracy are quite unlikely to give credence to the arguments made by proponents of the other vision. Each side is invested in its own view of what democracy should be, and it takes a major breakdown, perhaps repeated more than once in quick succession, as happened in New Zealand, to make the proponents of one of these visions rethink their priorities. Yet, some of the alleged advantages of each of these two visions lend themselves to empirical scrutiny: how successful are majoritarian systems in generating governments that are explicitly desired by the voters, and to what extent do proportional systems succeed in providing policies that voters actually want?

Dispersed versus concentrated power

In addition to their electoral system, countries can also be distinguished in terms of whether political power is concentrated or dispersed. This distinction is important for the expectations with which voters and political parties engage in the electoral process, and thus for the factors that they may take into account to realize their objectives. In countries with *concentrated power*, legislatures consist of only one branch (unicameral legislatures) or are characterized by the political dominance of one branch over the other. In such countries we also find that government parties control much of the legislative process. Countries where the legislature has a second branch with significant powers, and/or significant legislative power is placed in the hands of opposition parties, are seen in this classification to be systems with *dispersed power*. Federalism also contributes to dispersed power, as does the separation of powers inherent in a presidential system. Systems with dispersed power are sometimes characterized as *consensual* (Lijphart 1999; Powell 2000), but we think this an unfortunate term to employ because it is easily confused with the *consensus* politics often seen as characterizing the US. We rather see countries with proportional electoral systems and dispersed power as being *inclusive*. These are countries where minorities tend to have their voices heard and play a part in legislative decision-making, both because minority parties need to be included in governing coalitions, often being able to secure enactment of some of their preferred policies as a condition of coalition membership, and because dispersed powers widen the group of decision-makers beyond those explicitly included in the government coalition.

Perhaps partly because of the unfortunate confusion of 'consensual' and 'consensus' politics, and despite its FPTP electoral system, the US is often seen as conforming to the proportional vision (ibid.) because of its separation of powers. And it is true that the US is not really a majoritarian system. First, the separation of powers makes it impossible for the party that wins a majority in Congress to guarantee that it can carry its policies into law – even if the same party would be in control of the White House, which itself is not guaranteed. This is reinforced by the fact that American parties are not disciplined. Majorities have to be crafted on each and every issue as those issues come up. Second, the US has an extra stage in the creation of law that other countries do not have as a regular part of their legislative processes: the stage that occurs in Congress when interested groups and individuals can make themselves heard. In some ways this seems very democratic, extending the opportunity to take part in the legislative process beyond the members of the Congress, and it might be viewed as an American equivalent of the Swiss system where groups of citizens may force a referendum to be held on any piece of legislation of importance to them. The main difference is that public opinion is effectively represented in congressional proceedings by interest groups, not individuals. The interest group system is expensive and so is unavoidably biased towards wealthy interests, thus speaking with '"an upper class accent' (Schattschneider 1960).[2]

But while not truly majoritarian, the American system also fails to live up to the proportional vision in that it is easier to block legislation than to make legislation. So the prevalence of inclusive majorities that is a hallmark of the proportional vision is transformed in the American system into the prevalence of blocking minorities.

Making sense of the American anomaly is not hard, however, if we take separately the two classifications derived from a country's electoral system, on the one hand, and the extent to which it has concentrated power, on the other hand. When we do this we get the typology illustrated in Table 3.2, which well makes sense of the US anomaly: the US has a majoritarian system with dispersed powers (the only such system among established democracies). The typology also shows Westminster-type parliamentary systems distinguished from other parliamentary systems, on the basis of their FPTP electoral systems. Different PR systems are distinguished according to how strongly power is concentrated in the hands of the party or parties that control the government – generally a coalition government. Federal forms of government accentuate the effects of the power arrangements illustrated in Table 3.2 for Germany and the US, and they somewhat mitigate those arrangements in Spain, Australia and Canada (and increasingly in the United Kingdom).

The distinctive position of the US in this typology highlights the difference between the consensus politics practised in that country, where it usually takes a 'super majority' to enact legislation, and the inclusive politics of countries in which minorities can have their way on matters about which the majority does not feel strongly.

Presidents and monarchs in parliamentary systems

A presidential system like that in the US is totally defined by its constitution. The constitution lays down how a government will take office in every

Table 3.2   *Typology of political systems according to electoral system
classification and power dispersal arrangements*

	Electoral system	
Power arrangements	*Proportional (list PR, mixed PR-plurality or STV-PR) systems*	*Majoritarian/plurality (FPTP and run off) systems*
Concentrated	Exclusive governance (Israel, Sweden, Greece, Spain, New Zealand after 1996, etc.)	France and Westminster-type parliamentary systems (UK, Canada, Australia, New Zealand until 1996)
Dispersed	Inclusive governance (Italy, Netherlands, Germany, Norway, Finland, etc.)	Presidential systems with separation of powers (US)

circumstance that the Founding Fathers could conceive (and a few additional circumstances taken care of by constitutional amendment). Parliamentary systems are not totally defined. There are gaps in the organization chart, as it were. In particular there is a complete lack of determinism over what happens when no party wins an absolute majority of seats in the Parliament – a situation that is normal in many countries. Some would say it is a big defect for government formation to be indeterminate after an election. When no party wins a majority of seats the composition of the executive (in terms of parties as well as in terms of persons) is decided by coalition negotiations whose results are unpredictable. What constitutions can do is to establish procedures that will be followed in the (normal) event that such negotiations are needed – procedures we have not described in detail but which underlie the rules for coalition bargaining that we laid out earlier in this chapter. Gallagher *et al.* (2005) present an accessible description of these procedures. Constitutions in parliamentary systems can also provide a backstop – a sort of *deus ex machina* – in the shape of a non-executive head of state, a monarch or president (often an elder statesman elected by the legislature, but in some countries a popular figure directly elected by the people). Their mostly ceremonial role places them above the political fray, and exactly because of this they are occasionally able to prevent cabinets and political parties from bending rules and procedures in partisan ways, particularly in periods of coalition formation, allowing them to infuse the system with impartial wisdom that might be difficult for party politicians to muster. Finally, although this may happen only once in a couple of generations, the non-partisan Head of State is also expected to be able to assume a more active role in the event of some unexpected development that the system has not been designed to deal with. These occasions have become quite rare since World War II, but it is still not hard to come up with instances (see Box 3.7).[3]

One of the reasons why the Belgians (and so many others) keep their monarchy is precisely because monarchs have historically performed well in situations like the one described in Box 3.7. Over a period of nearly 200 years, monarchs have played a major role in the development of parliamentary democracy. In many of these countries a monarch saw the writing on the wall and sided with the people rather than with anti-democratic forces. In those countries where a monarchy has survived it has done so because the monarchs concerned were (or became) democrats. Kings can be democrats, as is clearly demonstrated in the constitutional monarchies which make up about half of the European parliamentary democracies. Elsewhere, a mechanism is needed for producing a quasi-monarch, generally a president, who is mostly a ceremonial figure but who does occasionally have the possibility of playing a more substantive role. These occasions occur rarely, however. Most of the time parliamentary systems work just as predictably as presidential systems. In both types of system the critical role in determining who will govern the country is played by voters in elections.

Box 3.7   The Belgian King takes a role in government formation

On 15 July 2008, Belgium's Prime Minister, Yves Leterme, tendered his resignation to King Albert II because he (the Prime Minister) had been unable to secure agreement in his coalition government regarding a divisive issue about regional autonomy and minority language rights. A week later the King had not accepted the Prime Minister's resignation, but was still trying to broker a compromise that would enable the Prime Minister to continue in office. According to *The Economist*, 'the King's hesitation was not due to any lack of practice: this was Mr Leterme's third resignation within a year'. Here we see a monarch using his own judgement in an attempt to resolve a constitutional crisis.

Chapter 4

Voters and Parties

We have established that there are a great many differences in the arrangements adopted in particular countries for organizing elections and for the
translation of election outcomes into functioning governments. What are the
consequences for the way voters behave at election time of different kinds of
party system, electoral arrangements and legislative–executive relations? In
this chapter we will flesh out the ideas that have been suggested regarding
the way in which voters reach their voting decisions.

Party identification

The process of habituation, discussed in Chapter 2, under suitable circumstances manifests itself in terms of voting for a particular political party. In
the US this habit is known as 'party identification' or 'partisanship'. As
mentioned, the concept of party identification was invented in the US, where
people report that they identify with a party more readily than they will actually vote for it. In other countries it is more customary to vote than to report
any sort of identification with the party voted for, so the concept does not
travel well outside the US (Budge *et al.* 1976). Nevertheless, in all established
democracies many voters acquire a habitual attachment to one or a small
number of ideologically similar parties (see Box 2.7) that carries over in their
voting behavior (Holmberg 2007). Though these voters do not themselves
refer to this habitual support as party identification (some might refer to
themselves as 'party loyalists' but this has a different connotation), as a
matter of convenience we will refer interchangeably to 'habitual support'
and 'party identification' or 'partisanship' when what we mean is the habit
of supporting one or a small number of similar parties (cf. Grofman *et al.*
2008). In countries such as France and the Netherlands, where switching
within a 'party family' is quite common, it would still be unusual to switch
between one party family and another, just as it is between parties in two-
party or quasi-two-party systems.

Party identification is particularly important in the US, where it is customary to have voters decide a whole series of elections at the same time, which
produces a ballot of great length and complexity: president, senator,
congressman, governor, state senator, state representative, school board

member, alderman, justice of the peace, sheriff, members of the board of trustees of the state university, and so on, sometimes down to the dog catcher. America is the only country that combines elections in this way. In other countries elections for different offices are usually separated, rather than conducted concurrently.[1] But in the US, if voters did not have a party to give them cues, what would they do when they got beyond the top two or three offices that are at stake and turn over the ballot to the 23rd office for which they have to make a choice? Who do you want for judge? Who do you want for state senator? This is why, even though these are candidate-centered elections, the party still has an important role to play: it helps with choices between candidates the voter has never heard of, like a brand label or a franchise. The party is an essential aid for dealing with this complicated ballot that demands more from ordinary citizens than they are possibly capable of delivering.

It has been argued that party identification is so important in the US precisely because so much is asked of voters. Still, party identification is important in other countries that do not have such complex ballots and which do not ask so much of voters. This is because having a complicated set of issues (in policy-centered elections) is not so different from having a complicated set of offices to fill (in candidate-centered ones). So the ballot is not the only factor responsible for the importance of party identification in the US. In all countries voters tend to take cues from their parties once they have come to trust them; as long as that trust is not irrevocably damaged, the party (and its leaders) remain an important source of cues. Party identification explains how people can come to an election without having paid much attention, and still make what seem to be sensible choices – choices that fundamentally accord with their values and preferences. If there were no such thing as party identification, many people would not be able to handle the complexities of most electoral situations – unless there was an equivalent source of cues to perform the same function (Miller 1976).

The special importance of party identification in the US also derives, paradoxically, from the fact that Americans often do *not* support the same party for all the different offices on the ballot. In particular, they may support a candidate of a different party for president than for Congress. Such 'ticket-splitting' does not imply that voters' choices are haphazard or inconsistent. Particularly when looked at over the course of several elections, it becomes obvious that many voters most of the time choose candidates from one of the parties only, but that they occasionally deviate (perhaps because of the attractions of a particular candidate). The concept of party identification was invented by political scientists to capture this evident tendency to choose candidates from one of the parties, in spite of the occasional 'defection'. We will have more to say about ticket-splitting by US voters in Chapter 5.

As already discussed in Chapter 2, the functions performed by party identification in America, in terms of cue-giving and reducing the need for information, in other countries are sometimes performed by identifications with particular groups (ethnic, religious, class) or with political ideologies that are the source of inspiration for multiple parties – each of which will then function as a source of cues. The way in which party identification is acquired, through processes of socialization and immunization, has already been discussed (pp. 49–50), but there are some aspects of these processes that we need to elaborate upon in the context of the present chapter.

Age, immunization and generational differences

The concept of immunization (against change) is one that many find hard to grasp. For example, the idea that 'people become more conservative as they age' suggests that they do indeed change rather than that they are immunized against change. To avoid confusion here, we have to make a distinction between two meanings of the term 'conservative'. One meaning is that the older people get the more likely they are to become stuck in their ways. It is not that everyone gets stuck in this way. People who change their party choice at least once every so often (for whatever reason) are less likely to become habitual supporters of any party. But, generally speaking, the more opportunities a voter has had to do the same thing a number of times, the more likely it is that he or she will indeed have done the same thing a number of times before, possibly for very good reasons each time. So older people will have had more opportunities to become habituated in this way – something we tend to think of as conservatism with a little 'c'. People become more conservative in this sense as they get older because they're less likely to embrace new ideas, new fads, new fashions, and so forth. But sometimes conservatism with a small 'c' gets confused with conservatism with a big 'C', which is about political values and policies, not about being stuck.

When American political scientists first started to investigate the political behavior of the American electorate, they noticed that older people tended to be more conservative with a big 'C', and from this deduced that people became more Conservative as they aged. More careful analysis, however, revealed that this was not true at all. Rather, the world in which these individuals had been socialized was a predominately Conservative one before the New Deal of the 1930s. So older voters of the 1950s bore the imprint of the pre-New Deal era. They were Conservative with a big 'C' because their small 'c' conservatism had preserved the values they had acquired when they were young, not because they had become more Conservative as they aged. Of course, today it is no longer true that older people grew up before New Deal ideas became commonplace. Those voters are now long dead. During the

1990s in the US older voters tended to be more liberal, if anything, than younger voters because they were young during the Great Depression when New Deal ideas first began to spread (Miller and Shanks 1996). Ten years later the youngest US voters once again appear to be by far the most liberal. So the myth of people getting more Conservative (with a big 'C') as they age is just that: a myth. What is true is that the youngest voters are the most responsive to whatever winds of change may be blowing at the time they enter the electorate (and for a few elections thereafter) – and then they become living time capsules, taking with them as they age the formative influences of their era.

What happens when individuals who have become stuck in their ways are presented with new information? This depends on whether the new information confirms or contradicts their established opinions. If it fits they embrace it; otherwise they tend to reject it (see pp. 52–3). This could be regarded as quite unfortunate. Many people learn the habit of voting for a particular party long before they've had time to give any real thought to which party that should be. After that, every time they read something which should have, perhaps, given them some help in making a decision, the information is colored by their party identification.

This process not only affects party choice but also all sorts of other information and beliefs about politics. The more firmly people's beliefs and opinions have become entrenched, the more likely they are to avoid being exposed to information that might contradict these beliefs. If forced to confront the information in question, they are likely to reject it and most unlikely to remember it. In studies of communication these processes are generally referred to as selective exposure, selective acceptance and selective retention.

Ideally we would like to have an electorate that made its political decisions on a carefully considered basis. But that would require people to have nothing else to be concerned about – to have endless time (and energy) for pursuing relevant information and for engaging in political discussion and reflection. The real world, however, does not conform to such ideals, and citizens (and politicians as well) have to find shortcuts. It is here that cues (based on trust) are of importance, and thus party identification. At the same time, however, accepting cues from parties (or other cue-givers) on the basis of trusting them may degenerate into blind and uncritical acceptance, with no space for any deliberative process. Where individuals, and entire electorates, are located on this axis – between independent and detached deliberation on the one hand and blind trust on the other hand – is a matter for empirical assessment. It will not be the same for all individuals or for all societies (or for the same society at different moments in time). However, one of the best-established findings in electoral studies is that people who are entrenched in a particular partisanship tend to be those who otherwise would be best equipped for independent deliberation: the better educated, the better informed and those who are most interested in politics (van der Eijk and Niemöller 1983; Sniderman 1993). In other words, party identification is a mark of political sophistication. In contrast, those with the least knowledge, experience and interest are also the ones least constrained by party identification. Of course, today the latter group contains a disproportionate number of citizens who have recently reached voting age. Most of these individuals will become better educated and more interested in politics with the passage of time, especially if they do cast a vote at the first opportunity; but, in the process of doing so, they lose some of their 'innocence' and freedom of judgement – and gain a party identification.

As we have said, those who have not yet got stuck in their ways and who thus have the best chances to effectuate electoral change are predominantly young people. They may have a strong inherited partisanship from their parents, but this is not locked down until they have voted repeatedly for the same party. Until that happens, any number of things can come along to override inherited partisanship – not that it happens that often. In stable party systems, parental transmission is a good predictor of partisanship, and it remains a good predictor throughout people's lives, but it gets weaker over the course of a young adult's first few elections as they gain their own experience of the political world, sometimes overriding initial partisanship.

The fundamental roles of immunization and party identification have been confirmed in all the research that has been conducted over 50 years or more in virtually all established democracies. The problem is reconciling this with what people see around them. Why, if that is where the possible gains are highest, do politicians not focus in their campaigns more closely on young voters? Why are we much more likely to see them focusing on older voters who are quite unlikely to vote for any other party? One reason why politicians often focus on those who would not be at all likely to vote for another party is to motivate them to actually turn out to vote when the time comes. Party supporters have been known to stay home rather than vote. If they do so in sufficient numbers, then their party will suffer at the polls. This happened in 1994 in the US when many Democrats were so frustrated by the poor showing of Bill Clinton's first two years as President that they just couldn't bring themselves to go and vote. The result was a landslide for the Republicans; not because the world had turned Republican suddenly, but because Republicans proved much more successful at getting out their voters (Center for Voting and Democracy 1995). So differential turnout is an important concern for politicians: a justification for politicians paying attention to people who probably would never vote for anybody else, but who might not vote at all. As a consequence, however, the attention given to the truly undecided (disproportionately young voters) is often less than would be expected in view of the potential they offer for making new 'converts'.

A second reason for talking to the faithful is that it makes good television. An audience full of hecklers, such as politicians would find on many a college campus, yields bad publicity for a party. The party wants to put across an image of having overwhelming support in the electorate. It is more likely to promote such an image by talking to the faithful than by talking to those who do not yet have a strong party identification. The unfortunate consequence is that those who might be converted tend to be ignored – one reason for the low turnout among young voters in more countries than just the US (recent US elections have seen more attention given to young voters, with the result that there was a higher turnout among such voters than at the elections in the 1980s and 1990s).

Group loyalties

Another really important reason why people vote the way they do is to be found in their membership in and loyalty to social groups defined by differences in class, religion, ethnicity and the like. If such groups are an important basis for social conflict and for social organization, and if membership in them is an important part of people's consciousness, then these groups are referred to as social cleavage groups and the dividing lines between them as 'social cleavages'. In established democracies social cleavages are often more relevant for understanding voting behavior in past eras than for understanding voters today; but in newer democracies group loyalties can be critical (think of the religious/ethnic cleavages in the former Yugoslavia, in South Africa or in Lebanon, for example). However, there are some established democracies, such as Northern Ireland, where social cleavages still have considerable strength (see Box 4.1). With *cleavage politics* people are voting on the basis of group membership. But what is the link between group membership and cleavage politics?

The groups we are talking about – Protestants, Catholics, workers, farmers – have distinctive political interests that political parties often were founded to represent (Lipset and Rokkan 1967). Repeated voting for those parties by the groups concerned will of course have led to the development or strengthening of identifications with the parties concerned. A party that plausibly represents a cleavage group will earn the loyalty of that group. Eventually the members of the group will become stuck in their party preferences. The cleavage group – itself an object of social identification – will then have become translated into a politically relevant identification linked to a particular party.

Of course, the same social group may be linked to more than one party. Traditionally, this used to be the case in European democracies for the relationship between the working class and socialist and communist parties.

Box 4.1   Cleavage politics in the Netherlands and Northern Ireland

These two countries illustrate well how conflicts between cleavage groups can be worsened or ameliorated by electoral arrangements.

The Netherlands entered the 20th century as a country where two different social cleavages had become strongly politicized: a religious divide that separated Protestants from Catholics, and a class divide that – amongst the less religious – set the working class against the middle class. Each of the four major cleavage groups constituted a minority at the national level, without any realistic hope of acquiring government power by itself, but fearful of being dominated by some other group. The severe tension between the groups was reduced by a compromise – known as the 'Pacification' of 1917 – giving each of the groups something they wanted (or wanted to avoid) and changing the electoral system from FPTP to PR, which removed the likelihood that any of the groups would be able to dominate the others. The Pacification guaranteed each group meaningful political representation and necessitated a 'give-and-take' style of national politics that helped gradually to dissipate the cleavage conflicts.

In Northern Ireland – a constituent part of the United Kingdom – it proved more difficult than in the Netherlands to defuse conflict between cleavage groups, partly because one of the two major cleavage groups (the Protestants) enjoyed a numerical majority over the Catholic minority. The FPTP electoral system effectively locked the Catholic minority out of political power. Increasing political frustration eventually exploded into an armed conflict (euphemistically known as 'The Troubles') between paramilitary groups on both sides of the religious divide during the late 1960s and early 1970s. The situation was ultimately defused by invoking cooperation of the Irish government in a historic Anglo-Irish Agreement in 1985, which led to the Good Friday Agreement of 1998 and the cessation of active violence. One of the central elements of this agreement was the adoption of a new electoral system giving real political representation to the Catholic minority. Ironically, the STV electoral system adopted had been mandated by the British Government at the time of the partition of Northern Ireland from the rest of Ireland in 1922 but had been abolished by the Northern Irish Parliament in 1925. It is quite possible that, had this change not taken place, the Troubles would never have occurred.

Those parties both claimed to represent the working class, but they offered different solutions to working-class problems. In the context of our present discussion, the fact that two parties can appeal for support from the same group of voters means that group identification is not strictly the same as party identification. This in turn implies the possibility that some people will identify with more than a single party – a phenomenon referred to as multiple party identification (or as ideological identification – see Box 2.7). In turn this means that more than one party can serve as a source of cues and authoritative pronouncements that voters use when orienting themselves in the political world. The development of multiple party identifications is promoted in multiparty systems, where it is common for parties to share their programmatic and ideological background with one or several other parties. But even in the two-party context of the US we also find indications for the existence of multiple party identification (Weisberg 1980), with some voters claiming an identification with both Republicans and Democrats.

Not only can we find the same group supporting multiple parties, we can also find a single party defined in terms of support from multiple groups. In most countries we find at one period or another parties that represent groups defined by the intersection of several cleavage lines. In such a country one party would target working-class churchgoing urban people, while another would target working-class churchgoing rural people, and yet another would target working-class non-churchgoing urban people, and so on. A good example was France at the time of the Fourth Republic, from 1944 to 1958. It is only a slight exaggeration to say that, in order to enumerate all the parties in the Republic, one just had to cycle through all the permutations and combinations of social cleavages because each intersection of the cleavage structure saw a different party appealing to voters at that intersection (Duverger 1964: 231—2). This system did not survive into the Fifth Republic, and after 1958 in France we find a rearrangement of the party system in which parties no longer focused on such narrowly circumscribed social groups.

Over time new cleavages can compete in importance with old cleavages and even replace old cleavages in terms of political importance. In Britain, in the first half of the 20th century, class replaced a religious divide between the state-supported Church of England and independent 'non-conformist' churches as the dominant cleavage that structured the political system. This accompanied a political realignment in which the Labour Party replaced the Liberal Party as the dominant opposition to the Conservative Party (Butler and Stokes 1974; Franklin and Ladner 1995). In the Netherlands, by contrast, the emergence of the class cleavage in the late 19th century did not lead to the replacement of the religious cleavage as the dominant one. Instead it gave rise to a party system in which some parties competed for votes on the basis of the class cleavage – but only in the more secularized segments of society – while the religious parties tried to accommodate the working-class as well as the middle-class components of their support base. How political systems reacted to the emergence of new cleavages differs from country to country, depending on the degree of politicization of earlier cleavages, on the behavior of political elites, and on the opportunities afforded by institutional arrangements such as the electoral system (Lipset and Rokkan 1967).

It has been theorized (Duverger 1964) that the differences between the outcomes that we observe in different countries might be related to differences in electoral systems of the kind discussed in Chapter 3: a majoritarian system such as the British tends to promote two party dominance, whereas proportional representation (PR) can easily accommodate multiple parties of roughly equal strength, as in the Netherlands. The first half of the 20th century provided repeated evidence of the importance of the type of electoral system in producing different responses to social developments that were the same in different countries. The class cleavage became important in all European countries during this time, but political systems reacted differently to this development, depending in part on whether they were majoritarian or proportional political systems. The tendency of electoral systems to promote particular types of party systems was so strong that it became known as Duverger's Law (ibid.).

The decline of cleavage politics

Interestingly, in what we now consider to be established democracies, cleavage politics reached a peak soon after the middle of the 20th century, after which socially anchored cleavages declined in importance as forces that structured politics in democratic countries (Dalton and Wattenberg 1993). This decline happened both in majoritarian and in proportional systems; and, though it happened somewhat earlier in majoritarian systems, we are talking about differences of only a decade or so, as can be seen in Figure 4.1.

Figure 4.1 provides an idealized view of the decline over time in the importance of social cleavages for voters' electoral behavior in ten countries. The horizontal axis is a time line, measured in decades, while the vertical axis expresses the importance of cleavages for the choices that voters made in elections. The scale on the vertical axis relates to how tied down the voters are to the social cleavages in terms of the parties they support – how well we can explain differences in party choice on the basis of social cleavages. At its height, cleavage politics explained some 30 per cent of the variance in voting for parties of the left.[2] Thirty per cent of variance explained corresponds to a multiple correlation above 0.5, which is a very strong correlation in survey-based research. After the decline of cleavage politics, variance explained is down to 10 per cent at most, less than a third of what it was only a few decades previously, and people's party choices are no longer dominated by their social group memberships, although social cleavages are still quite important even in established democracies. This is shown in Figure 4.1 in terms of the height of each line on the vertical axis. The line belonging to a particular country is shown high up the chart when cleavages are powerful explanations of party choice and low on the chart when cleavages are less

Figure 4.1   *Idealized view of a 20-year decline of cleavage politics*

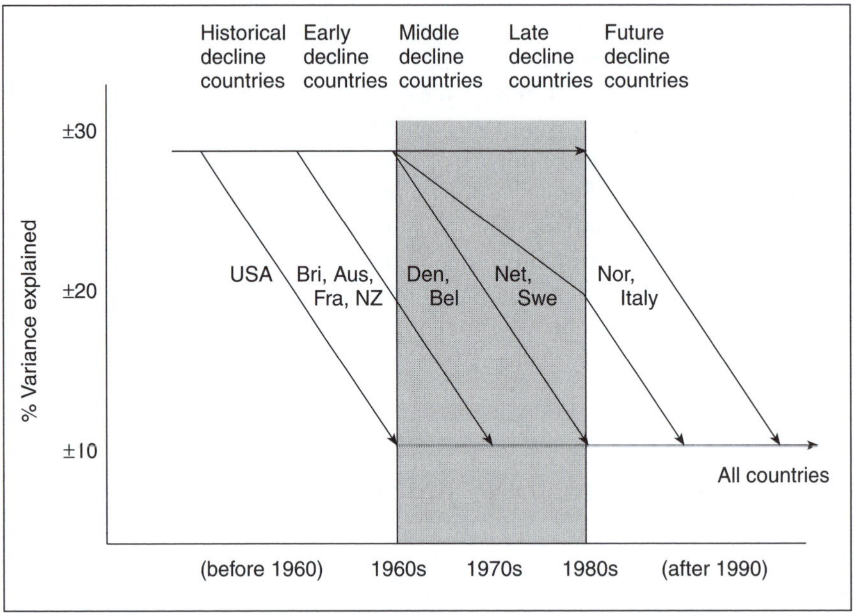

| | Historical decline countries | Early decline countries | Middle decline countries | Late decline countries | Future decline countries |

±30

% Variance explained

±20   USA   Bri, Aus, Fra, NZ   Den, Bel   Net, Swe   Nor, Italy

±10

All countries

(before 1960)   1960s   1970s   1980s   (after 1990)

Note: Extrapolated to encompass years before 1960 and after 1990.
Source: Adapted from Franklin *et al.* (1992).

powerful. We see that, generally speaking, the height of the line for each country drops with the passage of time.

Not everything that is displayed in Figure 4.1 was actually observed. The period for which data were available is indicated by the shaded 'window'. The patterns before and after that window are inferred from an in-depth analysis of cohort differences in the available data. One of the interesting things about this chart is that it was drawn in part as a prediction of future developments. Now, the future at the time the chart was drawn has become our current past and present, and we can verify that the developments projected in that picture did in fact occur. Countries where the importance of cleavage politics was expected to decline did indeed see a decline, and countries where the decline appeared to have run its course have indeed seen little further decline in cleavage politics (Franklin 2009).[3]

At the top left of the chart, before 1960, all countries appear to have had strong cleavage politics – even the US which had had strong cleavage politics going back to the 1930s and 1940s, when working people voted Democrat, and farmers, business people and old money voted Republican, except in the South. Cleavages decline in importance as we move across the chart, shown by the movement of lines representing different countries. These movements indicate (i) increasing votes for other parties, more than would be expected on the basis of group memberships, and (ii) increasing numbers of people in ambiguous social positions (caused by cleavages becoming increasingly uncorrelated or, in social science jargon, the increasing importance of 'cross-cutting' cleavages). Another way to look at this is in terms of parties becoming more and more successful at appealing across group boundaries, winning supporters who had previously given their votes to the party of a different group (with strong implications for the strength of party identification among different cohorts of voters). This appears to have happened in all established democracies, though at different times in different countries.

What does this mean in practical terms? It means that, whereas before the decline of cleavage politics the most parsimonious explanation for why people would support one party rather than another came from considering their group memberships (in Britain a working-class individual would most likely vote Labour, in Holland a Catholic would most likely vote for the Catholic Party), after the decline of cleavage politics these expectations became much weaker.

Why did social cleavages decline in their ability to structure partisanship in most established democracies? Various reasons have been suggested. The rapidity of social change may have played a role, since people born into one social group could find that group transformed in its character and relations to other social groups within the course of their lifetimes. Attempts by political elites to insure themselves against declining support due to social change certainly led some of them to appeal to voters across group lines, sometimes creating what were referred to as 'catch-all' parties (Kirchheimer 1966) and thereby accelerating the process. It has also been suggested that one reason for cleavage decline in established democracies was the coming of new cleavages (Inglehart 1971), though evidence for this is mixed (we will return to Inglehart's theories later).

In *Electoral Change* (Franklin *et al.* 1992) all of these theories and many others were evaluated, and none of the existing theories were found adequate to explain more than a small part of the changes we have described. Our own view (developed as a result of failing to find evidence in support of other theories) is that the advent of the franchise and the development of effective representative democracy provided mechanisms for resolving cleavage-based and other conflicts through innovative policy-making which, along with social changes (such as increasing affluence, modernization, urbanization, etc.), helped to ameliorate or resolve the conflicts between cleavage groups. In our opinion such developments lead inevitably to a decline of cleavage politics, as depicted in Figure 4.1 (van der Eijk *et al.* 1992). In particular, what appears to have changed in country after country is that the transmission of cleavage loyalties to new generations failed after cleavage-based conflicts were effectively resolved, thus making space for other, more contemporary, political considerations. Thus it may be no accident that the period of major change is one in which the baby-boom post-war generation first became eligible to vote. The coincidence of large numbers of new voters at the time of a reduction in the strength of traditional group loyalties might well account for the timing of the change.

In new and consolidating democracies, cleavages are often of greater importance than in today's established democracies, as we have already mentioned; but we believe that here too democratic processes will play the same role in the resolution of cleavage-based conflicts.

The rise of issue voting

Because of this evolution of party support away from a strong grounding in social cleavages, political scientists have needed to search for other explanations for why people choose to support the parties that they vote for. What seems to have happened is that, instead of acquiring votes on the basis of people's social identities, parties have started to gain support on the basis of the positions they take on contemporary issues, on the general values that they emphasize, or on the personal appeal of their leaders. It is not that these factors were unimportant before the decline of cleavage politics, but rather that then they tended to coincide with (and reinforce) group loyalties. Socialist parties stood for various forms of worker protection and job security, Catholic parties for traditional morality, and so on. After the decline of cleavage politics it was no longer possible to predict policy preferences (either of parties or of voters) adequately on the basis of these simple social stereotypes. The same issues initially remained important (protection for working people versus business-oriented policies, religious versus secular values, and so on), but they started to appeal across the boundaries of social groups. Apparently issues themselves had become more important than the groups that had previously been identified with those issues – for which reason political scientists started to refer to 'issue voting' (e.g. Franklin 1985b).

However, while they remained important, these old issues also appeared to have lost their urgency for many people, leaving room for new issues to increase in importance. So we started to see what Russell Dalton (1999) has called a 'New Politics'. Putting the two nomenclatures together we could call the development a 'new politics of issue voting'. The graph in Figure 4.2 shows how issue voting in Britain increased more or less in step with the decline of cleavage politics there. (See Franklin (1985a) for a discussion of why the changes occurred when they did and Franklin (2009) for a discussion of later developments.) Much the same appears to have happened in all established democracies – though in the US any decline in cleavage politics

Figure 4.2   *The rise of issue voting in Britain after 1964*

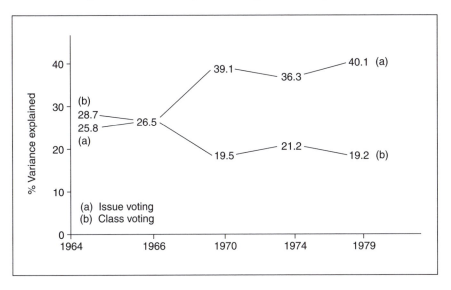

Source: Adapted from Franklin (1985a)

happened before we had opinion polls that could document it, and there are strong suggestions that in Canada social cleavages never did have much importance beyond the provincial level (Clarke and Stewart 1992, 1998).

Many of the new issues that rose to salience since the decline of cleavage politics – issues such as gender equality, the environment, 'life style' issues and nuclear armaments – appear to be interrelated, in that voters who favor one of these issues will also favor others. This complex of attitudes has been dubbed 'post-materialism' (Inglehart 1971, 1977, 1990) or more recently 'post-modernization' (Inglehart 1997), and an elaborate theoretical edifice has been constructed to account for these interrelationships, based on a supposed shift among those born after World War II away from material concerns and towards concerns for quality of life and self-actualization. The argument is loosely based on a combination of the enduring effects of early socialization with the historically unique conditions of unprecedented mate- rial security and prosperity under which new generations were socialized at this time. Analogously to Maslow's 'hierarchy of needs' (Maslow 1943) this was hypothesized to have produced a shift in values away from 'materialist' and towards 'post-materialist' concerns.

This explanation seems too simplistic, however, as Inglehart's own find- ings show a rising post-materialism even in generations that grew up during the Great Depression and World War II (Inglehart 1997: Fig. 5.2). It seems to us that the interrelationships between the various kinds of issues that are often seen as manifestations of post-materialism are more likely to have arisen simply because younger generations had not become 'stuck' in the frames of reference associated with older issues, thus providing the space for these newer issues to be embraced. The mechanisms of generational replacement that we outlined earlier in this chapter evidently make it almost inevitable that new issues will be taken on board most easily and most rapidly by new generations of voters, and these mechanisms seem quite potent enough to have produced the observed differences between the issue concerns of different generations.

Considerable controversy persists in the literature about the role of cleavages in the politics of today. For some commentators, any political issue that separates people into two or more camps can be called a cleavage. Yet Lipset and Rokkan (1967) were quite precise about the requirements that had to be fulfilled before a political dispute would be interpreted in terms of a social cleavage. The most important additional requirements were that protagonists should line up for and against the issue along some recognizable line of social demarcation that went beyond positions on the issue itself; that people should be conscious of this line of demarcation and identify with the group on 'their side' of the line; and that there should be some means of 'political expression' (generally by means of a political party) to mobilize and take advantage of support on the issue (cf. Bartolini and Mair 1990). Only if these preconditions were present did an issue difference acquire the longevity associated with cleavage politics.

On the basis of this definition of cleavage politics, it is not only hard in today's world to find old issues that any longer fulfill the requirements for social cleavage status but also hard to find any new issues that do this. Youth is not a social division, *pace* Inglehart, but a mechanism by which new issues enter the political world – because young people are more open to new issue concerns. Inglehart's (1977) identification of youth with a social cleavage misunderstood the nature of both cleavages and cleavage change by confounding one with the other. So the materialist versus post-materialist distinction he drew attention to is not and never was a social cleavage. Other new issues seem equally far from fulfilling the requirements for social cleavage status.

Even though loyalties to social groups, and the association of these groups with specific political parties, have declined in recent years, still the ubiquitous mechanisms of immunization and habitual behavior that helped to perpetuate these loyalties continue to exist (see pp. 89–91). As will be documented in Chapter 7, those mechanisms do provide a degree of immobility to the political attitudes and preferences of older voters, mimicking to some extent the role of social cleavages in earlier times. Some contemporary scholars refer to such durable distinctions as cleavages (e.g. Enyedi 2005). But it is important to realize that the mechanisms at work today are not the same and do not have the same political implications as the mechanisms that once were at work and used to be referred to as cleavage politics (Franklin 2009). In particular, it is important to understand the way in which the contemporary political world permits change to take place in a way that was previously impossible.

Long-term changes in electoral competition

New generations of voters bring into the electorate new patterns of party preferences and thus new opportunity structures for electoral competition. This happens in a number of ways. First, new voters may – as a consequence of different experiences during the period of their socialization – position themselves differently from older voters in terms of values, goals, policy preferences, and so forth. It is this insight that led Inglehart to the theory that we have just discussed. Second, political parties do not mean the same things to people of different generations. New voters are less constrained by past events that they did not witness themselves – events that for older voters color perceptions and evaluations of what parties stand for. The Great Depression of the 1930s, for example, colored the perceptions of a whole generation of voters in many countries regarding party stances. Voters of later generations associate the same parties rather with what they did or failed to do in the 1950s or 1980s. Third, young voters are themselves more changeable in their preferences. These preferences have not yet become locked down by repeated reaffirmation, and the way in which locking down occurs, when and if it does, contributes to long-term changes in patterns of electoral competition.

This provides a first way in which long-term changes to parties' baseline levels of support come about. A second way has to do with the cumulative effect of the actions of political parties, their leaders, interest groups and the media. These collectively define the agenda and the terms of political debate, in the process of which some parties will become more favorably positioned in the minds of some voters and others less so. The events of 9/11 in the US enabled the ruling party of the day to capture the political high ground in terms of framing the issue as a 'war against terrorism' and actions in response to that event as 'patriotism', thereby defining the Republican Party in such a way as to position it for electoral advantage or disadvantage, depending on how its policies played out. It is in this sort of way that political leadership is of particular relevance.

How much influence can politicians have? This brings us back to the question we posed in Chapter 1 about top-down versus bottom-up representation. In a bottom-up world, where voters determine the policies of the parties that they vote for, there would be little room for political influence on voters by political leaders. In reality it seems that the political world contains, to say the least, a very large component of top-down influence from parties (and their leaders). This is because of the extent to which voters identify with and remain loyal to the political parties that they have become used to supporting. When this type of loyalty is sufficiently strong a party can change its policy stances and ideological positions while hoping to largely take its voters with it. This is normal in two-party systems and is exemplified particularly by the American case, where the Republican Party has since the 1980s adopted radically new policies that focus on social and religious values without losing the bedrock support that it enjoyed when it was a more secular and less populist party. But we can see the same thing happening in multiparty systems too (see Box 4.2). This kind of relationship between voters and their parties is what leads political scientists to talk of top-down representation.

However, loyalties to parties are not always strong enough to give party leaders this sort of power. In the French Fourth Republic, for example, the kaleidoscope of changing party names over the years left voters with little choice but to focus their loyalties on ideological positions. Political posters at election time were couched primarily in terms of left and right, with party names added as a cue to voters regarding what party currently occupied a given position in left–right terms. In multiparty systems it is quite common for several parties to overlap partially in their ideological and policy positions. In such a political system, when parties change their policies (and hence their ideological locations) they are likely to lose the support of voters whose loyalties are defined in terms of that location, particularly if another party exists in that location (van der Eijk and Niemöller 1983; Converse and Pierce 1986). Most countries fall somewhere between these extremes, with parties able to take some or most of their supporters with them if they change their positions not too drastically.

Parties that change their political profile generally do so in the hope of acquiring new support from voters who did not previously find that party sufficiently attractive. Parties thus have an opportunity to reinvent themselves in terms of ideology, policy and personnel in order to be better placed in terms of electoral competition, as the British Labour Party managed to do under Tony Blair during the 1990s, completely putting behind it the legacy of left-wing dogma that had characterized its policies only ten years earlier. Still, a party's success in such an enterprise depends not only on its ability to take old supporters with it while acquiring new ones on the basis of its new issue stance, but also on its situation in relation to other parties with whom it competes for votes. One consideration that looms large in multiparty systems is the need to maintain good relations with other parties with whom coalition agreements might need to be forged. That is a *strategic* concern for political parties. Voters also have strategic concerns, however, as will now be explained.

Box 4.2   The Danish Social Democratic Party brings its voters along

The Danish Social Democratic Party (SDP) has proved itself remarkably successful in taking its voters with it when it changes position on major issues. When Denmark (along with Britain and Ireland) applied for membership of the (then) European Economic Community (EEC), the Danish SDP urged its followers to vote in favor in a national referendum (1972): 61 per cent of its supporters loyally followed the advice of their party (Svensson 2002). By the time Danish citizens were again called upon to vote in a referendum about Europe, in 1986 regarding the Single European Market, the party had changed its mind about the benefits of European unification and urged its followers to vote against. Only 19 per cent failed to follow their party through this major switch in policy orientation. Six years later (in 1992) the Danes were again called upon to vote in a referendum on a European issue – this time the Maastricht Treaty of European Union – and the SDP again changed its mind, urging its followers to support the treaty. But in 1992 the party was in the midst of a leadership crisis (ibid.), and the policy switch was not communicated very emphatically or unambiguously to its supporters. Nevertheless, 35 per cent gamely followed their party through this second switch in European orientation. The failure of the SDP to bring more of its supporters to vote for the treaty was partly responsible for Denmark's 'no' to Maastricht, but the party continued to work away at its supporters, and a year later, when Danes were asked to revisit the Maastricht Treaty a second time, 55 per cent of SDP supporters voted 'yes' (almost as many as had voted for EEC membership 20 years earlier) – contributing to the turn around that resulted in ratification of the treaty. That any Danish party would be able to lead its voters through a U-turn on Europe is surprising, given the supposed sophistication of Danish voters on the European issue (Siune and Svensson 1993); but to effectuate two U-turns in quick succession, bringing the bulk of their supporters with them, is truly astonishing. In doing so the party almost whiplashed its supporters, first one way and then the other, demonstrating in no uncertain terms the leadership that a party can exercise over its supporters even on a major issue (Franklin 2002b).

Strategic considerations

In an election at which a single party is expected to win a majority of seats in the Parliament, votes for any party that is not in the running for majority status are votes that are wasted in the contest to control the executive. Many voters consider government power to be the real prize in a parliamentary election, and most want their vote to count in this contest. So they hesitate to vote for small parties – even parties that they would otherwise feel considerable affinity for. Taking account of party size in this way is said to be a 'strategic consideration'.

Strategic considerations do not apply only in parliamentary democracies where single-party governments are the norm. Even in a country in which coalition governments are usual, it will be apparent to voters that any party they vote for is going to have to make a deal with other parties if it wins enough votes to become part of a government. So voters need to have one eye open for the likely coalition partners of the party they plan to vote for. This too is a strategic consideration. Voters might hesitate to vote for a party that they thought likely to join in coalition government with a party they abhor. Party leaders know this and have one eye on their voters when they are thinking about which coalitions to join.

Coalition associations may affect a party in other ways as well. The classic example is that of the German FDP. Because it formed coalitions both with the (leftist) Social Democrats and with the (rightist) Christian Democrats, voters started to think of it as being in the political center, even though it is a liberal party, and liberal parties in Europe are today generally thought of as being parties of the right. So centrist voters in Germany, who are not averse to either the Social Democrats or the CDU/CSU, may vote for the FDP in the belief that this party will moderate the policies of either of its possible coalition partners. Any such vote would also be a strategic vote, depending on judgements about likely coalition bargaining that would follow the election and not just on affinities for the party voted for.

This effect of parties' associations with other parties is an important feature of countries with coalition governments: voters are not only deriving cues about the political world from parties they identify with, but also from the patterns of interparty collaboration. As this latter kind of cue is virtually absent in systems with single-party governments, one can expect voters in those systems to make less use of (as well as having less need for) ideological cues, compared to their counterparts in coalition systems.

The other things that voters react to are all the things mentioned in the previous chapter that politicians have to bear in mind when they're making a coalition. Why will politicians agree to policy compromises after a few weeks that they were reluctant to consider earlier? Because voters will remember which parties were overly recalcitrant, just as they will remember which parties too willingly compromised their principles. Voters will judge parties partly on this basis – which is yet another type of strategic consideration.

There is another thing important in the coalition bargaining process that is also really important to voters. This is the thing that gives parties weight in the bargaining process. It is the thing that makes parties able to promise convincingly to their voters that they will be able to deliver their campaign promises. This is the centerpiece of everything to do with coalition formation and, moreover, everything to do with the difference between majoritarian and coalition governments: party size. Party size is critical. If a party is big enough it doesn't need a coalition: it can form a government on its own, as generally happens in majoritarian systems. But, even when coalition government is needed, the big parties are the ones that are most likely to be members of a governing coalition. And the largest parties in a governing coalition are going to have the most weight in that coalition. They will have the most cabinet members; they will have the most opportunities to introduce their policies.

What does this mean to voters? Frequently forgotten by commentators is the fact that many voters not only care about what policies their party has *proposed* but that they also care about getting those policies *enacted*. For them it is often pointless to vote for a party that is so small that it has no conceivable prospect of ever getting any of its policies enacted. Most voters like big parties. This is not just a tautology arising from the fact that big parties are big because lots of voters support them. When voters enter the electorate by reaching voting age, each of them sees the available parties as more or less an established fact of life. Seen by the new voter, these parties have various characteristics, one of which is their size. When we use these characteristics, as we will in Chapter 7, to try to explain why voters choose one party rather than another we discover that the larger a party is – while keeping all its other characteristics the same – the more it will be attractive to voters (van der Eijk *et al.* 1996). This is true in all systems.

From an American perspective, the relevance of party size is not always so clear. This is because in America there are only two parties and both of them are capable of winning, so party size is not an obvious issue. But scholars who study parties and party choice in other countries need to take account of the sizes of parties because voters take account of the sizes of parties. With the benefit of these insights it is possible to see party size as critical in American elections as well – it is the major force that keeps new parties from acquiring the support of voters.

Yet another aspect of strategic voting arises from the fact that voters care not only about the policies that parties propose and whether these parties can enact those policies; they also care very much about whether there is a government or not. Without a government invested on the basis of the latest election outcome, none of the promises made at that election will be carried into law. During the period that parties spend bickering about which of them will join together in what governing coalition, everyone loses. And voters in a parliamentary system bear – indirectly – a large part of the responsibility for whether there is an effective government or not. If they elect a parliament that cannot get its act together to form a government, then there is no government other than the caretaker one that was in place at the time elections were held. This government, of course, only reflects the previous election outcome, not the most recent one. Voters are often aware that if they choose to vote for small or inflexible parties they will complicate the coalition formation process. So such votes would not only be unlikely to contribute towards the choice of valued policies, they might even increase the length of time that their country has no effective government.

In their campaigns, parties attempt to make voters aware of unintended consequences that their votes might have, by pointing to the strategic implications of different election outcomes. So, in coalition systems it is common for large parties to warn voters who might be tempted to vote for small parties that their votes will be 'irrelevant' because those small parties will in all likelihood not be part of a governing coalition (see Box 4.3). Similar strategic concerns apply in first past the post (FPTP) elections, where small parties can easily fail to gain any representation at all, causing votes for them to be 'lost'. Small parties in both types of system will of course try to convince voters that a vote for them will not be irrelevant, but will force large parties to take account of policy concerns they might otherwise have ignored. That too is a strategic argument. We have seen that ignoring new issues may help large parties maintain party discipline, leaving voters who become frustrated with this behavior with no option but to vote for a small party. This has the effect of punishing large parties by taking votes from them and gives those larger parties an incentive to adapt their policies in order to prevent further erosion of their support and perhaps to get those votes back. This happened in the US in 1992 when Ross Perot won 15 per cent of the vote, mainly by attracting voters concerned about NAFTA and the budget deficit – topics that the two dominant parties had largely ignored. After that election, the winning Democrats turned their attention to the budget deficit which, by 2000, had been turned into a surplus. Small parties often play the role of gadfly to large parties in established democracies – in recent decades a particularly important role for green parties in many countries.

Getting voters to think about the strategic implications of their votes is a common way for parties in multiparty systems to pursue their competition for votes. It is an attempt to change the balance of considerations for voters who might otherwise find two parties equally acceptable. Usually one of the parties involved in such a 'tug of war' uses pragmatic arguments – cast in terms of power and the likelihood of actually being able to influence policy – whereas the other will emphasize its sincerity uncorrupted by pragmatism. Such strategic arguments are, of course, not only used by parties but also by candidates in multicandidate elections, such as American primary elections. Much of the discourse there is about which candidate can win in the general election that will follow. During the 2004 American campaign, before the primary elections, some people argued 'Vote for Kerry. You may prefer Edwards, but he's not going to be able to beat George Bush'. And because

---

Box 4.3   Strategic voting in the Netherlands

The relevance of strategic considerations for voting in multiparty systems is illustrated well by the following episode from the 1981 Dutch election campaign. Just before the parliamentary elections of 26 May, Dutch voters found a page-size advertisement in their newspapers which read 'A vote for Jan is a vote for Joop, so vote for Hans'. This minimal text was perfectly intelligible to Dutch voters: Jan, Joop and Hans were the first names of the leaders of three major parties: the left-centrist Democrat Party (D66), the Social Democratic Party (PvdA) and the more right-wing liberal party (VVD). The incumbent coalition consisted of the VVD along with the center-right Christian Democrats (CDA), and had ruled since 1977 with a paper-thin parliamentary majority of only two seats. During the election campaign, the CDA had neither ruled out a continuation of this coalition nor an alternative one with the PvdA. For the VVD, however, only a continuation of the coalition with the CDA would give them a share in government. In this situation D66 was not a possible coalition partner, so votes for D66 would not help decide who would form a government. In the Dutch proportional electoral system a loss of only 1.3 per cent of the total vote would suffice to deprive the coalition of its two-seat majority, so the VVD was anxious that none of its supporters defected to D66. Hence the advertisement was a warning that voting for (Jan's) D66 might lead to a center-left coalition (including Joop's PvdA) and that the most certain way to avoid this would be by voting for (Hans's) VVD.

---

voters care not only about the policies being proposed and how nice the candidates are but, above all, about whether they can win in the real election for president, some voters will be sensitive to such arguments and support a candidate who might not be the one whose policy proposals they prefer most. On the other hand, arguments about which candidate or party is best situated to deliver valued results will be contested by other candidates. As a consequence, when there are multiple parties or candidates, election campaigns tend to emphasize a mixture of substantive policy proposals and strategic arguments.

So political parties try to focus voters' minds on the important things at issue, which is having a government and having an effective government that has acceptable policies, even if not perfect policies. And because this requires in parliamentary systems a legislature that can invest a government, these dual considerations are necessarily both on voters' minds.

When there are only two choices available, it would seem logical that strategic arguments will be less important. That is particularly so when the two options are substantively far apart in policy terms. The more that the two parties or candidates propose similar policies, however, the more scope there is for arguments of a somewhat different type that center, again, on capacity to make good on good intentions.

The role of the Prime Minister in parliamentary regimes

Because of the importance of strategic considerations in party choice, the position of the Prime Minister in parliamentary systems has its own consequences for relations between voters, parties and governments. This can be best illustrated by what happened when Israel adopted what Lijphart calls 'the balanced system' (Lijphart 1999). The Israeli constitution was changed in 1996 so as to make the Prime Minister directly elected. Each voter was given two votes, one to cast for a party list (which would decide on the composition of the legislature) and one to elect (in an FPTP manner) a Prime Minister.

It is not clear exactly why the Israelis adopted this reform. The idea of having a Prime Minister directly elected by the people at the same time as the Parliament is elected has dire consequences that can be deduced logically from what we have already explained about how a parliamentary system works. A parliamentary system hangs together because of a complex relationship between the people, the Parliament and the cabinet led by the Prime Minister. Giving each voter a second vote to elect the Prime Minister freed them from having to take into consideration the consequences for government formation of what normally would have been their only vote. Because they were given a separate vote for Prime Minister they were guaranteed a chief executive of their choice, just like in America. But, just like in America, they were not guaranteed a government that could actually govern.

In this new system, the Prime Minister was instantly placed in an impossibly difficult position. Normally any party leader can try to put a coalition together. So if the first person to try fails, each remaining party leader in turn can try his or her luck. But the new Israeli system took away those other options. The elected Prime Minister was charged with the task of forming a coalition. By being absolved of their responsibility to take into account the consequences of their vote for government formation, Israeli voters were free to use their vote for a party in any way they wished, without heeding its consequences for the formation of a viable government. This meant that they were able to use that vote to support the party they liked best on other grounds than contributing to a viable government – a party whose policies might be incompatible with those of their preferred candidate for Prime Minister. If the electoral system so clearly suggests that the two votes have two different functions, and only one of these is related to the choice of government, it is little surprising that the other will express something different and unrelated to the formation of a government.

In practice what happened in Israel is that the number of seats going to minor parties in the Parliament exploded and the number of seats held by the biggest parties, the ones that might have formed a governing coalition (including the Prime Minister's party) plummeted to the point where the Prime Minister's was no longer the party with the most seats (Brichta 2001). So the person elected as Prime Minister found himself leader of a party that was unable to dominate the Parliament or even a set of prospective coalition partners. After two elections, when the Israeli political establishment figured out what was happening, it changed the system back and Israeli voters in 2003 did them the honour of starting to vote again in a manner that allowed the formation of viable coalitions (Rahat and Hazan 2005).

There are three lessons to take from this story. First: when asked to make separate choices for ostensibly different political functions, the implications of those separate choices will not necessarily be consistent in terms of government formation and government viability. Second, the viability of a coalition government depends in large measure on the willingness of the constituent parties to make compromises and to have the discipline to stick to them. Having separate electoral mandates for Prime Minister and for the legislature is a disincentive for parties to arrive at sensible compromises or to stick to them. Third, the functioning of a parliamentary system depends on a subtle balance of forces that cannot be rearranged at will.

What happened in Israel when it changed to an elected Prime Minister could have been foreseen on the basis of the logic of parliamentary government that we have set out in this book. Indeed it was foreseen by Israeli political scientists who predicted that the reform would completely wreck the Israeli party system. What surprised them, however, was the speed with which these consequences manifested themselves. The speed with which voters adapted to the new situation tells us something about their orientations to political parties. If most voters had had identifications with only a single party, not much would have changed when the constitution changed. But if – as happens to be the case in Israel – there are many parties largely arranged along a single ideological dimension, then for most voters there will be at least two parties whose proposed policies are reasonably attractive to them. By removing the strategic considerations that originally made many voters choose relatively large and pragmatic parties, voters could thus easily switch to ideologically similar, but less pragmatic, parties, with dire consequences for coalition formation.

Tactical voting

We have just seen that party choice in parliamentary elections is infused with strategic considerations because of the fact that, in such elections, one vote has to achieve different things. Voters must decide before they vote what they want in the way of an electoral outcome, and how their vote might contribute to that outcome. Such elections are not just beauty contests in which voters can happily vote for the party or candidate they most prefer in terms of policy proposals or the charisma of a leader. American primary elections have somewhat the same character. But the considerations we have been discussing occur uniquely at the national level and have to do particularly with whether a party will be in a position to take part in government (or adopt other roles that it might play vis-à-vis government parties). In parliamentary systems with FPTP elections such considerations are not only relevant at the national level but also at the constituency (or district) level. In such countries, each individual contest brings with it the chance of a wasted vote if the party voted for has no chance of winning. In each constituency voters have to address the question whether they should vote for the party they prefer most on the basis of national considerations or for a party that can win in that constituency. When voters take account of the strengths of parties in their local districts or constituencies it is customary to refer to this as tactical rather than strategic voting. Figure 4.3 illustrates the different forms of voters' sensitivities to strategic and tactical considerations and may also help to explain why the literature on 'voter preferences' can at times be quite confusing.

Starting at the left of Figure 4.3, we see that voters evaluate each of the parties in a number of different ways, each of which may lead to a certain

Figure 4.3   *Strategic and tactical considerations in FPTP elections*

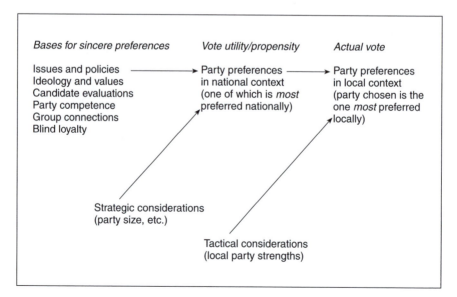

Bases for sincere preferences

Issues and policies
Ideology and values
Candidate evaluations
Party competence
Group connections
Blind loyalty

Vote utility/propensity

Party preferences
in national context
(one of which is *most*
preferred nationally)

Actual vote

Party preferences
in local context
(party chosen is the
one *most* preferred
locally)

Strategic considerations
(party size, etc.)

Tactical considerations
(local party strengths)

degree of preference for that party. Only considering issues and policies leads to issue-based preferences for parties. Keep in mind that such preferences need not be of a black-or-white character (total agreement versus total rejection). It is more likely that one or more of the existing parties will be preferred to a greater extent, and others to a lesser extent, on this criterion. But issues are not the only criterion that voters can use to evaluate parties. They can also use ideological (and value) considerations, evaluations of candidates and other key personnel, their perception of parties' track records or the extent to which a party represents a group with which the voter identifies.

Finally, we have included the identification with a party 'right or wrong' among the kinds of considerations leading to sincere preferences (first column).[4] When all these different single-aspect preferences are taken in conjunction, we get an overall *sincere* preference for each of the parties. These sincere preferences may be differentially affected, however, by how voters take account of the general (national) political context. A high sincere preference may be dampened by the realization that the party in question has virtually no chance of being part of the government (either because it is deemed to be 'beyond the pale' by other parties or because it is too small to be a likely coalition partner). Such strategic considerations modify the 'sincere' preferences and result in what Downs (1957) termed electoral utilities, which can be regarded simply as preferences for political parties, given the existing political context in the country as a whole. Often these form the immediate basis of the vote decision. Actual choice is then seen as choosing the option that is *most* preferred (in terms of utilities or propensities) which implies that the rank order of these preferences matters.

In some instances, however, there is an additional factor to be taken into account when deciding for whom to vote: the local political context. In spite of the fact that we focus in this book on national elections (and not on local ones) this local context is nevertheless relevant when elections for national office are conducted on a district or constituency basis, as is the case in FPTP or single transferable vote (STV) systems. What if party A (the party really preferred) is particularly weak in one's own district, while parties B and C are in a neck-and-neck race? It is here that what we refer to as *tactical* considerations kick in, making some voters support their second-best preference in order to try and avoid a victory of an even less preferred option (below we will address the terminological confusion in the use of the words 'strategic' and 'tactical').

It is obvious that tactical considerations (in our use of the word) can only occur in district elections and only when there are more than two options available. Even then such considerations are only relevant to voters whose first preference is not likely to win. Strategic considerations on the other hand are potentially relevant in all electoral systems and so matter to all voters. Both are more likely to occur when a voter has more choice options that are viewed favorably; however, it must be borne in mind that voters may differ between themselves in the extent to which they are sensitive to strategic or tactical considerations. More pragmatically oriented people will, *ceteris paribus*, be more sensitive to the overall context within which they make a choice (and thus more sensitive to both strategic and tactical considerations), while 'true blue' believers and ideologues will be less so.

Distinguishing 'strategic' from 'tactical' considerations is made harder by the fact that many authors use the words interchangeably. Yet the two types of considerations need to be kept separate. In Britain during the 1980s and 1990s the Liberal Democrats were a serious competitor for Labour votes, which suggests that many Liberal Democrat supporters had a higher preference for Labour than for the Conservatives, as well as that Labour supporters generally preferred the Liberal Democrats over the Conservatives. This made tactical considerations very relevant in some constituencies. In a constituency where Labour was ahead of the Liberal Democrats but behind the Conservatives, a Liberal Democrat might prefer to vote Labour rather than risk allowing the Conservatives to win. In a constituency where Liberal Democrats were ahead of Labour, a Labour supporter might similarly prefer to vote Liberal Democrat rather than risk a Conservative victory. To vote tactically in such a situation, voters had to be aware of the relative strengths of different parties in their own constituencies, and it appears that anything up to 10 per cent of voters (half of those for whom a tactical vote might be appropriate) did in fact vote tactically in this sense (Niemi *et al.* 1992). This type of behavior is quite different from the strategic behavior that was our concern earlier in this chapter. In constituencies where tactical considerations played no part, strategic considerations may yet have advantaged the larger Labour Party at the expense of the smaller Liberal Democrats.

Still, the prevalence of tactical voting in suitable circumstances tells us that voters are concerned about more than just voting for their sincerely most preferred party. Such behavior demonstrates the fact that individual voters see their votes as potent and are reluctant to waste them on a party that they do not feel can win. This is important evidence for the fact that while the objective value of one vote may be vanishingly small, the subjective value to the voter is far greater. Otherwise voters would not exercise this degree of effort. Nevertheless, no more than half of all voters who find themselves in a position to vote tactically do so in practice, which tells us that the electorate contains a mix of individuals, some of whom take the tactical situation into account and some of whom do not, a topic we will return to when we investigate the forces that shape party preferences and voting choice.

Figure 4.3 also illustrates why the term 'party preference' is used in so many different ways in the voting behavior literature (and occasionally even within the same text). Preferences can relate to a single aspect that is taken into account (such as 'issue preferences'), but also to an overall sincere preference. These are different again from the preferences when strategic considerations are taken into account. In all these cases, preferences have an 'absolute' character (they are high or low for a particular party), while in the case of rank orders the term preference acquires a relative meaning, which it also has in the case of actual choice. So there is terminological confusion in the literature referring to party preferences, and most likely we ourselves have not been fully consistent in our use of the term. The only advice we can give is therefore to always interpret the meaning of party preferences in a given text by taking account of the distinctions provided in Figure 4.3.

Candidate evaluations

Considerations very like strategic considerations (though usually considered separately) can apply to what are sometimes known as 'candidate evaluations' or 'candidate traits'. Candidates can appear more or less competent to achieve the objectives that they espouse. The (alleged) competence of candidates or parties as decisive leaders with a successful track record is often at issue in a campaign. And the perception that one candidate is considerably more competent than another may – again – result in voters not supporting the party or candidate whose policy proposals they like best. This contrast has been important in certain US elections – for instance Reagan versus Mondale in 1980 or Bush (senior) versus Dukakis in 1988. The importance of candidate traits – not only perceived competence, but also traits such as warmth or likeability, honesty, decisiveness, compassion – has been a focus of much scholarship, particularly in the US (e.g. Patterson 1989; Lodge *et al.* 1995). But it is obvious that candidate traits are also important elsewhere, particularly for those voters who have relatively strong preferences for more than just one party (Anker 1998; Schoen 2007; Dinas 2008).

In a parliamentary system, the role of the US presidential contenders is taken by party leaders who are the politicians who would become Prime Minister if their parties won a majority of the votes – or at least enough votes to become the largest party in a coalition government. In a country like Germany, where it is clear that any coalition must contain one or other of two large parties, or a country like Britain where one or other of two large parties is expected to gain a majority of the seats in the Parliament, the identity of the likely Prime Minister is known well ahead of any election. Indeed, party leaders in parliamentary systems are generally far better known than US presidential contenders, because to become a party leader one has generally to work one's way up through the ranks, taking first minor and then more important party positions and often serving as a cabinet minister before reaching the pinnacle of party leadership. The spectacle of a virtual political unknown (like Silvio Berlusconi) becoming leader of a party he invented for the purpose, and then Prime Minister, is so unusual in Europe as to be virtually unprecedented. Arguably it only happened because Italy's political system was in meltdown at the time (see Box 3.4).

In the US, by contrast, it is often seen as advantageous for candidates to run specifically as outsiders, untainted by the 'wheeling and dealing' of Washington DC. So the prevalence of previously unknown politicians as US presidential candidates is high and is yet another reason for the long campaign season that is apparently needed in that country.

Implications

In this chapter we have seen why, in previous chapters, we needed to pay attention to institutional arrangements, on the one hand, and their implications for the behavior of voters, on the other. Without that knowledge we could not have understood why the Israeli party system started to unravel as soon as voters were given a separate vote for the Prime Minister. Voters react to institutions as much as politicians do, so when looking at elections we have to understand voters in relation to politicians and both in relation to the institutional setting. Obviously this is equally true if we want to understand why voters behave differently in the Netherlands than in Britain, or in Britain than in the US. Understanding elections and voters is a quintessentially comparative exercise. More specifically, along these lines, we have seen that the strategic implications of electoral systems and institutional arrangements are understood and taken into account by voters, at least collectively. This is partly because politicians (and perhaps the media) help voters to do this, but the main point is that voters are quite sensitive to the implications of the institutional arrangements in their country. The Israeli example in particular teaches us that, if electoral verdicts are fragmented across different institutions, these separate verdicts may easily lead to inconsistencies and thus to a disempowerment of the electorate – exactly what we see in the American system which was designed to be that way.

Finally, in conjunction with what we have learned in earlier chapters, it is obvious that elements of presidential and parliamentary government cannot be mixed at will without the risk of creating chaos. Each has its own logic. Presidential systems require the cabinet to be subject to a president with his own electoral mandate, and a separation of powers between the executive and a separately elected legislature. In parliamentary systems executive and legislative functions are intimately linked, but this requires that both derive from a single electoral verdict. Of course there is nothing to stop individual systems from inventing idiosyncratic embellishments (especially in terms of electoral systems) as long as this primary logic is not violated.

Still, electoral behavior in different countries is similar enough that it can be characterized in common terms. This is best shown with a diagram (Figure 4.4) that was created to illustrate the theory at the heart of *The American Voter* (Campbell *et al.* 1960). This diagram (Budge *et al.* 1976), though published 16 years later than *The American Voter*, succeeds in putting on paper and systematizing a theory that is somewhat amorphous in the book itself. At the left is the prime cause, conceived by the authors of *The American Voter*, as it was by more recent authors, as group membership. Group membership is the only source pictured in the diagram with an effect on party identification, whose central importance is most clear: it is linked to everything later in the causal sequence. This diagram is essentially the same (though a little more detailed) as the bottom row in our own model of electoral behavior in Figure 1.2.

Starting at the far left of Figure 4.4 we see, as already mentioned, social group membership. In many countries it is common to have a religious party (which might call itself Christian or Christian Democrat) that seeks the support of Catholic or Protestant voters; a Labour party (which might call itself Socialist or Social Democratic) that expects working class support; and so on. Even when the parties do not refer in their own names to a particular

Figure 4.4 *The structure of causal relations contained in* The American Voter

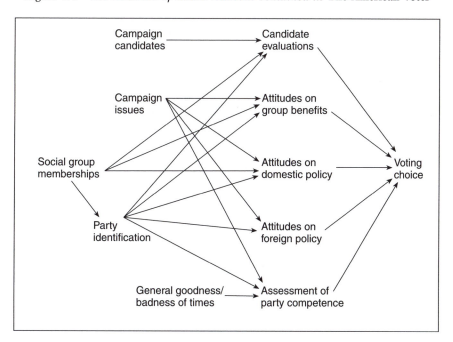

Source: Adapted from Budge *et al.* (1976), p. 6.

social group, historically most political parties have had close linkages to social groups, although not necessarily the same ones in each country. For example a liberal party (a pretty vague title) might be linked to Protestant voters in one country and middle-class voters in another. It is often a matter of historical happenstance what linkages became established in different countries (Lipset and Rokkan 1967: ch. 1). In the US, of course, the names of the major political parties are completely lacking in any content that might hint at the social groups that would be attracted to each party. Nevertheless social groups have been important historically in being tied to one party or another. Notice that this figure relates to a theory of American voting, and social group memberships are the first things on the left of the chart, even in a chart about America. In the US, Democrats have historically been the party of organized labor and more recently of various minorities. Republicans have historically been the party of farmers, business interests and more recently of Christian fundamentalists.

As we move to the right in Figure 4.4 we come to party identification. Here we see that people acquire their party identification, at least in part, from the social groups within which they are socialized, as explained. The other things that decide elections flow both from group memberships and from party identification: mainly evaluations of candidates and attitudes towards issues – items that fall towards the right-hand side of the diagram. These are the things that election campaigns are supposedly about and the things which conscientious citizens are supposed to educate themselves about so as to be able to make good electoral decisions. Two problems arise in practice, however. To a large extent people gain their attitudes towards issues and their evaluations of candidates from their party identification. Insofar as this is not the case, those evaluations and attitudes have largely idiosyncratic origins – arising, for example, from a voter's personal experience and knowledge about a particular issue. Finally, of course, some of these orientations are influenced by the campaign itself.

What Figure 4.4 cannot convey without undue complexity are the dynamic processes of immunization (or lack thereof) over time that may reinforce or undermine party identification – unless or until voters become 'locked in' after a sufficient number of successive affirmations of that identification (though this does not have to occur for all voters).

The role of party identification as a cue for voters and as a screen for the information that reaches voters makes the political world into an echo chamber – or more specifically into several echo chambers, one for each party – in which party leaders have immense power to color the attitudes of those who are supposed to pass judgement on them at election time and to obfuscate the clarity of debate on political issues. If the entire electorate were to consist of voters with clearly defined party identifications (an ideal type that has probably never totally described the real world), then the whole electorate would be tied down in its partisan preferences and elections would be quite different phenomena than when no one has their party choice locked down in this way (an opposite ideal type that might have existed in some new democracies). In political systems of the first type, parties do not vie with each other for votes, as each voter has only a preference for a single party. Psychologically, in such systems, elections are non-competitive and the only thing that parties can do to maximize their vote share is to ensure that all their potential supporters turn out. Those supporters are well represented in such a system, but elections are relatively futile as mechanisms for holding politicians (and the political parties that they represent) to account. If, however, a sizeable segment of the electorate is not locked in to a preference for only a single party or party family, then parties really have to compete with one another for the support of the available voters. In that case elections are competitive at the individual level, and many individual voters will be hesitating between several options that they find attractive to roughly the same degree. To the extent that electorates resemble this type, elections are not such definitive mechanisms of political representation (the links between voters and their parties are not so clear cut), but they are much more effective as mechanisms of political accountability.

In this chapter we have described how political life in mature democracies underwent a transition, that we described as 'the decline of cleavage politics', during the last part of the 20th century, from a world that approximated to the first of these ideal types to a world much more like the second of them. In the 21st century voters do have the opportunity to affect the course of political events. To the extent that they change their views they can effect change in the policies proposed and enacted by governments. How and why voters change will be the subject of Chapter 7. But first we need to discuss how elections enable voters to affect the course of public policy (the subject of the next chapter) and the nature of public opinion (the subject of Chapter 6).

Chapter 5

Outcomes of Elections

Election outcomes can be viewed in a number of ways, though we will focus on just three. First, they can be seen as deciding (or strongly influencing) whether office holders remain in office or are replaced. More specifically, they can be seen as more or less successful in holding governments to account. Under this heading we discuss matters such as the power of incumbency, term limits and phenomena associated with the possibility of 'throwing the rascals out'. Note that some offices that have little or no decision-making autonomy can nevertheless be filled by election (the Irish, for example, elect their national President whose role, however, is purely ceremonial, much in contrast to the Office of President of the United States).

Second, elections can be seen as influencing whether policies are initiated, continued or terminated. Often a change of personnel goes along with a change of policy, but sometimes an election can result in a change of policy even though the personnel are unchanged. The reverse is also possible. Elections involving parties or candidates that offer identical policies do not provide opportunities for meaningful policy choices. To some extent the meaningfulness of the choices (and the responsiveness of the government to the election outcome) depends on features of the electoral system and the way votes are translated into policy, as we shall see. These ways of typifying possible election outcomes are strongly associated with different ways of answering the question whether elections can be considered meaningful – a central concern of this chapter. These two ways of looking at elections are interconnected. If we throw the rascals out this is often so as to punish them for bad policy-making. Similarly, we generally put a new government into office hoping that it will correct errors of past governments and/or introduce better policies.

Third, the results of elections can also be considered in terms of the functioning of the political system. This perspective focuses less on specific outcomes (personnel and policy) and more on the process that generates these outcomes. By ensuring government responsiveness, or failing to do so, elections can help bolster support for democracy, or undermine it. We start by considering what it takes to have a government replaced.

Consequences of electoral shifts

How much do parties have to gain or lose in an election in order for this to change the political complexion of the government? Obviously, electoral landslides in which the incumbents are swept away will result in government change; the much rarer case where incumbents totally crush opposition parties will generally see no change in government. But landslides are comparatively rare, and the more interesting question is how moderate changes in parties' electoral successes affect government composition. What sort of shifts in party support are we talking about?

Powell (2000: 49) presents a chart showing how much vote loss or gain by incumbents results in government change, comparing majoritarian systems with proportional ones. Figure 5.1 is a stylized simplification of his findings, where the vertical axis gives the percentage of governments that change – which we can also interpret as the probability of a change of government – and the horizontal axis shows the change in electoral support for the party or parties that make up the government. The solid line in the chart represents election outcomes in majoritarian countries and the dashed line represents

Figure 5.1 *Impact of vote shift for incumbent parties on likelihood of government change, proportional and majoritarian systems*

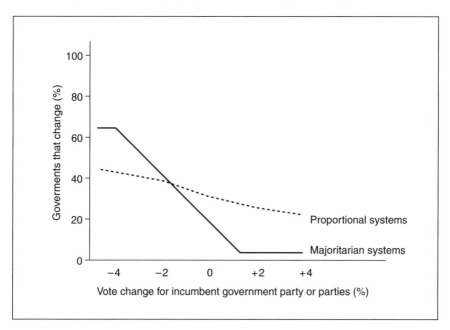

Note: Value of vote change should not be used to estimate effects beyond the range of vote change indicated, –4 to +4 per cent.
Source: Adapted from Powell (2000: Fig. 3.1).

outcomes in proportional countries. With majoritarian designs, we see that a loss of more than 3 per cent will cause a change of government more than 60 per cent of the time, though greater shifts do not increase that probability. Less than a 3 per cent loss of votes and the government is unlikely to change – very unlikely if it loses less than 1 per cent. Evidently this is because, with first past the post (FPTP) elections, small changes in support need not threaten a government's majority. At the other end of the horizontal scale we see that a government that gains votes in a majoritarian system is virtually never changed.

For proportional systems, the story is rather different. In these systems an incumbent government that maintains or even increases its share of the vote still has no less than a 20 per cent chance of being changed following the election. However, the chances of a change in the (party composition of the) government increases in line with government vote losses. The shift in the proportion of governments changed turns out to be pretty much proportional to the shift in votes, though even the largest vote shifts are associated with government change no more than 40 per cent of the time. In proportional systems, overall electoral losses by incumbents appear to be a less necessary condition for government change than they are in majoritarian systems. Evidently it is quite possible for individual parties that are members of a governing coalition to suffer loss of support even while other coalition members gain. This might lead the governing coalition to change in minor ways in response to a change in electoral support for the parties in the coalition; perhaps swapping or eliminating one partner while other partners remain the same. Indeed, the fact that there is considerable change in the composition of governments, even when there is no overall loss of votes for the incumbent coalition taken as a whole, suggests that governing parties quite frequently respond to electoral shifts, which may help to keep coalition governments well attuned to the preferences of the legislature as these reflect changes in the preferences of the voters – and in any case may give voters the impression that the election was consequential.

The tendency to consider gains or losses in a coalition government's vote share as indicative of the voters' evaluation of the coalition as a whole is particularly popular among Anglo-Saxon political scientists, who are accustomed to think in terms of single-party governments and who impose the same perspective on coalition governments. But the electoral fortunes of partners in a coalition rarely change in lockstep (van der Brug *et al.* 2007a; Urquizu-Sancho 2008). On the contrary, it is much more common for some coalition parties to lose votes while others from the same coalition gain. Even if a coalition as a whole gains votes, if one or several of the constituent parties register losses a change in coalition composition is not only likely but may very well indicate responsiveness. Viewing a coalition government in the same fashion as a single-party government is often misleading. Still, it is evident that more than half the time coalition governments are unaffected by vote shifts no matter how great those shifts may be. Shifts of overall support as great as 4 per cent, which would bring about a change of single-party government about two-thirds of the time, affect the composition of coalition governments less than half the time.

Even in majoritarian systems we have seen that the ability of voters to penalize a government is very hit-and-miss. Enough of a shift in votes will send a government packing, but a smaller swing has no effect whatsoever. In the US there is an additional factor that makes it hard to dismiss either a president or individual members of Congress – something called the 'incumbency advantage', to which we now turn.

Incumbency and term limits

In the US, incumbent politicians are generally thought to have an enormous advantage not shared by those in parliamentary regimes. A large part of the difference surely comes from the advantage that incumbents have in terms of name and face recognition. Two differences between parliamentary and presidential systems are relevant here. When it comes to the highest office, a sitting president has an enormous advantage not shared by a sitting prime minister, because other presidential contenders will not have had the same opportunities to become known as do party leaders in parliamentary systems.

When it comes to seats in the legislature a different contrast is important. In the US each candidate, even when only running for a legislative seat, has to fight a separate election campaign that cannot simply be piggybacked on the national campaign for her or his party. This fact puts a premium on name and face recognition even among candidates for the US Congress. For an aspiring Member of Parliament in other countries, by contrast, elections provide few benefits to those with face or name recognition because campaigns are much more party centered (see pp. 2–3).

This is even true in those parliamentary systems where elections are ostensibly for candidates rather than for party lists (in single transferable vote (STV) systems such as Ireland and FPTP systems such as the UK). In any parliamentary system, party discipline can only be maintained if the ultimate sanction for breaking ranks is failure to gain re-election, so parties in such systems make sure that they maintain effective control of the nominating process. Incumbents in parliamentary FPTP and STV systems may benefit electorally from doing services for their constituents and even through local name recognition in the district that they represent but to nothing like the extent found in the US.

Constituency (or district) service is a phenomenon that exists only in FPTP and STV systems (also to some extent in mixed systems), where districts are represented by MPs who thus stand to benefit from indebting their constituents to them by helping them individually (assistance in dealing with grievances) or collectively (promoting policies that are specifically beneficial to the district or constituency in question). In PR systems no such logic exists, hence the absence of constituency service there. The consequence is that the actual daily activities of representatives in these systems differ considerably, as do the expectations of citizens about what a good representative should do. In Scandinavian political systems the need to have someone to provide services for voters and respond to their grievances has led to the creation of a so-called 'ombudsman' (who may have a large staff). This idea has been widely copied and it is hard to find a contemporary democracy that has not adopted this method of addressing citizen complaints. In the US there is a Citizenship and Immigration Services Ombudsman to address problems for a class of residents who have no congressman because they are not citizens.

The incumbent's advantage in the US plays out differently at different levels of elective office. When we think of contests for the American presidency, the advantages are probably less than they are for individual members of the House of Representatives. Sitting presidents are sometimes defeated. Still, the advantage they are deemed to gain from incumbency is sufficient to have given rise to a constitutional amendment in 1944, limiting the number of terms a president can serve to two. The existence of term limitations at the presidential level in turn gives rise to the concept of a 'lame duck' president: a president precluded by law from running for re-election. Such a president partakes of the disadvantages that are felt by any leader who has announced her or his impending resignation. A lame duck president will not be around to protect or reward loyal followers, and such a leader finds it significantly more difficult to achieve policy or other objectives. The big difference here is that lame duck presidents cannot keep the public guessing as to when they will step down. In parliamentary systems, party leaders can often maintain their power until very close to the time they step down, simply by keeping quiet about plans for resignation. This probably enhances their effectiveness, though there is little actual evidence of this.

Members of the House of Representatives have the additional benefit of a 'locality rule' which in most parts of the country (not New York City or the Philadelphia suburbs) limits contestants in a congressional race to those who live in the district that they are contesting. The consequence is that an incumbent House member will rarely in the ordinary run of things be faced with an equally experienced challenger. Only after a change in district boundaries is there any chance of an incumbent having to run for election against a challenger who has gained prominence from past election campaigning. Ordinarily the incumbency advantage (enhanced by the willingness of state legislatures to redraw district boundaries so as to protect the re-election chances of the incumbent party) is such as to make incumbent members of the House of Representatives virtually unassailable,[1] and in most House elections only about 5 per cent of the contests in individual districts could be described as competitive – usually because the incumbent has retired, died or become embroiled in some kind of scandal. The incumbency effect is responsible in large part for the lack of competitiveness of US house elections (Fiorina 1977).

The lack of credible and well-known challengers that creates the incumbency problem in US presidential elections is largely absent elsewhere. In parliamentary systems the individual (or individuals) who might have hoped to become prime minister if their parties had been more successful are not without resources. Most of them are still members of their national parliament with positions of responsibility as party leaders – and they may even be sharing government power as member of a coalition. They have faces, characters and concerns that are familiar to voters because of the efforts they made at previous elections. In some countries, one of these individuals even has an official (paid) position as 'Leader of the Opposition' from which she or he is well able to counter official government pronouncements and build support for himself or herself in anticipation of the next election.

Accountability

Elections are important in a democracy to the extent that they permit voters some control over the direction of public policy. For such control to be meaningful, voters must have some awareness of the policies pursued by governments and proposed by opposition parties, and must be able to judge their consequences. For this it is generally thought that we need an educated and politically interested electorate. Or do we? We will see that the electorates of established democracies, however well educated they may be in other respects, know remarkably little about politics and about the government policies they are supposed to be overseeing at election time. This provides us with a puzzle that is the subject of the next chapter: how does an apparently uninformed and uninterested electorate do what appears to be quite a good job in directing the course of public policy?

Even leaving the skill and knowledge of the electorate aside, there are very real questions as to whether individual preferences can be aggregated into a collective decision of the sort that an election is supposed to give rise to. For example, Arrow's (1951) theorem stated that it may not always be possible to derive a unique ranking of social objectives by aggregating individual preferences for those objectives. In other words, there can be many different sets of outcomes that come equally close to (or remain equally far from) satisfying the preferences of all of the members of a group (a group of party supporters, for instance, or even a whole society). In turn this means that someone must be given the role of choosing between equally desirable (or undesirable) ends. One function of elections in practice is thus to decide who that person (or persons) shall be. As another example, in a multiparty system there is the very real possibility of an election giving rise to an outcome in which a government takes office, proposing a set of policies none of which are the preferred policies of a majority of the electorate. This is called a 'coalition of minority stands' and it was considered a theoretical anomaly until such a coalition actually took office in Israel in the 1990s. In some ways the disparate groups of Republicans who elected George Bush in 2000 and 2004 in the US, though not formal political parties, can be regarded as constituting a coalition of minority stands since the groups that supported him were prepared to tolerate policies wanted by other groups, provided those groups reciprocated. This is a common feature of party politics, more so the smaller the number of parties in a system. Thus, not many of the American religious right will have explicitly favored tax cuts for the wealthy, but they were willing to tolerate such in order to have a president whom they saw as sharing their moral views. Of those benefiting from the tax cuts, on the other hand, many were not enamoured of Bush's stand on abortion or gay rights, but they were prepared to put up with policies pleasing to the religious right in return for those tax cuts and the various benefits for American business. Since about half the electorate voted against George Bush, if those who voted for him included significant numbers of individuals who actually opposed particular policies, it is likely that those particular policies were actually opposed by a majority of the American electorate.

Electoral coalitions of minority stands are not unusual in American politics. The Democrats used to build their majorities on such a coalition, linking right-wing Southerners and liberal Northerners. That coalition lasted from shortly after the American Civil War in 1865 until the Voting Rights Act removed the basis for the implicit deal that had kept the two wings of the party together for a hundred years: a deal in which Southern Democrats were given a free hand with race relations in the South in return for supporting liberal policies in the North. Similar coalition processes have been documented in Europe during the period between the world wars (Luebbert 1991).

The frequently contradictory strands contained within each of the American political parties is often considered an inevitable price that has to be paid for a two-party system, but the fact that other countries have the same (or effectively the same) systems without the same lack of coherence suggests that there is some other reason for this feature of American parties. We have already mentioned that the locality rule and, above all, the fact that a presidential system does not require disciplined parties, are more persuasive explanations. But the overriding lesson is that election outcomes are enormously colored by the nature of the party and electoral systems within which they are conducted. These different sorts of outcomes have nothing to do with differences between voters. They are entirely the result of differences between countries in the contexts within which elections are held.

Luckily, elections are not the only route by which voters can make their opinions known, and we have already mentioned the fact that politicians look to opinion polls for guidance as to the state of public opinion. The guidance given by public opinion can be regarded as taking effect by way of two different routes: an electoral route and what might be termed a 'rational anticipation route', as illustrated in Figure 5.2. This route comes into play when governments react to shifts in public opinion by adopting new policies in an attempt to avoid the electoral outcome that they anticipate might otherwise occur. In the next chapter we will focus more closely on this topic (see pp. 172).

Fairness in election outcomes

Both majoritarian and proportional parliamentary regimes can suffer from a lack of reliable connection between votes and outcomes. If we start with majoritarian parliamentary systems, it is clear that the extent to which policy outcomes in such systems are responsive to changes in voter choices is highly dependent on circumstance, especially the margin of victory of the winning party in terms of votes, compared to the previous election, and the extent to which the vote margin is magnified when translated into a seat margin. A party may control enough parliamentary seats to support a government even

Figure 5.2   *The electoral route and the rational anticipation route to policy change*

though it receives far from a majority of the votes, and there would be no change in this situation if it received additional electoral support to the point of gaining a majority of the votes. Much more importantly, a swing against the government may have no effect at all if the swing in votes is not large enough to cost the party its parliamentary majority in terms of seats. Majoritarian systems can fail to respond to changes in electoral support precisely because of the magnification that occurs when votes are translated into seats, and because of the all or nothingness of the result. This lack of responsiveness can be very frustrating to voters if they swing against the government in one election and then swing still further in the next two elections – and still nothing happens when the same government continues to be re-elected despite this progressive reduction in its electoral support.

The putative strength of the majoritarian vision is a strong direct connection between voters' choices, the distribution of legislative seats and the composition of governments. Its main weakness is its tendency to distort the legislative representation of voters' choices (the connection between votes and seats). So the majoritarian vision is thought to provide a strong electoral connection at the cost of distorted representation. On the other hand the putative strength of the proportional vision is the fair reflection of voter choices in the legislature. Its weakness is the dependence of policy-making on coalition formation and hence on elite bargaining among the representatives of different parties. In order for an election outcome to give rise to policy change in response to changes in voters' choices, proportional systems depend on something that happens behind closed doors that may take two or three months to conclude. There is nothing definitive about this outcome, and a different outcome (in terms of a different coalition becoming the government) will give the voters a different set of policies as a result of the *same* election. So, for the electorate, there is no tight link between the votes they cast and the policies they get. Moreover, voters for a particular party may find their party represented in government (or not) almost irrespective of whether it gained or lost votes, emphasizing the vagaries of the coalition formation process that were described in Chapter 3.

However, because any coalition government is likely to contain the median legislator, this uncertainty is not often going to result in really dissatisfied voters. And in the long run, the majority of voters in proportional systems appear to get about what they voted for, at least in terms of the ideological complexion of the governments they get. With majoritarian outcomes, on the other hand, the extent of the change from election to election can be much greater, and there is no guarantee that things will cancel out even over quite long periods of time. The distortion resulting from the majoritarian translation of votes into seats can remain the same at election after election, engendering considerable dissatisfaction on the part of voters (often a majority of voters) subjected to a government very different from the one they would have chosen had their preferences not been underrepresented. The bias in majoritarian systems is one that systematically advantages large parties, and voters who support smaller parties are systematically disadvantaged. Even supporters of the second largest party are disadvantaged, and this could last for a considerable number of elections before things change. Indeed, there is no guarantee that a given disadvantage will ever change (see Box 4.1). A majoritarian system that gives no representation to a minority at election after election can cause that system to come under such stress that the aggrieved minority ceases to abide by the democratic process. Unfortunately, majoritarian systems not only exaggerate the winner's margin in terms of seats, they also tend to engender a 'winner takes all' mentality that sanctions the use of majority power even to the detriment of minority interests.

Trade-offs between proportional and majoritarian systems

The fact that there is a trade-off between proportional and majoritarian systems should by now be clear. In countries where the parties are represented in the Parliament in close proportion to the votes cast, we do not often find one party winning a majority of the seats (a majoritarian outcome). But as we have pointed out different countries have electoral systems that yield more or less proportionality depending on how much weight they give to other features that constitution writers value (or on unintended consequences that constitution writers had not considered).

Powell (2000: ch. 6) points out that to the extent that countries with proportional representation (PR) elections depart from delivering seats in exact proportion to votes, they depart in the direction of overrepresenting the party that receives most votes – in other words they depart in a direction that makes such countries more majoritarian. Indeed, there are countries with PR elections, such as Spain, that regularly find the largest party receiving so many additional seats in the Parliament, over and above what that party should have received on a perfectly proportional basis, that it is able to form a single-party government. Even where the departure from proportionality is not enough to deliver control of the legislature into the largest party's hands, such deviations from the proportional ideal always strengthen the hand of the largest party in any needed coalition bargaining, which can be regarded as consistent with the majoritarian ideal. So, to the extent that countries in the proportional vision camp fail to live up to proportional vision ideals, they deviate in the direction of ideals espoused by proponents of the majoritarian vision.

On the other hand, to the extent that countries with FPTP elections depart from the majoritarian ideal, they usually do so in the direction of inadequately boosting the seat share of the largest vote-winning party, failing to give it enough seats to form a single-party majority government. Such failures to achieve majoritarian ideals can be seen, according to Powell, to be deviations in the direction of the ideals espoused by proponents of the proportional vision. When this happens, a minority government almost invariably forms – a government that exists on the sufferance of other parties in the legislature. This tempers the policies that the minority government party might have introduced had it won a majority of the seats and it forces that government to be sensitive to the policy preferences of other parties in the legislature – a feature of proportional-vision governments.

These two kinds of departure from ideal-type election outcomes can be seen as mitigated failures: proponents of both majoritarian and proportional ideals can be found in all countries and, to the extent that proponents of one ideal are disappointed by an election outcome, proponents of the other ideal who live in the same country may be correspondingly pleased. Indeed, many of the mitigated failures among countries with PR electoral systems of one kind or another are probably failures that result from deliberate constitutional design. Constitution writers may well have wanted a system that would boost the seat share of the largest vote winner, precisely in order to improve accountability or some other majoritarian feature of their electoral process.

But Powell also points out that there can be a third kind of departure from ideal-type outcomes – a departure that occurs only in countries with FPTP, where the electoral system malfunctions and delivers majority control of the legislature into the hands of a party that was not the largest vote winner. Several examples of such cases have already been mentioned: two each in the United Kingdom and New Zealand, so the existence of such failures is not a surprise. The big surprise is how many of them there are. Out of 46 majoritarian outcomes illustrated by Powell (2000: 148) six are failures of this type, which amounts to 13 per cent. Whatever the benefits that majoritarian systems are supposed to yield, it is clear that on such occasions they do not live up to their own standards. On these occasions millions of people repeatedly failed to get the governments they voted for. Proponents of both the majoritarian and the proportional visions would regard them as failures – unmitigated failures – which are not fair from either perspective.

Failures among proportional systems are relatively small, according to Powell's data. The largest party in such systems never gets more than some 25 per cent more seats than its proportional due, half the disparity seen in the most majoritarian systems. Proportional electoral systems thus yield results that, if they are less proportional, are more majoritarian (often much more). Most majoritarian deviations are also quite benign, since the greater part of such deviations produce minority governments. However, the small number of deviations of the other type are far from both ideals – neither proportional nor majoritarian.

Ironically, the unmitigated failures of majoritarian systems are so dramatic precisely because of their inherent biasing effect. These systems boost the number of seats won by one of the parties and, in the case of these failures, that advantage accrues to the 'wrong' party. From one point of view these failures of the majoritarian design are not very important. These are election outcomes that were accepted as legitimate in the countries concerned. The people voted, they reached a verdict, the verdict gave rise to a government. There was no civil war. No one was killed. In that sense the outcome was a success. And the most blatant case of unacceptable outcomes leading to a virtual civil war was in Northern Ireland where the majoritarian system did not fail (see Box 4.1).

Nevertheless, with these facts in mind, it is not unreasonable for constitution writers to try to design a system with features of both types: a proportional system that makes it possible to hold its governments to account. And Powell's data shows that most proportional systems do boost the size of the largest party by 10 per cent or more, making it easier for its voters to do just that.

Bias in election outcomes

Even when an election is free and fair it is hard to be sure that its outcome is not biased. Bias could arise from many factors: the difficulty that some types of citizens find in getting to the polls, the lack of information that some citizens might have about politics, the advantage that might accrue to some citizens by virtue of strategic skills, and much else besides. One source of bias often mentioned is the advantages that accrue to wealthy individuals or well-heeled corporations and other businesses. Some political systems go to great lengths to control the power of money in elections, trying to ensure that all contestants have an equal chance of demonstrating the extent of their numerical support. In most established democracies, governments provide free air time on government-controlled television channels (or, as a condition of their licence, on private TV channels) for political parties to put their case before the voters (in Britain these are called 'party political broadcasts'). In many countries governments subsidize the electioneering expenses of legitimate political parties. And most countries drastically limit the expenditures of candidates and political parties. But countries do vary in the lengths they go to in trying to reduce bias caused by unequal expenditures by different parties and their supporters. The US is particularly liberal in allowing private money to play a large part in financing elections, often to the benefit of one candidate or another (if not always the same political party). There the freedom to spend one's money fighting an election campaign is considered to be part of the constitutionally protected freedom of speech, and efforts to achieve campaign finance reform are perennial and regularly fail to achieve their objectives.

The importance of money in elections is intimately linked to the type of party system a country has. With policy-oriented parties, elections need not be very expensive and it is not hard to limit campaign expenditures. With candidate-centered elections, expenditures are much harder to limit. This is rather like the problem regarding disciplined parties (to which it is intimately linked). A parliamentary system requires disciplined parties, for reasons explained in Chapter 3 and, because such parties are needed, party leaders find ways to achieve party discipline. A candidate-centered party system, in somewhat the same way, needs money in order for each candidate to be able to put her or his message before the voters. Candidate-centered elections are inherently expensive and, because candidates need money to stand a chance of being elected, they find ways to obtain it. Those who would reform the American system to reduce the role of money there would do well to think of ways of changing what the current system requires candidates to do in order to compete effectively, rather than vainly trying to stem a tide that is generated by the logic of the system as it currently exists. In Chapter 8 we will suggest one way in which the logic of the system (and hence the motivations of candidates) could be changed.

Still, the major requirement for a successful democracy in regard to these matters is that the overwhelming majority of citizens accept an electoral outcome as legitimate, whatever biases it might contain. This is indeed the case in the countries studied in this book.

Turnout and bias

One aspect of elections that is often thought particularly liable to be an indicator of at least potential bias is the level of voter turnout. In Chapter 1 we mentioned that the biases introduced by an FPTP electoral system can be exacerbated by low turnout. Turnout has been found to be lower in FPTP systems than in PR systems. Certain other institutional and quasi-institutional factors also have strong effects on turnout, as we shall see. This could have important implications for the outcomes of elections if those who failed to vote were not a random sample of the electorate. If certain groups or types of people are particularly prone to low turnout and if those groups or types of individuals have distinctive policy interests, then those policy interests will be less well represented. Considerable controversy surrounds this question and attempts to estimate the consequences of low turnout have generally found few effects in practice, but the analyses have usually been done using sample surveys that themselves fail to include many of the people who did not vote.[2]

This research has mainly looked at how those who did not vote would have evaluated the choices on offer in particular elections. It has not looked at the question of whether different choices would have been offered in an election where more people voted. American parties position themselves to maximize support from those who are expected to vote. For example, it is unusual in that country even to send campaign literature through the mail to people who are not registered to vote – and, in a country where registration is voluntary, most people who do not vote are not registered (Erikson 1981). So the American political system probably would offer quite different policy choices to voters if turnout were higher, as long ago argued by Schattschneider (1960). In other countries there has been little definitive evidence that political choices would be systematically different if turnout were higher (Bernhagen and Marsh 2007; van der Eijk and van Egmond 2007), but some analyses of policy outputs in countries (and parts of countries) with different levels of turnout suggest that higher turnout is associated with more redistributive and more welfare-oriented policies (for a survey, see Marsh and Lutz 2007). But these cross-sectional findings might not be replicated in time-series analyses (in Chapter 6 we present examples of each of these). So the jury is still out on the question of the political effects of low turnout. Still, there is little question that the especially low turnout found in the US does have effects on the quality of representation (Griffin and Newman 2005). Be this as it may, even if it makes no difference – and van der Eijk and van Egmond (2007) show that turnout *can* make a difference even if not very often – it still matters whether certain groups of voters do not in fact make their voices heard. To argue that outcomes would have been no different had poor people voted, does not settle the question of why they do not vote, nor does it make the question moot.

It also matters if low turnout is the result of politicians securing themselves against the slings and arrows of outraged voters, either by making it hard for challengers to win against an incumbent (as in the US) or by making it hard or impossible to change the governing coalition (as in Switzerland, see Chapter 7). In these two countries low voter turnout serves as a signal that elections have become pointless for many voters because the link between voting and policy change has been cut (cf. Franklin 1999). This provides good reason to worry about low turnout in these particular countries, even if the policy consequences are uncertain.

Protest voting

So far we have been talking about ways in which elections can be seen to be immediately consequential in terms of changing the personnel occupying elected positions, leading to changes in existing policies or to new policies being introduced. But there are also other consequences of election results that are worth considering.

For one thing, party leaders may look at the success or failure of other parties as clues as to what they themselves should be doing. The success of the Republikaner (a right-wing xenophobic party) in the European Parliament elections in Germany in 1989 led established parties to think they should be doing something about immigration (see Box 5.1). A similar success for Le Pen in France led established parties to consider educating the public against listening to him. The comet-like rise of Pim Fortuyn in Dutch politics and the dramatic electoral success of his party after his murder in 2002 forced all Dutch parties to rethink their diagnosis of Dutch society and their ideas about the problems that have to be solved there. Voters know that party leaders pay attention when they defect to other parties and this is the basis of 'protest voting'.

Protest votes are votes that are cast in order to carry a message other than the ostensible message of support for the party voted for. Protest voting is often thought to be the basis of support for parties that cannot possibly win, especially in majoritarian elections. Why would anyone have voted for Ross Perot in the American presidential election of 1992? He could not possibly win and, indeed, we know that about a third of those who voted for Perot did so exactly because they understood quite well that he could not win. Clearly those voters were not voting for Perot in the ordinary way. We can only understand their votes as protest votes: votes intended to carry a message to the major parties. In this case Perot's main differentiating policies were his concern over the US budget deficit and the North American Free Trade Agreement (NAFTA). Of course, many of those voting for him would genuinely have liked him to win and those votes cannot be interpreted as protests. But many were more concerned to make a point: that the budget deficit and the possible ill effects of NAFTA were important problems and that a major party that took these problems seriously would be more likely to get their votes.

The Perot case is one where protest voters agreed with the candidate they voted for on at least some issues. But such votes can be more extreme than this, being cast even for candidates or parties that voters do not like in any way, if such votes are felt to be the only way to gain the attention of major parties. (It should be mentioned in passing, however, that protest votes can backfire by giving a party plausibility and making it more attractive to genuine supporters who might not have voted for it had it remained small.)

That is what a protest vote is thought to be: a message to the party or parties that a voter would normally support that they are ignoring some matter of importance to that voter. Votes for green parties in majoritarian

Box 5.1   The 1989 Republikaner success in Germany

At the time of the European Parliament elections in 1989, the right-wing Republikaner party won an unexpected number of votes. This caused the leaders of the major parties to wonder what they were doing wrong. The established parties, and the ruling CDU party in particular, thought that if they did not change their policies and provide some of the policies the Republikaner were promising, the Republikaner would get even more votes at national elections due the following year. The Republikaner's most distinctive policies related to immigration (from Eastern Europe and elsewhere) and the established parties took it that their own policies were upsetting the voters. So the CDU, the government party of the time, adapted their policies by restricting immigration from those still-communist countries – a policy shift that would have created much unhappiness had it not been rendered moot by the fall of the Berlin Wall a few months later.

systems are often seen as protest votes: signals that the major parties are ignoring ecological issues. In proportional systems such votes seem more likely to be genuine, however, as in such systems limited vote shares can still lead to parliamentary representation and coalition participation. Votes for extreme parties – especially extreme right-wing parties – are often seen as protest votes, even in proportional systems. They are often motivated by topics that major parties resist putting on the national agenda, such as immigration or race. In such cases the identification of these votes as 'only' protest votes may be little more than an excuse by mainstream politicians to continue to ignore the issues concerned and to try by other means to limit the electoral success of parties that promote those issues – for instance by refusing to collaborate with them in any way, thus reducing their coalition potential and their attractiveness to voters as potential governing parties (van Spanje 2009).

To party leaders, protest voting may or may not be identifiable as such. Elections are such blunt instruments of communication that it is possible for the messages sent by voters to be completely misunderstood by party leaders who might not have the faintest idea which policies are responsible for the protest votes. In the Republikaner example, party leaders might have thought their support was genuine, just as the reverse is also possible: that leaders could interpret sincere votes for a party – particularly a new party – as protest votes. The only people who are going to know are the political scientists who go out with a carefully crafted questionnaire and figure out to what extent the votes going to a particular party are, or are not, to be seen as protest votes. But we can only find this out with specially constructed survey studies, the results of which generally become known only long after the election is over.

In the case of the Republikaner Party in 1989 in Germany it eventually turned out that votes cast for them at the European Parliament elections of 1989 were not really about immigration at all. Their voters were actually upset about something else entirely (Schmitt 1996). But by the time German political scientists had analysed their data and published their first results, which was about a month and a half later, the CDU – the mainstream conservative party that was mainly hurt by Republikaner votes – had already changed its policies regarding immigration. Mutual incomprehension can go to extremes when unhappy voters are trying to express something that cannot be expressed through the regular operations of an electoral contest. Interpreting what it is that (groups of) voters meant to convey with their votes is impossible on the basis of the vote-tally itself. Yet, such moments provide irresistible opportunities for politicians to try and stamp their favorite interpretation of the election outcome on the public debate.

This is one of the great tragedies of representative democracy. Elections are amongst the main instruments by which our leaders are guided, but they are such blunt instruments that our leaders often end up being misguided. Survey research need not be so blunt because the questions can be more carefully crafted and there can be more of them. So voters are generally able to say something a bit more nuanced when carefully questioned for a survey than what they can communicate when they are simply given a choice of parties to vote for in an election. We will see in the next chapter that politicians generally do pay attention to what voters say when surveyed and that they do so because they are trying to anticipate what will happen at the next election. Elections encourage politicians to pay attention to survey findings, when available. However, it should not be forgotten that politicians are also prone to ignoring such information in the hopes that in the long run the virtues of their policies will become apparent and the voters will change their minds. Such wilful behavior carries great risks of ultimate punishment at the hands of the electorate.

We get a much better understanding of these sorts of indirect consequences from looking at elections that have no direct consequences for the allocation of executive power. Elections to the European Parliament, for example, do not involve government formation. Neither a voter's own national government nor the government of the European Union is going to be made or unmade by European Parliament elections. Yet these elections involve the same parties with roughly the same programs and policies as national elections do. That is why political scientists often call them 'second-order national elections' (see also p. 22). By investigating voting behavior at such elections we learn a lot about the role that government formation plays in the minds of voters in elections where such concerns are relevant. Indeed it is because party leaders suppose that voters are behaving in European Parliament elections as though in national elections, while voters know perfectly well that they are not faced with a national election, that party leaders are likely to misinterpret the outcome.

In some ways European Parliament elections are rather like US mid-term congressional elections. Elections for the US Congress occur every two years, whereas elections for the President occur only every four years. This means that every second congressional election occurs between presidential elections, at the middle of the presidential term of office (hence their designation as 'mid-term' congressional elections) at a time when executive power is not at stake. The importance of mid-term elections is often misunderstood both by politicians and by voters who think that, because executive power is not at stake, these are not 'real' elections; yet such elections are capable of producing a surprise result, as happened in the 1994 US mid-term election. That election was thought to be irrelevant by disgruntled Democrats. They thought it did not matter what they did in that election because it was 'just' a mid-term one. Consequently, because so many Democrats were disappointed with Clinton, a lot of them stayed at home. The result was to give control of the House of Representatives to the Republicans several elections earlier than would otherwise have happened. This was certainly not what the abstainers had anticipated.

Indeed, all elections presumably contain some mix of first-order and second-order elements. In some first-order elections the allocation of executive power plays an important role because the election is too close to call or because it is impossible to predict which of several potential coalitions will get most, or at least sufficient, support. In other first-order elections executive power plays a lesser role because some party is far ahead in the polls and almost certain to form the next government (this is particularly so in majoritarian systems). In such elections there is room for protest voting among those who suppose the outcome to be a foregone conclusion or do not care what the outcome is (e.g. the Perot vote in the 1992 US presidential election).

The study of European Parliament elections has given rise to a typology of voter motivations which have been called 'voting with the heart', 'voting with the head' and 'voting with the boot' (Reif and Schmitt 1980; Oppenhuis *et al.* 1996). 'Voting with the heart' is what unreflective commentators assume voters do: vote for the party whose policies or personnel they like best, not paying attention to questions of government formation or other consequences of election outcomes. In terms of Figure 4.3, these are votes cast on the basis of sincere preferences for parties, taking account of ideology, issues, candidates, and so on. 'Voting with the head' is what many voters actually do much of the time in national elections where executive power is at stake. They take strategic considerations into account in addition to their (sincere) preferences. Because government formation is at stake many prefer large parties and eschew small and extremist parties. 'Voting with the boot' is what voters do if they are really dissatisfied with the options presented to them and judge that the outcome of the election does not matter to them, either because it is a second-order election or because the main parties are indistinguishable to them, or because the outcome seems to be a foregone conclusion.

We have just mentioned the US mid-term election of 1994. This was a case of voters staying home to send an angry message at a time when they thought it would have no policy consequences. This example shows that voters can sometimes be wrong about the actual consequences of voting with the boot, and may regret their protest afterwards. Analogously, voters may afterwards regret having voted with the heart and having ignored strategic considerations, as in the case of many who voted for Ralph Nader (a minor party candidate) in the US Election of 2000, votes which made possible the narrow Bush victory of that year. This example emphasizes the point already made in regard to Perot voters, that it is often hard to distinguish sincere voters, who support a party despite its strategic weakness (who would be happy if, despite everything, that party were to win the election), from insincere voters who support a party because of its strategic weakness (those who would be quite rueful if that party were to win).

The structuring effects of strategic considerations

Linking this story of second-order elections with our earlier story of what happened in Israel when voters were freed from the need to take strategic considerations into account (see pp. 108–9) can help us understand a phenomenon that Americans refer to as 'mid-term loss' and what in other countries is seen as 'second-order effects'. The fact that government office is at stake in the first-order arena is seen to concentrate voters' minds and force them to take account of the realities of government, as opposed to simply voting with the heart for the party they (sincerely, see Figure 4.3) like the most. This syndrome of influences is generally referred to as 'second-order election theory', which has been quite well confirmed in empirical work, especially regarding elections to the European Parliament (van der Eijk and Franklin 1996).

The same mechanism appears to exist also in a presidential regime such as the US, giving rise to more structure, even to congressional elections held concurrently with presidential elections. Again the habits and routines of the presidential level serve to structure the congressional vote that many people do not focus on separately. To some extent this structuring can be regarded as what Donald Stokes (1966) called the 'nationalization of electoral forces'. A single contest conducted over the entire country, which a presidential election must be, focuses voters' minds on the agenda of national politics. A mid-term election in the US is missing this focus; and, even though presidents may attempt to create such a focus, the dramatic failure of Franklin Roosevelt to inject national issues into the mid-term election of 1934, despite almost superhuman efforts, stands as a marker to the futility of such attempts (Burns 1963).

Without the structuring features of a national campaign, US mid-term elections bear an uncanny resemblance to parliamentary elections in Israel when those elections were divorced from strategic concerns. When voters have no good reason to take national concerns into account, whether those be national issues or more strategic matters, their behavior becomes less structured. Repeated failure to assert such concerns leads voters to focus increasingly on local or idiosyncratic matters that, in aggregate, lead to behavior patterns that can appear increasingly random.

There is entropy in politics as in nature and things move from order to disorder unless some countervailing force is at work. In nature a major countervailing force comes from life processes building order out of disorder. In politics a major countervailing force comes from national policy concerns, which also build order out of disorder. To the extent that those concerns are absent, the mainsprings of a national political system wind down. In parliamentary regimes, second-order elections occur at different time-points between national elections and we can see the strategically imposed order of the national arena winding down with the passage of time, only to be reimposed with the occurrence of the next first-order election (Franklin and Weber 2009). Mid-term election results in the US appear, like second-order election results in parliamentary regimes, to be elections that take one step towards disorganized behavior, but the fact that there is never more than one mid-term election between presidential elections means that the process cannot go very far. The regular occurrence of presidential elections reinjects national concerns into American politics and provides structure to a system that would otherwise very soon degenerate into separate state or even district systems.

This perspective is quite the reverse of what in the American political science literature is called the 'normal vote'. American political scientists have tended to view mid-term elections as 'normal', with presidential elections injecting an abnormal pull (in terms of candidate or issue effects), creating results that can be out of tune with the 'normal' (i.e. uncontaminated) balance of partisan forces (A. Campbell 1966; J. Campbell 1985). But the semblance of a normal vote at mid-term elections is only created by the fact that such an election is surrounded by structuring national elections (cf. Cox and Kernell 1991: 242). The idiosyncratic character of issue-effects and candidate evaluations in numerous mid-term races results in their nation-wide effect cancelling out, leaving party identification as the major 'normal' structuring factor. If there were not another presidential election two years later, the next congressional elections would be seen to take another step towards random behavior and soon there would be no structure at all (let alone a 'normal' one) at mid-term elections.

In the US, structure is injected by national contests, just as it is in other countries, though the structuring effects of presidential elections is arguably less in the US than that of national elections in parliamentary regimes because the accompanying congressional election in the US is not the source of structure. People *can* vote for a different party in the congressional election without vitiating their choice for President (just as in Israel during the period of direct elections for the Prime Minister). In fact many voters do not vote differently and this injects some structure into the American system, though less than the structure injected in parliamentary regimes. But this fact should remind us that, in Israel, even if direct elections of the Prime Minister had not been abandoned, eventually the move towards disorder would have ended. Some structure would still have been injected into the system by the Prime Ministerial election even if not nearly as much as when voters had to choose a parliament that would then choose the Prime Minister. In all countries the regular occurrence of national elections limits the extent to which entropy can have free rein.

Split-ticket voting, 'balance' and mid-term loss

It has been suggested that a particular strategic consideration might operate in American national elections, where the fact that voters cast separate ballots for President and Congress permits them the opportunity to vote for a different party at different levels, much as Israeli voters were able to do when presented with the opportunity to directly elect their prime minister. So-called 'split-ticket voting' (with voters casting their ballot for a different party in Congress than for President) has been a feature of US elections for many years, but its increasing frequency after the 1960s led some political scientists to theorize that voters might be deliberately trying to achieve 'balance' by having a different party in charge of the Congress than the presidency. It is well known that there are more voters at the center of the political spectrum than at the extremes, and the idea was that these centrist voters might expect policies more to their liking if they forced President and Congress to compromise their policy goals (Fiorina 1977; Alessina and Rosenthal 1995). This theory also promised a solution to a different puzzle in American politics: the puzzle of mid-term loss.

A feature of mid-term elections in the US is that turnout is lower than at congressional elections occurring in conjunction with presidential elections.

Another feature is that the President's party generally loses seats at a mid-term election. This is the process we have described as being due to lack of structure in mid-term elections, but, as Alessina and Rosenthal theorized, this mid-term loss might be due to voters trying to 'balance' the previous election outcome by producing a mid-term victory for the other major party, resulting in what Americans call 'divided government' – a Congress run by one party while the presidency is controlled by the other.

This was a really clever idea, but it has a number of flaws. The first is that, perhaps because American voters have no need to concern themselves with government formation, they are remarkably ignorant about which party is the majority party in congress. At about the time that Alesina and Rosenthal were writing, only 54 per cent of American voters were able to correctly name the party with a majority in the House of Representatives (American National Election Study 1992) – a remarkably low rate considering that 50 per cent would have been expected to get the answer right by chance alone. A second flaw is that mid-term loss for the President's party is a feature of virtually all mid-term elections, even when the 'opposition' party already controls the Congress. Finally, mid-term loss (when seen as a second-order effect) is a feature of all established democracies, as we have seen. But other countries (with the possible exception of France and Germany) have no means of creating balance by electing a different party at mid-term, yet where these elections are held (for instance regional elections or elections to the European Parliament – elections that play no part in determining the direction of government policy) governing parties lose in those countries too, for reasons perfectly well explained by second-order election theory. This calls the balancing hypothesis into question because there is no need for a uniquely American explanation for something that already has a widely accepted explanation.

Divided government in the US can be explained quite easily without recourse to ideas such as balancing. Divided government, in our opinion, is due to the fact that, while control of the presidency switches quite frequently from one party to the other, party control of the Congress seldom does so, due to the fact that sitting Congressmen are almost certain to be re-elected. Most seats in the Congress are safe seats. Indeed congressional elections are remarkably uncompetitive in comparison with legislative elections elsewhere. Since World War II the same party has retained control of the House of Representatives for decades on end, despite the losses observed at mid-term elections. By contrast, presidential elections are very competitive and the presidency seldom stays with the same party for more than eight years (two presidential terms) in a row. If congressional party control tends to remain the same while party control of the presidency changes, then divided government can be expected to occur about half the time (cf. Franklin 1996).

Consequences of party positions

One of the factors that determines the outcome of an election is the relationship between parties' and voters' positions in policy terms. Parties that propose policy positions shared by very few voters will, *ceteris paribus*, not attract many votes, while those whose positions are shared by many voters will generally do well. The electoral consequences of party positions have been elaborated by Downs (1957) who started from an idealized political world, characterized by having only a single policy or ideological dimension or 'spectrum', with only two political parties and most voters being located in the center of this spectrum –technically, this is known as a 'unimodal' (single-peaked) distribution at the center of which is located the so-called 'median voter'. In this world, according to Downs, 'parties formulate policies in order to win elections' (Downs 1957: 28); and so they tend to locate themselves at the center of the issue space, as close as possible to the median voter. Any party whose aim is to be elected will be pressed to take up that location, if only for fear that the other party would claim this middle ground first. This, of course, implies that they can expect voters to choose rationally by casting their votes for the party believed to provide more policy benefits than any other (ibid.: 36).

As we will discuss below, parties do not always conform to this expectation even when Downsean assumptions are met; but on average they can be expected to do so. However, the incentive for parties to move towards the center only exists as such in a two-party system. In multiparty systems, by contrast, counteracting any such incentive is the need for parties to take account of possible losses to less centrist parties that such a move might generate. Consequently, in multiparty systems, each party has to carve out a niche for itself at some point on the ideological dimension and then work to expand that niche through competition with other parties.

But even in systems where only two parties vie for government power, these do not in fact always locate themselves at the center of the policy dimension. In Chapter 6 we will give a British example of a party deliberately positioning itself far from the center, which allowed the other major party to do the same. In the US in 2004 George Bush (the younger) deliberately placed himself well to the right of what had previously been considered the center-ground, in a calculated (and, in the event, successful) attempt to move the electorate rightwards. What is it that allows parties in a two-party system to take up positions away from the political center? A critical component of the answer to this question arises from the behavior of the other party. If one party does not occupy the center-ground, then the other party has a choice. It can move to the center, in which case the first party might have to do the same, or it can take the opportunity to stay away from the center itself, trying to position itself just slightly closer to the center than the other party, but not adopting a stance that would force the other party to abandon whatever objectives might have led it to position itself away from the center in the first place.

One reason that might cause a party not to position itself at or close to the median voter would be that it misperceives where the median voter is located. Another reason would be because it believes that it can persuade voters to follow it in a move to another part of the political spectrum (through power of argument, charisma or other means), as George Bush did in 2004. Yet a third reason would be that parties at different moments in time have to placate different groups of people (cf. Grofman 2004).

Parties, especially in parliamentary systems, are generally formed with rather specific policy objectives. Some of these parties were founded in the days of cleavage politics (see pp. 95–8) in order to defend and promote the interests of a specific social group. Those days are over in most established democracies but, just as voters carry with them traces of the character of the era in which they entered the electorate, so parties bring with them something of the character they had in former times. It is hard for parties to change their traditional political stances because large numbers of voters have adopted the same stances and support the party on account of those stances. Especially in multiparty systems where voters have a plethora of options, a party may fear that changing its policy stance would cause it to lose voters to another party that is also close to those voters' preferences, and that it will find it harder to attract new voters at their new location than to lose voters at the location it vacated.

Even in two-party systems, where most non-centrist voters have nowhere else to go if their party moves towards the center, a party may still have incentives to take policy positions away from the center. Though the voters might prefer a centrist party, those who contribute money and help it at election time may work less hard and contribute less money if the policies it stands for are indistinguishable from those of the other major party. Many people go into politics in order to have an impact on the world. They want to get something done. That something is likely to be to the left or to the right of the center and, to the extent they are successful in using their party as a means to achieve their political goals, they will pull that party away from the center and hence away from the median voter. This insight is at the root of a dictum known as May's Law of Curvilinear Disparity (May 1973), which proposed that party activists have to be seen as having different objectives than party supporters, leading to the hypothesis that where parties position themselves vis-à-vis the median voter is governed by the interaction of these different groups, whose influence alternates over time (see also Kitschelt 1989). This 'law' derives from seemingly compelling rational choice theorizing, but empirical tests have so far largely failed to provide unambiguous support for it (Zielonka-Goei 1992; Narud and Skare 1999).

However, we believe the empirical problems derive from viewing the law in a too-strict rational choice framework (cf. Whiteley 1995). When reformulated in more general terms, it works better (Kennedy *et al.* 2006; Weldon 2008). Between elections the influence of party activists can pull a party towards particular policy positions, especially when their support is needed in internal party disputes. These loyalists are usually not at the position of the median voter, for reasons that we have just explained. During a general election campaign, by contrast, parties focus on all potential voters rather than only the faithful and this generates a pull towards the center. As soon as the elections are over, the imperative for this centrist posture ceases to exist and party loyalists and activists will be more successful again in having their positions adopted (Mulé 1997).

So parties in majoritarian systems behave at least to some extent like accordions. They squeeze in to the center as elections approach and then wheeze out again, away from the center, when the elections are over. That cycle keeps repeating and may well be linked to the popularity cycle that will be described in the next chapter, since parties become less palatable to voters as they respond to the greater extremism of their more activist supporters, and then more palatable again as the approach of an election forces them to focus on the need to please a more centrist electorate (cf. Maravall 2008). Superimposed on the short-term alternating pulls by party activists and voters, there are other longer-term processes that affect parties' positions.

In multiparty systems a similar dynamic affects party locations, although the specifics may be more equivocal. Here too, voters, party leaders and party activists will in general differ in their policy preferences and the influence of these respective groups varies over time. During general election campaigns parties are more inclined to take up locations that (they believe) will please their potential voters: so at the time of nominations and the drawing up of manifestos, activists are more influential. After elections have taken place the top leadership of parties is most influential, especially if the party did well. However, which of these will be most centrist and which the least may vary between parties. Moreover, because it is easier in most multiparty systems to found new parties than in two-party systems, the positioning of existing parties not only reflects the alternating pull by various groups, but also the (possibly anticipatory) reactions to attempts to launch new parties. In such instances parties have to weigh the advantages of moving towards the center (assuming that most voters are located at or near the center) and ceding voters to more extreme parties, versus competing with a more extreme party by moving outward and becoming less attractive to centrist voters.

Choosing a strategy is further complicated by the fact that in most proportional systems individual parties cannot entertain any realistic hope of gaining a majority on their own. As a consequence, they are dependent on others for acquiring government power by way of coalition formation. Potential coalition partners are usually located near by in ideological terms, owing to which they compete for the same groups of voters. This generates a dilemma: by waging an aggressive election campaign a party may gain votes that otherwise would have gone to its closest competitors, yet at the same time souring relations with those potential coalition partners.

Leadership

The idea that parties are pulled one way or the other by party loyalists who want their parties to stand for usually non-centrist ideals and policies shades imperceptibly into the notion of political leadership. Politicians not only react to what voters want, but they also try to influence voters' political preferences. When politicians try to persuade voters and party supporters to follow them towards a particular policy position, this is usually referred to as (one aspect of) leadership. In response to successful leadership we see voters moving to take up a different position on the left–right spectrum, a position they would not have taken except for the impact of a particular politician. Indeed, leadership can even affect what we think of as left or right (or liberal/conservative). This was seen vividly in Britain under the Conservative Prime Minister Margaret Thatcher. She came seemingly out of nowhere, produced a set of neo-liberal policy proposals that had hardly been dreamt of, and created the support for those proposals that won her a series of general election victories, all through the force of her personality, the absolute clarity of her convictions and her political acumen and persuasiveness. After 18 years of Conservative rule, neo-liberal principles had indeed redefined the meaning of the terms left and right in Britain to such an extent that the Labour Party found itself compelled to largely adopt them too, for fear of otherwise being seen as unelectable. Leadership can really matter, as we saw in Chapter 4, p. 101–2.

Political scientists have a penchant for thinking in structural terms and they often need to be reminded of the power of non-structural factors such as leadership. The likes of Franklin Roosevelt in the US, Margaret Thatcher in Britain, Frederik de Klerk or Nelson Mandela in South Africa – not to mention Slobodan Milosevic in the role of a Serbian evil genius – demonstrate that we cannot assert that leadership does not matter. Party leaders who have real leadership qualities can move their parties to new positions while bringing along their party faithful, and often others as well. Indeed, those responsible for initiatives that change the basis upon which party choices are made need not even be formal leaders of their parties (see Box 5.2). After such a change the regular order of things reasserts itself, and Downsean analysis regains validity.

Box 5.2   Karl Rove

The brains behind the Republican victories in the US Presidential elections of 2000 and 2004 was apparently a man called Karl Rove. He was President Bush's political advisor from 1978 until he officially resigned as White House Chief of Staff in August 2007 (reputedly Rove adopted George Bush as his vehicle for influencing American politics). As well as the two presidential campaigns, Rove advised Bush in his unsuccessful 1978 bid for the US Congress and his two successful campaigns for governor of Texas (in 1994 and 1998) – having failed to persuade Bush to run for that position in 1990. He is a genius at framing policies and political stances in such a way as to benefit his party. Supposedly he was the one who came up with the words 'tax relief' to describe tax cuts for wealthy Americans – words more generally associated with removing a burden from those unable to carry it. He is also reputed to be the author of the brilliant tactic of painting Bush's 2004 opponent, John Kerry, as a 'flip flopper' for trying to do what all Presidential candidates had done for decades – prevaricate about policy positions so as to try to occupy the center ground. This enabled George Bush to move well to the right in the American presidential election of 2004 and take his voters with him (this has no particular bearing on the policies that Bush actually proposed when in office, which were arguably not especially conservative).

Learning from elections

So far in this chapter we have discussed political behavior and election outcomes mainly in terms of their direct and indirect political consequences. But the electoral process has also consequences for people's perceptions, knowledge and understanding of politics, the relevance of which is not limited to a particular election, but which extends into the future.

Elections are potent educational mechanisms that help citizens to orient themselves in the political world. Irrespective of the amount of knowledge and understanding that voters have at the start of an election campaign, the barrage of information and communication directed at them during that campaign results in many going away from the election with more knowledge and understanding than they had before. Elections not only educate voters about the parties and candidates that win, but about all parties and candidates, including those who lose the election. This education is cumulative. It enables voters to come into the campaign for the next election with a head start.

This is particularly true in those parliamentary systems where parties are relatively homogeneous in their policy outlook and party leaders tend to be the same over long periods. It tends to be less true in the US than elsewhere.

In the US a candidate who loses an election often loses her or his opportunity to enter (or stay in) politics, or moves to a far less visible position. Whatever was learned about such a candidate during the election campaign will be of little help in future elections. Al Gore lost the 2000 election and became an adjunct professor in a minor New York college – and, later, a campaigner for climate change policy, being awarded a Nobel prize for this work. Many voters had learned a lot about him by the time he lost the 2000 election, but all that knowledge was no help at all when it came time to start assessing candidates in the election of 2004, because Gore was not a candidate for any elected post in that year. Instead, the candidate for the Democratic Party in 2004 was a relatively unknown senator, John Kerry, who in turn was not a candidate in 2008 when the story was repeated with a different senator, Barack Obama. The fact that American candidates for high office are often virtually unknown at the point in time when they announce their candidacies has the advantage of widening the pool from which candidates can be drawn, but it also hugely increases the cast of political actors whose personalities and policies voters need to come to grips with. And the fact that this cast of characters is constantly changing makes it difficult for voters to increase their knowledge in election after election.

The fact that knowledge about politics is more cumulative in parliamentary systems is arguably one of the reasons why election campaigns can be so short in those countries – often little more than a month, in contrast to ten months or more in the US. They can be so much shorter because voters do not have so much to learn. The cumulative nature of political knowledge in parliamentary systems may also account for differences in political sophistication (see pp. 153–4). And it may account for why in those systems there is more *shared* understanding among voters of what the political world looks like, which in itself helps them communicate effectively and which reduces the costs of expanding and updating their knowledge (cf. Granberg and Holmberg 1988).

Chapter 6

The Role of Public Opinion

As long as policy-makers submit themselves to regular elections, they have an interest in taking account of public opinion on matters of public concern – matters upon which they are making policy or might have to make policy. Public opinion manifests itself in many ways and not just at election time. In modern democracies opinion polls function as quasi-elections, providing a snapshot of the balance of preferences in an electorate without immediate implications for office-holding. Anticipating the possibility that this balance of public opinion might be mobilized at the time of the next real election, elected officials often react to an opinion poll as though to a real election. This is particularly so in the course of an election campaign, when political parties conduct many polls so as to pin-point sources of potential support and opposition, and so as to adjust their campaigns appropriately. The extent to which politicians adapt their policy stances on the basis of public opinion is dependent on whether they are more motivated by power considerations (vote-seeking) than by principle (policy-seeking) – a distinction that is related to the top-down versus bottom-up distinction made in Chapter 2. Even when the next election is a long way off, opinion polls can galvanize politicians into rethinking their actions just as though an election campaign were in progress (a phenomenon often referred to as 'the permanent campaign').

Not only opinion polls, but also elections for offices other than those of the national government, have these consequences for national politicians. Thus local, regional or state elections often serve as 'barometers' of public opinion that will be heeded at the national level (though perhaps mistakenly), as will non-electoral manifestations of public sentiment, such as demonstrations, protests, strikes, etc.

Ways of studying public opinion

Studying public opinion is complicated because it can be regarded in different ways, as a dependent variable (the result of other things) or as an independent variable (the likely cause of other things). It can also be studied over time or cross-sectionally. We will start by clarifying these distinctions.

As a dependent variable, public opinion has its sources in both long-term and short-term factors. Among the long-term factors affecting public opinion are values, identification with parties, groups or ideas, and so on. Among short-term factors, public opinion might be affected by events, including shifts in the economy, foreign developments, natural disasters, pronouncements (explanations of events) by governments and other actors, and so on. As an independent variable, public opinion might affect party support, support for particular candidates, support for particular policies, media attention paid to events or policies, amongst others. It is even possible for public opinion to depend on something that it also affects. We have already indicated that party identification is both affected by issue concerns as well as the other way around. Aggregating this individual-level relationship to the electorate as a whole we get public opinion being influenced by party preferences as well as vice versa – an example of what is referred to as 'reciprocal causation'.

Another important distinction is between 'cross-sectional' and 'time-serial' research. When we study public opinion, we might want to know why some people have certain opinions while others have different ones. In this case we are taking a slice through the world at a particular point in time – a cross section – and evaluating differences between individuals. Or we might want to know how opinions change over time (either in particular individuals or on average over all individuals). In this case we are thinking time serially. Time-serial research is particularly useful for disentangling effects that are subject to reciprocal causation, since if we look at changes over time we can sometimes see causes preceding effects.

To start with we will view public opinion cross sectionally as a dependent variable. Why do people hold the opinions that they hold, and why do different people hold different opinions?

Why do people hold the opinions that they do?

Issues and party identification (again)

We have already pointed out that party identifications (seen broadly as the commitments that people have, for whatever reason, towards particular parties or political tendencies) are the lynch pins of voting behavior. Party identifications play this role because the parties that voters identify with influence those voters' own opinions. In earlier chapters we referred to this as 'cue-taking'. It is often thought that this runs counter to fundamental principles of democratic governance, because voters should choose their governments on the basis of the policies they would like to see those governments pursue. But, of course, democratic governance does not preclude voters from taking cues from parties or other cue-givers that they trust. Moreover it is not the case that all voters take all their views from the parties they support, let alone that they do this slavishly. And when they get their views from other sources these views may influence their choice of party. The trouble is that these influences are very hard to disentangle because all factors affecting party preference are subject to the possibility of reciprocal causation. To work out how much effect some issue has on voters' assessments of the parties, we have somehow to take account of the fact that many people will likely adapt their positions on that issue in the light of their party identification, and not the other way around. Reciprocal causation is a complicating factor in our attempts to understand the role of public opinion. Still, it is clear that issues do influence people independently of party identification, even if it is hard to pin down these effects.

Official pronouncements

Politicians are engaged in building support and public opinion reflects their success in doing so. Think about American public opinion regarding the war in Iraq. Attacking Iraq (both in 1991 and in 2003) was not something that either George Bush Senior or George Bush Junior was elected to do, but something they persuaded the public to support them in doing. These are examples of leaders being very successful at influencing public opinion. Almost all politicians are engaged in similar efforts. In parliamentary democracies the power of the government to shape public opinion is less than in the US because the power of party leaders (including opposition leaders) is much greater, as is the need for continuity in party programs (see p. 33).

Linked to this is the fact that public policies affect public opinion. When the government announces a new policy, or stresses the beneficial consequences that have come from an existing policy, this affects public opinion, as we will discuss later.

Opinion leaders and reference groups

A plethora of groups and institutions – sometimes even individuals – are important as 'shapers' of public opinion. These include churches, labor unions, professional associations, interest groups, cause groups such as Greenpeace, and influential individuals such as commentators and literary figures. Obviously the influence of such groups and individuals is not uniform over all aspects of public opinion or over all segments of the public. Churches, for example, may have little relevance in shaping public opinion about economic affairs, but more influence over matters of morality. At the same time, some people will be attracted to the values and arguments espoused by opinion leaders while others may be repelled. So the ways in which public opinion is shaped differs from individual to individual and from topic to topic.

The media

The mass media perform crucial functions in a democracy. These include the provision and interpretation of information, and helping the public to make sense of what is going on. Additionally, they provide a platform for political and social actors to voice their views.

With regard to the information that the media provide, it is obvious that they have to be selective in their coverage. 'All the news that is fit to print' is a nice slogan, but unworkable in practice. The media have to be selective because of lack of space and resources, but also because they would otherwise not be of any use to their audiences. This selection can take quite different forms, however, which is obvious when comparing the contents of different newspapers, radio and TV stations. How the media fulfill their information function depends, among other things, on the selection criteria that they employ. Ideally, information should be unbiased and relevant, but little agreement exists on what this actually means. What is relevant to one person is not seen that way by others. And notions of relevance are closely related to what is or is not considered to constitute bias. What a particular part of the media considers to be relevant is to a large degree dependent on its view of the world.

In addition to being relevant and unbiased, we like to think that information should be factually correct as well. This, too, is less straightforward than appears at first sight, particularly when differences of opinion exist as to what is 'true' and how facts should be interpreted. The media can fulfill their interpretative function in various ways. Different media often employ different perspectives on the world, as can easily be gauged from their contents. As stated above, this affects their selection of what they cover, but it also affects the way in which they cover it: the words they use, and the explicit and implicit judgements that are aired. Much of this is covered by the term 'framing', which refers to the interpretative perspective that (often implicitly) colors the information that media provide. Sometimes this is regarded as problematic, but that is naïve. Interpretative frameworks are both unavoidable and desirable. They are unavoidable because the simple act of choosing to treat something as news requires a frame for the information concerned. They are desirable because they allow disparate pieces of information to be connected, and thus to acquire more meaning than they would otherwise have.

The media help citizens to form their own opinions by providing the frames that help people make sense of the news, as well as by the explicit commentary and background information that they provide. The more varied all of this is, the more opportunity the media provide citizens to construct their own opinions. One way in which this happens is if different social groups and interests are able to voice their opinions in the media. The more that media outlets make this possible, the more they help reflect existing public opinion.

This is not to deny that there are concerns about the role that the media play in the politics of democratic states. These concerns focus on the media's relation to governments and the unequal access that different groups and interests have to the media (and thus to media audiences). Parties and politicians that are part of the government seem to be much better placed than others in this respect. The very fact that they can make actual policy, directly or indirectly affecting large numbers of people, means their pronouncements score high in 'news value' and thus survive the selection filters more easily than whatever is put forward by parties and politicians not in government, let alone by common citizens. As indicated above, this inequality is even more pronounced in systems - such as the US one – where there is not such a figure as a Leader of the Opposition to provide an authoritative alternative view. Because of the impossibility of providing information free of frames, this unequal access gives governments a strategic advantage in the way in which political affairs are framed, and thus also – because of the connection between frames and relevance – an advantage in determining which matters will be highlighted in the media and which will remain largely unreported.

Framing the news

George Bush framed his argument for a war against Iraq in terms of terrorism (suggesting that Saddam Hussein might have played a role in the 9/11 attack or might play a role in some future attack). He chose that frame in preference to available alternatives, such as Iraq's ignoring UN resolutions or the humanitarian need to get rid of a dictator without punishing his people through UN sanctions. The media play a role in allowing a particular frame to be placed on an issue and in contrasting that frame with other possible frames (or in failing to do so). To the extent that they fail to present alternative frames, they allow politicians a monopoly on the way in which public discourse is framed.

The problem becomes even more complex when pronouncements by government (or by other political actors) contain inaccuracies, either in the view of journalists or of other political actors. Drawing attention to, let alone correcting, inaccuracies or falsehoods cannot always be easily combined with accurate reporting, or be done in a way that reaches all those who were exposed to the misinformation. The media can counter this risk by providing space for the views and frames of opposition politicians, or by engaging in investigative journalism that is intended to expose lies and misinformation for what they are. But that takes time and money, and not all media organizations have those in large supply. For a society it is therefore important how the media system as a whole has evolved: the extent to which newspapers are 'quality papers' as opposed to 'tabloids' (generally considered such because they engage in sensationalism) or whether media organizations exist that (as in the case of public broadcasting organizations) regard it as their remit to provide 'balance' between different viewpoints in their coverage of political affairs (Gunther and Mughan 2000).

How influential are the media?

Does it matter what is and what is not covered by the media, and does it matter how this is done? The question as to how much influence the media have is frequently asked, but it is actually too imprecise to be answered. Influence *on whom and on what*? The media may influence citizens, and thus also politicians if they anticipate or react to public opinion. But then again: what exactly is influence? We can distinguish a number of different possibilities.

The first form of influence that the media may have is captured by the term 'agenda-setting'. This refers to the role of the media in determining what citizens and politicians deem to be important. In this respect the media often seem to be influential indeed. The more often the media pay attention to a particular problem or issue, the more people will be inclined to consider that issue or problem to be an important one. Political scientists use the words 'issue salience' to cover this. The more salient an issue, the more likely it is for that issue to get onto the agenda of political parties and governments. This form of agenda-setting via the media partly reflects the media's own choices in selecting the material presented, and it partly reflects the choices of other institutions and actors for which the media serve as an information conduit.

The impact of the media on what the public see as important does not imply, however, that their influence on *how* people think about that issue or problem is necessarily very large. In that respect, it is not so much the amount of coverage but the *framing* that potentially matters. How strongly citizens are affected by the framing of media information depends to a large extent on how many different frames are presented for the same information at the same time. Such differential framing may derive from differently 'colored' newspapers, radio or TV channels, but also from citizens' personal experiences (which may include experiences personally related to them by people whom they know and trust) or from the framing possibilities that exist in so-called 'popular wisdom' (Gamson 1992). Only when such alternatives are absent – as is the case with totally new and unexpected events that people have not previously experienced in some form – do the frames employed in media coverage have a strong impact on how their audiences frame (and thus interpret) these events.

There is a second reason, in addition to the availability of alternative frames, for the often modest effects of the media on how people think about issues and problems. Not only do the media have to be selective, citizens have to be selective too. They do not expose themselves to everything that is covered by the media, they do not believe and accept everything that they find there, and they are not inclined to use all media information for future reference. As mentioned earlier (see pp. 52–3), these phenomena are known as selective exposure, selective acceptance and selective retention. Ordinary citizens are not witless victims of what media 'inject' into their minds. On the contrary, they are actively engaged in finding meaning in political affairs. They do make use of what the media provide them, but only selectively so. The result is that media effects are generally small – often too small to measure in opinion polls of a size that is normal in election studies (Zaller 2002).

Does it matter what opinions people hold?

Here we want to think about public opinion as an independent variable: as an influence on policy-makers. Do policy-makers take account of public opinion? Are they even, perhaps, chosen on the basis of public opinion? For public opinion to be influential it would be necessary for people to vote in accordance with their opinions and preferences. If they failed to do so there would be no need for politicians to take any notice of what people want.

But for someone to vote on the basis of their preferences it is necessary, first, that they indeed have preferences for different possible policies and, second, that there is a politician or party offering to provide the policies this person prefers. In other words, preferences must be at least minimally aligned with the political options available, which is to say the party system. As explained earlier (pp. 13–14), a party system is usually thought of as being distributed across the political spectrum in left–right (or liberal–conservative) terms, with one party being to the right of the other in two-party systems and parties being arrayed from left to right in multiparty and quasi-multiparty systems. Parties are observed to adopt and propose policies that accord with this differentiation. In order for voters' preferences to be influential, those voters must hold opinions that are consistent with their party preferences: they must prefer a party of the right when they hold predominately right-wing policy preferences and a party of the left when they hold predominately left-wing policy preferences. The logic of the argument presented here is equally valid in party systems that are based on more than one dimension of competition (in addition to liberal–conservative or left–right) such as a regional or language divide. In multiparty

systems, parties of the center might be preferred by voters with mixed preferences or by voters whose preferences could be characterized as centrist (or
both).

If the attitudes of the mass public were not structured in some consistent
fashion, then it would be very hard for politicians to craft a set of policies
that would please their voters. Indeed, politicians who tried to take account
of voter preferences in such a world would very likely alienate (because of
certain policies) the same voters they were trying to please (with other policies). So, in such a world, there would be no point in politicians trying to pay
attention to what voters want.

Early research into the nature and structure of voter attitudes seemed to
find that the required consistency was largely absent and, therefore, that
voters were in no position to influence the direction of public policy. In a
seminal article published in 1964, Philip Converse set the tone for the mini-
malist approach to public opinion that was common until the late 1980s. In
that article he described the findings of early voting studies in the US to the
effect that the public is ignorant and that its attitudes have no coherence,
except for a small elite. Most people's attitudes appeared to show no consistency (what Converse called 'constraint'). These findings were a matter of
considerable concern for political scientists and those who worried about the
health of democracy. It appeared that voters (at least American ones) did not
have the intellectual skills or, apparently, the knowledge to judge policy-
makers on the basis of even a rudimentary understanding of what they were
doing or planning to do. Early research into public opinion in other countries did not go far towards contradicting Converse's characterization of
American public opinion. Early voting studies in parliamentary democracies
focused on social cleavages, not policy preferences, as determinants of the
vote. It was not until the mid-1980s that studies started to emerge in such
countries that challenged the notion that voters almost everywhere lacked
political knowledge and that their policy preferences lacked constraint (van
der Eijk and Niemöller 1983; Franklin 1985b; Granberg and Holmberg
1988). But by that time new American research was also putting early findings into a more favorable perspective (e.g. Nie *et al.* 1979).

It is true that most voters are ignorant about most of what goes on in politics for most of the time. This is true everywhere, though less true in parliamentary systems than in the US, where low voter turnout goes along with a
low interest in politics and a corresponding lack of information about politics. But if we focus only on those Americans who do vote and compare them
with Europeans and citizens of other established democracies who vote, the
differences in knowledge and sophistication are not great (Milner 2002). We
will be exploring the question of why the Americans (and the Swiss) have
such low turnout at general elections in a later chapter. Meanwhile the time
has come to focus on a puzzle already mentioned earlier in this book: how

does such ignorance of political matters coexist with what appear to be quite sophisticated electoral judgements?

The puzzle of the ignorant electorate

The puzzle of voter ignorance and lack of sophistication turns out to have been largely a matter of faulty expectations on the part of early researchers. These scholars started out with the assumption that a knowledgeable public requires all its members to be knowledgeable about all major political concerns. So the questionnaires these scholars used would ask about defence, social policies, welfare, space exploration, and so on. Respondents were then assessed on the basis of how many topics they could address knowledgeably. These assessments seemed to show that most individuals had no information regarding most issues. When looking more closely, it was found that people specialize – some knowing quite a lot about space exploration, for example, without knowing much about welfare or unemployment policy. But this received little attention at the time.

In retrospect the importance of specialization seems blatantly obvious. We all know that people specialize. When we watch a television program, when we listen to a talk show on the radio, experts are called upon to tell us about particular things – people who know a lot about those particular topics. These experts are not asked about topics outside their area of expertise. Not only experts specialize, so do ordinary people, as well as most politicians, journalists and other commentators. The more that ordinary people specialize the more they know about particular topics, but the worse they do across a broad spectrum of different concerns (Sniderman 1993). People are knowledgeable in patches. In areas about which they know little their answers lack coherence but, to the extent that they do have knowledge in more than one area, their attitudes in those areas show the sort of constraint that is needed for political effectiveness. So a critical question becomes: on what policies are people knowledgeable?

How many people are knowledgeable about any particular topic depends on its salience: the more salience an issue acquires, the more people there are who develop coherent ideas about that issue. And of course issues of high salience are the ones that we would expect to be most influential in deciding election outcomes. It thus turns out that the electorate, though generally quite lacking in general knowledge, is most competent in precisely those areas that matter most to them. Now we might want to worry about whether the areas that matter most are the areas that *should* matter most, but that is a different question. Political issues vary widely in their salience, and a new issue can acquire salience very rapidly in certain circumstances. In Spain in the spring of 2004 terrorism suddenly acquired enormous salience as a result of the bombing of four commuter trains near Madrid. Throughout Europe in the spring of 1986 nuclear power suddenly acquired enormous salience as a result of an accident in the nuclear power plant at Chernobyl in the Ukraine which released radioactive dust that spread over much of Central and Western Europe. In each of these cases, and in many other similar ones, voters very quickly acquired knowledge in this new area of interest (Lupia and McCubbins 1998). And on the basis of their new expertise they became able to play a part in directing the course of public policy.

There is a final point of great importance about the patchiness of public knowledge. No single individual voter needs to have knowledge on all subjects relevant to public policy. Public opinion is a collective phenomenon, not an individual phenomenon. Every member of the public does not need to know something about everything in order for the public as a collective entity to know something about everything. When individual opinions are aggregated to constitute public opinion, different aspects of it can come from different individuals, but the aggregate entity that is 'the public' can know quite a lot. That is the magic of aggregation.

So the mistake that many early scholars of public opinion made was to think that what they learned about individual voters would tell them what they wanted to know about public opinion. Converse did suggest that citizens specialize in their knowledge, referring to 'issue publics' (Converse 1964). The implication was less readily drawn, namely that public opinion can be consistently organized across a wide range of issues – and thus be politically effective – even if individual opinions are not.

Another finding from earlier public opinion research is worth mentioning. Converse established that most American citizens (in contrast to politicians and the media) do not use the liberal–conservative axis as an organizing principle, but he did observe that voters used such organizing principles as 'we' versus 'they' (insiders versus outsiders) in race and religion to create order among their opinions. But just because the American public does not generally think in liberal–conservative terms does not mean that they have no other abstract organizing principles to give coherence to their political knowledge than race and religion. Indeed, Rasinski (1987) showed that most Americans do use a couple of organizing principles: specifically, equity and egalitarianism. These are two organizing principles that are apparently much easier for ordinary citizens to handle, and, when we take them as the organizing principles, we find that people have much more constrained attitudes than when assuming that they were using the liberal–conservative axis as their organizing principle.

Of course, the fact that the American public uses a different organizing principle for making sense of politics than the American elite could create a problem if this were to stand in the way of a common political discourse. However, it seems that ideas of equity and egalitarianism map pretty well onto the liberal–conservative axis, with liberals being more concerned with equity and more egalitarian while conservatives are less so. So elites and publics in the US still manage to communicate with each other.

Outside America, in other established democracies, the organizing principles at work are not liberalism–conservatism (or equity and equality) but left and right; although countries differ greatly in how much use is made of this organizing principle. In countries with a multitude of parties (such as the Netherlands) or parties that are constantly changing their names and identities, as was not uncommon in Central and Eastern European democracies that emerged after the fall of communism (Rose and Munro 2002), the concepts of left and right with a continuum running between them is essential as an aid to making sense of politics. In the Netherlands party leaders, party members and ordinary voters all use the same left–right organizing principle to make sense of where the parties stand in relation to their own political preferences (van der Eijk and Niemöller 1983; van der Brug 1997). In France under the Fourth Republic, the same was even more true, since the French often could only make sense of what a party stood for by being told where it was placed on the left–right scale (Converse and Pierce 1986). In some Central and East European countries, the lack of a generally agreed notion of left and right will have stood in the way of the use of this cue by voters, as we will explain in Chapter 7.

On the other hand, there are countries like Britain and Canada where the political discourse makes relatively little use of the concepts of left and right. In these countries (generally Anglo-Saxon countries) there are sufficiently few parties that the public can apparently keep track of the major policy differences between them without having to resort to this organizing principle. However, it must be admitted that no political scientist in these countries has tried to emulate the work of Rasinski, done in the US, which established the importance of equity and equality as organizing principles for ordinary people. It may well turn out that the British and Canadians do make use of general concepts other than left and right to help them make sense of the political world.

Still, it seems that in all established democracies the public does make some collective sense of the political world in terms that map onto what most call a left–right scale but which Americans call a liberal–conservative scale. And there is sufficient collective coherence to permit a meaningful conversation to take place between the rulers and the ruled, although the extent to which this happens in practice is different in different countries, and even within the same country in different policy areas. Democratic publics are able to inform their political leaders about their general preferences and concerns, if those leaders care to look to their publics for this information. Later we will be asking whether political leaders do look for this type of guidance and what happens when they do.

From issues to issue spaces

Contemporary public opinion is particularistic, which means that the issues people are interested in – and even many of their policy preferences on those issues – are only weakly explicable from the location those people occupy in a society. This is quite different from what was seen at the start of the democratic era, and for most of the 20th century. That period was characterized by voters supporting parties on the basis of identification with a social group – what we have called 'cleavage politics': that members of the different social groups defined by social cleavages had different political interests, that party systems were organized so that most voters could find a party with their interests at heart, and that votes were primarily cast on the basis of group loyalties (see pp. 92–4).

During the second half of the 20th century much of this changed in established democracies and social cleavages declined in importance. What took their place was a new politics of issues, where the positions taken by individuals and political parties were no longer predictable on the basis of their location in the social cleavage structure. Instead, people started to focus on a plethora of different issues and concerns. Many of these concerns, of course, were adopted by voters because they were put forward by the parties that those voters supported but some of them presumably were adopted for other reasons. Certainly we know that concern about nuclear energy after Chernobyl resulted from an event – a nuclear accident – not from the proposals made by a political party (van der Brug 2001). Such events may be rare, but on a less dramatic scale they happen all the time and people do find themselves taking political positions for all sorts of idiosyncratic reasons. Indeed it is that very idiosyncrasy that characterizes contemporary public opinion in established democracies, giving rise to what has been called the particularization of political concerns (Tuckel and Tejera 1983; van der Eijk *et al.* 1992). It is this particularization that results in the patchy knowledge that characterizes contemporary public opinion. But, as already explained, this patchiness disappears when we look at public opinion as a whole.

When we do look at public opinion as a whole, there are a number of things we can do that cannot be done when looking at individuals. In particular we can make use of what citizens tell us in response to numerous survey questions designed to map out the locations of individuals, issues and parties on charts that depict the relative locations of different issue positions in an 'issue space', rather as a geographic map depicts the locations of cities and towns. To illustrate this idea we will look at two charts (Figures 6.1 and 6.2) in which an analysis technique known as 'factor analysis' (see Appendix) is used to show the changing issue space in Britain over a 15-year period.

Figure 6.1   *The British issue space in 1983*

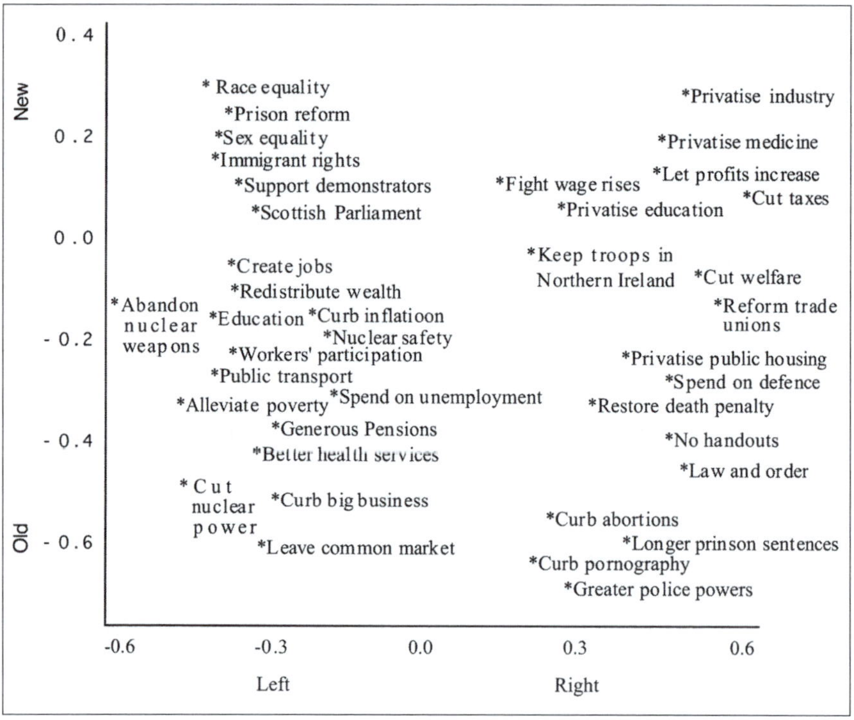

Source: British Election Study (1983).

In a map of the issue space policy preferences on issues are placed close together when they are likely to be held in common by the same people. So preferences for 'better health services' (at the left bottom of these charts) are close to wanting to 'alleviate poverty' because the same people who would like to see more money spent on health also want to see more money spent on alleviating poverty. The mapping procedure generates a configuration of policy preferences that reflects the extent to which these preferences are held in common by the same people. Figures 6.1 and 6.2 present these maps of preferences for policies on important issues in Britain in 1983 and 1997. The dimensions of these charts are labelled left–right and new–old, using these terms as described earlier (pp. 98–100). We see the issues associated with the old cleavage politics arrayed across the lower half of these charts, with traditional issues of the left in the lower left of the charts and traditional issues of the right at the lower right of the charts. Issues that rose to prominence with the decline of cleavage politics are arrayed across the upper part of the charts, with 'new left' issues towards the upper left and 'new right' issues towards the upper right of each chart (cf. Franklin 1989).

Figure 6.2 *The British issue space in 1997*

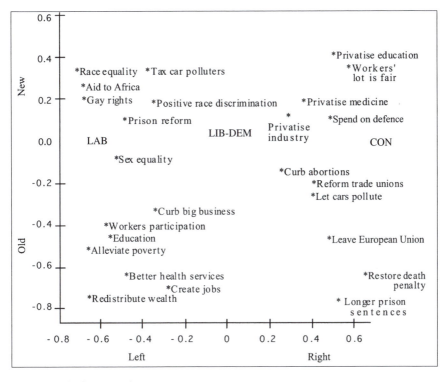

Source: British Election Study (1997).

When using mapping procedures to chart issue preferences, the researcher has to decide how many dimensions are needed to do justice to the observed co-occurrence of issue preferences. These charts are two-dimensional; a single dimension would – for these particular data – not have been sufficient to reflect accurately which preferences go together; a third dimension would not have improved on this accuracy and would thus mainly reflect 'noise'. For other countries, or for Britain at other moments in time, the number of dimensions that are actually needed could be more or less than two. How many dimensions are needed is thus a function of the observed patterns of preferences that people hold in common. Still, these findings tell us that there is constraint in public attitudes – at least in Britain when considered at the aggregate level – in terms of public opinion taken as a whole.[1]

A second decision that the researcher has to make is how to draw the axes on the chart and what they mean in substantive terms. The British charts have been labelled with dimensions left to right and old to new, but there is nothing in the statistical manipulations that tells us how to label the axes. It is up to the researcher to employ labels that make sense in terms of where the issues are located in relation to each other. Left versus right and new versus old seem to encapsulate the essence of the two dimensions in terms of which issues appear in what positions. Interpreting the dimensions can be facilitated by adding to the charts other objects (like political parties) whose relative locations on at least one dimension are known. This has been done in Figure 6.2, to which have been added the locations of the three major British political parties, as gauged from the issue concerns of their voters.

An important implication of the distribution of the parties across the middle of Figure 6.2 is that each of them is differentiated from the others (and the voters for each party are differentiated from the voters for the other parties) in terms of left and right, while not being differentiated at all in terms of the new/old distinction. Were any of the issues at the top or at the bottom of the chart to become highly salient, each of the parties would find its own voters (and probably its party elites as well) highly divided on these issues. The anticipation of the dire consequences of such internal divisions for their electoral prospects provides a strong incentive for party leaders to avoid, as far as possible, divisive issues becoming politicized. How difficult that task is depends – as we know from previous chapters – on at least two things. First, it depends on whether parties are 'disciplined', i.e. whether they can compel their MPs and other elected officials to toe a particular party line. Second, depoliticization of potentially divisive issues is more likely to succeed if the electoral system makes it difficult for new parties to gain electoral representation (as is generally the case in first past the post (FPTP) systems such as in Britain).

Because the parties are differentiated mainly in left–right terms, the British party space appears less complex (involves one less dimension) than the British issue space. This should not surprise us. After all, these figures chart a great number of issues but a small number of parties. In 1997, British parties were mainly differentiated in left–right terms and hardly at all in new–old terms. We will see that things were rather different in Britain at an earlier point in time.

With these charts before us we return to the question of constraint in voters' issue preferences. When early researchers were looking for consistency in the minds of each individual, they did not find it. We can understand this failure if we consider that, for any one individual, it is unlikely that all these issues will be salient at any one point in time. So the structure that we see is only valid for public opinion taken as a whole. It depicts issues in proximity to each other when concern for these issues is felt by the same person more often than not (even though the number of people with clear preferences on both of the issues in question might be quite small). People specialize, as we have said. But when we deal with an electorate as a whole we do see that issue preferences are structured, as shown in the charts in Figures 6.1 and 6.2.

We can use charts like these to study how the issue space evolves over time. Some policies move from year to year, but those that move do so in understandable ways that correspond to changing political realities. For example, the movement of anti-European attitudes in Britain (from low on the left side of the issue space in Figure 6.1 to low on the right side in Figure 6.2) corresponds to a change in party positions over the years, in which Labour became much more supportive of the EU while the Conservative party began expressing anti-EU concerns. For the most part, issues appear in very much the same places from year to year, not only for the two charts presented here but also for intervening elections (Franklin and Hughes 1999). This reflects the fact that under normal circumstances not everything can change at the same time.

The issue space and proximity (smallest distance) theory

What are issue spaces good for? They tell us that, in the aggregate, there is issue constraint and that issues go together in the public mind in a sensible fashion. They also help to picture (and perhaps to understand the import) of changes in public opinion. Much more interesting, however, is to use the issue space in order to discover how parties and candidates position themselves within that issue space and how those positions change over time.

As mentioned in Chapter 5 (pp. 140–1) Downs (1957) set out a theory of party competition in which he argued that parties would position themselves in an issue space so as to try to capture the votes of as many people as possible. The fundamental axiom that drives this *spatial theory* is that every member of an electorate will cast their vote for the party that is closest to them in policy terms: the party that is at the smallest distance from them in the issue space. Not surprisingly, this theory is often referred to as '*proximity*' or '*smallest distance*' theory (in recent years it has been challenged by a so-called '*directional*' theory which we will discuss a little later). Downs proposed his theory in the context of a one-dimensional issue space arrayed from left to right, where most voters have preferences somewhere in the middle and the number of voters gradually decreases when moving away from the center towards more extreme preferred positions. The theory is equally helpful, however, as a way of thinking about political competition in multiple dimensions. Downs stressed that, in order to win an election, parties would tend to locate themselves close to the position where voters are concentrated (often referred to as the location of the median voter – the voter with just as many other voters positioned to his or her left as to the right). If one party failed to do this while the other did so, the party taking the more extreme position would be overwhelmed in the election as citizens gave their votes to the party closest to them. Of course, movement away from the center by one party also permits movement away from the center by the other party which can still win provided it moves less far away from the center. Finally, a vacuum in the center constitutes an invitation for new party formation. There is a gap in the political market that some political entrepreneur will be tempted to fill.

All of these ideas are clearly illustrated in Britain during the period from 1974 to 1983 (see Box 6.1), as illustrated in Figure 6.3 (whose period has been chosen for this purpose), which, for clarity, zooms in on the central portion of figure 6.2 and focuses on the positions of the leaders of the various British parties, as these positions are located by respondents to successive surveys of the British electorate following elections in this period. To aid interpretation, reference lines have been added at the midpoint of each dimension.

The group of connected points on the left of the chart all refer to successive Labour leaders, while the group of connected points on the right of the chart all refer to the leaders of the Conservative Party in successive elections.

Box 6.1   Margaret Thatcher meets Anthony Downs

The election of 1979 saw a comfortable victory for Mrs Thatcher's Conservative Party, which was followed by even greater victories in 1983 and 1987. Meanwhile the Labour Party was tearing itself apart on the left of the political spectrum, selecting a leader, Michael Foot, who in 1983 took a position centered on older issue concerns (which also tended to be more left wing). This prompted a split in the party and the foundation of a new centrist party that called itself the Social Democrats and made an electoral alliance with the tiny Liberal Party (the two parties later merged). These developments were the most exciting that British politics had seen in half a century.

The appearance of the Lib–Dem Alliance (as it became known) as a new force in the middle of the British political spectrum had the effect of splitting the anti-Thatcher votes between two parties, making it easier for the Conservatives to win comfortable electoral victories in 1983 and 1987. The response of the Labour Party was to appoint a far more moderate leader, Neil Kinnock, who tried to move his party back towards the center ground of British politics and to mend fences with the electorate, though it was not until 1997 that the Labour Party was able to win another election. These developments almost perfectly illustrate the general principles of Downsean 'smallest distance theory', which is why we picked this period in history with which to illustrate these ideas.

Figure 6.3   *Perceived movements of parties and leaders within the British issue space*

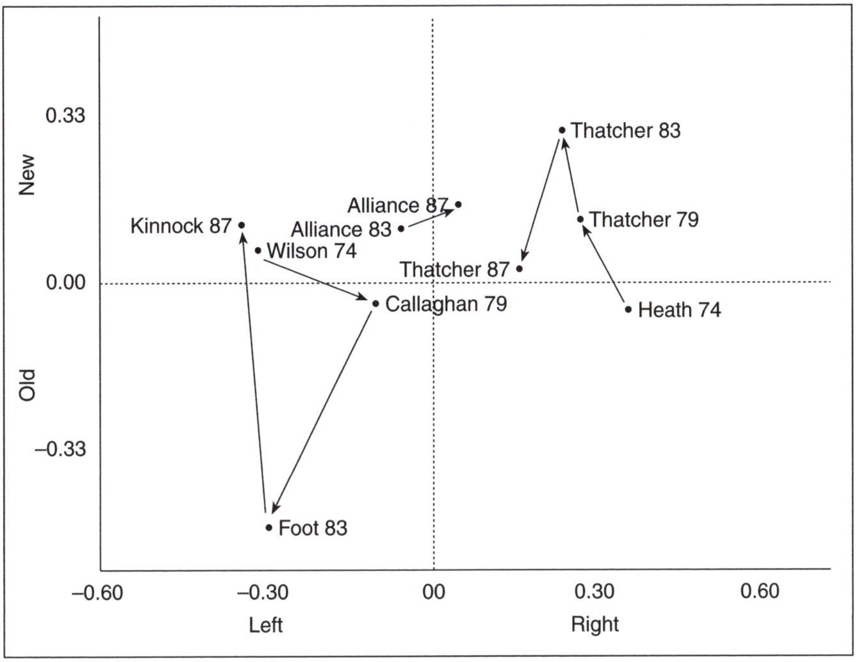

Source: Franklin and Hughes (1999).

In the center of the chart two additional points are plotted, showing the position of Alliance party leaders in 1983 when it came into being and in 1987. Restricting the chart to the names of party leaders reduces clutter and makes it easier to trace developments in the positions of the leaders over the period. Note that during the period encompassed by the chart (a period earlier in time than that encompassed by Figures 6.1 and 6.2), leaders are differentiated not only in left–right terms but also in new–old terms, with much of the movement from election to election being in a vertical rather than in a horizontal direction. Evidently the lack of differentiation of British parties in new–old terms that we remarked upon in regard to Figure 6.2 was not true of this earlier period. The period starts in 1974 – at which time the two major parties received an almost equal number of votes, though Labour had a bare majority – and extends to Mrs Thatcher's third electoral victory in 1987.

Between 1974 and 1979 we see both the Conservative and Labour leaders (Thatcher and Callaghan) moving towards the center of the issue space (the chart does not tell us which leader moved first but, whichever it was, we see the other leader countering the movement by also moving towards the center). Between 1979 and 1983 we see the new Labour party leader, Foot, positioning himself far down in the old left quadrant of the chart, while Mrs Thatcher took the opportunity to move somewhat higher (though no further to the right), laying claim to the center ground. Finally, in 1987 we see a third Labour leader, Kinnock, taking his party back to the center in new–old terms, and Mrs Thatcher's Conservatives doing the same, but continuing to dominate the center in left–right terms. We also see the Alliance candidates appearing on the scene in 1983, filling the center ground between Labour and Conservative.

The chart does not provide an explanation for why Mrs Thatcher won the election of 1979. Callaghan appears to be slightly closer to the center of the chart than Thatcher in that year, but the theory does not purport to provide a total explanation for everything that happens. Bringing contextual knowledge to bear we can explain the Thatcher victory in 1979 mainly on the basis of the swing of the pendulum, which we will examine in some detail below. In brief, by 1979 voters had become somewhat disenchanted with the policies that the incumbent Labour government had on offer. Mrs Thatcher, though she espoused some fairly radical policies, was close enough to the center to benefit from the voters' mood.[2]

In 1983 we might have expected a swing back towards Labour. Governments normally fall into disfavor as they put their policies into practice. However, the Labour Party put themselves out of the running by selecting as a leader a man who wanted to take the party back to its historical roots as a class-based socialist party: a position that was simply too far away from the center of gravity of British public opinion in 1983 to have any chance of winning. So Mrs Thatcher was able to enhance her lead over Labour despite a decline in personal popularity that was evident in opinion polls of the time and despite taking more extreme positions on a variety of issues. This moved her away from the center, but not nearly so far away as Mr Foot moved the Labour Party.

The configuration of the parties in 1983 provides a perfect illustration of Downsean electoral dynamics. If voters are supporting the candidate closest to them in the issue space and voters are concentrated in the center of that space, it follows that those who found themselves closer to Foot than to Thatcher were a much smaller group than those who found themselves closer to Thatcher than to Foot.

The only thing that complicates this calculation is the appearance of Alliance party leaders in the middle of the political spectrum, almost exactly at the zero point of each axis. Because these leaders find themselves closer to Mrs Thatcher than to Mr Foot, they would be expected (on the basis of Downsean logic) to take more votes from Thatcher than they took from Foot. Moreover, they would be expected to win the election hands down. But Downsean logic ignores party identification and strategic considerations (as well as the problems that voters might have in identifying the political character of a new party). In the real world, most people are set in their political ways and a new party cannot capture the votes of those who have already acquired a psychological attachment to an established party. Furthermore, the origins of the new political force as an offshoot of the Labour Party evidently would have colored its identity in people's minds, making it a competitor for Labour votes rather than for Conservative ones. On the other hand, the very appearance of the Alliance in 1983 is consistent with a different prediction of Downsean theory. Downs would expect to see a new political party position itself to fill a manifest gap in the political offerings, as already mentioned, especially if that gap corresponded to the location of a large number of voters – precisely what happened in this case.

Although not every aspect of Downs's theory is supported by the developments that occurred in Britain in 1983 and subsequently, still the theory goes a long way towards illuminating events and their repercussions on later developments. In Britain in 1983 the major parties both broke the Downsean rules. After 1983 we see them moving back towards the center, though the Labour Party's new leader, Kinnock, was still perceived as being further away from the center than Mrs Thatcher. But by then it was too late for the major parties to prevent the emergence of a third force in British politics, which soon became the Liberal Democratic Party.

Though this story does not constitute proof that the smallest distance theory correctly describes all the nuances of the translation of public opinion into party choice or of how parties position themselves vis-à-vis voters and issues, other research has repeatedly shown that one of the most important components in people's decisions as to which party to vote for is indeed the distance of that party from their own position in the issue space. People who find themselves towards the left of the issue space will tend to vote for left parties while people who find themselves towards the right of the issue space will tend to vote for right parties (van der Eijk and Niemöller 1983; Converse and Pierce 1986). The same is true of the liberal–conservative issue space in the US (Miller and Shanks 1996). It is as well that political science research has found this to be the case, because this is certainly what politicians and commentators assume to be at the center of the political process. If politicians want to win votes, they try to propose policies that they think people want. Such politicians assume that if they do this, rather than propose the policies being offered by other candidates, then (other things being equal) they will win more votes than other candidates will. Political science research has demonstrated that, other things being equal, this is indeed the case.

Of course, other things are not always equal and, in particular, two additional factors affect the relevance of an issue in proximity terms. The first is how important the issue is to voters – how salient it is. A highly salient issue matters more than a less salient one, and a party can have a huge advantage in terms of its position on some issue but find that advantage vitiated if it is unable to persuade voters that the issue is an important one. The second factor is how the issue plays among party supporters in contrast to groups that the party hopes to attract. Parties always need to balance the possibility of losing existing supporters (if they stress some issue that splits these supporters) against the chances of gaining new adherents on the basis of the issue concerned.

Political scientists have also found that not all of Downs's ideas apply to all voters everywhere. Some only apply with full force in two-party (or essentially two-party) systems. In particular, the idea that parties will all move towards the center does not apply in multiparty systems (see p. 140),[3] where it may pay particular parties to cultivate the voters in a specific portion of the issue space, focusing on protecting their own patch from incursions by other parties. In a multiparty system, a party of the right that moves too far towards the center is just as vulnerable to incursion (from the right, in that case) as, in all systems, is a party of the center that moves too far away from the center. So while in two-party systems the center is the focal point of the political battle, in multiparty systems both parties and voters can be much more widely dispersed. This has implications for the nature of public opinion and the adequacy of electoral representation in different systems, issues that we will explore more fully in Chapters 7 and 8. But before we move on to this topic we need to consider some alternatives and extensions to Downsean analysis that have been proposed in the political science literature as explanations for why voters choose the parties they do.

Party competence and issue ownership

It was long ago pointed out (Stokes 1963) that issues of public concern include not only issues on which parties take different positions, but also so-called 'valence' issues on which all parties (and almost all voters) take the same position. It is hard to imagine a party being in favor of more crime or of higher unemployment. These and many other issues are ones on which parties hasten to agree with one another. The question facing the voters is not which party is right but which party is most likely to be able to bring about a desired state of affairs. The party competence approach stresses that parties have or acquire reputations for competence in regard to certain issues. Some parties might even be said to 'own' certain issues, in that no other party has a chance of appearing more competent in terms of the issue in question (Budge and Farlie 1983; Clarke *et al.* 2004, 2006). Thus a socialist party might be said to own the issue of safety in the industrial workplace and a green party might own the environmental issue. We actually believe that it is not very helpful to distinguish issue ownership from party competence in terms of different issues. This is because – even though one might loosely speak of a party owning an issue, meaning that it was overwhelmingly advantaged by that issue – many voters would still disagree and maintain that their own preferred party (preferred on other grounds, no doubt) was best able to handle the issue in question. The extent to which a party's reputation for competence in regard to a specific issue overcomes loyalty to other parties is an empirical question that must be evaluated separately for each issue at each point in time, meaning that in practice issue-ownership must be treated just like party competence. Parties differ in the extent to which they are seen to be competent in dealing with specific valence issues. If a valence issue acquires high salience, the question of which party is seen as best able to handle the issue becomes a matter of major importance and the loss of a reputation for competence in regard to an important valence issue (as the British Conservative Party lost its reputation for competence in handling the economy in 1992) can have major repercussions for party choice (see Box 6.2).

In general, since voters differ in their opinions as to which parties are competent, it follows that valence issues need in practice to be treated in much the same way as position issues. We need to discover, for each voter, where he or she places each party in terms of its competence regarding each

Box 6.2   British withdrawal from the European Exchange Rate Mechanism

The European Exchange Rate Mechanism (ERM) was a method established in 1979 for fixing currency exchange rates among members of the (then) European Economic Community so that they varied by no more than 6 per cent relative to the German currency (the Deutsche Mark). It was seen by many as a precursor to a single European currency (introduced in most EU countries in 2002). Britain had originally spurned the ERM but joined in 1990. Unfortunately, differential interest rates between Britain and Germany made it increasingly difficult for Britain to keep the pound within its agreed limits and currency speculators such as George Soros sold huge amounts of British currency in the belief that the British government would be forced to devalue it. The British Treasury spent an estimated £3.4 billion propping up the pound at its unsustainable level, before announcing withdrawal from the ERM on 16 September 1992 ('Black Wednesday'). Opinion polls later showed that this episode cost the Conservative Party (then in government) the trust that average Britons had previously felt for its ability to manage international finance and hence the economy, contributing to its defeat at the next general election.

issue. A voter who regards a particular party as being particularly competent in terms of a specific issue is effectively a voter who places that party close to him or herself in terms of the issue concerned. For both kinds of issues, we need also to take into account how salient the issues are in order to evaluate how important they are to a voter. For both kinds of issues, salience functions as a factor that gives more or less weight to distances to parties (in the case of position issues) or to perceived party competence (in the case of valence issues). Low salience issues contribute little to overall evaluation of parties, high saliency ones are of crucial importance.

Actually, party competition on valence issues is about more than salience and competence. Underlying these factors, parties (and voters too) differ in their views about the means to be used in dealing with a valence issue, and about the priority to be given to it in relation to other pressing concerns. What seems to be party competition about valence issues is thus also competition in positional terms about *how* to attain universally desired goals and *at what cost*. And these aspects can be integrated seamlessly into a spatial framework of analysis. A party thought by a voter to have the right ideas about how to attain a valued goal is a party that can be seen (at least regarding that issue) as close to that voter in the policy space.

The directional theory of party support

We mentioned earlier some respects in which Downsean smallest distance theory taken alone can fail to explain political developments. We pointed out that party identification can count for more in certain circumstances than the smallest distance between parties and voters. This is another way of saying that there is considerable inertia in people's preferences for parties and that established loyalties are hard to break. Nevertheless, few theorists maintain that either Downsean theory or party identification theory can stand alone. Both explain aspects of the process by which parties position themselves to win votes and by which voters respond to party positions (see in particular Wayman 1996). However, there is a challenge to Downsean theory, sometimes seen as explaining both the fact that certain parties appear to be preferred that are not the closest to the voter and the fact that certain parties (particularly in the center of the issue space) receive less support than would be expected if voters were supporting the party closest to them. This so-called '*directional* theory' (Rabinowitz and Macdonald 1989) holds that parties and voters take policy positions that either favor one alternative (e.g. promoting nuclear energy) or its opposite (opposing nuclear energy). According to this theory, there is no such thing as a centrist position, as failure to favor one direction or the other on some issue simply indicates the lack of any policy preference on that issue.

In addition to direction, policy preferences differ in intensity. Directional theory expects voters to prefer a party which takes the same policy direction as they do themselves and, if several parties take the same policy direction, to prefer the one that is most strongly committed. Following this approach, what Downsean theory sees as different policy positions are actually only differences in intensity of commitment, so directional theory incorporates the notion of differential issue salience that has to be taken into separate account when thinking in terms of proximity theory and thus provides a straightforward way of thinking about valence issues. It is suggested by proponents that this theory makes fewer demands on voter sophistication and is more parsimonious than the combination of smallest distance theory and party identification theory taken together. The theory explains the generally small size of parties of the center because these are not committed to any direction of policy whatsoever (and thus not attractive to voters who have policy preferences).

An excellent statement of the differences between the directional and the smallest distance approaches to understanding voter choices has been made by Merrill and Grofman (1999), who developed what they called a 'unified theory of voting' that takes aspects of all three approaches (smallest distance, directional and party identification) and tries to demonstrate that the combined theory performs better than any of its components taken alone. Although we find the synthesis of the three theories inspiring, we are not convinced by it. We think that the anomalies that appeared to call for directional theory can easily be explained by known features of the two other models. In particular, the center of the political space is not nearly as populated by voters as it appears to be (many respondents to sample surveys place themselves in the center of the left–right scale, as an alternative to saying 'don't know', simply because they do not think of themselves in these terms), so the apparent mismatch between numbers of centrist voters and the support for centrist parties is not as great as it appears to be. At the same time, the fact that parties position themselves away from the center ground is particularly prominent in multiparty systems (where 'smallest distance' logic does not imply that parties are pulled to the center) as well as by the fact that parties do not exist only to win elections (an assumption of Downsean theory that is widely contested). Parties also exist to put forward (and if possible enact) policies wanted by their members.

Almost by definition those who care about politics will want policies that are distinct and those who care about politics are those who join and actively support political parties. Those who care less about politics may well prefer to see the government adopt centrist policies (if only to save them the effort of having to understand and choose between what to them appear to be arcane policy differences). The tension between more centrist voters and less centrist party activists is a real one that plays out in terms of movements of parties away from the center to please their most loyal supporters and back to the center to win elections (see p. 142). This oscillation is a feature of political life which we do not wish to have 'explained away' by a theory that has voters supporting parties far from them in the issue space. That would explain away a feature of political life that, in our opinion, is fundamentally present, at least in two-party (and essentially two-party) systems.

Still, proximity theory in its pure form does not exactly come out shining from this story either. Downs was right in the sense that the only ultimate equilibrium point in two-party systems is for both parties to compete for the center ground. But his analysis left out the fact that parties face constant internal pressures to move away from the center. Downs assumed that parties are homogeneous office-seekers (that is, uniquely interested in getting elected), whereas in fact they are much better regarded as heterogeneous policy-seekers (cf. Müller and Strøm 1999). Of course, both to win office and to make policy, parties need votes; but motive is also important. It is because parties want to make policy that differences arise between activists and voters. Moreover, many parties contain more or less recognizable 'factions' or 'wings' that differ amongst themselves with respect to the positions they want their party to adopt, and even – partly because of wishful thinking – with respect to what they believe their potential voters would prefer (while voters will in general not be very homogeneous either). Parties' positions are affected by who – which faction – acquires the upper hand.

The responsiveness of public opinion

So far in this chapter we have established two things that are particularly important for understanding the role of public opinion in a democracy. The first thing we have learned is that public opinion, in the aggregate, has a structure that corresponds recognizably to the nature of political discourse in a country. Though many voters individually might not understand even the important issues at stake in an election, an electorate taken as a whole does have this capacity. The second thing we have learned is that to the extent that parties and candidates are vote-seeking, they can position themselves so as to appeal to the largest possible number of voters (though what is large and what is possible depends to some extent on the nature of the electoral system in different countries). What we do not yet know is whether voters themselves respond only *prospectively* to the positions taken by parties and candidates – the *promises* they make about what they will do if elected – or whether they also respond *retrospectively* to the actual policies enacted by parties entrusted with government power.

It is not widely recognized, even by political scientists (though it has been repeatedly pointed out by theorists), that the whole idea of democratic government rests on the assumption that the public notices what governments do. If public opinion did not react to government policy, then there would be no incentive for the government to pay any attention to public opinion. If no one noticed whether parties and governments carried out their promises, then the whole premise of holding them accountable would fall to the ground. We do hear elected officials sometimes complaining that 'nobody notices what we do'. If they were right, then parties and governments could totally ignore the promises they had made. However, in spite of such complaints, there is quite a bit of evidence that voters react to what parties do when they make government policy (cf. Klingemann *et al.* 1994; Thomson 1999).[4] Recent work by Christopher Wlezien (1995, 1996; Soroka and Wlezien 2009) is particularly interesting in this respect.

In order to look at whether public opinion responds to public policy, it is necessary to take a longitudinal perspective, rather than the cross-sectional one that we have used so far. This involves observing variables changing over time and analysing whether changes in some variables go along with (or even lead to) changes in other variables. We will defer until the next chapter a discussion of where the malleability comes from that enables public opinion to change, even when many members of that public are locked down in their party choices by forces of habit and inertia.

If public opinion is responsive to policy-making, this implies that when the government produces policies wanted by voters, those voters will notice this and approve of the government action. At first sight, one might expect that this would lead to the government being rewarded at the next election. Indeed, many theories of electoral democracy seem to imply such a conclusion. The best known of these, the so-called *'responsible party model'* (APSA 1952; Schmitt and Thomassen 1999), is a normative theory that states that parties should have clear programmatic differences, which they should implement if they win executive office. Such differences would permit voters to make their choices on the basis of policy considerations and, if they did so, to enhance the policy relevance of electoral democracy. Although the model does not state this explicitly, we think it also implies that voters would cease to support a party that failed to implement the policies it promised when running for executive office. If we take such a view of electoral democracy then, if parties lose votes even when they did implement the policies that their supporters wanted, one might conclude that something was amiss in the operations of electoral democracy. Such a conclusion would, however, be naïve. In practice one can think of numerous examples of elections in which successful and highly appreciated governments were not rewarded by the voters for having instituted popular policies. The most famous of these examples was the rejection by British voters of Winston Churchill at the end of World War II. But the same thing happened to Churchill's successor, Clement Atlee, after his Labour Party instituted policies regarding social welfare that were highly popular. The same thing has happened in many other countries without the conclusion being justified that representative democracy does not function. Why is this?

This is because, when desired policies are implemented, the demand for those policies may be satisfied to such an extent that voters will cease to demand more of them. Expectations of this kind give rise to what we now call the *'thermostatic model'* (Wlezien 1995, 1996; Soroka and Wlezien 2009). Wlezien was not really studying elections and voting behavior – the subject of this book – but rather the way in which government policy evolves between elections. In other words, his research was related to what we called 'rational anticipation' (see Figure 5.2): governments reacting to public opinion in anticipation of repercussions should they fail to do so. Yet Wlezien's findings have implications for voter behavior at elections as well, even if those implications have never been clearly spelled out. Wlezien used repeated observations of policy and public opinion in the US to establish not only that government policy responds to change in public opinion, but additionally that influences also run the other way: public opinion responds to government policy. Taken together, these processes generate a feedback mechanism – exactly as proposed many years ago by the theorist Karl Deutsch (1963) – giving rise to the rather counter-intuitive idea that successful governments may create the conditions that lead to their replacement. Obviously this expectation would only hold for policies for which there can be 'too much of a good thing', for which the law of diminishing returns applies, or that compete for scarce attention by policy-makers. It appears, however, that many policies do fall under one of these headings.

It is an empirical question whether voters will reward governments who fulfill campaign promises. Wlezien's ideas might in practice be validated if we find a negative relationship over time between the provision of policy and the demand for it. Probably the extent to which this happens depends in part on the political system concerned, but not enough research has yet been done for us to be sure under what circumstances we will see the feedback cycle at work and under what circumstances we will see the responsible party model. We know that thermostatic feedback (responsiveness of public opinion to policy outputs) is highest in the UK, less strong in the US, and least strong in Canada, of the three countries investigated by Soroka and Wlezien (2009). By contrast, policy responsiveness (what we called rational anticipation) is found most clearly in the US, less clearly in Britain and least clearly in Canada. The lack of policy responsiveness in Britain ties in well with frequent references to British government as an 'electoral dictatorship' (ibid.) but these examples do not range very far over the spectrum of countries we are concerned about in this book.

Of course the feedback loop, where it exists, is not a closed one. Just like the thermostatic control of a heating system in one's home, there are external influences at work. In a home heating system the temperature outside is an external influence. If the outside temperature drops, the heating kicks in. Wlezien documented the same thing happening with policy. One of the policy areas he investigated was defence. He showed how public demand for defence spending reacted not just to how much the government was already spending, but (in the period of the Cold War) to changes in the perceived threat from the Soviet Union, with the public supporting greater defence spending when they perceived the Soviet Union as being more threatening. Wlezien also found demands for policies in one area responding to changes in policy in another area. Thus, when the public decided that more should be spent on defence, they would moderate their demand for social spending, as though they realized that they could not have both guns and butter at the same time.

Puzzlingly, however, Wlezien did not find equal degrees of public responsiveness to policy in all policy areas. He surmised that this might be because some areas were more salient to voters than other areas and that voters would only respond to government activities in areas that were salient to them. He corroborated this idea by looking at voters' responses to European unification, an issue that is known to have evolved from complete lack of salience in the early years of European unification to considerable salience today. Voters were indeed found to respond in a thermostatic fashion to policies bringing further unification, but only after the issue of unification became salient. Figure 6.4 shows the European public responding to the amount of legislation promulgated from the capital of the European Union in Brussels (the actual supply of policies that effectuated further unification). This figure has time along the horizontal axis and it shows the evolution over time of two different phenomena. The first is the extent to which European voters would prefer a more (or less) unified Europe than existed at that point in time (the line labelled in the graph as 'relative preference for policy'). The other line (referred to as 'difference between preferred and actual policy' in the graph) shows the extent to which the volume of EU legislation in each year approximates to what we assume (on the basis of another measure, not shown) that voters want. As actual policies become more than voters want so this line drops. We see that when this happens the relative preference for policy generally falls in step. To the extent that actual policies are less than what voters want, the line rises.

The figure shows two things that are relevant to our story: (i) there is no relationship before 1978, in the days when the policies of the European Economic Community (as it then was) are not thought to have been salient to European publics; and (ii) there is a relationship after 1978 that is staggeringly precise, with only a single exception (1990–91). The starting point

Figure 6.4   *Responsiveness of European voters to EU policy-making*

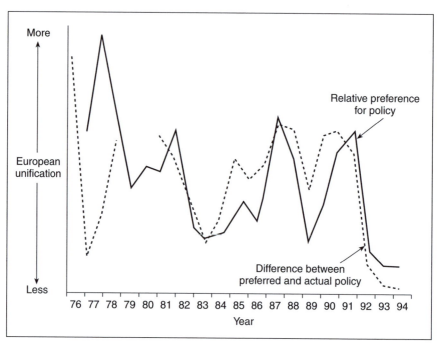

Source: Adapted from Franklin and Wlezien (1997).

for this strong relationship was expected to come at a date later than 1971, when European integration was not yet a salient issue to European publics, and earlier than 1986 when new-found enthusiasm for Europe was manifested in the Single European Market act and the push to complete the single integrated European market by 1992. The actual point of inflection appears to have occurred roughly in the middle of that period.

These findings show clearly that public opinion responds to government policy-making in a domain that is salient – and this despite the low visibility of policy-making in the European Union. This being the case, we should be able to understand movements in public opinion over quite long periods in the same terms, helping us to explain something that has often puzzled political scientists: something sometimes referred to as the 'swing of the pendulum'.

The swing of the pendulum

The phrase 'the swing of the pendulum' refers to the fact that governments tend to fall out of favor with the passage of time. This tendency is ubiquitous in contemporary democracies, and often causes politicians to characterize the voters in their country as fickle or ungrateful. But the swing might have nothing to do with gratitude if what is happening is that voters are responding in a thermostatic fashion to the provision of public policy. Voters presumably cast their votes in the hopes that resulting electoral victories by certain parties or candidates will yield certain policies, but once those policies have been enacted why would voters continue wanting more of the same? Of course any government can come up with new policies, and sometimes these new policies may be attractive enough that voters are induced to support governing parties for a second or even third time. But eventually voters will be satiated with the kind of policies that those parties stand for and look to some other party or parties to satisfy needs that have been neglected.

This idea has not been very rigorously tested by political scientists so far. Investigations of thermostatic responsiveness documented in the previous section have not yet been taken to the point of investigating election outcomes, but it seems promising to do so. Figure 6.5 shows the average extent of liberalism in US public opinion over time, as indicated by a composite measure averaging large numbers of opinion polls on different topics. The vertical lines in the figure correspond to elections at which the Presidency changed hands. In 1952, the starting point of the graph, the

Figure 6.5 *Swings in political mood in the US, 1952 to 2006*

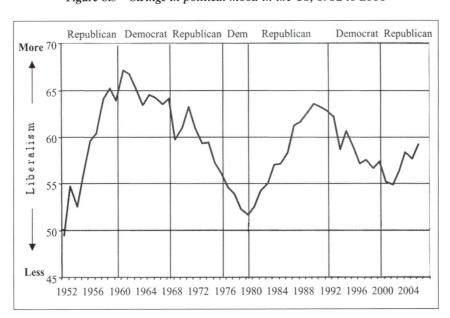

Source: Adapted from Stimson (1999) with extension from www.unc.edu/~jstimson.

Republican President Eisenhower had just been elected for the first of two terms in office. The 1960 vertical line corresponds to a switch to the Democrats, and so on.

Under a Republican president we can expect the policies coming out of Washington to be generally less liberal than under a Democratic president, from whom we can expect public policy to be generally more liberal. The thermostatic ideas we get from Wlezien's research lead us to expect a reaction against the policies of each era: a reaction that should move the electorate in a conservative direction during a Democratic era and in a liberal direction during a Republican era (cf. Erikson *et al.* 2002). With the exception of the period during Nixon's second term and the ensuing Ford presidency (1972–76), this is exactly what the chart shows. From 1952 to 2004, with just that one major exception,[5] if we look at periods when there was a Democratic president, we see the mood moving towards less liberalism. In periods when there was a Republican president, it moves towards more liberalism, exactly as though the public mood were responding thermostatically to the policies being produced.

A less elaborate analysis conducted in the United Kingdom (Franklin and Hughes 1999) strongly suggests the same thing: that periods of Labour rule saw a swing towards the right in public opinion, other things being equal, and that periods of Conservative rule saw a swing towards the left, other things being equal. Wlezien's later work has confirmed the operations of the thermostatic model in Britain and also in Canada (Soroka and Wlezien 2009). Indeed, as suggested earlier in this chapter, it is hard to make sense of the evolution of electoral choice in Britain without understanding the swing of the pendulum, which is one way in which thermostatic behavior manifests itself. Evidently the term 'swing of the pendulum' is itself somewhat unfortunate, implying a mechanistic process with a strict regularity, unaffected by circumstance. In practice this swing appears to be the response of public opinion to particular circumstances, of which the provision of public policy is only one. The influences on public opinion that contribute to (or sometimes counteract) this movement back and forth include:

1. Downs's (1957) 'costs of governing' – the idea that as soon as a party starts to make policy it also starts to make enemies and to lose electoral support.
2. The policy pay-off lag – governments are regularly advised to take tough decisions early in their term of office so that there is time for the benefits to become clear (and the costs to be forgotten) before the next election falls due.[6]
3. The tendency of partisans to 'rally around the flag' and support their party 'right or wrong' as the day of an election draws closer and brings a swing back towards the government in the run-up to an election.

4. The so-called 'promise-fulfillment cycle', which refers to the fact that voters react to whether governments fulfill their campaign pledges. This cycle has different implications if the public reacts thermostatically than if it behaves according to the predictions of the responsible party model, as explained earlier.

These four driving forces yield innumerable different combinations of circumstances, explaining why the supposed swing of the pendulum does not in fact have the strict regularity that the term implies. In the next chapter we will present an additional reason why elections are particularly likely to see a swing against government parties, helping to explain why the various effects listed above do not simply balance out.

A sophisticated electorate?

Wlezien's findings, and the extrapolation of those findings to areas investigated by others, are encouraging. They show us an electorate which, in aggregate terms, is considerably more sophisticated than most politicians and commentators would credit. But the extent of its sophistication is still very limited. It is certainly not the case that we have an all-seeing, all-powerful citizenry that has its finger on the pulse of everything that the government is doing. That is not what Wlezien found. What he found is a very hit and miss type of control mechanism where certain things are hit and many things are missed. We only see responsiveness in areas of high salience. People have only limited information about politics. Even when we get rid of most of the noise in the data by aggregating to the level of the electorate, the range of political affairs about which the electorate is informed does not extend beyond the big ticket items.

The public knows about education. It knows about defence. It knows about welfare. There are enough people who know about those things that their expertise comes shining through when we aggregate the data. But when it comes to space exploration or (up until recently) drug costs, aggregation to the level of the electorate does not help. There are just not enough interested people in these policy areas. However, these days drug costs are becoming a salient issue, at least in the US. If Wlezien would repeat his analysis today, he might well find a hugely more sophisticated response to health care costs than he found in his original analyses. This underlines the fact that the hit-and-miss electorate is highly flexible and can take on board new policy areas as they become salient. What we do not see is very much control by the public over what should be salient. In that respect the public is largely at the mercy of the media, politicians, interest groups, commentators and dramatic events. If an issue fails to become salient, the public will never hear about it and will never get any sort of grip on government policy in that area.

The public is also utterly dependent on the quality of the information it receives. No amount of sophistication can overcome this problem, which greatly limits the ability of the electorate to direct sensitively the course of public policy. We will revisit this question in our final chapter, where we will consider whether parliamentary democracies offer better protection against inadequate information than does the American presidential system.

Chapter 7

Voter Orientations

Over the course of the previous chapters it has become clear that the inter-action between voters, parties and electoral institutions is a complex one. An election outcome can be understood from different perspectives. From one perspective, it can be seen in terms of what voters do – how they evaluate parties and candidates. Alternatively it can be seen in terms of what parties do – how they choose policies, exercise leadership and strategically position themselves. Yet again, it can be seen in terms of the institutional setting in which voters and parties interact. So an election outcome is the result of a dynamic interaction between voters, parties and institutions. We have already discussed parties and institutions in earlier chapters. In this chapter we will consider voters.

Voter orientations evolve in a number of ways and for a number of reasons. We have already dealt in Chapter 6 with one of those ways (ther-mostatically) and one of those reasons (responsiveness to policy). Given the important role we earlier gave to habits and routines, there might be thought to be a puzzle involved in understanding how public opinion can be as malleable as we have seen it to be. Part of the answer arises from changes that are always occurring in the composition of the electorate, though the electorate also contains at any point in time a large number of individuals whose preferences are not (yet) locked down by forces of habit and inertia.

Though voters with an established partisanship can be induced to change their votes, they make poor converts and are likely to return in due course to their habitual party preferences. Thus it is predominantly in the malleability of younger voters that we find the potential for long-term change (see pp. 89–91; 101). Attracting uncommitted voters is an important task for politi-cal parties, who constantly seek to position themselves to attract such voters. However the extent to which they can adjust their policy positions to this end is constrained by their need to 'keep the faith' with their established supporters – generally older ones.

The decline of partisanship

Because the potential for long-term change arises mainly from individuals who do not have a firmly established partisanship, the size of the group of uncommitted voters relative to the electorate as a whole is of fundamental importance. In the days when party loyalties were largely established on the basis of social group memberships, newly adult voters essentially inherited their partisanship and entered the electorate with their loyalties almost fully formed. In such a world there was little room for change other than as made possible by enlargements of the electorate (see pp. 92–4). Once universal suffrage had been established it appeared as though party systems had become 'frozen', to use a famous expression coined by Lipset and Rokkan (1967). However, the declining power of social cleavages to structure partisanship that occurred in many countries in the last part of the 20th century also led to a decline in the strength of partisanship, with weaker effects of group loyalties giving rise to weaker identification with political parties (see pp. 95–8). In Britain, and presumably in most European countries, a decline in the strength of party loyalties followed immediately upon the decline in cleavage politics, giving rise in Britain to a phenomenon highlighted in the title of a widely read book, *Decade of Dealignment* (Särlvik and Crewe 1983), which focused on the declining strength of partisan identification with Britain's two major political parties. We have already asserted that the same thing would have happened in the US, where the decline occurred earlier than in Europe.

Figure 7.1 shows this indeed occurring. The chart plots the percentage of strong partisans in successive electoral cohorts over time. At the left of the chart we see the pattern for cohorts that were already members of the electorate (or who entered the electorate) in 1952, the date of the earliest US election study containing the appropriate information. As we move rightwards across the chart we see additional cohorts of voters entering the electorate with varying levels of initial partisanship, and we also see the evolution of partisanship for each cohort. The fluctuations in partisanship are partly random, due to the small number of people interviewed in each cohort at each point in time, so these fluctuations have been smoothed by taking overlapping averages of each trio of adjacent cohorts. The figure shows a progressive decline in the percentage of strong partisans among cohorts that entered the electorate from 1948 to 1968, along with a temporary downward swing, in 1968 and 1972, among older cohorts – especially those that had not been members of the electorate for long enough for their initial level of partisanship to become locked down. After 1968 there ceases to be a clear decline in initial partisanship (there might even have been a slight rise). It seems as though, whenever it began (presumably before the advent of academic election studies), the overall decline in the percentage of strong identifiers in the American electorate had come to an end by the time the first members of the post World War II baby-boom generation reached adulthood in 1968 – though some studies have seen a particularly strong decline of party identification in the 1964 and 1968 cohorts (Nie *et al.* 1979).

Figure 7.1 *Percentage of US strong partisans by electoral cohort, 1952–2004*

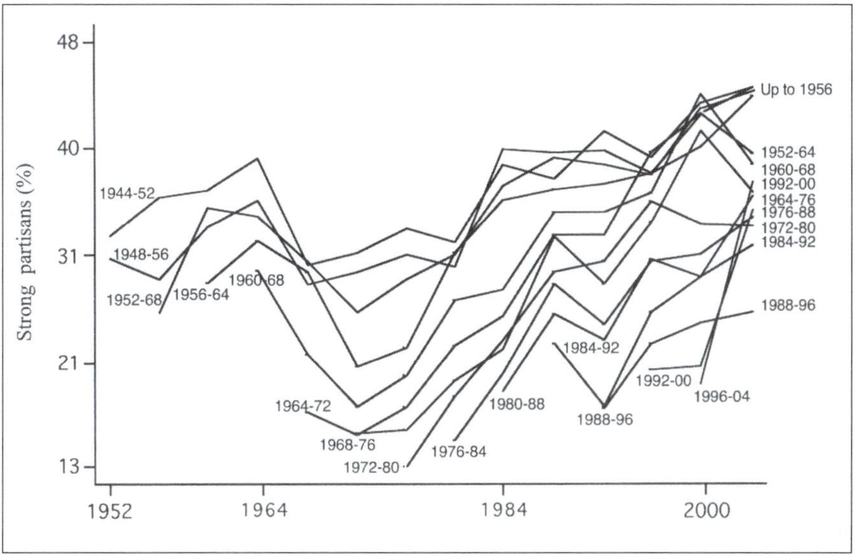

Source: American National Election Studies, 1952–2004, cumulative file.

From about 1968 onwards, the percentage of strong partisans among young adults entering the electorate (shown by the starting height of each successive line in the graph) appears to be less than half what it was in 1948 and earlier (top line in the graph), and this lower partisanship among young adults has continued to characterize the American electorate in more recent years. The corresponding drop in partisanship among older cohorts, which also occurred after 1968, was not so long lived, however. By 1988 party identification among cohorts that entered the electorate in 1960 or earlier had returned to more or less its pre-1968 level. This brings us to an even more striking feature of the graph than the lower level of partisanship among young adults after 1968: the fact that, from about 1976 onwards, the difference between younger and older adults is rapidly made good as each cohort ages. Older voters today are no less partisan than they were 50 years ago even though young voters are much less so. So there are more weak partisans in the American electorate today than there used to be because younger members have lower partisanship than used to be the case.

The age differential in the 'locking down' of partisanship, which we have mentioned repeatedly in past chapters, turns out to be a much more marked feature of the contemporary American electorate than it was half a century ago, which is probably the case in other countries also. This is because young voters are much less committed to political parties than used to be the case, providing the raw material for greater volatility of election outcomes in the modern era (and greater potential for long-term change). The same pattern that we see among strong partisans in Figure 7.1 exists also (but is not shown here) among weak partisans and those who lean towards a particular party. All of them show the same evolutionary pattern over time.

Generational replacement and electoral change

Because an electorate is a constantly evolving entity, with voters leaving in a constant stream through incapacity and death and entering in a constant stream as children grow up to become young adults old enough to vote, it is not actually necessary for any individuals to change their mind about what they want politically in order for the electorate collectively to change its mind. All that it takes is for new voters to want different things than voters who are leaving the electorate. To the extent that there is a systematic difference (that is not an effect of ageing) between the political complexion of those leaving and those entering the electorate, over time there will be a change in the political complexion of the entire electorate. This is obvious if we consider the extreme case of an electorate in which people born before a particular point in time all support one party and people born later all support a different party. Over time, support for the former party will dwindle to nothing as its supporters progressively leave the electorate, while support for the latter party will increase to encompass the whole electorate. This would take about 60 years to accomplish – the time that the average voter remains in the electorate.

In practice, generational change is seldom as dramatic as this, but even a quite small difference in political orientations between younger and older cohorts of voters can shift the electorate significantly to the benefit of the party or parties that are supported by more recent cohorts. In Western countries in recent decades, at each election roughly 10 per cent of the electorate has been new. If new voters favor a given party 30 per cent more than the oldest voters do, then at each election the shift in votes will be about 3 per cent in favor of the party supported by new voters. Elections are often won or lost by margins less than this (see Figure 5.1). If the difference between younger and older voters is only 10 per cent then it will take three elections for a 3 per cent shift in votes to occur – keeping all other things equal. Smaller differences between younger and older voters will slow down the speed with which aggregate political change takes place, but the changes induced by generational replacement are inexorable. The fact that they cumulate over time gives them immense power over the long term.

Political change and political realignments

But generational replacement is surely not the only way in which the electorate changes. There is controversy about this in the political science literature, but in some countries it is clear that generational replacement is far from being the dominant force in electoral change. Van der Eijk and Niemöller (1983) found that in the Netherlands party switching by established voters in consecutive elections caused three times as much political change as generational replacement. However, to the extent that this switching was due to older voters changing their party support, many of those changes are likely to have been short term in nature, with converts being reconverted at subsequent elections. And much of the switching that occurred was limited to shifts within particular 'party families', as discussed in Chapter 4 (p. 87), rather than between parties with radically different policy postures. Consequently, over longer periods the replacement effect is likely to have been greater, as was indeed established in a longer-term study by the same authors (van der Eijk and Niemöller 1992: 268). But there is an important question as to whether the customary situation that we have described up to now also applies at times of massive change in party support – changes that are known as 'political realignments'. Realignments are rare, but many suppose that they occur precisely because the normal forces for continuity in party support go into abeyance at such times.

A classic treatment of political realignment in the US (Key 1955) suggested a typology of patterns of change that distinguished between elections that (a) maintain the alignment of political forces (such that the parties continue to be supported by their established clienteles); or (b) loosen the relationship of party attachments to a previous clientele (dealignment); or (c) alter those relationships (realignment). Key (1955, 1959) suggested that realignment had to be preceded by dealignment – that the bonds of loyalty had somehow to be loosened so that they could be reconstituted in a different configuration, yielding a new long-term equilibrium of party forces. However, elections are generally not very easy to classify according to Key's typology, as they tend to exhibit mixtures of maintaining, dealigning and realigning tendencies among different groups of people. Yet no research has been able to establish that Key's suggested sequence of election types actually characterized historical realignments in the US or anywhere else. As a case in point, one contemporary account of the 1930s realignment in the US (Lubell 1952) reported that the author, after talking to hundreds of voters over the course of several years, had failed to find even one whose party loyalties had been weakened and transformed.

The problem for political scientists is that no realignment of the classic type has occurred in any country since the advent of academic election studies based on random samples of the mass electorate. By reconstructing electoral loyalties of the 1930s from academic surveys conducted in the 1950s, Andersen (1979) was able to validate Lubell's failure to find voters who had changed their party allegiance during the US 'New Deal' realignment of the 1930s. Her reconstruction seemed to show that the realignment of the 1930s in the US took place as a result of the mobilization of large numbers of previously non-voting individuals rather than the conversion of existing voters. The new voters, according to Andersen, were predominantly drawn from the pool of first- and second-generation immigrants who had acquired citizenship prior to the Depression years but had not previously been mobilized to vote. This argument is also consistent with Lipset and Rokkan's (1967) view of expansions of electorates as the motor of European electoral change in the late 19th and early 20th centuries. Newly enfranchised voters provided time and again a pool of electoral newcomers available to be mobilized especially by new political parties. According to this account, what President Roosevelt managed to do during the 1930s in the US was to motivate people to vote for the Democratic Party who otherwise would not have voted at all.

This interpretation of the 1930s realignment in the US has been contested. It is hard to be definitive about what happened because the realignment occurred over the course of three presidential elections (1928, 1932 and 1936), which has allowed political scientists to argue about what should be considered the proper base from which to calculate the changes that took place (Erikson and Tedin 1981). Arcane definitional problems remain unresolved and different scholars today describe the events of the 1930s in different terms. Less ambiguity surrounds the British realigning election of 1945, when the Labour Party definitively replaced the declining Liberal Party as the major competitor to the Conservatives. Because there had been no election in Britain since 1935 (an election that should have been held in 1939 was cancelled at the outbreak of World War II), the realignment of 1945 took place at a single election. There is thus no argument about the base from which the realignment took place and there has been no controversy regarding the only research so far conducted on the topic, which attempted to reconstruct the 1945 British electorate on the basis of 1960s election study data. The reconstructed data (Franklin and Ladner 1995) showed exactly the same pattern of change in the British realignment as had been found by Kristi Andersen for the earlier realignment in the US: the major source of change was generational. Citizens who had not been old enough to vote in 1935 were entirely responsible for the huge increase in votes for the British Labour Party in 1945. There is no need to suppose that normal bonds of party loyalty were somehow weakened through dealignment in order to explain the British realignment of 1945. It happened not because voters switched their party allegiances but because new voters were sufficiently numerous and sufficiently different from established voters to bring about the realignment.

Generalizing from the British and American cases, it would seem that realignments, even of the classic type, did not in fact require that normal forces of party loyalty go into abeyance. Instead, such political realignments appear to have been long-term consequences of electoral enlargements that increased the sizes and political distinctiveness of new cohorts, boosting enormously the normal effects of generational replacement. When the franchise was extended to new groups of citizens, or (in the US) when large numbers of immigrants started to take advantage of their recently acquired citizen status, the result could be large swings in the electoral fortunes of political parties. With the enfranchisement of virtually all adult citizens in established democracies in the contemporary world, there would seem to be little room for further realignments of this kind.

However, the modern world is also different in another way from the world in which realignments of the classic type occurred. Because of the decline of cleavage politics (and consequential decline of partisanship documented earlier in this chapter), a window has opened during young adulthood in which partisan forces for most young adults are much less than they used to be. Because of this development, large swings in support are possible in contemporary electorates without requiring a corresponding enlargement of the electorate. A tentative assessment of the sources of the realignment that is known to have occurred in the southern states of the USA after 1948, where a pre-1948 hegemony of the Democratic Party gave way to almost universal Republican electoral victories in later years, illustrates how this can happen.

In Figure 7.2 we show a subset of the electoral cohorts involved in the realignment that took place between 1948 and 1984 among white voters in the Southern US (starting with the earliest election for which we have adequate data and continuing to include the Republican electoral victories of Ronald Reagan in 1980 and 1984). We omit the election of 1972 and cohorts after 1968 (the missing year and cohorts would have muddied the picture because of the Watergate scandal in 1972–73 and the resulting Democratic victory in 1976). The cohort movements have also been smoothed by taking three-cohort overlapping averages in order to dampen fluctuations due to the small numbers of Southern whites in US election studies.

These cohorts show three clear patterns of movement over time. The first is a post-1960 swing to the Republicans and back again (and then back to the Republicans a second time and the apparent start of a second reversal) among the oldest cohorts (those who had entered the electorate in 1956 and earlier). This pattern is typical of what we expect from cohorts who have acquired a partisanship – members may be induced to defect from that partisanship, but only temporarily. Such movements contribute towards the 'swing of the pendulum' that we discussed in Chapter 6, but not to long-term

**Figure 7.2   *Republican vote among Southern white 1948–68 cohorts, 1952–84
elections***

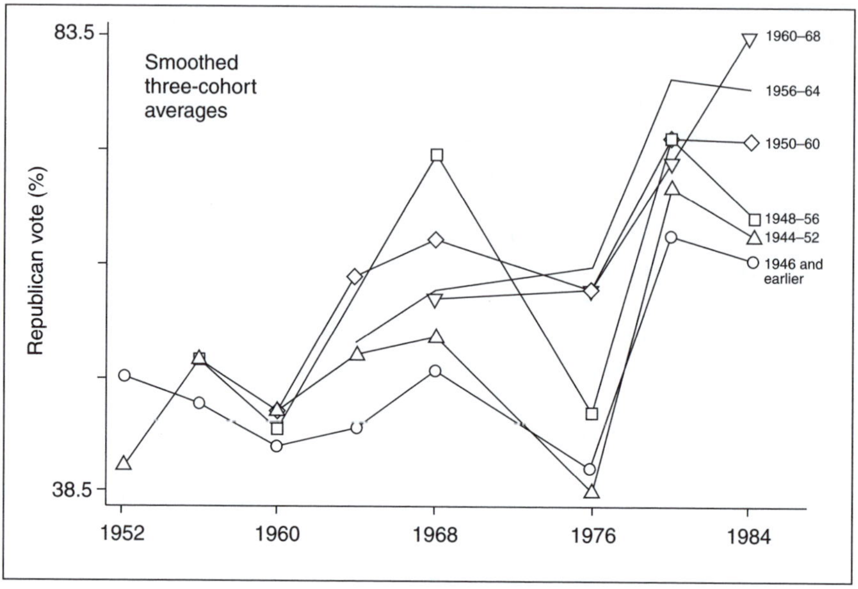

Source: American National Election Studies, 1952–84, cumulative file.

electoral change. The second pattern is of a progressive movement towards
the Republicans among cohorts who entered the electorate in 1960 and later.
Because the cohorts concerned began this move while still quite young, it
was possible for them to vote for a different party and even to acquire a
different partisanship – a pattern we expect from voters who are not yet
locked down in their partisanship. The third pattern is a clear pro-
Republican movement among successive cohorts of voters, each of which
either enters the electorate with a stronger initial Republican complexion
than the previous cohort, or rapidly acquires such a complexion (in the case
of the 1952 cohort) and maintains this cohort differential in succeeding elections. Thus each line in Figure 7.2, representing the extent of Republican
voting in a particular group of cohorts, acquires a position higher on the
chart than the line for the previous cohort group. This progression is what
we expect to see during a period when some group (southern US whites, in
this case) is changing its partisan identity. Each successive group of cohorts
reflects the trend more clearly than the preceding group. The final line-up of
these cohorts in 1984 is clearly arranged in sequential order, with the
1960–68 group of cohorts as the most Republican at the top of the chart in
1984 and the cohorts from 1946 and earlier as the least Republican at the
bottom of the chart in 1984.

This example shows how a new long-term equilibrium can come about in the contemporary era. It happens incrementally, requiring a number of consecutive elections for it to become manifest. The search, especially among American political scientists, for 'the next realignment', while only considering pairs of consecutive elections, is therefore bound to be fruitless. In the absence of a massive influx of new voters (such as following a franchise extension), only over a sequence of elections can we expect to find sufficient electoral replacement to provide the basis for a realignment (if there is one).

On the other hand, it also needs to be borne in mind that in the modern world large swings in party support no longer mean what they meant before the decline of cleavage politics. When party preferences were largely locked down and large swings in support could only come from massive increases in the size of the voting population, realignment really meant something. Today, large swings in party support no longer require a change in the complexion of the electorate – but the very flexibility of contemporary electorates that facilitates such large swings also makes it likely that they will soon be reversed. So large swings in party support do not necessarily herald realignments (Franklin and Hughes 1999). Only a study of the cohort structure of political orientations can determine whether a realignment has occurred or is in the process of occurring.

The hand of the past

We have seen that a voter's early experiences tend to become 'locked down' with the passage of time. A cohort that gives strong support to some party when its members are young usually continues to do so in the future and the reverse happens for a cohort that avoids voting for a particular party when its members are young. This results in a baseline vote in any election that is largely set by the electorate's past history. The same is true for turnout. A high turnout era will tend to perpetuate itself among the cohorts that entered at that time, as will an era in which a turnout was low. Only a portion of the electorate is truly free to vote or not, or to choose any one of the political parties competing for their votes. Remaining voters are set in their ways and those settled ways reproduce in the present the political orientations of years gone by (cf. Miller and Shanks 1996: 22–35). Because voters are most responsive to the politics of their formative years, those politics continue to affect the future for as much as 60 years ahead (the length of time the average voter remains in the electorate after first casting a ballot).

Of course, even established voters are not all immunized and immunization can be overcome. Certainly, voters set in their ways of voting for a particular party may fail to go to the polls in a given election if the party really disappoints them. In these ways we can expect short-term deviations from the baseline, but those deviations are liable to reverse themselves in the near future. More permanent changes among formerly immunized voters occasionally occur too, given strong enough motivation. Voters whose immunization is neutralized later in life again become free to adopt new partisan identities (as appears to have happened in France for many of the generation that supported left parties in the late 1960s – see Box 7.1). Another example occurred when the Dutch Labour Party, in government in the early 1990s, was forced to take the lead in a neo-liberal restructuring of welfare arrangements in the country. This caused widespread disenchantment, particularly among its oldest and most established supporters, who withdrew their electoral support in sizeable numbers, not to return again (Hillebrand and Irwin 1999). Similar problems were felt some years later in Germany where the Social Democratic Party, while in government, needed to bring the country into line with an already restructured pattern of welfare arrangements in neighboring countries, and instituted policy changes which helped in the rise of a new party (*Die Linke*) to the left of the center-left Social Democrats (SPD). These are instances of changes in the baseline itself, which therefore have permanent effects on turnout or on party choice (or both).

Circumstances that may bring about an increase in the number of unimmunized voters can also include changes in the institutional context. The abolition of compulsory voting in the Netherlands in 1970 is a likely suspect

---

Box 7.1   *President Mitterrand's U-turn*

In 1981 the Gaullist monopoly on presidential power in France, which had lasted since the inauguration of the Fifth Republic in 1958, was brought to an end by the electoral victory of François Mitterrand, the perennial candidate of the French Socialist Party. On taking power, Mitterrand set about bringing to fruition the 'socialist project', strengthening civil liberties, extending the powers of local governments and improving welfare entitlements. The cornerstone of his policy was the nationalization of the banks, bringing them under the control of the state. The program was a spectacular economic failure, leading to soaring inflation, a weakened currency and rising unemployment. In 1983 Mitterrand retired from public view for several days to 'think things through' and returned with the announcement of a U-turn on economic policy which abandoned the socialist project. The beneficial effect on the French economy was rapid and served as a vindication for capitalist policies in what was regarded by many as a head-to-head competition. The result was also extreme disillusionment of many left voters in France, who regarded Mitterrand as a traitor to the socialist cause and led others to turn their backs on socialism as a realistic program for social change.

in our attempt to explain the increasing volatility of Dutch voters since the 1970s (Irwin 1974; Wolinetz 1988); large-scale change in the set of choices on offer is a likely suspect in explaining the melt-down of the Italian party system in the 1990s.

Not much research has been conducted on the way in which baseline party choice can shift over time, though the research into policy mood by James Stimson (see pp. 175–7; 213–14), is relevant. But Stimson does not investigate why the baseline changes, and certainly does not investigate the influence of the past on the present balance of political forces. We will return to that research in the next chapter.

Rather more research has been done on the way in which changes in institutional arrangements and other fixed features of elections can change the level of turnout progressively over the course of future years. Turnout at any particular election reflects a dynamic balance of long-term forces reinforcing or counteracting each other to create a baseline turnout level, from which short-term forces can cause deviations. These findings are suggestive of the sorts of analyses we should be pursuing in order to understand the dynamics of political partisanship.

The dynamics of generational replacement

For the sake of brevity we will consider only two prototypical effects that have long-term consequences for the evolution of turnout levels (see Franklin 2004): effects due to (i) the extension of the franchise (which happened when women were given the vote in Switzerland in 1971 and in several other countries immediately after World War II); and (ii) the abolition of compulsory voting (which happened in the Netherlands and in Italy during the last half of the 20th century).

We start with the extension of the franchise. When this happens, the right to vote is given to a group of citizens who previously were excluded from voting. Because that group reached adulthood without being allowed to vote, they did not learn the habit of voting as other groups will have done. Indeed, many members of the newly enfranchised group are found to behave as though they had learned the habit of non-voting. They do not take advantage of their new right to vote when it is accorded to them. Since turnout is calculated in terms of the proportion voting out of the entire electorate, extending the franchise means increasing the denominator used in this calculation. So if the newly enfranchised group is voting at a lower rate than groups that gained the franchise earlier, turnout will fall. The youngest members of the newly enfranchised group, however, learn to vote at the same rate as other members of that new cohort and, as time goes by and additional cohorts of the previously disenfranchised group reach voting age, they too will presumably learn to vote at the same rate as everyone else. So the lower turnout that resulted from the franchise extension should gradually disappear. Figure 7.3 illustrates this expected pattern. As these groups of new voters learn the habit of voting, they presumably also need to learn the habit of voting for a particular party, in the meantime providing additional malleability to public opinion.

Unsurprisingly, compulsory voting keeps turnout higher because citizens who might otherwise have abstained in an election will turn out to vote. The abolition of the legal requirement to vote does not affect established members of the electorate who are already set in their ways. Only voters facing one of their first three elections – those not yet set in their ways – are expected to react immediately to the change (Figure 7.4). So there should be an immediate fall in turnout as these voters respond to the change in the law, after which the level of turnout should continue to decline as successive cohorts of voters enter the electorate with no compulsion to vote, and therefore learn to vote at a lower rate than their elders did. Eventually the whole electorate consists of voters who learned the habit of voting after the abolition of compulsory voting, and turnout settles down at a steady but lower level.

Various other reforms can be expected to create footprints in the electorate of a similar nature (or its reverse). The lowering of the voting age may have long-term effects if the acquisition of the habit of voting and of party identification is less propitious at the lower age than at the higher one (as explained at pp. 47–8). Institutional reforms may also have positive effects on turnout. For example, the introduction of postal ballots, or any other reform that reduces the difficulties of casting a ballot, should not affect those

Figure 7.3   *Expected long-term evolution of turnout following extension of franchise to a previously disenfranchised group*

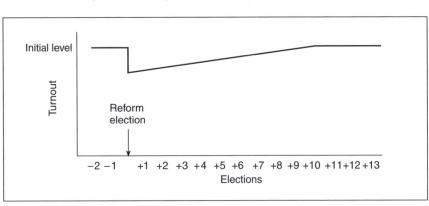

Source: Franklin (2004: 85).

Figure 7.4   *Expected long-term evolution of turnout following abolition of compulsory voting*

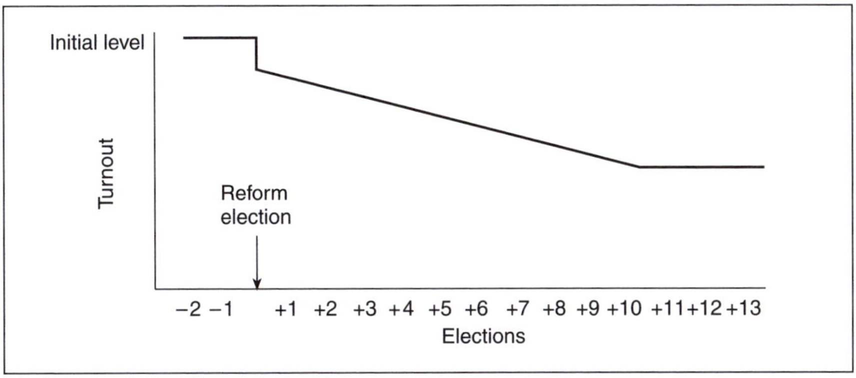

Source: Franklin (2004: 84).

already established in the habit of non-voting, but young adults might be expected to start voting at a higher rate, a rate that would come increasingly to characterize the entire electorate as additional cohorts are socialized into turning out at the higher rate.

These are the principal types of long-term effect on turnout that set the baseline about which short-term forces can cause temporary deviations. We can illustrate how this works by looking at two countries where electoral reforms gave rise to changes in the baseline turnout level. The first country is the Netherlands. There, compulsory voting was abolished in 1970 and the first national election held after this was that of 1971. This reform gives rise to expectations of declining turnout following the pattern displayed in Figure 7.4. Immediately following this reform, the Netherlands also lowered the voting age to 18. The theoretically expected effect of these two reforms jointly is plotted as the 'expected turnout' line in Figure 7.5 – which controls for a number of other effects detailed in Franklin (2004). As can be seen, actual turnout deviated somewhat from these expectations (with a single large deviation, in 1971). But over the long term, turnout has declined largely along the trajectory that could be expected as a consequence of these two electoral reforms, each of which is driven by the distinctive behavior of new cohorts socialized under the new institutions.

Another case is Switzerland, where the vote was extended to women in 1971. This development should have caused an initial drop in turnout, although ever-increasing female electoral experience should gradually have raised turnout in later years along the lines illustrated in Figure 7.3. But things are more complicated than that. About ten years earlier the Swiss had

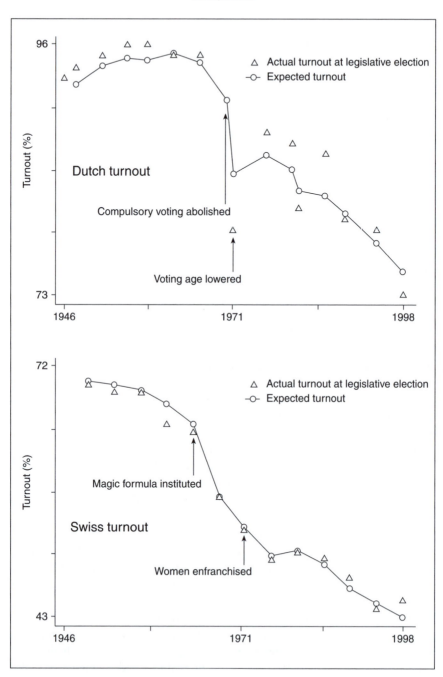

instituted an informal agreement between the national parties with even more dramatic implications for turnout than the abolition of compulsory voting would have had: the institution of a governing cartel in which the same parties took office, sharing power in the same proportions, whatever the outcome of parliamentary elections (this arrangement was marginally adjusted in 2003, but it is as yet too early to know what effect this might have on turnout). This so-called 'magic formula' effectively removed the relevance of parliamentary elections for the allocation of government power. In elections without consequences there is no point in voting, so turnout in Switzerland can have been expected to drop suddenly – as younger cohorts (those not yet locked down in the habit of voting) saw no point in casting a ballot – and then decline progressively as additional cohorts learned the habit of voting (or, more properly, of non-voting) at elections with no purpose – elections which, however, did not divert older cohorts from their ingrained habit of voting. The two reforms that the Swiss introduced so quickly on each others' heels will have generated both of the dynamics for the evolution of future turnout that were illustrated in Figures 7.3 and 7.4, and both of these dynamics have to be taken into account when calculating values for expected turnout in that country – as do additional considerations described by Franklin (2004). The lower graph in Figure 7.5 shows the baseline for expected turnout in Switzerland on the basis of these developments, together with actual turnout. As can be seen, actual turnout after these reforms follows closely the expectation that results from the combination of the two long-term trends (the fact that we do not see the rise in turnout that would have been expected following the extension of the franchise to women is because this rise is overridden by the much stronger effect of the government cartel).

The hand of the past can be seen to have powerful effects in these cases, as it does in every country. There is a delay built into the reactions of electorates to new circumstances. That delay brings about progressive effects as new cohorts of citizens enter the electorate and those progressive effects are not the result of something happening now: they are the result of things that happened at times past – often at times long past. These examples show the importance of past events in shaping current turnout. We can expect past events to influence current party choice in a similar cohort-related manner, but this has simply not been studied as such. Realignments and the decline of cleavage politics both reflect generational replacement. What has not yet been done is to use these insights to generate expectations for a baseline balance of partisanship – a baseline around which voting at particular elections would vary under the impact of short-term forces – another important avenue for future research.

Events and economic news

Short-term forces are epitomized by the impact of events. When asked by a young reporter what were the greatest challenges he had encountered as Prime Minister of Britain in the early 1960s, Harold Macmillan is famously reported to have answered 'Events, dear boy. Events'. Events come in many forms and achieve salience for voters to different degrees. A nuclear melt-down or near meltdown, such as occurred at Three Mile Island in the US or at Chernobyl in the Ukraine, can command the front pages of every news-paper and galvanize opinion, as can a terrorist attack such as occurred in the US in 2001, Spain in 2004 and Britain in 2005.

An important feature of certain events that makes them interesting politi-cally is the fact that they tend to act in the same way on people of all politi-cal persuasions. A nuclear meltdown makes everyone concerned about the dangers of nuclear energy; a terrorist attack can provide the 'rally around the flag' effect that enables a government to change completely the course of public policy. A somewhat different kind of event that provides a constant backdrop to political activity is news about the economy. Events that consti-tute good economic news are generally considered to be good for govern-ment parties, since managing the economy is one of the most important things that governments are expected to do (despite the fact that their powers to actually achieve particular economic outcomes are probably more limited than voters suppose). Bad economic news is made much of by oppositions and downplayed by governments. And the fact that it is continuously forth-coming on a regular cycle means that economic news, unlike other kinds of news, is always with us. In the next sections we will put economic news together with the other factors we have been discussing and look at the effects of different sorts of factors on party preferences.

Studying party preferences

At an election, voters are expected to make a choice between the available options. As mentioned earlier in Chapters 1 and 2 (see pages 12–13 and 50–2) the voting act consists of two stages, the first of which establishes or updates voters' preferences for parties and candidates; the second of which is to arrive at a choice, which boils down to picking the party that is most attractive or, in Downs's (1957) terms, the party that would yield the highest 'utility' if voted for. Because the term 'utility' has acquired many additional associations since Downs's time, we prefer to talk of preferences or party support propensities. The first stage of the process may yield various patterns in terms of these propensities: a voter may consider all parties to be very attractive as options to vote for, or only some, or (conceivably) none at all.

A voter may prefer a single party by far to all others, or more than one party may be tied for first place (see p. 52).

It should be clear from that discussion that early learning experiences inculcate preferences that may (or may not) be reinforced later by various agencies and by the experience of voting. In stable party systems, preferences become generally more focused on a single party as people age and that party becomes more strongly preferred (see Table 2.3). Voters with strong preferences for a single party can be regarded as providing the bedrock support for that party. These are the 'party faithful' who will turn out reliably at election after election without the need for appeals from party leaders. Voters with weaker preferences are also more likely to have multiple preferences and are probably only mobilized by election campaigns in which parties vie for their support. Relatively weak first preferences for multiple parties are evidently common among younger voters and may also exist among older voters in societies where political instability has uprooted their established patterns of preferences or prevented patterns of preferences from becoming established. Because only voters with more than one almost equally preferred party are readily available to switch parties, it follows that parties will be differently situated in the competition for votes, depending on how many voters they can appeal to who have multiple competing preferences (see Box 7.2). When focusing on parties, we can say that they have 'potential electorates'. These consist of groups whose votes each party will inevitably receive together with groups whose votes they might only receive to the extent that they are successful in their competition with other parties for these votes.

Parties in highly competitive situations will find that their potential electorates have a large overlap with that of other parties, which presents opportunities for losses as well as gains. Parties whose potential electorates overlap less with those of other parties will find it harder to increase their vote shares because only few supporters of other parties fall within their potential electorates. Equally, they are less likely to lose supporters to competing parties.

Figure 7.6 illustrates the concepts of potential electorates and overlapping electorates for Britain. There, five parties are arrayed from left to right and from new to old according to the same mapping conventions as were used in Chapter 6. In this figure, however, the parties occupy an area of space rather than being represented as points. The amount of space within each oval suggests the size of the potential electorate of the party concerned and the overlapping parts of those ovals correspond to overlapping electoral potentials. This figure is based on Table 7.1. Though drawn only approximately to scale, it illustrates clearly the overlaps between the groups of potential voters for British parties in the late 1980s.

The citizens with roughly equally strong preferences for both the Labour Party and the Conservative Party are located in the lightly shaded area in the

Box 7.2   Overlapping party preferences in Britain

Table 7.1 shows the extent to which British voters saw more than one party as a potential recipient for their vote at the time of the European Parliament elections in 1989 based on respondents' answers to the question as to how likely it was that they would 'ever' vote for each of the parties competing for their votes. These answers allow us to estimate the size of parties' potential electoral support (van der Eijk and Franklin 1996: 417–19). Of Labour's potential electorate (in the column with that heading) 44 per cent also belongs to the potential electorate of the Green Party, 35 per cent to the Liberal Democrats and 28 per cent to the Conservatives. The other columns can be read in a similar fashion.

Table 7.1   *Potential support and overlap between British parties in 1989*

	Labour	*Green*	*Lib Dem*	*Cons*
Conservative				
Labour	1.00	0.60	0.60	0.29
Green party	0.44	1.00	0.59	0.35
Liberal Democrats	0.35	0.46	1.00	0.30
Conservative	0.28	0.45	0.49	1.00
Size of electoral potential	0.42	0.31	0.24	0.40
Left–right median (1–10)	3.11	4.57	4.83	8.58

Note: The off-diagonal cells are not symmetrical as the 100 per cent base of each column (the size of the electoral potential) is different.
Source: Franklin and Curtice (1996, page 86).

Table 7.1 shows that people do indeed have more preferences than they can express on their ballots; otherwise all non-diagonal cells would be zero. Second, there is a clear pattern in these overlaps: they are generally greater when parties are closer together in the ordering of this table. That ordering reflects parties' left–right positions (indicated in the bottom row), as perceived by respondents in the survey. The Conservative Party is far away from the other parties (almost four points on the left–right scale), while those other parties are quite close to each other, which explains the smaller overlap of Conservatives with other parties.

middle of the picture. This area comprises about 28 per cent of the total Labour area but 29 per cent of the (slightly smaller) Conservative area. Nationalists share about 65 per cent of their area with Labour, 62 per cent with the Greens, and so on (see Table 7.1). Figure 7.6 also shows a small area

Figure 7.6   *Potential support and overlap between parties in the British issue space, 1989*

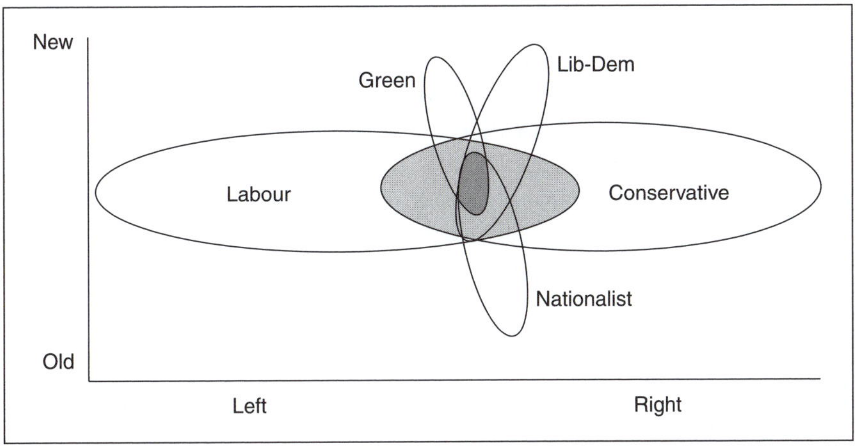

Source: Franklin (2004: app. C).

of more darkly shaded overlap between all five parties and several slightly larger areas of overlap between four parties. Voters in these areas fall within the potential electorates of all or almost all parties and are 'in play' in the competition for votes by all or almost all parties. Larger numbers of voters fall within the potential electorates of two or three parties. Still, for most voters their preferences for one of the parties is so much stronger than for any other party that they are highly likely to vote for that party; they fall within one of the large areas of space that 'belongs' to only a single party.

The area of overlap between the largest parties may change over time, but in the short run the size of this area limits the extent to which each party can be successful in an election and the extent to which each can lose. When focusing on the major parties, we can imagine the 'swing of the pendulum' of electoral politics (see pages 174–6), going back and forth through the area in which the parties overlap, yielding changes in the vote shares of different parties.

A critical point often overlooked by commentators is that no party can do better in the short run than to capture all the voters within its area. Once a party has done that it has realized its full electoral potential. Parties that do well in elections tend to do so because they have captured a large segment of their potential electorate. This means that, in the short run, such parties find it hard to improve further their positions, just as parties that do poorly may, in the short run, be protected from further losses. When focusing on the dynamic alternation between government and opposition, it becomes apparent that governing parties will generally have done well in the most recent election (parties that perform poorly compared to their potential will not win a majority in first past the post (FPTP) systems and will be unattractive coalition partners in other systems). This creates a natural asymmetry in the balance of political forces at any given point in time that makes it more likely for government parties to lose than to gain and more likely for opposition parties to gain than to lose, were it only on the basis of random events that otherwise might be thought to affect all parties equally. Such events may well affect all voters' preferences equally, but an increase in preferences for government parties will translate into only few additional votes if those parties have already largely exhausted their electoral potentials. Conversely, events that lower voters' preferences for government parties may easily result in large vote losses (see also the illustrative examples of the relation between preferences and vote choice shown in Table 2.3).

This built-in bias against ruling parties provides an additional reason for the swing of the pendulum effect. It is as though parties operate within guidelines established by their own past performance. However, this perspective is most relevant in the short run. The longer the time period under consideration, the less plausible becomes the 'other things being equal' condition and the more likely it is that events and other developments will change voter preferences and thereby affect the sizes of parties' potential electorates and the structure of their overlaps. Particularly as a result of changes in the composition of the electorate deriving from generational replacement, the structure of competition can change quite radically in the course of a few elections. Indeed, parties are constantly attempting, by their own efforts, to increase their pool of potential voters, creating opportunities to grow.

Distinguishing between preferences and votes and focusing on the extent to which parties compete for voters who fall within the overlap of their electoral potential with that of other parties helps to explain a number of things that otherwise would remain obscure. Returning to the topic of effects of economic news, an improving economy cannot help governing parties very much when they have already realized most of their electoral potential (or hurt opposition parties very much if they have already been reduced to their bedrock of support), but a deteriorating economy can quite easily hurt governing parties and benefit opposition parties, an asymmetry that has been misconstrued by commentators as implying that voters are more inclined to blame the government for a bad economy than they are inclined to credit it for a good one (Price and Sanders 1994; Nannestad and Paldam 1997, 2002; Stevenson 2002). It is obvious, however, that such asymmetries of vote share do not need to be interpreted in this way. They might be mere quasi-mechanical effects of the translation of multiple preferences into a single vote choice (cf. van der Brug *et al.* 2007a). Voters might well react differently to good news than to bad news, but discovering whether this is the case requires the study of preferences, not votes.

Table 7.2   *Effects of a changing economy on votes for parties in different positions regarding their potential support and their government/opposition status*

Standing of party relative to its electoral potential	Government or opposition party	Improving economy	Deteriorating economy
High	Government	No change	Fewer votes
High	Opposition	Fewer votes	No change
Low	Government	More votes	No change
Low	Opposition	No change	More votes

Table 7.2 lists the various outcomes in terms of votes for government or opposition parties that one would on average expect to see under improving or deteriorating economic conditions. What this table shows is that a party that would be expected to benefit cannot do so if it has already largely realized its electoral potential and a party expected to be hurt cannot in fact be hurt if its standing is already low. However, we should make it clear that these expectations hold only when all other things are equal which is, of course, rarely the case. Parties are not only affected by the economy but by a variety of other things that also need to be taken into account before making predictions in any specific case (ibid.).

What accounts for preferences?

There is an old saying to the effect that 'there is no accounting for preferences', but in fact the various factors that we have discussed in this and previous chapters do go a long way towards accounting for the preferences that people have for different parties. These are factors that were illustrated in the bottom row of Figure 1.2 and also discussed in some detail in Chapter 4 (Figure 4.3, p. 110).

In this section we illustrate the way in which such factors contribute to preferences for parties, using data obtained in Europe at the time of elections to the European Parliament. These might not be thought very appropriate occasions to study voters since no government power is at stake in European Parliament elections. However, these elections are second-order *national* elections, which means that voters' preferences are determined predominantly by the same factors that assert themselves in national parliament elections. It also means that specifically European factors are of marginal importance at best. These elections are therefore excellent windows into national political processes (van der Eijk and Franklin 1996; van der Brug and van der Eijk 2007). What we see in these data are baseline forces at work, uncontaminated by the hype and idiosyncratic events of a typical national election campaign. A more practical reason for using these data is that these voter surveys are the only ones that contain measures of party preference for all the parties that competed for votes over any large number of countries. The data employed here were collected following elections to the European Parliament in June of 1989, 1994, 1999 and 2004 and contain the answers from some 50,000 respondents to surveys conducted in EU member countries. These include long-established democracies (Austria, Britain, Finland, France, Germany, Denmark, the Netherlands, Belgium, Luxembourg, Ireland, Italy and Sweden), recently consolidated democracies (Spain, Portugal, Greece and Cyprus) and still consolidating democracies (Estonia, Latvia, Poland, Hungary, Slovakia, the Czech Republic and Slovenia). Although this selection of countries is limited to members of the EU, we have reason to believe that the conclusions we reach generalize quite widely, particularly because there are corroborative findings from other research covering a larger group of countries (Kroh 2003).

Table 7.3 reports two different analyses, based on different combinations of surveys, as not all independent variables were available for all years. The analyses concern the effects on party preference of many of the factors we have been considering in this and previous chapters. The table reports how differences in the propensities to vote for parties (the dependent variable) are shaped by differences in the independent variables. Party preferences were measured on ten-point scales from 'certainly would never vote for this party' to 'certainly would vote for this party at some time'. The independent variables are listed in the first column of the table, grouped according to whether they are characteristics of parties, individuals or 'the nature of the times'. Individual-level variables are measured in the same units; others are measured as specified in the table. The table reports two different analyses (labelled Model A and Model B), which are based on different segments of the data, as not all independent variables were available for all years. For each independent variable (and for each model) we get two coefficients, one referred to as 'b' (the so-called 'regression coefficient') and the other as 'beta' (the so-called 'standardized regression coefficient') – see Appendix. These coefficients tell us how strongly preferences are affected by differences in the corresponding independent variable. As a case in point, the coefficient 0.39 for 'left–right proximity' in Model A tells us first of all that parties closer to a voter's own position in left–right terms generate higher preferences (the coefficient is positive) and secondly that if we regard proximity to party in left–right terms as a cause of party preferences, as suggested by Downs, then a one point change in proximity brings about rather less than half a point (0.39) change in preferences, when controlling for all the other factors listed in the table. All the coefficients not marked with a dagger are significant, which means that they are unlikely to have been a happenstance of the particular sample (see Appendix). The corresponding beta, 0.26, tells us how

Table 7.3 *Effects of party-level, individual-level and nature of times variables on party preferences in established democracies, 1989–99*

Independent variables and interaction terms	Model A (1989)		Model B (1989–99)	
	b	Beta	b	Beta
Country and party-level effects				
Concurrent national election occurred (0,1 = yes)	0.25	0.03		
New politics party (0,1 = this is a new politics party)	0.99	0.09		
Government party (0,1 = this is a government party)			−0.29	−0.03
Party has extreme left–right location (0,1 = yes)	−0.07	−0.03		
Party size (proportion of votes at most recent election)	6.92	0.30	5.71	0.32
Less perceptual agreement on left–right party locations (0–1)	−0.45	0.02	0.00†	0.03†
Years since last national election for government party (0–5)			−0.06	−0.01
(Years since last national election)^2 for government party			0.01	0.04
Individual-level effects				
Previous national vote (whether voted for this party)			0.77	0.40
Class	0.52	0.12	0.36	0.06
Religion	0.55	0.13	0.31	0.06
Postmaterialism	0.32	0.05		
Left–right proximity	0.39	0.26	0.33	0.24
Issues	0.54	0.18	0.47	0.11
EU approval	0.21	0.04	0.27	0.04
Government approval	0.50	0.17		
Government approval where concurrent national election	0.19	0.03		
Issues where no perceptual agreement on l–r party locations	0.24	0.01	1.21	0.03
Left–right proximity where no perceptual agreement	−0.48	−0.04		
Left–right proximity where party has extreme l–r location	0.05	0.04		
Nature of the times effects				
GDP growth, per cent			0.03	0.02
Unemployment growth, per cent			0.07†	0.02†
Inflation, per cent			−0.04	−0.04
GDP for government party			0.07	0.02
Unemployment for government party			−0.01†	−0.01†
Inflation for government party			−0.08	−0.03
Adjusted R^2		0.430		0.462
Weighted *N*		9,736		27,505

Note: All coefficients significant at 0.01 level, except those marked †.
Source: European Election Studies 1989–99.

important this effect is, when taking account of the way left–right proximity is distributed across cases, in comparison with other effects. For a more detailed exposition of these findings see van der Eijk and Franklin (1996) and van der Brug *et al.* (2007a).

Readers who are unaccustomed to tables such as this one (as well as Table 7.4) should feel free to focus on the text and ignore these tables. But a little effort will be rewarded by a more detailed understanding than can be given in words of the relative impact of different forces we have been discussing in this and previous chapters.

The coefficients for class and religion show the role still played by social structure in determining party preferences even after the decline of cleavage politics. These appear to be quite strong effects (the bs are quite high) but the much lower betas tell us that the distribution of religious and class characteristics across respondents is such as to limit the overall impact of these variables (most people do not vary in class and religious terms). Indeed, in terms of betas we see far more important effects of issues and, especially, of left–right proximity. These policy-related concerns appear even more important if we regard government approval and EU approval as policy-related and postmaterial values as a surrogate for new politics issues. Voters do by far prefer parties that are close to them in left–right terms and this preference may be reinforced or weakened by specific issue preferences. The relatively weak effects of group loyalties (in terms of betas) should be seen in light of the fact that social structure has indirect influences via factors later in the causal sequence (as we saw in Figure 4.4). When those later factors are included in the analysis, as we have done, their coefficients partly reflect their role in channelling the effects of social structure, explicating some of the effects that otherwise would have been attributed to class and religion. What we see in Table 7.3 are only the direct effects of class and religion, not the effects that these variables have indirectly by way of variables later in the causal sequence.[1]

Some interesting fine-tuning occurs if we take account of a number of interactions that are indicated by the use of the words 'for' or 'where' in the names of the variables in Table 7.3. For example, 'Years since last election for government party', towards the end of the group of country and party level independent variables, is used to identify a coefficient that applies only to government parties. In evaluating interactions, the beta coefficients are less helpful since these are affected by the distribution of the conditioning variable (in this case the proportion of government parties); yet our concern with interaction terms is precisely to focus on the cases picked out by the interaction (government parties in this instance), no matter how many or few these may be. A more interesting interaction, 'Government approval where concurrent national election', refers to the effect of government approval in the case where the European election (the occasion of the research reported in the table) occurred in conjunction with a national election. We will discuss this effect shortly. 'Issues where no perceptual agreement' tells us about the effects of issues in countries where perceptual agreement on left–right locations of parties is lacking, as will now be explained.

Perceptual agreement about left–right location plays an important role in conditioning the effects of both issues and left–right placement. Countries differ in the extent to which voters agree as to where they see parties being located in left–right terms. Where voters are less in agreement about this, left–right proximity is less helpful to voters in making their evaluations and, at the same time, issues gain compensating importance.[2] This effect will become especially relevant when we study the difference between established and consolidating democracies below.

The first of the interactions listed under individual-level effects deserves special attention. This is the interaction between the occurrence of a concurrent national election and government approval. The data in the table were collected following elections to the European Parliament. As already pointed out, these are elections where government power is not at stake, neither in the EU, nor in the member states of the EU. This hugely reduces the salience of such elections. Nevertheless, we see such elections as windows into national electoral processes because of the fact that their European content is so slight as to hardly divert voters from the matters that concern them in their national political contexts. Still, we do expect certain variables to have different effects in national elections. In particular, voters should be more concerned about the performance of government parties if the election is a national one. We can check this expectation because there are occasions when national elections coincide with European Parliament elections. In 1989 there were simultaneous (concurrent) national and European elections in Greece, Ireland and Luxembourg, so for three countries out of the 12 represented in Model A in Table 7.3 our surveys were conducted in the political context of national elections in which government power was at stake. Incidentally, we see in such countries that all parties get higher scores for propensity to vote (the effect of concurrent national election, taken on its own towards the top of the table, is to increase the probability of voting for any party by a quarter of a point on the ten-point propensity scale) a difference that helps to account for higher turnout at national elections than at elections for the European Parliament. If the effects we measure on party preferences are different in such contexts, we would discover this by interacting the presence of a concurrent national election with independent variables. We did this for every individual-level variable, and only one of these interactions proved significant: the interaction with government approval, as expected. When the composition of the national government is to be decided (in those instances where national and European elections occurred concurrently), government approval affects party preferences rather more than if the election is 'merely' an election for the European Parliament. Other effects in Table 7.3's Model A are not different when government power is at stake than when it is not. What is striking about this interaction is that its magnitude is so small and that it is the only significant interaction of seven possible interactions between concurrent national elections and independent variables. These findings justify our use of surveys of voters conducted at European Parliament elections as though they were surveys conducted at the time of national elections.

A few party-level effects are also significant in this model. One of these is the most powerful effect in Model A, that of party size. For this variable, the beta is the more useful coefficient, since the effect is measured on a different scale than other variables (giving rise to its enormous b coefficient), but even the lower beta is still the largest beta in Model A. This huge effect of party size on preferences underscores the importance we gave to party size as a basis for party choice in Chapter 4 (see pp. 103–5). Another significant party effect comes from what we have called 'new politics parties'. In 1989 these parties (notably green parties) did particularly well in the European Parliament elections, evidently because in that year preferences for these parties were abnormally high. Our independent variables do not fully explain the attractiveness of new politics parties to the voters we interviewed in 1989 and these parties score virtually a full point (0.99) better on a ten-point scale than we would have expected them to score given their other features. The importance of this discrepancy is not so much in signalling our ignorance about what made new politics parties so attractive at that election as it is in pointing up the fact that no similarly significant effects were found for any other class of parties – implying that this model is equally capable of explaining preferences for parties on the left as on the right, religious as secular, and so on. Moreover, it was only in 1989 that any party type required this kind of special treatment. Model B in Table 7.3 required no similar interaction and neither were any such interactions found to be significant for the individual years 1994, 1999 or, indeed, 2004.

A third party-level effect is that parties with extreme positions to left or right are less preferred than moderate parties (shown by the negative coefficient for 'Party has extreme left–right location') except for voters who themselves take an extreme position (shown by the positive effect on the corresponding interaction of 'Left–right proximity where party has extreme l–r location', which comes close to matching in magnitude the negative effect that such parties have on the preferences of most voters). It has often been suggested that voters in general dislike extreme parties, and Table 7.3 shows this to be the case.

Towards the top of Table 7.3 we see three significant effects having to do with government parties. These effects can be estimated more reliably when using data for several elections, which is done in the table's Model B using information from the 1989, 1994 and 1999 European Parliament elections. Government parties are found to be disadvantaged in terms of voter preferences, other things being equal. The negative coefficient for this variable tells us that government parties are preferred somewhat less than we can account for on the basis of their other characteristics. This is a tiny penalty for being a government party, but it is statistically significant and is magnified by the additional effect of months elapsed since the previous national election. Downs predicted this by reasoning that parties cannot fulfill all their promises and moreover cannot avoid making increasingly more enemies over the course of their tenure. But this is evidently true only up to a point. The positive coefficient on the square of the elapsed time variable indicates that, after a certain point, the standing of government parties again starts to rise. So government parties are subject to a frequently observed cycle in popularity that declines during the first half of their term of office and then improves as the next election approaches, for reasons associated with the swing of the pendulum. Note that this cost of governing is quite separate from the asymmetry in support for government parties that was the subject of the previous section. Changes in preferences may or may not translate into changes in support, depending on where parties stand in relation to realizing their potential support, but here we are just talking about preferences.

Finally we turn to the 'nature of the times'. These are constant at any one election for any one country and thus need to be studied using data that include as many different electoral contexts (natures of the times) as possible. For this reason we again employ Table 7.3's Model B, which is based on information from 1989, 1994 and 1999. Unfortunately those studies did not have as many independent variables as the study of 1989, making it impossible to include postmaterialism or government approval as independent variables. These studies also included a smaller set of issue questions. In order to compensate for the relative paucity of individual-level variables, our study of the effects of the nature of the times includes, as a surrogate measure of omitted variables whatever they might be, an indicator of whether a party was the one voted for in the most recent national election. This variable, of course, replaces not only the variables we know to be missing from the studies of 1994 and 1999 but any that were missing from the study of 1989 as well. The measure is naturally correlated with all the effects that are more specifically measured (which will also have influenced previous votes), accounting for the fact that effects of substantive variables are generally lower in Model B. The inclusion of previous national votes in the model accounts for the fact that two of the interaction terms (left–right distance with perceptual agreement and left–right distance with extremity of party) prove not significant in Model B and were thus excluded from that model. It is also because of the inclusion of previous national vote that Model B explains more variance than Model A (the R^2 is higher), not because this model includes effects of the nature of the times.

We measure the nature of the times in Model B with three variables obtained from OECD data (www.oecd.org): the rate of GDP growth, unemployment increase and inflation – all measured over the year prior to the European Parliament election. GDP growth yields higher preferences for all parties, but especially for government parties (taking the relevant interaction effect into account), and inflation reduces the preferences for all parties, especially government parties. Unemployment does not show the negative effect that might have been expected (its effects are not statistically different from zero and one of these effects actually has the wrong sign). This anomalous result was the subject of detailed investigation by van der Brug *et al.* (2007a) who find that unemployment only really reduces voters' preferences for large left government parties, not for government parties in general. Because of the small numbers of such parties in our data, we do not see these effects when all government parties are taken together (ibid.: 98).

A more important feature of these effects is that they are relatively small (less than any of the individual-level main effects, and an order of magnitude smaller than left–right proximity) – a finding corroborated by a new study (Duch and Stevenson 2008) which shows changes in party support due to economic voting of almost identical magnitude to the effects found by van der Brug *et al.* (2007a). Though effects due to the nature of the times are small, these effects play a unique role in determining election outcomes because all voters are affected equally by such influences. Even a small effect can have large consequences when it moves all voters in the same direction, and other research has shown that even the small effects of economic conditions that we see in Table 7.3's Model B are quite enough to change election outcomes, so that governing parties lose office and/or opposition parties become governing parties as a consequence of changing economic conditions, other things being equal (ibid.: ch. 6). Other forces are shown in the model to be more powerful, but they often tend to cancel out, pushing different voters in different directions. The nature of the times, by contrast, by pushing all voters in the same political direction, sometimes does determine election outcomes.

Bill Clinton was not wrong in 1992 when he had his campaign staff erect a banner in their headquarters reminding them of their key campaign theme: 'It's the economy, stupid!'. But equally, the small magnitude of these effects explains why the economy does not always determine election outcomes. Elections such as those of 2004 in the US (which re-elected President George Bush the younger for a second term) or that of 1992 in Britain (where the Conservatives under John Major were re-elected) were won by incumbent parties despite poor economic conditions; and the elections of 1997 in Britain and 2000 in the US were lost by the governing party, despite booming economic times. Many other examples could be cited. The small effects of economic conditions relative to other effects, and the certainty that other effects will not always cancel out, make this easy to understand (see also our discussion in Chapter 2 with respect to Table 2.3).

Mandates versus accountability (prospective versus retrospective voting)

One enduring question in electoral behavior is whether people vote retrospectively, holding governments to account for their performance while in office, or prospectively, giving mandates to particular parties to introduce or amend particular policies (cf. Fiorina 1981). In a two-party (or effectively two-party) system it is hard (but not impossible) to determine which objectives were motivating voters. Punishing the governing party requires voting for the opposition party, and it takes appropriate survey data to tell us whether the motive was punishment for past government policy-making or a desire to see enacted the policies promised by the opposition – a reason why the controversy endures (and a reason for the possibility of confusion regarding the motives of voters). However, with coalition governments it is possible to distinguish to some extent between these different motivations that voters might have when they cast their ballots.

Powell (2000) has pointed out that a focus on government accountability is really a feature of the majoritarian vision, and it is logically hard to reconcile an accountability orientation with the fact that partners in a coalition government do not generally see their vote shares moving in step at election time. If some parties gain and some lose after being in government together, on what basis are they being held accountable? In a study of this very point, van der Brug *et al.* (2007a) conclude that in coalition governments it is not really government status that voters were taking into account when retrospectively judging parties on their past performance, but party size. Large parties (including large opposition parties, who are also 'players' in the proportional vision) are those held responsible for economic conditions, not government parties. Moreover, ideology is just as important as party size in determining how voters credit or blame individual parties for good and bad economic times. In coalition systems, voters react to changes in economic conditions in a very prospective fashion, taking account of likely party policies in the light of whatever economic problems might be paramount. Their preference for right parties increases when inflation is a problem and their preference for left parties increases when unemployment is a problem, as though they see a party's ideological stance as a sign of its priorities should it take government office. The retrospective punishment model seems to be a better fit in countries that are characterized by single-party governments;

but it is possible that this is apparent only, given the just-mentioned difficulty of distinguishing retrospective from prospective orientations.

Here we see an echo of our findings in Chapter 6 regarding the apparent punishment of parties that fulfill their campaign promises (see pp. 170–2). It is clear that voters quite often focus on what parties offer in the way of future prospects rather than on bestowing credit or blame for past performance. Fiorina (1981) suggested that voters use past performance as a guide to future performance so that retrospective and prospective orientations are merged; but when we look separately at the parties that are members of a coalition government or when we look at public reactions to policies that a government has enacted, we see clear signs of prospective orientations on the part of voters many of whom, when prospective and retrospective orientations would have led to different choices, apparently choose prospectively rather than retrospectively.

Effects on preferences in newly established and consolidating democracies

We are mainly focused on established democracies. We adopted this focus because much less is known about transitional and consolidating democracies. We reported in Chapter 4 that learned behavior is important and, earlier in this chapter, that (at least in established democracies) older voters retain the imprint of influences felt when they were young. But we do not know what to expect in countries that were not democracies when older members of their electorates were young. Research on this topic is in its infancy. Nevertheless, the enlargement of the EU in 2004 to include eight consolidating democracies that are Central European ex-communist countries provided an opportunity, in the European Parliament elections of that year, to compare the voting behavior seen in those countries with that seen in more established democracies. On the basis of a study of those elections, we can answer a number of questions that could not previously be answered.[3]

What differences do we expect to find between the behavior of voters in established as opposed to consolidating democracies? The fundamental expectation that underlies all research on voting behavior, though seldom stated so baldly, is that people are people wherever they are found, and that in general they will behave in similar fashions unless prevented by specific circumstances, such as their social structure, institutional arrangements, economic conditions or historical experiences. If they behave differently in some countries than in others, it is because they find themselves in different circumstances such that, if those circumstances were replicated in another country, the behavior of the voters in that country would respond accordingly. Research on political behavior in different political systems has repeatedly vindicated this expectation.

We expect two kinds of differences when comparing established democracies with consolidating ones: differences in the extent to which voters preferences for parties can be explained (we expect more idiosyncrasy in preference formation among voters in consolidating democracies) and differences in the relative strengths of explanatory factors. Historically speaking, the countries that became democracies in the late 19th and early 20th centuries had electorates with very strong group loyalties, which boosted the effects of social structure. In the countries of Central Europe that became democracies in the 1990s, the same importance of group loyalties does not appear to have characterized voting behavior, partly because the communist regimes that preceded democratic governance in these countries did all they could to suppress group identifications, which they regarded as incompatible with communist objectives. In established democracies, the decline of cleavage politics led to increases in issue voting, but we do not necessarily expect to see this in new democracies, mainly because of the instabilities in their party systems. In new democracies parties are often seen to adapt their policy positions and ideological profiles in the face of rapid social changes and changing opportunities for political mobilization. This, however, prevents voters from learning where parties stand in left–right and policy terms, making it more difficult for voters to develop stable preferences and decide which party to vote for.

This said, we do not expect all consolidating democracies to have the same characteristics, any more than we expect this of all established democracies. Countries differ in the speed with which their party systems consolidate and in the extent that consolidated systems present voters with clear choices that are well-structured in terms of policy differences.

Table 7.4 is laid out in the same way as Table 7.3, though with models in different columns for established democracies, former communist states and a joint analysis of both types of country taken together. Because our interest with this table is mainly in comparing the coefficients for established democracies with those for consolidating democracies, the first two models include only regression coefficients (bs). Betas cannot be used in comparisons between models because their effects are calculated relative to the effects of other variables in the same model, as already mentioned (see Appendix). When comparing these two models, we see first that there is considerably more idiosyncrasy in preference formation in consolidating democracies – variance explained (the R^2 coefficient) at the foot of the table is down by about a third (0.244) in consolidating democracies compared with established democracies (0.339), as anticipated. Secondly, we see that the effects of most variables (the b coefficients) are remarkably similar across the two groups of countries. These similarities suggest that the independent variables giving rise to these coefficients play much the same role in party preference formation in each type of country.

Two effects for consolidating democracies are significantly different from those in established democracies in readily understandable ways. This is shown by the interaction effects at the bottom of Table 7.4, which apply to the analysis of all EU countries taken together in the last columns of the table. The reduced effect of party size (shown by the negative coefficient on the interaction 'Party size for former communist state') suggests that voters in these relatively new democracies have not yet learned the same strategic preference for large parties that we see in established democracies – or perhaps, more simply, that the sizes of parties are so unstable in consolidating democracies that voters find it harder to take party size into account. In any case the difference is not great, given the scale on which party size is measured.

There is also a small reduction in the effect of left–right proximity in former communist states. This difference between the two groups of states would have been greater but for another significant interaction – that for left–right proximity where there is less perceptual agreement – which helps to explicate the lesser effect of left–right proximity in former communist states by telling us that it reflects the circumstances in which voters find themselves. The particular aspect of people's context that matters here is the degree to which agreement exists on the positions of parties on the left–right dimension. We have already discussed this variable in the context of Table 7.3. In the analysis of all EU countries reported in the last columns of Table 7.4, we see from its interaction with left–right proximity that this variable reduces the effect of left–right proximity where perceptual agreement is low. Had we not included this interaction then 'Left–right proximity for former communist state' in the model for all EU countries would have had somewhat greater effects than those indicated by the small coefficients ($b = -0.05$, Beta $= -0.02$) that we see in the table.

So the weaker effect of left–right proximity that we see in former communist states is largely due to the same factor that causes variations between established democracies in the importance of left–right proximity: the extent of perceptual agreement about where parties stand in left–right terms. The small number of elections so far conducted in these consolidating democracies, and the instability of their party systems, has somewhat limited the extent to which voters have been able to acquire a common understanding of where their parties are located in left–right terms (and perhaps also of their sizes). As a consequence, in such countries, the terms 'left' and 'right' are less helpful as aids to understanding political affairs and as factors contributing to the formation of preferences for parties[4] and strategic considerations appear to play a smaller role.

We should stress, however, that the important finding to take from this comparison of established with consolidating European democracies is that

Table 7.4 *Effects of different variables on party preferences in established and consolidating democracies taking part in European Parliament elections in 2004*

Independent variables and interactions	Established democracies	Consolidating democracies	All EU countries	
	b	b	b	Beta
Social class	0.54	0.50	0.52	0.08
Religion	0.61	0.75	0.65	0.12
Gender	0.72	0.84	0.75	0.04
Issues	0.64	0.69	0.64	0.08
Government approval	0.64	0.68	0.63	0.20
Satisfaction with democracy	0.36	0.44	0.37	0.06
Left–right proximity	0.39	0.32	0.39	0.34
Proximity on European unification	0.08	0.11	0.08	0.06
Party size	4.29	3.74	4.36	0.23
Former communist state			0.03†	0.00†
Party size for former communist state			−0.60	−0.02
Left–right proximity for former communist state			−0.05	−0.02
Less perceptual agreement			0.00†	−0.00†
L–R proximity where less perceptual agreement			−0.43	−0.04
Adjusted R²	0.339	0.244	0.313	
Weighted N	11,247	5,209	16,436	

Note: All coefficients except those marked † are significant at 0.01.
Source: European Election Study 2004.

the differences between these two groups of countries are slight and largely not statistically significant when considering the importance of factors that generate preferences for parties. Voters in both kinds of countries evidently use very much the same considerations when evaluating parties as potential recipients of their votes. Our findings strongly support the notion expressed earlier in the phrase 'voters are voters wherever we find them'. The only significant differences we see are 'things about countries' not 'things about people' and are readily explained from lack of opportunities in consolidating democracies (due to the flux in their party systems) for acquiring a common understanding of the political world.

These findings provide a fitting conclusion to this chapter since they reinforce the lesson that voters respond to the political environments in which they find themselves, but that otherwise much the same forces are at work in all elections. One important factor that helps voters make sense of their political environment is their experience with that environment. And one important difference between political systems is the extent to which the political environments found in different countries do encourage and make possible a lifetime of learning experience for voters. The findings for consolidating democracies in this chapter reinforce our diagnosis of the difference between the sophistication of voters in parliamentary democracies and the US. In the latter country it is also hard for voters to learn their way around the political system – not because it is new but because it is constantly changing, with new protagonists contesting for high office at virtually every presidential election (cf. Grönlund and Milner 2006).

An interesting implication is that the way in which new and consolidating democracies differ from established democracies is essentially the same as the way in which new and recently adult voters differ from established voters. A new democracy is different in the same way that new voters are different, which makes sense because in a new democracy all voters are 'new'. Only after the passage of 60 years will a new democracy gain a full complement of voters, with every different degree of experience found in established democracies, but even then the early political experiences of the oldest voters may well have lacked coherence (if the early party system lacked coherence) compared with older voters in democracies that have been established for an even greater length of time. Confirmation of these conjectures must wait on future research.

Chapter 8

Assessing Electoral Democracy

Apart from their consequences for policy and selection of personnel, elections affect the relationship of citizens to their political system. In Powell's (2000) words they are 'instruments of democracy'. To what extent can we judge how well they fulfil this role? And, to the extent that we can do so, how do various systems perform in relation to each other?

A primary aspect of this question is whether elections lead to the formation of governments that are more acceptable and, on average, better suited to the preferences of citizens in some countries than in others. In this chapter we will consider this and other aspects of electoral democracy in terms of how well different types of political systems perform. This requires yardsticks on the basis of which judgements can be made. A primary yardstick suggested in past research is the extent to which the policy preferences of citizens are matched by the policies produced by democratic governments.

Representing citizens' preferences

In a democracy political decisions are supposed ultimately to reflect the wishes of a country's citizens. If this is the case, then government policies should to some extent reflect popular sentiments. How responsive are governments to what voters want? This question motivates much research and theorizing about the electoral process. In our discussion we will refer particularly to Powell's *Elections as Instruments of Democracy* (2000), which puts this question at its heart, and to Stimson's *Public Opinion in America: Moods, Cycles and Swings* (1999) and some of the work that has been inspired by it.

In *Public Opinion in America* Stimson tried to depict the opportunity structure of American electoral politics in terms of a mood cycle that swings backwards and forwards between liberalism and conservatism over the course of many years. As discussed at the end of Chapter 6 (and illustrated in Figure 6.5), when the mood is liberal, democrats tend to win elections. When the mood is conservative, Republicans tend to win – all other things being equal.[1] The idea of a liberal–conservative public mood frames American electoral politics in a predominantly one-dimensional issue space analogous to the left–right issue space of European politics, and provides evidence that public opinion moves over time in a cyclical fashion within this issue space. Stimson did not investigate the sources of changing mood, but he ascribed it to political leadership. We have already noted the work of one of Stimson's successors (Wlezien 1995) who established that at least one reason for the cycle in public mood is a countervailing cycle in public policy: Republican governments tend to satisfy the demand for conservative policies while Democratic governments tend to satisfy the demand for liberal policies, causing the mood that brought them to office to change as its demands are met. We saw that much the same mechanism could be seen at work in British politics. This creates something of a paradox, as politicians appear to be 'punished' for fulfilling their campaign promises, quite in contrast to what is generally expected. However, the fact that voters react to the policies that governments produce does not mean that nothing else is involved in changes in public mood. Certainly, political leaders play a role in generating a demand for their policies in the first place. We already saw how, in Britain in the 1970s, Margaret Thatcher played an important role in creating a demand for her policies – a demand that she then proceeded to satisfy. Similar processes occur in other countries.

Stimson's work uniquely addressed politics in the US, but his perspective inspired others to address electoral politics more widely. However, most of this work focuses on the dynamics of representation within specific countries. Powell's work, by contrast, is explicitly comparative. *Elections as Instruments of Democracy*, like *Public Opinion in America*, saw electoral politics as framed in an issue space, but its concern was not so much to demonstrate movement by voters within this issue space as to investigate the extent to which governments give to voters the policies that they want, which is one of the central themes in the study of representative democracy. How well voters' desires are satisfied by government outputs is sometimes referred to as 'output representation' or 'policy representation' (cf. Wessels and Schmitt 2008).

This concern with whether governments actually provide what voters want can be addressed by measuring both the locations of governments and the locations of voters on a variety of issues. The underlying idea is that parties may try to win elections by taking up positions that represent what (most) voters want. Obviously, no government can provide policies that will satisfy all voters alike and those whose desires are not reflected in government policy will be dissatisfied. But, if voters are clustered around the center of the issue space, then providing policies that satisfy the median voter will minimize the total amount of dissatisfaction and, moreover, will satisfy the democratic requirement of majority rule. The possibility of parties and governments to devise policies that will satisfy the median voter is enhanced by the fact that in most countries issues are customarily structured along relatively few dimensions which represent more general, ideological distinctions. Usually, one of these dimensions is of overwhelming importance, because democratic politics generates a dynamic towards unidimensionality – a dynamic in which second and higher dimensions add interesting detail but without distracting from the overriding structuring importance of the first dimension (Schattschneider 1960). This is quite fortunate, as theorists have shown that, in a multidimensional issue space, there is no unambiguous best strategy for parties in terms of positioning themselves to win elections – in other words, no particular incentive for office-seeking parties to produce policies that satisfy voters' desires. Moreover, the usually overriding importance of the first dimension in structuring issues makes it possible to investigate output representation in terms of the relationship between government and voter locations on this dimension, avoiding the need to take account of a multitude of separate issues.

Voters' positions on ideological dimensions can be measured using survey questions about left–right positions, from which the position of the median voter can be determined. Parties' positions can be measured in a variety of ways (see Marks *et al.* 2007). Powell used experts to place parties on the same scale as used for voters. From this information an average location can be calculated for a legislature as a whole, as well as for segments of the legislature, such as the parties that constitute or support a government and those outside the government who nevertheless hold policy-making power by chairing a legislative committee or controlling an 'upper' house of the legislature (where that exists).

Taken together, all this information allows a researcher to chart simultaneously the positions of voters, of the parties they vote for, of the governments that ensue, and even of policy-makers that are not members of the government, in order to find out how well these actors represents voters' desires. Figure 8.1 is the result (generated from the data presented in Powell's book). The horizontal axis gives the position of the median voter in each country; the vertical axis gives the position of the median policy-maker and the median member of a governing party or coalition. Country names represent the government in each country (i.e. the position of the median member of the party or parties supporting the government). Triangles located with each country name, or linked by a line to a country name, give the position of the median policy-maker in the same country (including members of governing parties and those who informally support those parties, as well as any members of the opposition who might hold policy-making positions in certain countries). Lines linking governments and policy-makers only occur where the two are not the same. This happens with countries where power is dispersed according to the proportional vision as described in Chapter 3; for these countries (the US and certain proportional representation (PR) countries – see Figure 3.2) the name of the country is located at a distance from the triangular country marker in the diagram. In countries with concen-

Figure 8.1   *Adequacy of representation by policy-makers and governments, early 1980s*

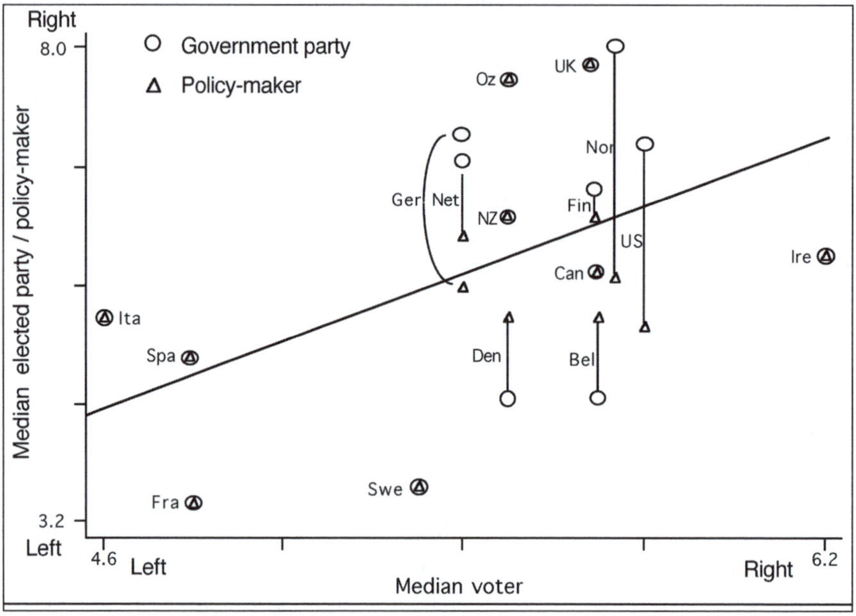

Source: Constructed from Powell (2000: Figures 7.1 and 9.1).

trated power the triangles and country names are together, because the government contains all the policy-makers.

The line drawn across the graph (which would be a 45 degree line if both axes were drawn to the same scale) shows where both policy-makers and governments would fall if they were perfectly representing the locations of the median voter – the position where governments or policy-makers would have the same left–right location as the median voter (4.6 on the horizontal axis corresponding to 4.6 on the vertical axis, and so on). In practice we see that policy-makers are generally more representative than governments (triangles are generally closer to the line than are their corresponding country names). In proportional vision countries, where it makes sense to distinguish between governments and policy-makers, it is evident that governments do not reflect the median voter as closely as does the wider group of policy-makers.

The implication of what is portrayed in Figure 8.1 – supported by a variety of additional analyses – is that there are distinct differences in policy representation between majoritarian and proportional vision countries. The left–right distance between policy-makers and voters is systematically smaller in proportional vision countries than in majoritarian ones. Similarly, legislatures (not displayed as such in Figure 8.1) are systematically closer to the median voter in proportional vision countries. Powell argued that, since proportional vision countries are the ones where the government is likely to encompass the median legislator and a larger segment of the legislature is involved in policy-making than only government parties, these countries will on average do better in providing policies that cater to the median voter, and thus are as close as possible (which might not be very close) to the wishes of the entire electorate.

This finding is based on a notion of policy representation defined in terms of proximity of the position of the policy-makers to the median voter, as mentioned earlier. This view of representation is widespread in the literature. It holds that policy representation is best when governments (or, more generally, policy-makers) are located close to the median voter. This point of departure is so ingrained in the extant literature on policy representation – and we have used it ourselves at times – that it merits some critical attention, as it is not without problems.

In the first place, who is this median voter that governments are applauded for resembling? Evidently the median voter is a statistical abstraction, like the average family. And just as the average family may include some fraction of a child, who could not be alive in the real world, so the median voter may well have characteristics that are not found empirically. Whether the median voter is a useful abstraction depends, moreover, on the shape of the distribution of voter preferences. If that distribution happens to be bimodal, with a concentration on each side of the midpoint but no one at the midpoint, then the 'median' voter would not resemble anyone at all and it would be doubtful that policy at such a midpoint would be considered better from a democratic perspective than any other policy. Admittedly, most established countries do yield a voter distribution between left and right that appears to be reasonably unimodal. We would expect a bimodal distribution only in countries that are so polarized as to risk civil conflict (see Box 4.1 regarding Northern Ireland). However, other voter distributions that are empirically more plausible – highly skewed ones, for example – would also render the median voter less useful as an abstraction than is usually assumed.[2]

Another problem with the dominant definition of what constitutes a responsive government is that it disregards the intensity of voters' policy preferences. Policies that are not 'ideal' may still be quite acceptable and how large a discrepancy between ideal and actual policies that voters can tolerate depends to a large extent on (and is inversely related to) how passionately those preferences are held. The presence of a minority passionate about its preferences, along with a majority that is not very committed to its own, would undermine the idea that the median voter's preferences were optimal. In such situations the majority might very well acquiesce in government policy that did not reflect the preferences of the median voter but which was biased towards the preferences of the passionate minority and such policies should not necessarily be regarded as unresponsive or unrepresentative of voters' desires.

We have referred to an alternative to Downsean proximity theory, namely directional theory (see pp. 168–70). That theory proposes that issues should be seen as dichotomies, and that the 'position' of voters and of parties on a scale such as the left–right scale is actually a measure of strength of commitment. As a consequence, voters choose not on the basis of which party is 'nearest' to them (a notion which has no relevance if policy dimensions are actually dichotomous) but rather on the basis of which party is on the same side of the ideological or issue divide as they are themselves. Moreover, if voters care about what is at stake in this dimension, then they would rather vote for a party that is strongly committed to its issue stance than for one that is less committed. To the extent that this theory is correct, the median voter position has no particular relevance as a criterion for adequate representation. Much theorizing about policy representation thus begs the question of *how* voters evaluate parties, governments and actual policies – a question that is still a matter of debate among political scientists. Our own critique of the directional theory (see p. 170) leads us to continue to make the Downsean assumptions that have characterized most of this book, but those who take the alternative view would likely reject the methodology that enabled Powell to provide such unequivocal evidence in support of the proportional vision.

Another problem with much of the kind of research that is exemplified by Powell is that it is not about policy-making at all. The locations of governments and policy-makers are determined by the perceptions of expert witnesses. It is far from certain that those experts arrived at their perceptions by assessing the policies actually produced rather than by considering all kinds of other things such as manifestos, policy intentions and more or less established stereotypes. And even if those manifestos and intentions were to be useful proxies for policy intentions, they still leave open the extent to which such intentions are converted into actual policies – a question that relates to the effectiveness of governments at producing policies (including policies that the median voter might have liked) and also to the time lag between formulating policy intentions and the conversion of these intentions into actual outputs.[3]

One of the purported strengths of the majoritarian vision is that it is supposed to produce 'governments that can govern': effective governments that readily implement their policy intentions and deal with new contingencies without the delays and difficulties engendered by coalition bargaining. Coalition governments might conceivably score worse in this regard because the need for bargains to be struck might impede their ability to actually legislate the policies they apparently stand for. On the other hand, if we focus not on decision-making by governments but on the actual implementation of policy decisions in real life, effective implementation usually requires support by (or at least the acquiescence of) a larger group than only those who voted for a government. We might expect that systems operating under the proportional vision would be particularly good at cementing a broad base of acceptance, which is necessary if government decision-making is to be implemented effectively. This ties in with the question of whether policies are reversed by successive governments. Countries in which decisions are made by narrow majorities (or by minorities boosted into majority status by the workings of a majoritarian electoral system) are liable to see new governments undoing many of the policies introduced by the previous government (Dur and Swank 1997), as famously occurred in Britain in 1951 and again in 1970, when new Conservative governments undid policies that had recently been introduced by the outgoing Labour Party. This type of policy reversal is also common in the US, at least in regard to regulations that are within a president's prerogatives to change. It is obvious that such policy reversals are a most inefficient use of government resources and greatly detract from the long-term effectiveness of a political system in terms of policy representation.

A quite different concern when considering what kind of systems are best in achieving policy representation is the breadth of representation that is achieved. Who do we think should be represented: all voters, or just those who voted for the parties that acquired government power? A central precept of the majoritarian vision is 'to the victors belong the spoils'. But who are the victors and can the voters who supported the parties that won an election be counted amongst them? Do majoritarian systems indeed have the advantage ascribed to them by their proponents, namely that they represent the wishes of those who supported the winning parties? It is not certain at all whether they actually manage to do this. Figure 8.1 and Powell's other findings suggest that majoritarian governments more often take extremist positions than do coalition governments, but whether these positions adequately represent the preferences of their own supporters (i.e. the median of those who voted for the winning party) remains open and in need of being addressed empirically. It is not impossible that majoritarian systems would be found to perform quite well in this respect (but this would not address the criticisms of those who point out that in these systems the supporters of the winning parties can constitute a rather small proportion of the electorate, opening the way for dissatisfaction with democracy, especially if the government proves hard to unseat).

But despite all these methodological quibbles, we should stress that there are many indications – from Powell's analyses, as well as from the work by Lijphart and others – that the proportional vision produces better policy representation, more responsive government and, in Lijphart's words, 'kinder and gentler' societies – even if proof for such a general statement is not fully conclusive, partly for the reasons noted above.

Do elections matter?

We can hardly avoid addressing this question in the final chapter of a book about elections and voters, even though few people imagine that elections do not matter. On this score we have merely corroborated conventional wisdom. Yes, elections matter. Most importantly, governments are often replaced as a result of elections. Even if the same government is returned to office, the policies of that government are often changed as a result of election outcomes. The wishes of voters – particularly in terms of what they do *not* want – are brought to bear on the behavior of political elites because of election outcomes. Governments proceeding in unpopular directions are reined in or replaced as a consequence of election outcomes. And the anticipation of possible future outcomes has multiple ramifications by way of making politicians more solicitous of, and responsive to changes in, public opinion, knowing that otherwise they risk being voted out of office. Of course, notable exceptions exist and it would be folly to suggest that a direct line of command exists between voters on the one hand and policy making on the other. Voters and electorates do not always have clear 'wishes' and, even when they do, those wishes are not always discernible in election results. And sometimes politicians, parties and governments feel justified in blatantly ignoring such wishes. But still, the general pattern is that we see political elites reacting to voters –sometimes by way of anticipation.

We find such responsiveness to public opinion even in policy-making situations where elections are not effective in producing changes in government personnel to match the policy preferences of voters. European Parliament elections do not determine who holds executive power. Yet there are strong indications that, even so, policy-making in the EU responds to changes in public opinion (Arnold and Franklin 2006; Thomassen 2009). But the EU contains other mechanisms for bringing changes in public opinion to bear on EU policy-makers – not least elections in member countries that result in changes in the complexion and policies of the governments that constitute the European Council and Council of Ministers, the supreme governing bodies of the EU. It is by no means clear that without any electoral connection in member countries any such policy responsiveness would be evident.

Those who decry elections generally do so for one or other of two sets of reasons. In the first place, sceptics point out that most of the things that call for policy responses are events and developments beyond the control of individual states and hence beyond the control of individual sets of policy-makers. Of course, this is true. But how well or badly policy-makers respond to external events and developments is certainly something that voters can and do react to, with political elites responding to voter reactions. The second reason for scepticism relates to the effectiveness of the electoral process in bringing about precisely the consequences listed earlier: policy change, policy responsiveness and government accountability. Yet in this book we should have made it abundantly clear that such scepticism is often unwarranted. We have seen that, while it would be hard to overstate the ignorance of voters, it is easy to understate the sophistication of electoral behavior. Voting is a collective activity that brings the magic of aggregation to bear in producing a verdict that does not (as often supposed) reflect the lowest common denominator of individual competence but rather something more like the highest common multiple. Unlike the behavior of crowds, which appear often to manifest the worst of human folly, the behavior of electorates appears to manifest, if not exactly the best of human wisdom, certainly wisdom of a far higher order than would be expected from indi-vidual voters taken separately. There are major deficiencies in the electoral process, particularly as regards issues of low salience, which simply play no part in determining election outcomes. Moreover, the role of political leaders and the media in determining which issues are salient and which are not is far too great. Even more worrying is the ability of leaders, at least occasion-ally, to fabricate complete deceptions that mislead not only electorates but also legislatures and the media (for example, the steps that were apparently taken by the Bush administration in the US to legitimate an attack on Iraq in 2003). Although such manifest untruths are – in liberal democracies – gener-ally uncovered in due course, this can easily take too long to prevent adverse policy consequences. These types of deficiencies arise not so much from defi-ciencies in the capacities of voters as from deficiencies in the institutional and quasi-institutional arrangements that structure the information that voters need. These often make it easier than it should be for politicians to obfuscate their responsibilities for responding to events and even (as in the case of the Iraq war) sometimes to actually generate false information that voters then base their decisions on.

Nevertheless, while it is clear that much that happens in the realm of policy-making is beyond the reach of elections to control, we would contend that the Iraq example actually demonstrates the importance of popular control in a democracy. If public opinion did not matter and voters had no power to control the policies of the executive, the Bush administration would not have needed to create such an elaborate apparent deception in order to go to war against Iraq. It is also true that elections as such are not enough to fulfil the promise of representative democracy. The details of what we have learned in this respect deserve to be summarized.

What we have learned

Above all we have learned that understanding elections is not just about understanding voters. We cannot just look at voters alone, but have to take account of parties and politicians. We cannot look at them alone either. Politics is a multi-actor game in which the actors have different purposes, motivations and goals. Their behavior is guided by anticipation or reaction, or both, and is aimed at making other actors do something that they would not otherwise have done. The electoral process must thus be understood in terms of a system of interconnected elements, rather than in terms of any of these elements in isolation.

Common questions such as 'Why did Al Gore lose the US Presidential election of November 2000?' (or similar questions for other times and other political systems) cannot be answered by looking only at what Gore did or failed to do. We have also to look at what his opponent – George W. Bush – did or failed to do and at the background against which their competition played out, such as the state of international affairs, the state of the economy and the nature of the electoral system which allowed the winner of the popular voter to be the loser in the Electoral College (see Box 1.1). So addressing the question by just asking what the Democrats did wrong underplays the fact that they are not the only ones in the game. The US election of 2000 was not just a game of Democrats against nature and neither is any other election in the US or anywhere else. So the questions of the kind 'Why did Gore lose?' are misspecified questions.

Another thing we have to bear in mind is that not all candidates want the same thing. Politicians want power, of course, but there are different sorts of power. In particular there is not only executive and legislative power but also agenda power. A candidate for US President, such as Ralph Nader (who ran on behalf of minor parties in all US presidential elections since 1996), did not suppose for one moment that he would be elected President, but by running as a third party candidate he hoped to get a different sort of power – the power to put the issues he cared about on the public agenda. In many political systems there are parties running on principle rather than in any serious attempt to gain political power. In other words, we cannot assume that all politicians – or, for that matter, all voters – are motivated by the same factors. Ignoring such differences will obstruct our understanding of the interactions between the various actors.

But elections are not just about politicians. They are also about voters, parties, party systems, electoral systems and political institutions more broadly. We began this book by talking about the institutional setting in which elections are held, then moved down to the electoral systems that provide the rules of the electoral game, and finally to voters and parties which constitute the actual protagonists. What we found is that both voters and parties are strongly influenced by the nature of the electoral and institutional settings in which they find themselves. Change the setting and one changes the behavior of both voters and parties in often fundamental ways (as we saw most dramatically in our analysis of what happened in Israel when they changed to a directly elected Prime Minister – see pp. 108–9). But people's behavior changes not because of any change in the people themselves. One of the most important findings of recent research is, in the words used in an earlier chapter, 'voters are voters wherever we find them'. Differences between one country and the next lie primarily in the constraints and incentives that govern voters' actions. Voters' responsiveness to changes in the institutional setting in which they find themselves is surprisingly strong and rapid. Change the menu of choices on offer or the rules of the electoral system and we see immediate and marked changes in voter behavior – at least on the part of those who have not become locked down into habitual patterns of behavior.

The responsiveness of voters to the setting in which they find themselves provides opportunities for what is sometimes called 'electoral engineering' (Sartori 1997) or 'institutional engineering' (Norris 2004). We can think of the Israeli political establishment as performing the role of institutional engineers when they introduced direct elections for the Prime Minister and New Zealand governments as institutional engineers when they introduced a mixed member proportional (MMP) electoral system. Such attempts at institutional engineering may have the effects anticipated by the engineers (as in New Zealand) or not (as in Israel). But the fact that institutional engineering can have such far-reaching consequences raises the important question whether political scientists should be more forthcoming with advice for re-engineering the political systems of the world to improve their performance. It is hard to persuade politicians to change the systems under which they were elected, but the fact that changes are hard to achieve does not absolve us from the duty to suggest changes that we think would be beneficial. For that it is necessary to evaluate systematically the quality of electoral processes in different countries.

The quality of electoral processes

The contribution of electoral processes to democracy can be evaluated in a variety of ways. The criteria we consider important have generally been extensively discussed, in various different contexts, in previous chapters. Here we recapitulate those discussions with a focus on the criteria we think important as ways to evaluate the performance of electoral democracy taken as a whole.

Above all, elections should be meaningful: they should be about matters that affect the lives of citizens. This implies on the one hand that the choices on offer should encompass the major political concerns of the population and provide as wide a choice as possible; on the other hand it implies that the consequences of the choices made in an election should be as unequivocal as possible. In the process, electoral arrangements should foster political community, regime support and the mitigation of social conflict. These overall objectives have a number of subsidiary components, some of which are interrelated. In no very strict order of importance we can mention the following.

Adequate representation

Elections should provide for adequate representation. How much weight should be given to social representation (see p. 15) depends on the heterogeneity of the society in question, especially with respect to socially embedded inequalities of power and resources. In general, majoritarian systems are worse at representing a variety of social divisions and social interests than proportional systems are, especially when the various groups and interests are not strongly concentrated geographically. However, in a homogeneous society, majoritarian systems will do quite well at social representation.

More generally, elections should provide voters a relevant menu of options, which relates to the number of viable parties on offer and their diversity. Obviously, majoritarian systems score worse than proportional ones in this respect and, to the extent that the competition between the two dominant parties in a majoritarian system leads both of these to converge towards the median voter, may offer no more than a choice between Tweedledum and Tweedledee, which might be fine for voters at the center of the political spectrum, but utterly disappointing for those with less centrist views. Comparative studies amongst European countries find that a small effective number of parties leads to a large group of voters who find none of the options on offer attractive (van der Eijk and Oppenhuis 1991).

Policy representation – the extent to which elections will provide policies that voters want – is generally the focal point of discussions about adequacy of representation. Recall from our earlier discussion in this chapter the difference between systems operating according to the majoritarian or proportional visions of democracy. Proportional designs do better on average in terms of producing policy proposals that represent the median voter and thus, usually, large segments of the electorate. As parties in government tend to implement the policies that they promised in their manifestos, this representation extends to actual policy outputs (Klingemann *et al.* 1994). It must be stressed, however, that the empirical evidence about the responsiveness of policy to voters' concerns is not unambiguous. A recent analysis (Hobolt and Klemmensen 2008) distinguishes between responsiveness in terms of announced policy intentions and in terms of actual policy implementation. It establishes – not surprisingly – that intentions are not necessarily carried out in practice and that this gap between promise and performance is not the same across countries. As a consequence, the results of evaluations of the responsiveness of different types of system are strongly dependent on what one focuses on.

Accountability

A second desirable feature of electoral processes is that they yield accountability, which has at least two components. One is that electoral processes encourage policy-makers to account for their actions between elections – for there to be clarity about who did what. The other aspect of accountability is that electoral processes should allow voters to hold politicians to account in terms of rewarding or punishing them (generally by removing them from office or not) for their performance since the last election. Particularly desirable would be electoral arrangements that provide governments with mandates to govern in a certain fashion – mandates which supply a benchmark against which to hold them accountable for their exercise of power. Voters hand over power to politicians not as a blank check but in order to get certain things done. Although new problems certainly arise in the course of a term of office that are not covered by a mandate, still the presence of any kind of mandate should constrain the power of those holding elective office. Fulfilling a mandate is, of course, no guarantee of being rewarded at the next election (as Wlezien's thermostat model makes clear – see pp. 172–4), but incumbent parties that fail to live up to their campaign promises should be punished electorally. Majoritarian systems tend to be better at this. Only 20 per cent of proportional design systems provide clear accountability through mandates, as contrasted with 80 per cent of majoritarian design systems (Powell 2000: 87; and see pp. 207–8).

Still, it is worth noting that the countries that do worst in terms of policy representation are precisely those that do best in terms of accountability. In countries with poor accountability systems it is generally difficult for voters to know who should be credited or blamed for policies. Repeated failure to punish poor policy performance may lead to the feeling that elections are not a relevant way to 'throw the rascals out' (but only a mechanism to replace them by another set of rascals), which would erode support for the whole political system, as happened in Italy towards the end of the Cold War and possibly still pertains today.

Legitimacy

The third common standard of evaluation of electoral processes is their contribution towards providing legitimacy for the exercise of power. There are yet again two aspects to this. One is that the claim to wielding power should not be contested. Countries in which protesters take to the streets, and/or law suits are regularly brought that contest the outcomes of elections, are not countries that perform well on this criterion. The second is that legitimacy would lead policy outputs to be accepted and respected, thus avoiding policy reversals. In established democracies legitimacy in these terms is pretty much taken for granted as a by-product of having a functioning democracy. But if we broaden the field to include all systems that hold elections, legitimacy cannot so easily be taken for granted. Nevertheless, even amongst functioning democracies it cannot be assumed that all electoral arrangements are equally good at imparting legitimacy to authorities and policies. There are numerous indications that systems operating under list PR and other proportional arrangements perform better than first past the post (FPTP) systems in this respect, were it only because governments in those systems have a larger electoral base.

Equity and openness

Yet another aspect from which electoral processes can be evaluated is the extent to which electoral competition between parties and candidates is fair, unbiased and open to new entrants. The unbiased and fair aspects are often taken for granted in established democracies, although they perhaps should not be (the American presidential election of November 2000 produced particularly troubling charges of fraud, intimidation and selective disenfranchisement; British elections in recent years have seen more fraud with postal voting than many had thought possible, and so on). As far as openness to newcomers is concerned, there are large differences even among established democracies. The so-called 'costs of entry' are very high in majoritarian systems, leading to a smaller number of effective parties in such systems. Costs of entry are much lower in proportional systems, especially if they have low electoral thresholds. The debilitating effects of high costs of entry are particularly great if they occur in systems with strong party discipline where party leaders work hard to keep new issues (that might provide a challenge to party discipline) from making it onto the political agenda. These two features go together particularly in Westminster-style political systems, where new issues can rather easily be suppressed, making these systems potentially unresponsive to newly emerging policy concerns of the electorate.

Government effectiveness

Another important consideration is whether electoral arrangements promote effective government. Here too there are a number of more specific considerations. One element is (i) anticipatory responsiveness to new issues and concerns, which is more likely when there is a threat of new entrants into the competition for votes, as just mentioned. But the fact that the US does particularly well in terms of this type of representation (see also Soroka and Wlezien 2009) emphasizes that anticipatory responsiveness can be brought about in other ways. Further elements are (ii) the smoothness of transfer of power after an election; (iii) the extent to which existing arrangements avoid gridlock and stalemate; (iv) the extent to which they promote effective implementation of decisions by executive and legislature; and (v) the extent to which they prevent policy reversals by successive governments. All of these concerns relate to government efficiency. Governments are not efficient when matters requiring urgent decision can be kept from the agenda or lead to gridlock or can be blocked at the implementation stage or are reversed as soon as a different government takes office. In systems with any or all of these deficiencies, time is wasted, decisions are delayed or vitiated, and good government is impeded. We have said that Westminster-style majoritarian systems are particularly subject to lack of responsiveness, because of the ease with which new issues can be effectively avoided in such systems. But proportional design systems can also suffer from lack of responsiveness if there is not sufficient agreement about how to deal with particular problems as to permit a coalition government to take those problems on board. Arguably the American system is the one least subject to inbuilt pathologies that can limit its openness to new issues, since in that system interest groups and individuals find it relatively easy to bring a problem before Congress and have it discussed. Whether the issue will be effectively dealt with is, of course, another matter since the American system has sources of gridlock beyond any seen in parliamentary systems, but at least it is relatively easy to confront parties and politicians with issues (new as well as existing ones).

Communications between citizens and elites

Finally, representative democracy requires intelligible, interpretable and unambiguous communication between elites and citizens, requiring shared frames of reference. Moreover, it also implies that electoral arrangements should promote a learning process among voters that leads them to acquire adequate knowledge and understanding of the workings of their political system and of the choices on offer. Here the media clearly play a crucial role. Since two-party systems are those in which parties have an interest in contesting the center ground, which requires parties and candidates to play down their differences, it would seem that elections in proportional design systems should have an edge – on average – in their ability to promote intelligible, interpretable and unambiguous communication between elites and citizens (Granberg and Holmberg 1988). Moreover, the party discipline that is necessary for the functioning of parliamentary systems facilitates voters' learning their way around their political system by ensuring that all those speaking on behalf of the party do so with one voice, in contrast to candidate-centered systems that do not require party discipline. In addition, we have pointed out that there are political systems in which opposition parties and candidates (i.e. those not in government) lack spokespersons who are seen to represent legitimately 'the opposition'. Such spokespersons, because of their status, enjoy 'natural' access to the media. Among established democracies, the US most conspicuously fails to provide such clear figureheads for the opposition, while it also fails to subject the chief government policy-maker to rigorous questioning by other party leaders. Presidents are only questioned by the press, not by political opponents (except for stylized 'debates' held every four years during the run-up to presidential elections).

These six criteria (along with their several component subcriteria) provide a broad basis for evaluating different electoral arrangements.

Evaluating the institutional arrangements for electoral democracy

How well do different kinds of political systems do in terms of the quality of electoral democracy? How would we assess different systems in terms of their performance? Such assessments involve the aspects in which PR, for example, performs better or worse than an FPTP system. We do suspect, however, that neither PR nor FPTP systems always perform equally well or poorly, but that this is dependent on what other systemic arrangements are in place. We therefore also distinguish between dispersed and concentrated power, along the lines discussed in Chapter 3 and illustrated in Table 3.2, effectively distinguishing between 'packages' of institutional arrangements as they occur in particular established democracies. This leads to Table 8.1 in which four types of political system are listed across the columns (the same four as were distinguished in Table 3.2) and in which the rows are allocated to the various criteria for evaluating the quality of electoral democracy that we set out above. In this table evaluations are made very broadly by scoring each type of system either with a '+' if it is evaluated positively, a '–' if it is evaluated negatively, or a zero if neither of those evaluations applies.

Most of the scores given to particular criteria arise from assessments contained in this and previous chapters and will not surprise our readers. Some may agree with these evaluations, some may disagree, but the arguments have generally been made and can be evaluated on their merits. A few of the evaluations relate to criteria that have only been dealt with in passing, if at all, and these do deserve some explication.

Legitimacy of the outcomes of elections is evaluated negatively in the US because only in that country, amongst established democracies, is it at all

Table 8.1   *Assessing the strengths (+) and weaknesses (−) of different constitutional designs for the quality of electoral processes*

Evaluation criterion	Proportional systems with concentrated power (e.g. Sweden, Ireland)	Proportional systems with dispersed power (e.g. Germany, Switzerland)	Majoritarian systems with concentrated power (e.g. Britain, France)	Majoritarian systems with dispersed power (US)
Input (social) representation	+	+	−	+
Output (policy) representation	+	+	−	+
Clarity of accountability	0	−	+	−
Ease of obfuscation	0	0	0	−
Legitimacy of outcomes	+	+	+	0
Fairness of outcomes	+	+	0	0
Costs of entry for new parties	+	+	−	−
Smoothness of power transfers	0	0	+	−
Openness to new issues	0	0	−	+
Susceptibility to gridlock	0	0	+	−
Adequacy of implementation	+	+	+	+
Susceptibility to policy reversals	+	+	−	0
Learning/ communication	+	0	+	−

common to find defeated contestants engaging in litigation because of alleged irregularities in procedures and counts – of course there are multiple examples of non-legitimate outcomes in democracies that are not well established (such as Georgia or the Ukraine), or in non-democracies where elections are staged in attempts to gain legitimacy (such as Zimbabwe, Algeria, etc). The most famous US case was Bush vs Gore, which was decided in 2000 by the US Supreme Court in favor of George Bush who therefore became the 43rd President of the US (see Box 1.1). But that legal contest was only the most visible of a large number of legal challenges to declared election outcomes which are, indeed, so frequent in the US as to seldom get much publicity. In other established democracies legal challenges to election outcomes are rare.

Adequacy of implementation has not been discussed at all in this book. All regime types were given a positive score because all established democracies have effective civil services. *Susceptibility to policy reversals* has only been briefly touched on. Here we distinguish FPTP regimes from those in other countries. In most of the proportional systems there is a convention that policies enacted by one government should not be reversed by the next but should be allowed to remain in force to be evaluated in the light of performance. In the US and in Westminster-type parliamentary systems there is no such convention. Instead the notion that 'to the victors belong the spoils' is taken as a licence for a new executive to feel no compunction in overturning policies of a previous administration, to the extent to which this is in its power (although in the US legislation, by consensus, this is not easily overruled). The generally more inclusive nature of proportional government – particularly in the case of coalitions – makes policy reversal uncommon there, except in those few instances where the issue was an explicit topic of contention on which parties fought their campaigns.

The US also gets a negative score for *ease of obfuscation*, because that system contains no person with the stature or opportunity to challenge routinely administration claims, as already explained. No constitutional design gets a good score on this item, however. We are particularly concerned at the way in which national politicians in the EU take advantage of the fact that the EU itself has no person of stature to challenge exaggerated claims and outright deception by national politicians. These often take advantage of the secrecy surrounding EU decision-making to obfuscate their own complicity in EU decisions. Such decisions are, after all, the outcome of negotiations in which all member countries have a role, but one would never guess this by listening to some politicians blaming 'Brussels' for unpopular policies – which sometimes have nothing to do with Brussels at all (van der Eijk and Franklin 1996: ch. 21). The so-called 'democratic deficit' in the EU is in this respect very real and could have dire spill-over consequences for the quality of democracy in member countries – but this is a problem relating to EU institutions, not national ones.

We have written elsewhere of the deficiencies of EU institutional arrangements (van der Eijk and Franklin 1996), which far outweigh the deficiencies of US institutional arrangements from an electoral perspective. But in this book we are concerned with national institutions and Table 8.1 only scores those institutions. If the deficiencies of EU institutions were allowed to count against the institutions of its member countries, Table 8.1 would look very different. More importantly, allowing the deficiencies of EU institutions to count against the scores we have given to the institutions of EU member countries would obscure our assessment by suggesting that US style institutions might be the solution to Europe's problems. Our objective is to allow different institutional types, each seen in its best light, to show their relative strengths and weaknesses.

As can be seen, the system types are ranked from left to right in terms of the number of plusses versus minuses in each column, with concentrated power proportional systems (list PR, MMP or single transferable vote (STV)) scoring best (eight plusses and no minuses), and the US scoring worst (four plusses and six minuses). Though PR systems with concentrated power do best (cf. Gerring and Thacker (2008), the differences between proportional systems are not great and all of them do better than majoritarian systems. Moreover, among majoritarian systems there is as large a difference between parliamentary systems and the US as there is between parliamentary systems of the proportional and majoritarian varieties. The US scores better than parliamentary systems in terms of openness to new issues and of input and output representation and no worse than other systems in terms of adequacy of policy implementation. In every other respect, however, the US system is rated as bad as or worse than other systems.[4] Its deficiencies bring to mind another criterion used by some to rate political systems but not included in Table 8.1: voter turnout. Franklin (2004) has argued that voter turnout is so low in the US mainly because of the lack of competitiveness of American elections; but that lack of competitiveness is intimately connected with many of the deficiencies in electoral arrangements highlighted in Table 8.1. We referred in Chapter 3 to Bingham Powell's insight that the trade-off in the design of political systems arises from the incompatibility of the two great visions of what democracy should be like – the proportional and majoritarian visions. It is hard or impossible to design a system that would provide for clarity of accountability and also for policy-making that closely adheres to the desires of the majority of the electorate, but the US constitution essentially provides neither of these benefits, thus giving to its citizens the worst of both worlds, a vision neither strictly majoritarian nor strictly proportional, which we have described as a majoritarian system with dispersed powers.

We are not the first to give to the US a poor score related to criteria such as these. One of the grand old men of American political science, Robert Dahl, describes the American system of government as neither majoritarian nor consensual but as 'a hybrid that possesses the vices of both and the virtues of neither' (Dahl 2002: 149). However, we should again mention recent research (Soroka and Wlezien 2009) that gives the US a good score for anticipatory representation – policy change that tracks public preferences in anticipation of possible electoral repercussions – in comparison with Britain (and also with Canada). This is a type of representation that classic critiques of the US system (by Lijphart or Powell or Dahl, for example) do not take into account. In contrast, our assessment of US electoral politics does take this advantage of the US system into account. Arguably, however, this type of representation should not be counted as an aspect of electoral democracy at all. Indeed, it can be asked (as we will ask in the next section) whether the US, like Switzerland, cannot be regarded as a perfectly well-functioning democracy – but not as an electoral democracy.

We have not given consideration in this book to two other parliamentary systems with arguably dispersed powers (Canada and Australia) which have single-party governments but federal power arrangements – systems that Britain has become much more akin to in recent years, with the establishment (or re-establishment) of devolved parliaments and administrations in Scotland, Wales and Northern Ireland. It may be the case that such systems perform worse than does a majoritarian system with concentrated power because of the tendency of dispersed power to reduce clarity of accountability. Indeed, it is possible that they perform even worse in some ways than the US dispersed power system, if the nature of the devolved powers is such as to make it difficult for voters to determine whether responsibility for specific policy areas rests with the central or regional governments (Soroka and Wlezien 2009).

What role for electoral democracy?

This is a book about elections and voters. As such it has focused on electoral democracy, and in this chapter we have rated countries according to how well they perform as electoral democracies. The US performs relatively poorly on these criteria. It might be argued, however, that these criteria are perhaps not the appropriate ones to apply to the US when assessing its democratic credentials. In this, the US might be rather like Switzerland. These might both be seen as well-functioning democracies, but with their democratic credentials coming from something other than the contribution of the electoral process to their systems of government.

The easier case to make in these terms is the case for Switzerland. In that country the government takes the form of a cartel of parties that share power between them in the same proportions election after election without reference to election outcomes (except that, in 2003, the proportions were marginally adapted to give additional weight to one of the parties). The institution of this cartel effectively cut the link between elections and their outcomes, as argued at length in Franklin (2004: 92–7) accounting for the dramatic decline in turnout that followed this institutional change becoming effective (see pp. 191-3). In many ways the Swiss magic formula can be seen in the same light as the direct election of the Israeli Prime Minister (see pp. 108–9) – an experiment whose results demonstrate something that would have been hard to do in any other way. In the Swiss case, the experiment shows the need for elections to have policy consequences if they are to be

taken seriously by voters. The effect of the sudden removal of policy consequences from Swiss elections reinforces what we thought we knew about
elections to the European Parliament –elections that have never had any
evident policy consequences – and also sheds light on the low turnout seen
in US elections.

In brief, if voters see no point in voting (as evidenced by low turnout) this
seems to be because they see no evident connection between their votes and
policy consequences. Policy consequences are absent in Switzerland because
the complexion of the government is not changed by elections there and are
largely absent in the US because even a government with a new complexion
cannot necessarily get new policies enacted. Recent declining turnout in
Britain may perhaps one day be explained on the same basis. Because
repeated loss of electoral support by first Conservative and then Labour
governments was unable to unseat these governments, this might have given
the strong impression to voters that elections are not effective there.

However, the fact that elections perform poorly as instruments of democracy does not mean that democracy itself is not functional. There are more
components to democratic governance than elections. In Switzerland, citizens are involved in democratic processes in a manner unparalleled
anywhere else, being called upon to vote in referendums to propose or ratify
particular policies virtually on a monthly basis. Turnout in these referendums is often far higher than in Swiss Parliamentary elections. Evidently
Switzerland has a functioning democracy, but elections appear not to play a
large role in this. Rather, even though the parties recruit and provide career
paths for politicians virtually without reference to voters, still, when it comes
to policy, these politicians require the advice and consent of the citizenry at
large, making this country more of a direct democracy and less of an electoral democracy.

What of the US? There elections, even if their policy consequences are
muted to say the least, do at least function as mechanisms for selecting the
individuals who run the machinery of government. Moreover, elections there
provide the incentives that lead these individuals to try to anticipate the
wishes of the electorate by adjusting policy during the period between elections in the light of evidence (perhaps from opinion polls, but perhaps also
from their extensive connections) regarding public preferences. This anticipatory responsiveness to policy preferences does not amount to direct
democracy of the kind seen in Switzerland. Nevertheless, it is a very positive
aspect of the American system of government and has been taken into
account when scoring the US for output representation in Table 8.1.

Some would also regard as positive the fact that when the American
government does manage to put together a bipartisan majority in support of
some new policy, the majority concerned is generally a large one (Mayhew
2005), suggesting the achievement of an extensive consensus in support of

the measure concerned. Clearly, this is the sort of political system that the writers of the American Constitution had in mind and the forging of consensus policies is not in itself undemocratic. What is undemocratic about the American system is the corresponding ability of minorities to obstruct the desires of a majority. So the US does not pass the test that Switzerland passes of having a democratic process that involves in a formal way the majority of its citizenry and that enables that citizenry to pass into law legislation that a majority of them support. The US is an anomaly among democratic countries in placing a high premium on consensus government (remembering the distinction we have repeatedly made between consensus government and inclusive government – often misleadingly referred to as 'consensual', see p. 83). This stands in the way of the democratic notion of majority rule, and the consequences (for example the long delay in securing health care for all American citizens) are generally seen as unfortunate (cf. Dahl 2002).

Possibilities for reform

In the columns of Table 8.1, one set of institutional arrangements stands out in terms of its disadvantages – the FPTP electoral system with all of its concomitants. And one country stands out as having deficiencies in its electoral arrangements that are even worse than in other FPTP countries – the US.

The US, it is true, because it does not have disciplined parties, does not suffer in the same way as do other FPTP countries from lack of articulation of new issues. In this respect it scores better than other FPTP countries. To get an issue on the agenda in the US requires the availability of politically relevant resources (money in particular), which is necessary for exactly the same reason: the absence of disciplined parties and the generally limited role of policy orientations in the electoral process. These are problems in their own right, because policy-oriented elections, as we have already pointed out, give voters much more power to influence the direction of public policy than candidate-centered elections do. Candidate-centered elections are also expensive elections (Scarrow 2006) as each candidate has only limited opportunities to piggyback his or her own campaign on a national political campaign organized by the party leadership. The fact that media time has to be purchased by candidates, rather than being supplied free by television stations as a condition of their licence to broadcast, also contributes to the problem, of course, but the main reason why money plays such an important role is that policies generally do not – at least not explicitly. Policy-oriented elections in the US would be cheaper because, instead of having to get their message heard from scratch at each presidential election, candidates could build on the familiarity with their party's program engendered by previous election campaigns. This also would ensure a politically more sophisticated electorate, better educated in both abstract ideologies as well as in the issues of the day (cf. Granberg and Holmberg 1988).

A number of political reforms have the potential to improve party discipline and policy orientation in the US, but none would serve the American electorate better than the introduction of PR in elections for the House of Representatives. This is because many of the ills that plague the US system at the present time would be alleviated or removed by PR of the parties in the House of Representatives. We can consider these ameliorations by going through Table 8.1 row by row.

Starting at the top, 'social representation' would be improved if minor parties no longer found it so very difficult to gain representation. PR would have to be instituted state by state (in the absence of a constitutional amendment) and would make no difference for states with less than three seats in Congress. But indirectly the reform might even affect small states because the presence of small party representation in larger states would reduce the disincentive for supporting such parties even in small states.

Moving down the table, 'policy representation' would also be improved because of increased responsiveness of Congress to changes in popular sentiments. The separation of powers would still stand in the way of the sort of link between electoral change and policy change that is to be expected in parliamentary systems, but PR elections call for coordinated party messages and thus a mechanism to ensure that each party speaks with a single voice. 'Clarity of accountability', 'legitimacy' and 'fairness' would probably not be improved enough to warrant a change of score on any of these three items, but 'ease of obfuscation' would be reduced to the extent that the number of party leaders with an interest in challenging administration assertions – and their responsibility as party leaders for doing so in order to keep their party's message before the voters – were increased. 'Costs of entry' for new parties would be hugely reduced, for obvious reasons. This would be particularly so in the larger states, but should also have overflow effects into smaller ones, as was the case for social and policy representation – and for the same reasons.

The remaining cells of Table 8.1 would mainly be unaffected by a change to PR; however 'learning/communication' would be improved – though not to the levels found in some other systems. Finally, PR elections would improve the prospects for 'legitimacy of outcomes' free of legal challenges were it only because, in the absence of the 'winner takes all' character of election outcomes, there are fewer contestants who have an incentive to go to court. PR elections would also increase the likelihood of policy-oriented elections for all the reasons spelt out at various places in this book, which would take away from individual candidates the expensive need to get their own messages before voters. It is true that elections to the US Senate could not be reformed in the same way, but Senatorial elections are not as subject to incumbency advantage as House elections and historically there has been more frequent change of party control in the Senate than in the House of Representatives. So elections to the House are the major problem in this regard and these are the elections that this reform would address.

In summary, the introduction of some form of PR in elections to the US House of Representatives would address a number of problems that afflict the extent to which elections can be seen as an instrument of democracy there. The idea is not at odds with the constitution nor with what seems to have been the logic of the American Founding Fathers who might have bequeathed the US a proportional electoral system had such a system been known to them. Unfortunately, PR was not invented until the late 19th century, so the Founding Fathers had no opportunity to propose it. But we have pointed out that the American system of government is in other respects very much a proportional vision country.

The main reason for making this suggestion is not in the expectation that the suggested changes will be brought into being, but rather to illustrate how one aspect of the institutional framework can have multiple repercussions. Moreover, the list of changes that would result from our suggestion also make it clear that there are different routes to achieving any given assessment of the performance of electoral democracy. With these reforms the democratic credentials of the US system would be on a par with (or perhaps even exceed) the British, but mostly for different reasons. Even if unlikely, this reform should be seriously considered. Major reforms in the American system have been made before and can be made again. This is a reform that could unite the proponents of term limits and non-partisan redistricting with those who want to reduce campaign finance abuses and those who feel that minor parties do not get an adequate chance in the system as it stands.

Other majoritarian systems are less in need of reform, but the adoption of PR would benefit them also. All of the other FPTP countries tend to suffer from issue sclerosis, as new issues are kept from coming onto the political agenda by politicians who find it easier to stifle issues that threaten to split their parties than to provide adequate leadership (see p. 160). Moreover, particularly in Britain, we see increasing popular dismay with a system that provides a substantial overall majority in the Lower House for a party that acquired (in 2005) only just over one third of the vote – amounting to approximately 20 per cent of the adult population when taking a relatively low level of turnout into account – while at the same time failing to provide remotely adequate parliamentary representation for parties that between them received almost a quarter of the votes (see Box 2.1 and also our discussion at pp. 69–71). But such reforms are not hard and have already occurred in countries (Italy, Japan and New Zealand) where existing electoral systems were producing the most unfortunate consequences.

Britain, home of the Mother of Parliaments, has been flirting for some years with proportional elections, adopting them for the Welsh, Scottish and Northern Irish assemblies and for elections to the European Parliament. It is not far-fetched to suppose that in due course they may be introduced for general elections to the British Parliament as well. A good time to introduce such a reform would be in anticipation of an election that the incumbent party fears that it might lose. At present the British employ four different electoral systems – only two in England and Northern Ireland but all four in Scotland: MMP in Scottish Parliament elections, FPTP in British Parliament elections, list PR in European Parliament elections and STV in local elections in Scotland and Northern Ireland. Whereas some of these systems might be preferable to the FPTP system (see Table 8.1), instituting several of them at once completely vitiates any cumulative learning that elections might otherwise stimulate among voters and which is a requirement for voting sensibly, as we have discussed at several points in this book. To bring about sensible electoral representation in Scotland drastic simplification is needed, which would be easier politically in conjunction with nationwide reform to produce the same system everywhere.

Turning to countries that already adhere to the proportional vision, the fact that they score higher in our assessments than majoritarian countries does not mean that all is well there. Improvements are still possible in these countries on a piecemeal basis and one of the reforms that is often discussed is moving from pure PR to an MMP system. However, we also hear occasional proposals that PR countries adopt aspects of the FPTP system, which we would regard as quite unfortunate.

One lesson of this book should be that proposals for reform cannot be evaluated only by looking at the problems that the proposal purports to ameliorate, but requires attention to likely effects on other aspects of electoral democracy that might not be so favorable. In particular, the lack of clarity of accountability in proportional vision countries occasionally gives rise to proposals for reforms that would adopt elements of the Westminster system – especially FPTP elections, as reported in Box 8.1. This example from the Netherlands illustrates how proponents of reform often fail to appreciate the self-correcting features of proportional vision countries. These countries are especially vulnerable to obfuscation by politicians who – wittingly or unwittingly – contribute to the lack of clarity of accountability that we have described as being endemic to such countries. The threat of a loss of clear policy options and clear responsibility is a persistent weak point in coalition systems. Yet PR (without an artificially high threshold) also provides new political entrepreneurs with realistic opportunities to blow the whistle on such obfuscation. The resulting cycle of obfuscation leading to a shake-up may at times appear problematic, yet these spasmodic episodes do not so much call for reform as represent a self-correcting mechanism at

Box 8.1   Electoral shake-ups in the Netherlands

In the Netherlands a new party – D66 – was founded in the 1960s that advocated a variety of institutional reforms intended to improve accountability and give rise to more decisive election outcomes in terms of government formation. Some of its proposals included changing to a district-based FPTP system and instituting a directly elected prime minister. This party's critique of the obfuscation of political responsibility that characterized Dutch politics in the 1960s was well justified, but its preferred remedies would, in our view, have done more harm than good. The score sheet in Table 8.1 suggests that an FPTP system falls short on more criteria than a PR system does and our analysis of the short-lived Israeli experiment with direct elections of the Prime Minister (see pp. 108–9) shows the damage that such a reform can inflict on the entire electoral process. But the appearance of D66 in the Dutch political arena in an (as of then) unrivalled electoral landslide did demonstrate the openness of the Dutch system to new contestants and to new issues. The resulting shake-up forced established parties to pay attention and inaugurated a period of much greater political clarity. Much the same thing happened again in the 1990s, with increasing obfuscation by major parties leading eventually to an electoral revolt in 2002, instigated by the firebrand Pim Fortuyn, which again shook things up and forced the major parties to define themselves in more distinct terms.

work. The larger danger is that a mistaken desire for reform would lead to the institution of a less responsive system.

Still, there are proportional vision countries with more clarity of accountability than the Netherlands. If would-be-reformers were to look to such countries for ideas, rather than to majoritarian systems, it is quite likely that improvements could be made that would reduce the need for spasmodic self-correction.

We should end by saying that, although we see clear avenues for reform available in several countries, it does not seem likely that one of them will be the US – at least not any time soon. American elections would no doubt perform better with PR, but it is very hard to see how sufficient political leverage can be brought to bear to accomplish such a reform. Still, by setting out the advantages we hope to shift the odds just a little. Reform in majoritarian systems has already begun with major changes in New Zealand and more tentative steps in Britain. It does not seem far fetched to imagine these leading in due course to a full-fledged reform of the electoral system in Britain and perhaps in Canada and Australia as well. Reform in PR systems should focus on relatively minor adjustments that are consistent with the proportional vision and designed to increase clarity of accountability in countries that employ PR electoral systems.

A work in progress

In this book we have set out to describe the nature of electoral democracy in terms of the interconnections between its central institutional arrangements and the behavior of its central actors – its parties, voters and media. Our theme has been that neither elections nor the behavior of parties and voters can be considered in isolation, either from each other or from the institutional and quasi-institutional arrangements found in the political systems in which these elections occur. Many of the most important influences on voter behavior derive from these institutional arrangements, which means (among other things) that they remain invisible when studying elections country by country. To understand electoral democracy requires a comparative perspective, since only from such a perspective can we identify and evaluate the import of influences that are largely constant within any single country. A comparative perspective has allowed us, in this chapter, to assess the functioning of democracy in particular types of political systems (and thus – explicitly or implicitly – in particular countries).

We said in an earlier chapter that electoral democracy is a work in progress. Our assessment of the current state of play in regard to the performance of electoral democracy is also a report card on the progress being made. As we have seen, the verdict must be that there is scope for improvement.

Appendix

Use of Statistical Analysis

At several places in this book we have presented results from statistical analyses or referred to such results presented elsewhere in the literature. Electoral studies are by their very nature empirically oriented and it is almost impossible to understand the literature in this field without some familiarity with statistical analysis of empirical data. In fact, parts of this literature are among the most advanced in the social sciences in terms of application of statistical methods. It is therefore recommended that endeavors in electoral research beyond this book be complemented by adequate training in social-science research methods and the application of statistics in data analysis. As far as this book is concerned, this appendix intends to provide some assistance in reading and interpreting the sections of the book that rely most heavily on statistical analyses.

Background: analysis of empirical data

Much empirical research in the study of elections and voters involves large numbers of observations. The study of voter behavior, for example, is often based on surveys where hundreds or even thousands of people are interviewed. Comparative studies of political parties – for example across the 27 countries of the European Union – deal with more than a hundred parties at any single moment in time. Analyses of media content and campaign communications customarily involve thousands of news items, press releases, etc. In all such instances it is impossible to analyse exhaustively the available information with the naked eye, let alone to arrive at convincing conclusions in that way. For such conclusions, statistical analysis is required.

Empirical information (usually referred to as 'data') relates to *units* or *cases*; these may be voters, candidates, parties, governments, newspapers, or whatever. More particularly, the information relates to specific traits of all those cases, which are referred to as *variables* (sometimes also as 'measures'). Variables relating to voters include, for example, whether or not they turn out to vote, their age, and the strength of their partisanship. For parties, variables might include whether or not a party is a member of the government, its size, and its ideological orientation. In general, researchers try to get information about their cases for as many variables as possible and the number of variables can easily run into hundreds. Finally, at the level of each particular case, empirical information relates to the *values* of that case on each of the variables in question, sometimes also referred to as 'scores', categories or measurements.

The analysis of empirical information usually starts with summaries (across the cases) of the values of the available variables. Such summaries might include a mean, or a median, and some measures of the extent of variation: how much the observed cases differ from each other in terms of each variable. In subsequent stages of analysis, questions of *correlation* between one variable and another are addressed: the extent to which particular values of a variable tend to occur in conjunction with particular values of other variables. For example: 'To what extent do young people differ from older ones in terms of whether or not they turn out to vote?' can also be expressed as the relationship between the variables 'age' and 'electoral participation'. Such relationships can sometimes be shown by means of a cross-tabulation, sometimes by a graph, sometimes by a coefficient, depending on the character of the variables involved (e.g. how many values or categories the variables have). Finally, in order to distinguish between the many substantive interpretations that such correlations allow, empirical studies often involve 'multivariate analysis' in which the values of cases of three or more variables are investigated simultaneously; regression analysis is a particularly popular form of multivariate analysis.

Uncertainty

All empirical research – irrespective of whether or not one conducts statistical analysis – is confronted by uncertainty and, as we will see, statistical tools are particularly useful in making explicit how large this uncertainty is. Uncertainty arises from two factors in particular: noise and sampling.

The term 'noise' or 'error' is used to convey the notion that any particular score of a unit on any variable will in general deviate from what we are really interested in: the 'true' value or 'true' score. The difference is called 'error', which results from not only such mundane things as human mistakes during the collection and recording of data, but also the unavoidable limitations of whatever measures we use. One can think of, for example, a survey question about one's preference for a political party, to be expressed on a scale from 1 to 10. If a respondent's true score would be 7.5, this cannot be reflected on the scale in question, thus yielding error. These differences between the observed values and the unknown true values (also known as 'unreliability') do not matter very much if we are interested in many cases and if these differences are random – meaning equally often positive as negative and, in general, without any particular pattern. If we are interested in the mean of a variable and we have many cases, these errors will average out to a very large extent, so that the observed mean will be very close to the true mean. The same holds for other kinds of analysis, such as correlational and multivariate analysis. Yet, one of the consequences of error is that we cannot expect 'perfect' relationships between variables to be found in our data. Even if there were to be a perfect relationship between the true values of variables, then error would preclude this from being reflected in our data.

'Sampling' refers to the procedure by which we select cases in a study. In many instances it is impossible (and not cost effective) to try and include all possible cases. When millions of people are eligible to vote in a particular country, it is often sufficient if our information about them derives from a relatively small group: the sample. Particularly interesting are *random* samples where every unit in the target population has a given probability to be selected ('to be drawn', as in a lottery). In such instances, the cases selected are not dependent on the whim of the researcher or on the fact that they tend to exhibit certain characteristics. Provided the sample is truly random, it can be used to arrive at conclusions about the target population. That sample is, of course, not the same as the population. It is only a (randomly drawn) limited number of cases and every other sample that we could draw with the same procedure would look slightly different. The variations between different but similarly drawn samples is known as 'sampling variance' or 'sampling error'. But, if the sample is randomly drawn, then statistical tools can inform us about the uncertainty involved in any generalization from sample to population. This allows us to decide whether or not the findings in the sample will hold 'beyond reasonable doubt' in the population in which we are really interested.

Significance

The 'doubt' referred to above is in statistical terms often expressed as a 'confidence interval', or as a 'probability' of finding a particular pattern of data by mere chance, or as 'significance'. These three ways of expressing uncertainty can be seen as different views on the same phenomenon, so we will discuss here only the concept of significance.

Any property that we can calculate from the data in our sample (for example a mean, a correlation, a regression coefficient – such properties are generically known as 'parameters') has an equivalent (its true value) in the population. As stated above, the parameters from each sample will differ a bit from the true ones, because the sample is only a (randomly drawn) subset from the population. With any particular sample it is possible that we have had random 'bad luck', which would mean that the sample parameters deviate quite a bit from the population parameters; on the other hand they might not differ much. We cannot know which is the case as that would require us to already know the population parameters, so there would have been no need to do the research in the first place. But statistical tools can tell us what the probability is of finding a particular parameter value in the sample, supposing that the true value in the population has a specific value. Particularly in the case of correlation and regression coefficients, we often want to know whether the population parameter value is different from zero (if it was zero there would be no correlation between two variables, no effect of one variable on another). So we calculate the probability of finding by mere chance (i.e. sampling variation) the observed sample parameter value, supposing that the true value is zero. If that probability is large, we would be in doubt as to whether the sample parameter reflects anything real (we cannot plausibly reject the possibility of the true value being zero). But if that probability is very small, then the sample finding is very unlikely to have been generated by mere chance and we would conclude that the sample parameter – beyond reasonable doubt – indicates a population parameter different from zero. The sample parameter is then said to be 'significant' (or, in full, significantly different from zero). What would constitute 'reasonable doubt' is up to the analyst to specify. Customarily it is seen as a probability larger than 0.05 (sometimes as larger than 0.01) of being mistaken when asserting that the true value is non-zero.

Significance thus expresses the probability that mere chance (sampling variance) generates the difference between a specific parameter value in the population (usually, but not necessarily zero) and the value of that parameter in the sample. In this context it should be noted that:

- The larger this difference, the smaller the probability that it is generated by mere chance (in other words: it is quite possible that a sample will deviate somewhat from the population, but unlikely that it will be totally different).
- The larger the sample, the smaller the probability that a given difference will have been generated by mere chance. This implies that, when testing for significance against a population parameter value of zero, a small sample parameter (but not zero) may be significant with a large sample, but not with a small one. What this means in practical terms is that large samples are needed in order to establish the significance of coefficients that are little different from zero.

Regression

One of the most common methods of statistical analysis in electoral research is regression analysis. Regression is a form of multivariate analysis in which one variable is viewed as the *dependent variable*, and all others function as *independent variables*. The aim of the analysis is to establish in what way the independent variables (interpreted as causes) affect the dependent variable (the consequence). In its most straightforward form, the method assumes that all the variables are quantitative, that the dependent variable is continuous, and that the effects of each of the independent variables can be combined by adding them up. (Specific forms of regression analysis exist to handle dependent variables that are not continuous, such as logistic analysis for dependent variables that are dichotomous. The logic of the procedure remains the same, however.) The dependent variable is customarily referred to as Y, the independent variables as X (if there are several independents, these are X_1, X_2, X_3, etc.).

The model can be written as follows:

$$Y = a + b_1 X_1 + b_2 X_2 + b_3 X_3 + \dots + e.$$

The variables in this equation are Y, X_1, X_2, X_3 (and any possible further X variables) and e, which is what is termed the 'residual'. Each case has a value on each of these variables. For Y and the Xs these values are observed (they are part of the data); the value of e for each case is not observed, but calculated. The elements a, b_1, b_2, b_3 (and for each subsequent X an additional b) are regression parameters (often also referred to as regression coefficients). On the basis of these coefficients, a value of Y can be predicted for each case. The difference between this predicted Y and the actual Y for each case is a residual. The parameters are calculated in such a way as to ensure that the values of the residuals over all cases are as small as possible.

The regression model states that for all cases, their individual value on the dependent variable (Y) can be seen as composed of summed contributions of each of the independent variables (the Xs, which values are multiplied by the respective b-coefficients), plus a constant (the 'a'), and finally of a residual (calculated as explained above) which ensures that both sides of the equal sign are in balance.

The importance of the independent variables (the Xs, seen as causes of Y) can be gauged in different ways. One way is by inspecting the b-coefficients, which can be interpreted as effects of X on Y. All other things being equal, a larger b implies that the X in question is more consequential in terms of the dependent variable (Y). It is said to have a larger *effect* on Y. But, as always, all other things are often not equal. The b for a particular X tells us how much Y changes when that X changes by one point on the scale (e.g. from 1 to 2, or from 4 to 5). But how much of a difference in X corresponds to a one point difference in Y depends on the scales that are used to measure these two variables (for example, one might be measured in years and the other in dollars or pounds) and these scales often differ not only between an

X and the Y but also between different Xs. The more categories that are distinguished for an X (the more refined is its scale in terms of gradations) the smaller the b generally will be. As a consequence, if different Xs are measured on different scales then their respective bs cannot be directly compared.

A second way to assess the importance of independent variables is by assessing to what extent they account for differences between cases in terms of the dependent variable –their explanatory power. The bs tell us how much is the average difference in Y for cases that are one unit apart on X, but they do not tell us how often such differences in scores on X occur in the data. If differences in X are infrequent, such differences will explain fewer of the differences (less of the variance) in Y than if there are frequent changes in X over the cases in the data. Stated differently, for any given effect size (b), the importance of an independent variable as an explanation of differences in the dependent variable varies with the distribution (and in particular the variance) of X. The contribution of each independent variable to the overall explanatory power of a regression is expressed in the standardized regression coefficients – the betas. Betas can, in general, not be compared between different samples, as the distributions of the variables involved will rarely be the same between those samples.

Collectively, the explanatory power of the entire set of Xs can be gauged by the size of the residuals. Each residual represents the portion of Y that cannot be accounted for by the independent variables (the Xs). If all the residuals are small, then the independent variables were able to 'explain' the scores of the cases on the Y quite well. How large the residuals are is commonly expressed in the so-called coefficient of determination, R^2, also often referred to as the (proportion of) explained variance.

When inspecting the results of a regression analysis (such as in Tables 7.3 and 7.4) there are thus a number of aspects to focus on:

- The magnitude of the b-coefficients (the effect sizes), and of the beta-coefficients (their explanatory power).
- The sign of the coefficients, which tells us whether higher scores on an X-variable correspond to higher scores on the Y-variable (in which case the coefficient is positive), or higher scores on an X-variable correspond to lower scores on the Y-variable (in which case the coefficient is negative).
- Whether or not the coefficients are significantly different from zero (as explained earlier). If they are not, we cannot dismiss the possibility that they are merely the product of chance, rather than of any real effects in the world beyond our data.
- The degree to which the variation in Y-scores between the cases is accounted for ('explained') by the differences in the X-scores, which is reflected in the R^2. For a variety of reasons we can usually not expect R^2

to be 1 (which would imply a perfect explanation of Y in terms of the Xs). We may lack information on some independent variables that matter (so called 'omitted' variables) and our data will contain a certain amount of noise, which in itself cannot be explained. The realistic maximum for R^2 depends on particular characteristics of the variables that we use but, in the case of the kind of voter surveys customarily used in electoral research, a realistic maximum value for R^2 seems to be around 0.5.

In addition, it should be noted that the comparison of b-coefficients assumes that all independent variables were measured on the same scale. If they were not, then one can use standardized regression coefficients (betas) instead, which express all variables (Y and the Xs) in normalized form, without changing in any way the logic of the model. But because we cannot compare betas between different subsets of the data (or between different samples) we often need to use both bs and betas in conjunction. This was the case with the regression analyses reported in Tables 7.3 and 7.4 in this book.

Factor analysis

In Chapter 6 we reported results from a multivariate analysis method known as factor analysis. In this method there is no distinction between dependent and independent variables. The question is not whether some variable(s) can be explained by other variables, but rather to what extent the scores on all the variables can be seen as reflecting a smaller number of underlying and unobserved ('latent') variables. The analysis is usually based on correlations between all the observed variables and yields, first, an indication of the number of underlying variables that would be required to account for the observed scores and their correlations. Subsequently, the method shows how each of the observed variables is related to these underlying variables (which are referred to as 'factors'), which helps in interpreting the substantive nature of the factors and permits the variables to be located in the 'factor space' and plotted on a chart in terms of these locations, as was done in Figures 6.1 and 6.2.

Similarly, correlations between the factors and any other variable, not included in the factor analysis, can be used to 'place' additional variables in the factor space in order to visualize their positions relative to variables that were included in the analysis. This was done with party variables in Figure 6.2 in order to place parties in the issue space on the basis of their correlations with the two factors that defined that space.

Notes

Chapter 2

1. The effective number of parties, N, is defined as $1/(\sum s_i^2)$, where s_i is the proportion of votes (or seats) of party i.
2. We picture the two houses of Congress separately because they are of roughly equal political importance and often find themselves in conflict, reducing the policy consequences of elections in the United States – an important theme in this book. Figures 2.1 and 2.2 are, of course, simplifications of more complex realities –omitting for example the role of the Senate in the confirmation of members of the Cabinet in the US – but they capture all the relations that are relevant for our argument.
3. Our descriptions are stylized versions of procedures that vary in detail from country to country. Sometimes there is no provision for early elections to be called; sometimes a change of the party composition of the government is expected to be legitimated by early elections. In some countries a government has to resign after a vote of no confidence, but elsewhere this only happens after a 'constructive' no-confidence vote (which implies that a new government has to be appointed before the old one resigns). The powers of the Prime Minister also vary by country, as are the methods by which 'upper houses' or 'senates' are elected, and so on.
4. This peculiarity is not inherent of a presidential system per se, but a reflection of the kind of bureaucracy that has evolved in different countries. Because governments can change at short notice, parliamentary systems require an apolitical bureaucracy that loyally follows the wishes of whatever government is in office (irrespective of its political color), whereas in the US the norm is for a politicized bureaucracy to show loyalty to the government that appointed it.
5. Unfortunately, the propensity-to-vote questions were not asked in Belgium, Luxembourg or Sweden in 2004.
6. Statistically astute readers may be aware of multinomial and conditional logit regression as methods for analysing party choice in multiparty contexts. Those methods actually use preferences as their dependent variable and thus seem to be compatible with the logic of our argument. Their problem is, however, that those preferences have not been observed empirically. Instead, they are estimated from observed party choices. This procedure is fraught with difficulties in ways that are only now becoming apparent to researchers (see van der Eijk et al. 2006 for a detailed exposition). In brief, preferences can be translated into choices quite easily, but choices cannot readily be translated into preferences, even in well-specified models that control for all relevant influences on choice, as Table 2.3 makes clear. This is why, in this book, we focus on analyses that employ voter preferences that have been observed empirically by means of questionnaires that explicitly ask

people how likely it is that they would ever vote for each of the parties in their party system.

Chapter 3

1. In many systems voters can override the ordering in which candidates on a list are elected by casting a so-called 'preference vote' for a particular candidate. How many preference votes are needed to change the order of the list varies between countries.
2. In Switzerland, it is true, interest groups play an important role in the referendum process, but these groups need to focus their attention on persuading voters to support or oppose a referendum issue, whereas in the US the voters as such play no part in this stage of the proceedings.
3. The most important recent example occurred in Spain in 1981 when King Juan Carlos faced down an attempted coup by a small group from the Spanish armed forces. This is an excellent example of a monarch siding with democratic forces, but not as good an example of the exercise of political judgement in the face of a hung parliament (the usual reason for intervention by a head of state). Note that the reverse situation, of a monarch siding with a military dictatorship in Greece in 1967, resulted in the demise of that monarchy when democracy was restored in 1974. Monarchs in the modern world need to be democrats if they are to keep their crowns.

Chapter 4

1. Occasionally in some of these countries different elections are conducted on the same day, perhaps local and national elections or national and European elections. But then voters have just two choices to make, still a far cry from the normal American election.
2. An estimate derived from multiple regression analysis – a technique that will be described further in Chapter 7 and in the Appendix.
3. There is considerable controversy in the literature on voting behavior over the extent to which cleavage politics actually declined during this period. Political scientists, being in need of an explanation for the rise of new parties and new issues in the 1970s and later, generally accept that the decline in cleavage politics removed a 'straightjacket' that would have stood in the way of such developments (Franklin *et al.* 1992). Sociologists, on the other hand, stress the continuing strength of group differences in electoral terms (Evans 1999). We believe that the controversy really turns on what is to count as a group-based party. Sociologists are happy to call a party's support group-based if the party gets its support from any group – even one that had previously supported a different party. Political scientists are more interested in continuity of group support (Franklin 2009).
4. We do not claim to be exhaustive, but we think that these six types of considerations cover most of what is suggested in the literature. All but one have been

touched upon in previous chapters. We will discuss candidate evaluations later in this chapter.

Chapter 5

1. Abramowitz *et al.* (2006) find no effect of redistricting on competitiveness, but our argument relates to long-standing party advantage in district geography, not the changes to that advantage that might or might not accrue as a result of repeated redistricting in response to population changes or court decisions.
2. Conventional wisdom in survey research is that the underrepresentation of non-voters in election surveys is caused by the tendency of respondents to misreport having voted when in fact they did not. This factor is, however, not always the prime cause of the underrepresentation of non-voters. It is also caused by the fact that those who do not vote are also very unlikely to find their way into national samples of the electorate (cf. Voogt and Saris 2003).

Chapter 6

1. The number of required dimensions is also a function of the degree of accuracy that the analyst desires: some are mainly interested in painting with a broad brush the general contours of the issue space (which requires few dimensions), others want to add a lot of detail (which requires more dimensions). Whether the issue space for a country *can* be depicted adequately using only one or two dimensions is an empirical question, as is our finding that issues take up much the same positions in charts made from surveys conducted at different points in time, but all extant research shows constraint of this kind in different countries.
2. Readers familiar with British politics may be surprised to see Margaret Thatcher located closer to the center in Figure 6.3 than her predecessor Edward Heath, because the latter is generally regarded as more centrist. This is partly because Mrs Thatcher proposed policies that were further from the center in a quite new direction (up instead of rightwards on the chart). It is also partly because of Mrs Thatcher's ability to dominate the political debate to such an extent that she effectively moved voters' issue preferences somewhat towards her own position. Mr Heath was – in his day – less effective in this respect, and hence was perceived as more distant from the center (see also our discussion on political leadership in Chapter 5, pp. 143–4). The analyses on which this figure is based were not calibrated to account for this phenomenon.
3. It has been argued (Grofman 1993) that a careful reading of Downs does not lead to the expectation of parties invariably seeking the center-ground.
4. Such complaints are more often justified when voiced by politicians elected to institutions that are generally overshadowed by the national political arena, such as regional assemblies or the European Parliament. Owing to the low visibility of those institutions, voters are generally uninformed about what parties and politicians do there and the second-order national elections for those institutions are

unable to provide an adequate electoral connection between voters and parties. This is a fundamental reason for what is sometimes referred to as the 'democratic deficit' afflicting such institutions (e.g. van der Eijk and Franklin 1996: ch. 21).

5. The anomalous 1972–76 period was dominated by the Watergate scandal and its aftermath. Arguably, during much of this period a distracted and then discredited Republican president (and his temporary successor) were not actually making public policy which was, rather, in the hands of the Democrat-controlled Congress.

6. Sometimes, however, the lag is longer than expected, so that the next government reaps the benefits of (or pays the cost for) the policies of an earlier one.

Chapter 7

1. Adding indirect effects to the direct ones reported in Table 7.3 increases the estimated effect of class by about half, and of religion by about two-thirds (cf. Oppenhuis 1995: 161), making the effects of religion comparable to those of issues or of government approval.

2. Indeed, if we take the effect of left–right proximity where there is less perceptual agreement at face value, it would appear that, in countries where there is no perceptual agreement, people are actually repelled by parties close to them in left–right terms: the amount by which effects of proximity need to be reduced in such countries appears greater (0.48) than the effect of proximity elsewhere (0.39). However, this appearance is misleading. No country scores zero on perceptual agreement, and all countries in the real world exhibit substantial positive effects of left–right proximity.

3. The data needed for the analyses presented in this section are not available for Lithuania, Malta, Belgium, Luxembourg or Sweden – for more details see van der Brug *et al.* 2008.

4. The magnitude of the reduction in left–right proximity where perceptual agreement is low suggests that there might be situations where this proximity plays no role at all in forming party preferences; but, in practice, there are no countries in such a situation (see footnote 2). The lesser effect of left–right proximity in some consolidating democracies is not different from what we see in established democracies, where the role of left–right proximity in preference formation is also much less in low agreement countries.

Chapter 8

1. In reality, all other things – the distribution of partisanship, which of the parties is the incumbent, etc. – are not equal. Such differences have to be controlled for by statistical methods and Stimson does this in order to bring out the importance of 'mood' for the support that parties receive.

2. Empirical distributions of voter positions – as derived from surveys – are unfortunately not fully conclusive. It has often been observed that respondents who are

actually unable to place themselves on a scale pick the mid-point. The center of the left–right scale thus contains a mixture of genuinely centrist voters along with an unknown number of voters who are unable to place themselves, and who cannot for that very reason be assumed to be 'centrists'. So it is possible that the real distribution of left–right self-placements is less unimodal than would appear at first sight. No systematic evidence is available on this point which is thus in urgent need of research.

3. The usual critique in the literature is that experts' assessments of professed party positions might be contaminated by their having observed the actual policies produced by these parties. From Powell's perspective, the greater this sort of contamination the better, since he assumes these ratings do measure actual policy rather than mere intentions.

4. In these scores, all elements have been weighted equally. One could disagree with the weighting of the various criteria. But it is highly unlikely that any reasoned deviation from the equal weighting that we applied will be able to bring the US presidential system to an equal level with parliamentary systems. It would also be hard to find an acceptable weighting scheme that would bring the Westminster system up to par with PR systems.

Further Reading

This book is, of course, only an introduction to an important and fascinating field of study. As a consequence, some important topics have not, or have hardly been, discussed. Moreover, even at an introductory level it is impossible to discuss in depth all matters to which the text refers. Hence this guide elaborates and extends the references inserted in the various chapters, suggestions which, for the same reasons, are not exhaustive but which should help the reader to find his or her way through the vast literature, should he or she wish to engage in further study.

The suggestions for further reading that follow are largely organized along the distinction between individual, party and system-level phenomena, which was also the basis for Figure 1.2. There we elaborated schematically our view of the ways in which topics are linked between these different levels of analysis. In addition to topics that are defined in terms of the levels of analysis, this guide also includes a header on 'elections' and a 'miscellaneous' category to accommodate topics that transcend these distinctions. Because many of the topics that we discussed are recurring themes – not confined to a single chapter – it follows that many of these suggestions are not related uniquely to separate chapters. Nevertheless, starting from the topics that are discussed in the various chapters, one can quickly find relevant suggestions for further study by navigating through the headings that are used to distinguish topics.

Potential voters

Theoretical approaches to study of voter behavior

Theoretical approaches to the study of voters and elections can be distinguished by the nature of their central explanatory concepts leading to the distinction between so-called sociological, social-psychological and economic approaches.

The *sociological* approach (originally also known as the Columbia model), emphasizing the importance of people's social position, is exemplified by *The People's Choice* (Lazarsfeld *et al.* 1944) and *Voting* (Berelson *et al.* 1954). More recent studies that emphasize sociological determinants of voter behavior include Evans (1999, 2000), Nieuwbeerta and De Graaf

(1999), Andersen and Heath (2002), Knutsen (2004, 2006) and Brooks *et al.* (2006).

The *social-psychological* approach (or the Michigan model) focuses on attitudes and party identification as central variables (see Chapters 4 and 7); its emblematic publications are *The American Voter* (Campbell *et al.* 1960), *Elections and the Political Order* (Campbell *et al.* 1966) and in the British context *Political Change in Britain* (Butler and Stokes 1969, 1974). The *European Journal of Political Research* (vol. 25, 1994) provides a comparative overview of the importance of the Michigan model in Europe in a special issue. Lewis-Beck *et al.* (2008) revisit the approach of The American Voter for later elections.

The *economic* approach – often also referred to as a rational choice approach – uses the market analogy to analyse elections with voters as consumers and parties as suppliers. This approach, which has become increasingly influential, started with Downs's *An Economic Theory of Democracy* (1957). In contrast to the sociological and social-psychological approaches, its relevance is not limited to the analysis of voter behavior, but extends also to the analysis of parties' competition for votes. Its original formulation emphasizes distances between voters and parties, a perspective that has been challenged by the directional theory (see Chapter 6), which also belongs to this 'economic' tradition. Since the 1980s there is an increasing tendency to combine elements of these approaches in models of voter behavior (cf. Merrill and Grofman 1999).

Social background, cleavages and group loyalties

Voters' social characteristics affect their electoral behavior by reflecting differences in politically relevant resources (gender, age, region and ethnic background) or because they reflect specific group interests (e.g. class, religion, ethnic background). Such distinctions are particularly important when politicized and organized in social cleavages (cf. Lipset and Rokkan 1967), and thus prominent in studies of contexts where cleavages are of great importance (cf. Lijphart 1968; Rose and Urwin 1969; Rose 1974). The electoral importance of cleavages declined sharply in most established democracies somewhere between the 1960s and 1980s (see Chapter 4), a process documented by, amongst others, Dalton *et al.* (1984), Crewe and Denver (1985), Franklin (1985a) and, particularly, Franklin *et al.* (1992) who also offer, in their final chapter, a theoretical explanation for the observed declines in cleavage voting. Social characteristics also lie at the heart of sociological models of voter behavior in the US (Lazarsfeld *et al.* 1944; Berelson *et al.* 1954; Alford 1967). See also Evans (1999, 2000), Nieuwbeerta and De Graaf (1999), Andersen and Heath (2002), Knutsen (2004, 2006) and Brooks *et al.* (2006).

Party identification

The concept of party identification (see Chapters 2, 4 and 7) is the corner-stone of the so-called Michigan model of electoral research (Campbell *et al.* 1954). It acquires its central place in the seminal volume by Campbell *et al.* (1960; cf. Campbell *et al.* 1966). In later years the concept was reconceptualized (cf. Fiorina 1981; Weisberg 1980) to address conflicting empirical findings. Its 1960s' use in European voter studies soon estab-lished that the concept does not travel well to multiparty contexts, see Budge *et al.* (1976) and Box 2.7. It has been repeatedly shown that meas-ures of party identification may lack conceptual validity and are sensitive to minor changes in question-wording; see, amongst others, Budge *et al.* (1976), van der Eijk and Niemöller (1983), Johnston (1992), Franklin (1992), Heath and Pierce (1992), Krosnick and Berent (1993), McAllister and Wattenberg (1995), Bartle (1999) and Blais *et al.* (2001). The prag-matic reconceptualization of party identification as a relatively stable loyalty to politically relevant entities (parties, reference groups, values and ideologies) has replaced earlier, somewhat dogmatic, discussions. See Kaufman (2002), Sanders (2003), Weisberg and Green (2003), Greene (2004), Goren (2005), Burden and Klofstad (2005), Berglund *et al.* (2005), Ikeda *et al.* (2005), Tilley (2006), Marsh (2006a), Grynaviski (2006) and Abramson (2008).

Ideology

The concept of ideology is commonly used to refer to a more or less coher-ent set of political ideals or values, sometimes conceptualized in terms of '-isms' such as liberalism, socialism, conservatism, fascism, communism. In electoral studies, however, it has been found that political ideals and values can often be summarized adequately in one dimension, which is commonly labelled 'liberal–conservative' in the US and 'left–right' in Europe. The importance of ideological dimensions for party choice is demonstrated in many studies, including Klingemann and Inglehart (1976), van der Eijk and Niemöller (1983), Middendorp (1989), Fuchs and Klingemann (1990), Shamir (1994), Inglehart and Abramson (1994), Knutsen (1995), Jacoby (1995), van der Eijk *et al.* (1996, 2005), Bartle (1998), Kim and Fording (1998), MacKuen *et al.* (2003) and Kroh (2003). In most of this literature the substantive meaning of these ideological dimensions is hardly addressed. Studies on the origins and meaning of citizens' ideological self-identifications include, Conover and Feldman (2004) and Freire (2006). A highly stimulat-ing framework for understanding how these meanings change over time is provided by Silverman (1985).

Short-term factors: issues, candidates and strategic and tactical considerations

Orientations towards specific *issues* are among the important short-term factors that can influence voters' choices. Much of the relevant literature focuses on their overall impact and the question of how to distinguish this from other factors. Interesting publications include Conover *et al.* (1982), Borre (2001), Evans and Andersen (2004), Steenbergen and Scott (2004), Aardal and van Wijnen (2005), Whiteley *et al.* (2005) and Kim *et al.* (2005). Economic conditions constitute a much researched short-term factor, with a number of important recent contributions, in particular a special issue of the journal *Electoral Studies* (vol. 19, no.2, 2000), Dorussen and Taylor (2002), van der Brug *et al.* (2007a) and Duch and Stevenson (2008).

Recent publications about the impact of *candidates* in candidate-centred elections include Ottati and Deiger (2002), McGraw *et al.* (2003), Steenbergen and Lodge (2003), Blais *et al.* (2003), Druckman (2003), Stroud *et al.* (2005), Hayes (2005) and Baumgartner and Morris (2006). For candidate effects in parliamentary democracies see Huddy and Capelos (2002), Anker (1998), Lavine and Gschwend (2006), Rosema (2006), Schoen (2005, 2007), Johns and Shephard (2007), Shephard and Johns (2008) and Marsh (2007).

Many authors devote considerable attention to untangling *strategic considerations* from other factors. See Niemi *et al.* (1992), Franklin *et al.* (1994), Heath and Evans (1994), Blais and Nadeau (1996), Ordeshook and Zeng (1997), Alvarez and Nagler (2000), Blais *et al.* (2001), Fisher and Curtice (2006) and Hermann and Pappi (2007). For the particular role of strategic considerations linked to party size see Tillie (1995) and van der Eijk *et al.* (1996, 2006).

Protest voting

In Chapter 5 we discussed the concept of protest voting, which is hard to distinguish empirically from sincere voting. Recent US studies include Southwell and Everest (1998). For Australia and New Zealand see Denemark and Bowler (2002), and for European countries see van der Brug *et al.* (2000) and van der Brug and Fennema (2003) – the most convincing, in our view. Kang (2004) investigates the effect of electoral systems on protest voting, and Oppenhuis *et al.* (1996) attempt to estimate the aggregate incidence of protest voting ('voting with the boot').

Electoral participation and turnout

Whether or not citizens use their right to vote is a central questions in electoral research. Some of the classic comparative studies are the pioneering aggregate data study by Tingsten (1963 [1937]), and the survey-based studies by Rose (1980), Powell (1986) and Verba *et al.* (1987), who look at electoral participation in the context of other forms of political activity. Geys (2006b) provides a wide-ranging overview of results from aggregate-level analyses of turnout. Recent comparative studies include Oppenhuis (1995), Jackman and Miller (1995), Blais and Dobrzynska (1998) and Franklin (2001). Franklin (2004) and Franklin *et al.* (2004) model the evolution of turnout over time in a number of countries as a function of electoral reforms and cohort replacement (cf. Rubenson *et al.* (2004), Plutzer (2002) and Fowler (2006).

A recurring debate is whether or not turnout is on the decline, particularly in established democracies. See Wattenberg (1998), Patterson (2002) and McDonald and Popkin (2002) regarding the US. For similar debates in other countries see, amongst others, Blais *et al.* (2004), Grey and Caul (2000) and Franklin (2004); for an overview see Blais (2006).

Lijphart (1997) considers extensive non-participation (and thus unequal participation) to be a major problem of representative democracy, partly on normative grounds. The question whether non-participation distorts political representation is another recurring theme, which is addressed in a special issue of *Electoral Studies* (2007, vol. 26).

Regarding the so-called turnout paradox (Chapter 1) see the very thoughtful collection by Benn (1978), and also Grofman (1993), Kanazawa (1998), Franklin (2004: ch. 2), Dowding (2005) and Geys (2006a).

Distinguishing party preferences and party choice

As we emphasized in Chapters 2 and 7, it is important to distinguish electoral preferences from actual party choice. The logic of this distinction (in the context of voting) dates from Downs (1957), yet has been widely ignored until recently. Practical applications require valid measures of electoral preferences for parties on the one hand and appropriate designs for analysing them on the other. The criteria for measurement validity and the logic of relevant analysis designs have been extensively documented in van der Eijk *et al.* (1996, 2006); interesting applications include van der Eijk *et al.* (1996), van der Eijk and Oppenhuis (1991), van der Brug *et al.* (2000, 2007a, 2007b), Marsh (2006b) and Kroh *et al.* (2007).

Habituation, immunization, socialization and learning

In Chapters 2 and 7 we emphasized that repeated behavior (such as turning out to vote or voting for a particular party) can become habitual. The psychological processes involved have been theorized by Bem (1967, 1970) to be related to the effect of behavior on self-perception. Various forms of habit formation have been widely investigated, cf. Franklin and Jackson (1983), C. Franklin (1992), Ajzen (2002) and Wood *et al.* (2002, 2005). Applications to voting and party identification include Butler and Stokes (1974), Jennings and Markus (1984), Gerber *et al.* (2003), Green and Shachar (2000), Shachar (2003), Plutzer (2002) and Grynaviski (2006). Research on the wider processes of political socialization and learning has been summarized by Sears (1975); cf. Dudley and Gitelson (2002), Campbell (2002), Sapiro (2004), Hess (2005) and Beck and Jennings (1991). Morton and Williams (2001) report a unique study of how changes in the organization of voting arrangements in US primary elections affect voters' ability to learn about the candidates.

Constraint in political opinions and sophistication of the electorate

The extent to which voters have real and structured opinions on political matters – implicitly or explicitly a debate about the political sophistication of ordinary citizens (Converse 1964) – remains a topic of academic contention. Early contributions were muddled by political overtones, poor conceptualization and often flat-footed analysis. We therefore recommend starting with reviews of the debate that have appeared since the 1990s, e.g., Sniderman (1993), Converse (2000), Kinder (2003, 2006) and Bennett (2006). Cf. Hill and Kriesi (2005), Hansen (2007) and Saris and Sniderman (2004) for a helpful mix of substantive issues and methodological pitfalls in this field.

Political parties

Political parties in established democracies

An excellent starting point are the recent wide-ranging overviews of the role of political parties in democracies and the political process: e.g. Gunther *et al.* (2002), Webb *et al.* (2002), Webb (2002) and Katz and Crotty (2006). The academic journal *Party Politics* is a further excellent source for research on all matters related to political parties.

Party motivations and party strategy

How the behavior of parties and politicians has to be interpreted depends on their motivations. In the jargon of political science, it matters whether they are 'policy seeking', 'vote seeking' or 'office seeking'. See Wittman (1983), Budge and Laver (1986), Ware (1992), Schofield *et al.* (1998), Müller and

Strøm (1999), Adams and Merrill (1999), Crisp *et al.* (2004, 2007) and Adams *et al.* (2005). Linked to the question of motivations is that of electoral strategies. Much of the literature is of a formal nature – arguing on theoretical grounds what party strategy should be given particular goals – and often requires considerable mathematical skill. More empirically oriented research includes Grofman *et al.* (1999), Sitter (2002), Meguid (2005) and Bakke and Sitter (2005).

Party locations

Parties' positions on issues and ideological dimensions are a crucial component in the study of representation and parties' electoral strategies. How those positions are to be measured is less clear. Several approaches are used. One is to infer party stances from what parties say and do. Party *manifestos* are extensively employed to derive party positions on specific issues or on ideological dimensions. The Comparative Manifesto Research Group has produced and analysed such material for many countries over most of the period since World War II. See in particular Budge *et al.* (1987, 2001), Volkens (2001) and Gabel and Huber (2000). In contrast to the expert coding used in these studies, others advocate the use of computerized coding of manifesto contents: Laver *et al.* (2003, 2006) and Proksch and Slapin (2006). Rather than looking at what parties profess in their manifestos, one can also look at what they actually do by analysing *how they behave in a legislature*: Poole and Rosenthal (1997), Jackman (2001), Hix (2001), Clinton *et al.* (2004) and Hix *et al.* (2006).

A second approach is to measure party positions according to the perceptions of political experts or of voters. *Expert judgements* are used extensively, see, amongst others, Castles and Mair (1984), Huber and Inglehart (1995), Laver and Mair (1999), Marks *et al.* (2002), Steenbergen and Scott (2004) and McElroy and Benoit (2007). For measures based on *voter perceptions*, see van der Eijk and Franklin (1991, 2004), van der Brug *et al.* (2000), Alvarez *et al.* (2000) and van der Brug (2001). Not surprisingly, each of these approaches yields somewhat different results and a lively debate concerns the relative merits of each; see Laver (2001) and a special issue of the journal *Electoral Studies* (2007, vol. 26, no.1).

Party responsiveness to different groups

As we emphasized in Chapter 5, political parties are not homogeneous entities. Party leaders, middle-level party elites, activists, members and (potential) voters often differ in their preferences. Such differences in political orientations have been studied by Kitschelt (1989), Herrera and Taylor (1994), Norris (1995), Narud and Skare (1999) and Kennedy *et al.* (2006).

Political systems

Constitutions, constitutional design and constitutional engineering

A useful general overview of the importance of constitutional arrangements is provided by Bogdanor (1988). On the relations between constitutional design and the working of democracy, see Foweraker and Landman (2002), Reynolds (2002), Lutz (2006), Diamond and Plattner (2006); and see Lijphart (1991) and Lijphart and Waisman (1996) for constitutional design in new democracies. The specific question of how to design a constitution so as to maximize desired effects and minimize undesired effects is generally referred to as constitutional engineering. A classic text is Sartori (1994, 1997); a more recent text is Reynolds (2002). Lijphart has spent much of his life investigating the most appropriate form of constitutional arrangements for deeply divided societies (e.g., Lijphart 1968, 2004; Lijphart and Grofman 1984).

Regarding choice of or change in electoral systems see, Norris (1997), and, regarding particular cases, the special issue of the *International Political Science Review* (vol. 16, 1995), focusing on New Zealand, Israel, Italy and Japan.

Cleavage structures

Social cleavages are important determinants of party systems, and membership in social groups is an important factor in voter behavior. The classic discussion is by Lipset and Rokkan (1967). See also Bartolini and Mair (1990), Crewe and Denver (1985), Dalton *et al.* (1984), van der Eijk *et al.* (1992), Inglehart (1984), Rokkan (1970), Rose and Urwin (1969, 1970), Marks and Wilson (2001), Bartolini (2000), Shamir and Arian (1999) and Enyedi (2005).

Electoral systems

The general labels that we used in Chapter 3 do not detail the ways in which votes are defined, counted and transformed into election outcomes. For more detail see Carstairs (1980), Massicotte and Blais (1999), Farrell (2001), Horowitz and Goals (2003), Doorenspleet (2005) and the impressive handbook by Colomer (2004). For the consequences of electoral systems, see Rae (1967) and Lijphart (1990) regarding the distribution of political power, Rule and Zimmerman (1994) regarding impact on women and minorities, Reynolds *et al.* (2005) regarding consequences for fairness of elections, and Lijphart (1995) regarding the link between electoral systems and party systems. For electoral reform, see also constitutional engineering.

Party systems

As we discussed in Chapters 1 and 2, a party system is more than the sum of the parties comprising it. The most profound discussion of the characteristics and dynamics of party systems is still – more than 40 years after its publication – Sartori (1976, republished in 2005). More recent literature – including research on party system change and the emergence of new parties – includes Mair (1997), Pennings and Lane (1998), Anckar (2000), Tavits (2006), Bardi and Mair (2008) and Dalton (2008). The number of parties in a party system continues to generate research regarding (i) ways of counting them, (ii) updates of country descriptions, and (iii) the unravelling of factors that determine this number. See Gaines (1997), Taagepera (1997, 1999, 2002), Moser (1999), Herron and Nishikawa (2001), Benoit (2001) and Dunleavy and Boucek (2003).

Coalition and minority governments

The literature on the formation of coalition governments is extensive. Early and classical studies include Riker (1962), Browne and Franklin (1973), de Mesquita (1979) and the large-scale study by de Swaan (1973). More recent studies of the formation, composition and operation of coalition governments are, among others, Laver and Schofield (1990), Budge and Keman (1990), Laver and Shepsle (1996), Martin and Stevenson (2001) and Laver (1998). Pre-electoral coalition formation has been studied by Golder (2005, 2006).

Minority governments are investigated in a seminal study by Strøm (1990), and in later studies by Bergman (1993), Green-Pedersen (2001) and Cheibub (2002). An very useful source of comparable data is Woldendorp *et al.* (2000).

Issue spaces and party spaces

Mapping issues and parties in a 'spatial' fashion (see Chapter 6) requires more than just information on party locations (see earlier entry in this guide). Additionally, we need to know how party locations on different issues or policy dimensions are related to each other, helping to diagnose parties' competitive advantages or disadvantages or their potential for taking part in governing coalitions. Such spaces can be constructed in a variety of ways; see Dow (2001), Kato and Laver (2003), Benoit and Laver (2005), McElroy and Benoit (2007) and Aarts and Thomassen (2008).

Elections

Non-democratic elections

As stated in Chapter 1, elections are also held in non-democratic states. See Schedler (2006), Zaslavsky and Brym (1978), Diamond (2002), Diamond and Morlino (2004) and Levitsky and Way (2002). Related to this topic is the question as to what distinguishes democratic from non-democratic contexts. See Linz (1975); more recent discussions include van de Walle (2002), Munck and Verkuilen (2002) and Zakaria (2003).

Do elections matter?

This question (see Chapter 8) has been addressed in a volume edited by Ginsberg and Stone (1996), particularly in connection with the 1994 elections in the US. For how electoral processes and outcomes affect citizens see, amongst others, Ginsberg and Weissberg (1978), Ginsberg (1982), Clarke and Acock (1989), Nadeau and Blais (1993), Rahn *et al.* (1999), Banducci and Karp (2003) and Anderson (2005); Taagepera (1998) looks at effects on democratization and Cigler and Getter (1977) at depolarization of conflict.

Types of elections

The first- and second-order distinction was first made by Reif and Schmitt (1980) and this has been invaluable in the comparison of different kinds of elections. See also Anderson and Ward (1996), Marsh (2000, 2005) and Marsh and Mikhaylov (2009). See also Berkman and Plutzer's beautiful (2005) study of elections for school boards in the US.

In this book we did not discuss referendums. Useful overviews of these kinds of elections can be found in Butler and Ranney (1994), Gallagher and Uleri (1996), LeDuc (2002, 2003) and, with a view on the particularities of campaigns, de Vreese and Semetko (2004).

Conduct of elections (free and fair)

Much literature discusses what would be 'free and fair' elections. Useful sources include Goodwin-Gill (2006) and Thompson (2004, particularly on the US). Most treatments of how this ideal of 'free and fair' is violated are of an anecdotal nature; but see Lehoucq (2003) and Wilson (2005, particularly relating to the post-Soviet world).

Organizations attempting to promote free and fair elections include the Inter-Parliamentary Union (www.ipu.org/english/home.htm) and IDEA – the

International Institute for Democracy and Electoral Assistance (www.idea.int).

Dealignment and realignment

Classic studies of critical (dealigning or realigning) elections are Key (1955, 1959), Burnham (1970), Andersen (1979) and Sundquist (1983). A useful collection of essays is in Clubb *et al.* (1990). See also Schofield *et al.* (2003), Abramowitz and Saunders (1998) and Campbell (2002). Discussions of the concepts themselves are in Shafer (1991), Rosenof (2003) and Mayhew (2004). For individual-level concomitants of de- and realignments, see Erikson and Tedin (1981), Dalton *et al.* (1984), Crewe and Denver (1985), Franklin (1985a) and, particularly, Franklin *et al.* (1992) and Franklin and Ladner (1995).

Other applications of the critical election framework include Evans and Norris (1999), Crewe and Thomson (1999), Denver (2000) and Dalton and Bürklin (2003).

Popularity cycle

In Chapter 6 we referred to an often reported cyclical evolution of government support over the period between elections, sometimes also referred to as a popularity cycle. See, amongst others, Norpoth (1984), Veiga and Fonseca (1998), Johnston (1999) and Byers *et al.* (2000). Lewis-Beck and Paldam (2000) and Nannestad and Paldam (1994) find massive variation in the specification of these cycles in the existing literature, as well as many anomalous findings; van der Brug *et al.* (2007a) diagnose these as resulting from the frequent failure to distinguish between party preferences and electoral choice (see earlier entry in this guide) .

The popularity cycle is often seen as a reason for government losses in second-order elections and of the President's party in US mid-term elections. See Marsh (1998, 2007) for empirical tests of rivalling theories about these second-order and mid-term losses. The classic arguments in this respect have been formulated by A. Campbell (1960), Tufte (1975) and J. Campbell (1997).

Miscellaneous

Comparative electoral research

The comparative study of elections requires a good understanding of elections in the political systems in which they occur. This can to some extent be acquired from concise election reports or from articles that focus on a particular election in a country in journals such as *West European Politics*, *Electoral Studies* or *Government and Opposition*; see also Widfeldt (2007) and Roller (2001). In addition, the EPERN website at the University of Sussex (UK) contains excellent papers on elections in many European countries (www.sussex.ac.uk/sei/1-4-2.html). Much more extensive insight is to be gained from book-length studies about elections in a particular country, often produced by the principal investigators of national election studies. Unfortunately in many non-English speaking countries such volumes are only available in the native language. Excellent and recent examples are *The Finnish Voter* (Borg and Sänkiaho 1995), *The Irish Voter* (Marsh *et al.* 2008), *How France Votes* (Lewis-Beck 2000), *Unsteady State* (Nevitte *et al.* 2000, about Canada) and *Political Choice in Britain* (Clarke *et al.* 2004). Moving beyond single elections one can find comparative studies on over-time developments in a single country, e.g., *The American Voter Revisited* (Lewis-Beck *et al.* 2008) and *Stability and Change in German Elections* (Anderson and Zelle 1998). Important and recent broad-ranging comparative analyses of elections in multiple countries are *The European Voter* (Thomassen 2005) and major volumes based on the European Election Studies: van der Eijk and Franklin (1996), Schmitt and Thomassen (1999), van der Brug and van der Eijk (2007) and Thomassen (2009).

Generations, cohorts, life-cycles

In Chapters 2 and 7 we emphasized the importance of generational replacement for electoral change and the need to distinguish cohort effects from life-cycle or period effects. Glenn (1977, 2003) provides excellent, concise and accessible introductions. A more in-depth text on the methodological issues involved is Mason and Fienberg (1985).

Recent studies that productively use these distinctions in the analysis of voting and elections include Cassel (1999), Lyons and Alexander (2000), Phelps (2004, 2005), Franklin (2004), Scappini (2006) and Wass (2007).

Media and electoral studies

Broad-ranging studies that cover many different aspects of the relation between the media and electoral politics include Blumler (1983), Gunther and Mughan (2000), Norris (2000), McCombs (2004) and de Vreese and Semetko (2004). Studies of the media at specific elections are Norris *et al.* (1999), Brandenburg (2002), Hillygus and Jackman (2003) and Gibson *et al.* (2003). For more detailed analyses of media functions such as information provision, agenda setting, framing and priming, and mobilization, see Dalton *et al.* (1998), Kleinnijenhuis and de Ridder (1998), Shaw (1999), Newton (1999), Soroka (2002), Banducci and Karp (2003), Aarts and

Semetko (2003), Norris and Sanders (2003), de Vreese *et al.* (2006) and Peter (2007). Media bias and its effects have been investigated by D'Alessio and Allen (2000), Druckman and Parkin (2005) and Barrett and Barrington (2005).

European Parliament elections

We have repeatedly referred to research on European Parliament elections, which have been used extensively as occasions for comparative research ever since they were first conducted in 1979. The major publications of this research are Blumler (1983), Reif (1985), van der Eijk and Franklin (1996), Schmitt and Thomassen (1999), van der Brug and van der Eijk (2007) and Thomassen (2009). A detailed bibliography can be found at www.piredeu.eu/public/Publications.asp.

Academic journals for electoral research

Publications on elections and electoral research can be found in many political science journals, particularly in the broad-ranging association journals such as the *American Political Science Review*, the *American Journal of Political Science*, the *European Journal of Political Research*, the *British Journal of Political Science*, *Acta Politica*, and so on. A few academic journals focus exclusively on matters relating to electoral research: *Electoral Studies*, the *Journal of Elections, Parties and Public Opinion* and the web-based *Political Institutions: Elections Abstracts*. A journal focusing exclusively on practical aspects of election campaigning (mainly in the USA) is *Campaigns and Elections*.

Other text books

Obviously, much of what has been presented in the chapters of this book will figure prominently in other textbooks as well. Yet each textbook provides its own perspective and its own selection of information. Therefore, after having read this book, further reading in other textbooks will prove rewarding because of the complementary information and viewpoints that they provide. We particularly recommend LeDuc *et al.* (2002), Gallagher *et al.* (2005), Evans (2004), Catt (1997), Lewis-Beck *et al.* (2008) and Denver (2007).

Bibliography

Aardal, B. and van Wijnen, P. (2005) 'Issue Voting', in J. Thomassen (ed.), *The European Voter: A Comparative Study of Modern Democracies* (Oxford: Oxford University Press): 192–212.

Aarts, K. and Semetko, H. A. (2003) 'The Divided Electorate: Media Use and Political Involvement', *Journal of Politics*, 65, 3: 759–84.

Aarts, K. and Thomassen, J. (2008) 'Dutch Voters and the Changing Party Space 1989–2006', *Acta Politica*, 43, 2–3: 203–34.

Abramowitz, A., Alexander, B. and Grunning, M. (2006) 'Incumbency, Redistricting and the Decline of Competition in US House Elections', *Journal of Politics*, 68: 75–88.

Abramowitz, A. I. and Saunders, K. L. (1998) 'Ideological Realignment in the US Electorate', *Journal of Politics*, 60: 634–52.

Abramson, P. R. (2008) 'Generational Change and the Decline of Party Identification in America: 1952–1974', Paper presented at the American Political Science Association, August, Boston, USA.

Adams, J. and Merrill, S. (1999) 'Modeling Party Strategies and Policy Representation in Multiparty Elections: Why Are Strategies So Extreme?', *American Journal of Political Science*, 43: 765–91.

Adams, J., Merrill, S. and Grofman, B. (2005) 'Does France's Two-Ballot Presidential Election System Alter Candidates' Policy Strategies? A Spatial Analysis of Office-Seeking Candidates in the 1988 Presidential Election', *French Politics*, 3, 2: 98–123.

Ajzen, I. (2002) 'Residual Effects of Past on Later Behavior: Habituation and Reasoned Action Perspectives', *Personality and Social Psychology Review*, 6, 2: 107–22.

Alesina, A. and Rosenthal, H. (1995) *Partisan Politics, Divided Government and the Economy* (Cambridge: Cambridge University Press).

Alford, R. R. (1967) 'Class Voting in the Anglo-American Political Systems', in S. M. Lipset and S. Rokkan (eds), *Party Systems and Voter Alignments: Cross National Perspectives* (New York: Free Press): 67–94.

Alvarez, R. M. and Nagler, J. (2000) 'A New Approach for Modelling Strategic Voting in Multiparty Elections', *British Journal of Political Science*, 30, 1: 57–75.

Alvarez, R. M., Nagler, J. and Willette, J. R. (2000) 'Measuring the Relative Impact of Issues and the Economy in Democratic Elections', *Electoral Studies*, 19, 2–3: 237–53.

American National Election Studies – data and documentation: http://www.election-studies.org/ (last accessed 26 March 2009).

American National Election Studies (2004) *American National Election Studies Cumulative File* (Ann Arbor, MI: ANES).

Anckar, C. (2000) 'Size and Party System Fragmentation', *Party Politics*, 6, 3: 305.

Andersen, K. (1979) *The Creation of a Democratic Majority, 1928–1936* (Chicago: Chicago University Press).

Andersen, R. and Heath, A. (2002) 'Class Matters: The Persisting Effects of Contextual Social Class on Individual Voting in Britain, 1964–97', *European Sociological Review*, 18, 2: 125–38.

Anderson, C. (2005) *Losers' Consent: Elections and Democratic Legitimacy* (Oxford: Oxford University Press).

Anderson, C. J. and Ward, D. S. (1996) 'Barometer Elections in Comparative Perspective', *Electoral Studies*, 15, 4: 447–60.

Anderson, C. J. and Zelle, C. (1998) *Stability and Change in German Elections: How Electorates Merge, Converge, Or Collide* (Westport, CT: Praeger).

Andeweg, R. B. and Irwin, G. A. (2009) *Governance and Politics of the Netherlands*, 3rd edn (Basingstoke: Palgrave Macmillan).

Anker, H. (1998) *Normal Vote Analysis* (Amsterdam: Het Spinhuis).

APSA (American Political Science Association) (1950) 'Towards a More Responsible Two-Party System', *American Political Science Review*, 45, Supplement.

Arnold, C. and Franklin, M. (2006) 'Heterogeneous Policy Preferences and Support for European Integration: Exploring the Dynamics of European Policy-Making', Paper presented to the American Political Science Association, Philadelphia.

Arrow, K. J. (1951) *Social Choice and Individual Values* (New York: Wiley).

Bakke, E. and Sitter, N. (2005) 'Patterns of Stability: Party Competition and Strategy in Central Europe since 1989', *Party Politics*, 11, 2: 243.

Banducci, S. A. and Karp, J. A. (2003) 'How Elections Change the Way Citizens View the Political System: Campaigns, Media Effects and Electoral Outcomes in Comparative Perspective', *British Journal of Political Science*, 33, 3: 443–7.

Bardi, L. and Mair, P. (2008) 'The Parameters of Party Systems', *Party Politics*, 14, 2: 147–66.

Barrett, A. W. and Barrington, L. W. (2005) 'Bias in Newspaper Photograph Selection', *Political Research Quarterly*, 58, 4: 609–18.

Bartle, J. (1998) 'Left–Right Position Matters, But Does Social Class? Causal Models of the 1992 British General Election', *British Journal of Political Science*, 28, 3: 501–29.

Bartle, J. (1999) 'Improving the Measurement of Party Identification in Britain', *British Elections and Parties Review*, 9: 119–35.

Bartolini, S. (2000) *The Political Mobilization of the European Left, 1860–1980: The Class Cleavage* (Cambridge: Cambridge University Press).

Bartolini, S. and Mair, P. (1990) *Identity, Competition and Electoral Availability: The Stabilisation of European Electorates, 1885–1995* (Cambridge: Cambridge University Press).

Baumgartner, J. and Morris, J. S. (2006) 'The Daily Show Effect: Candidate Evaluations, Efficacy, and American Youth', *American Politics Research*, 34, 3: 341.

Beck, P. A. and Jennings, M. K. (1991) 'Family Traditions, Political Periods, and the Development of Partisan Orientations', *Journal of Politics*, 53, 3: 742–63.

Bem, D. J. (1967) 'Self-Perception: An Alternative Interpretation of Cognitive Dissonance Phenomena', *Psychological Review*, 74, 3: 183–200.

Bem, D. J. (1970) *Beliefs, Attitudes, and Human Affairs* (Belmont, CA: Brooks Cole Publishing).

Benn, S. (ed.)(1978) *Political Participation: A Discussion of Political Rationality* (Canberra: Australian National University Press).

Bennett, S. E. (2006) 'Democratic Competence, Before Converse and After', *Critical Review*, 18, 1: 105–41.

Benoit, K. (2001) 'District Magnitude, Electoral Formula, and the Number of Parties', *European Journal of Political Research*, 39, 2: 203–24.

Benoit, K. and Laver, M. (2005) 'Mapping the Irish Policy Space: Voter and Party Spaces in Preferential Elections', *Economic and Social Review*, 2: 83–108.

Berelson, B., Lazarsfeld, P. F. and McPhee, W. N. (1954) *Voting: A Study of Opinion Formation in a Presidential Campaign* (Chicago: University of Chicago Press).

Berglund, F., Holmberg, S., Schmitt, H. and Thomassen, J. (2005) 'Party Identification and Party Choice', in J. Thomassen (ed.), *The European Voter: A Comparative Study of Modern Democracies* (New York: Oxford University Press).

Bergman, T. (1993) 'Formation Rules and Minority Governments', *European Journal of Political Research*, 23, 1: 55–66.

Berkman, M. B. and Plutzer, E. (2005) *Ten Thousand Democracies: Politics And Public Opinion in America's School Districts* (Georgetown: Georgetown University Press).

Bernhagen, P. and Marsh, M. (2007) 'The Partisan Effects of Low Turnout: Analyzing Vote Abstention as a Missing Data Problem', *Electoral Studies*, 26, 2: 401–13.

Blais, A. (2006) 'What Affects Voter Turnout?', *Annual Review of Political Science*, 9: 111.

Blais, A. and Dobrzynska, A. (1998) 'Turnout in Electoral Democracies', *European Journal of Political Research*, 33, 2: 239–62.

Blais, A., Gidengil, E., Dobrzynska, A., Nevitte, N. and Nadeau, R. (2003) 'Does the Local Candidate Matter? Candidate Effects in the Canadian Election of 2000', *Canadian Journal of Political Science/Revue Canadienne de Science Politique*, 36, 3: 657–64.

Blais, A., Gidengil, E., Nadeau, R. and Nevitte, N. (2001) 'Measuring Party Identification: Britain, Canada, and the United States', *Political Behavior*, 23, 1: 5–22.

Blais, A., Gidengil, E. and Nevitte, N. (2004) 'Where Does Turnout Decline Come From?', *European Journal of Political Research*, 43, 2: 221–36.

Blais, A. and Massicotte, L. (2002) 'Electoral Systems', in L. LeDuc, R. G. Niemi and P. Norris (eds), *Comparing Democracies 2: New Challenges in the Study of Elections and Voting* (London: Sage): 40–69.

Blais, A. and Nadeau, R. (1996) 'Measuring Strategic Voting: A Two-Step Procedure', *Electoral Studies*, 15, 1: 39–52.

Blais, A., Nadeau, R., Gidengil, E. and Nevitte, N. (2001) 'Measuring Strategic Voting in Multiparty Plurality Elections', *Electoral Studies*, 20, 3: 343–52.

Blondel, J. (1972) *Comparing Political Systems* (New York: Praeger).

Blumler, J. G. (1983) *Communicating to Voters: Television in the First European Parliamentary Elections* (London: Sage).

Bogdanor, V. (1988) *Constitutions in Democratic Politics* (Aldershot: Gower).

Borg, S. and Sänkiaho, R. (1995) *The Finnish Voter* (Helsinki: Finnish Political Science Association/Statsvetenskapliga fören).

Borre, O. (2001) *Issue Voting: An Introduction* (Aarhus: Aarhus University Press).

Borrelli, S., Lockerbie, B. and Niemi, R. (1987) 'Why the Democrat–Republican Partisanship Gap Varies from Poll to Poll', *Public Opinion Quarterly*, 51: 115–19.

Brady, H. E. and Stewart, J. (1991) 'Do Elections Matter?', in B. Ginsberg and A. Stone (eds), *Do Elections Matter?* (Armonk, NY: M. E. Sharpe).

Brandenburg, H. (2002) 'Who Follows Whom? The Impact of Parties on Media Agenda Formation in the 1997 British General Election Campaign', *Harvard International Journal of Press/Politics*, 7: 34–54.

Brichta, A. (2001) *Political Reform in Israel: The Quest for a Stable and Effective Government* (Brighton: Sussex Academic Press).

British Election Studies (1998) *British Election Studies Cumulative File*, Created by Anthony Heath for authors of chapters in G. Evans and P. Norris (eds), *Critical Elections* (London: Sage).

British Election Studies – data and documentation: *British Election Studies Information Site*: http://www.besis.org/Body.aspx (last accessed 26 March 2009).

Brooks, C., Nieuwbeerta, P. and Manza, J. (2006) 'Cleavage-Based Voting Behavior in Cross-National Perspective: Evidence from Six Postwar Democracies', *Social Science Research*, 68: 88–128.

Browne, E. C. and Franklin, M. (1973) 'Aspects of Coalition Payoffs in European Parliamentary Democracies', *American Political Science Review*, 67: 453–69.

Brug, W. van der (1997) 'Where's the Party? Voters' Perceptions of Party Positions', PhD thesis (Amsterdam: University of Amsterdam).

Brug, W. van der (2001) 'Perceptions, Opinions and Party Preferences in the Face of a Real World Event: Chernobyl as a Natural Experiment in Political Psychology', *Journal of Theoretical Politics*, 13, 1: 53– 80.

Brug, W. van der and Eijk, C. van der (eds) (2007) *European Elections and Domestic Politics: Lessons from the Past and Scenarios for the Future* (Notre Dame: University of Notre Dame Press).

Brug, W. van der, Eijk, C. van der and Franklin, M. (2007a) *The Economy and the Vote: Economic Conditions and Elections in Fifteen Countries* (Cambridge: Cambridge University Press).

Brug, W. van der, Eijk, C. van der, Schmitt, H. *et al.* (2007b) 'European Elections, Domestic Politics, and European Integration', in W. van der Brug and C. van der Eijk (eds), *European Elections and Domestic Politics: Lessons from the Past and Scenarios for the Future* (Notre Dame: University of Notre Dame Press): 226–61.

Brug, W. van der and Fennema, M. (2003) 'Protest or Mainstream? How the European Anti-immigrant Parties Developed into Two Separate Groups by 1999', *European Journal of Political Research*, 42: 55–76.

Brug, W. van der, Fennema, M. and Tillie, J. (2000) 'Anti-Immigrant Parties in Europe: Ideological or Protest Vote?', *European Journal of Political Research*, 37, 1: 77–102.

Brug, W. van der, Franklin, M. and Tóka, G. (2008) 'One Electorate or Many?', *Electoral Studies*, 27, 4: 589–600.

Budge, I., Bara, J., Volkens, A. and Klingemann, H. D. (2001) *Mapping Policy Preferences: Estimates for Parties, Electors and Governments, 1945–98* (Oxford: Oxford University Press).

Budge, I., Crewe, I. and Farlie, D. (eds) (1976) *Party Identification and Beyond* (London: Wiley).

Budge, I. and Farlie, D. (1983) *Explaining and Predicting Elections* (Sydney, Australia: Allen & Unwin).

Budge, I. and Keman, H. (1990) *Parties and Democracy: Coalition Formation and Government Functioning in Twenty States* (Oxford: Oxford University Press).

Budge, I. and Laver, M. (1986) 'Office-Seeking and Policy-Pursuit in Coalition Theory', *Legislative Studies Quarterly*, 2: 485–506.

Budge, I., Robertson, D. and Hearl, D. (1987) *Ideology, Strategy and Party Change: Spatial Analyses of Post-War Election Programmes in 19 Democracies* (Cambridge: Cambridge University Press).

Burden, B. C. and Klofstad, C. A. (2005) 'Affect and Cognition in Party Identification', *Political Psychology*, 26, 6: 869–86.

Burnham, W. D. (1970) *Critical Elections and the Mainsprings of American Politics* (New York: W.W. Norton).

Burns, J. M. (1963) *The Deadlock of Democracy: Four-Party Politics in America* (Englewood Cliffs, NJ: Prentice Hall).

Butler, D. and Ranney, A. (1994) *Referendums Around the World: The Growing Use of Direct Democracy* (Washington: American Enterprise Institute Press).

Butler, D. E. and Stokes, D. E. (1969) *Political Change in Britain: Forces Shaping Electoral Choice* (London: Macmillan).

Butler, D. E. and Stokes, D. E. (1974) *Political Change in Britain: The Evolution of Electoral Choice*, 2nd edn (London: Macmillan).

Byers, D., Davidson, J. and Peel, D. (2000) 'The Dynamics of Aggregate Political Popularity: Evidence from Eight Countries', *Electoral Studies*, 19, 1: 49–62.

Campbell, A. (1960) 'Surge and Decline: A Study of Electoral Change', *Public Opinion Quarterly*, 24, 3: 397–418.

Campbell, A. (1966) 'Surge and Decline: A Study of Electoral Change', in A. Campbell, P. Converse, W. Miller and D. Stokes (eds), *Elections and the Political Order* (New York: Wiley): 40–62.

Campbell, A., Converse, P., Miller, W. and Stokes, D. (1960) *The American Voter* (New York: Wiley).

Campbell, A., Converse, P. E., Miller, W. E. and Stokes, D. (eds) (1966) *Elections and the Political Order* (New York: Wiley).

Campbell, A., Gurin, G. and Miller, W. E. (1954) *The Voter Decides* (Evanston, IL: Row, Peterson & Company).

Campbell, D. E. (2002) 'The Young and the Realigning: A Test of the Socialization Theory of Realignment', *Public Opinion Quarterly*, 66, 2: 209–34.

Campbell, J. (1985) 'The Sources of the New Deal Realignment: The Contributions of Conversions and Mobilization to Partisan Change', *Western Political Quarterly*, 38: 357–76.

Campbell, J. E. (1997) 'The Presidential Pulse and the 1994 Midterm Congressional Election', *Journal of Politics*, 59: 830–57.

Carstairs, A. (1980) *A Short History of Electoral Systems in Western Europe* (London: George Allen & Unwin).

Cassel, C. A. (1999) 'Testing the Converse Party Support Model in Britain', *Comparative Political Studies*, 32, 5: 626–44.

Castles, F. G. and Mair, P. (1984) 'Left–Right Political Scales: Some 'Expert' Judgments', *European Journal of Political Research*, 12, 1: 73–88.

Catt, H. (1997) *Voting Behaviour: A Radical Critique* (Leicester: Leicester University Press).

Center for Voting and Democracy (1995) *Voting and Democracy Report* (Washington, DC: Center for Voting and Democracy).

Cheibub, J. A. (2002) 'Minority Governments, Deadlock Situations, and the Survival of Presidential Democracies', *Comparative Political Studies*, 35, 3: 284.

Cigler, A. and Getter, R. (1977) 'Conflict Reduction in the Post-Election Period: A Test of the Depolarization Thesis', *Political Research Quarterly*, 30: 363–76.

Clarke, H. and Acock, A. (1989) 'National Elections and Political Attitudes: The Case of Political Efficacy', *British Journal of Political Science*, 19, 4: 551–62.

Clarke, H. D., Sanders, D., Stewart, M. C. and Whiteley, P. (eds) (2004) *Political Choice in Britain* (Oxford: Oxford Scholarships Online Monographs).

Clarke, H., Sanders, D., Stewart, M. and Whiteley, P. (2006) 'Taking the Bloom off New Labour's Rose: Party Choice and Voter Turnout in Britain, 2005', *Journal of Elections, Public Opinion and Parties*, 16: 3–36.

Clarke, H. D. and Stewart, M. C. (1992) 'Canada', in M. Franklin, T. T. Mackie and H. Valen (eds), *Electoral Change: Responses to Evolving Social and Attitudinal Structures in Western Countries* (Cambridge: Cambridge University Press): 255–83.

Clarke, H. and Stewart, M. C. (1998) 'Partisan Inconsistency and the Dynamics of Party Support in Federal Systems: The Canadian Case', *American Journal of Political Science*, 41: 97–116.

Clinton, J., Jackman, S. and Rivers, D. (2004) 'The Statistical Analysis of Roll Call Data', *American Political Science Review*, 98, 2: 355–70.

Clubb, J. M. and Flanigan, W. H. and Zingale, N.H. (1990) *Partisan Realignment: Voters, Parties and Government in American History*, new edn. (Boulder, CO: Westview).

Colomer, J. M. (2004) *Handbook of Electoral System Choice* (Basingstoke: Palgrave Macmillan).

Conover, P. J. and Feldman, S. (2004) *The Origins and Meaning of Liberal/Conservative Self-identifications* (New York: Psychology Press).

Conover, P. J., Gray, V. and Coombs, S. (1982) 'Single-Issue Voting: Elite-Mass Linkages', *Political Behavior*, 4, 4: 309–31.

Converse, P. E. (1964) 'The Nature of Belief Systems in Mass Publics', in D. Apter (ed.), *Ideology and Discontent* (New York: Free Press): 206–610.

Converse, P. E. (2000) 'Assessing the Capacity of Mass Electorates', *Annual Reviews in Political Science*, 3, 1: 331–53.

Converse, P. E. and Pierce, R. (1986) *Political Representation in France* (Cambridge, MA: Harvard University Press).

Cox, G. W. and Kernell, S. (1991) 'Governing a Divided Era', in G. W. Cox and S. Kernell (eds), *The Politics of Divided Government* (Boulder, CO: Westview).

Crewe, I. and Denver, D. (1985) *Electoral Change in Western Democracies: Patterns and Sources of Electoral Volatility* (London: Croom Helm).

Crewe, I. and Thomson, K. (1999) 'Party Loyalties: Dealignment or Realignment?', in G. Evans and P. Norris (eds), *Critical Elections* (London: Sage): 64–86.

Crisp, B. F., Escobar-Lemmon, M. C., Jones, B. S., Jones, M. P. and Taylor-Robinson, M. M. (2004) 'Vote-Seeking Incentives and Legislative Representation in Six Presidential Democracies', *Journal of Politics*, 66, 3: 823–46.

Crisp, B. F., Jensen, K. M. and Shomer, Y. (2007) 'Magnitude and Vote Seeking', *Electoral Studies*, 26, 4: 727–34.

Dahl, R. A. (2002) *How Democratic is the American Constitution?* (New Haven: Yale University Press).

D'Alessio, D. and Allen, M. (2000) 'Media Bias in Presidential Elections: A Meta-Analysis', *Journal of Communication*, 50, 4: 133–56.

Dalton, R. (1999) 'Political Support in Advanced Industrial Democracies', in P. Norris (ed.), *Critical Citizens: Global Support for Democratic Government* (Oxford: Oxford University Press): 57–77.

Dalton, R. J. (2008) 'The Quantity and the Quality of Party Systems: Party System Polarization, its Measurement, and its Consequences', *Comparative Political Studies*, 41, 7: 899–920.

Dalton, R. J., Beck, P. A., Huckfeldt, R. and Koetzle, W. (1998) 'A Test of Media-Centered Agenda Setting: Newspaper Content and Public Interests in a Presidential Election', *Political Communication*, 15, 4: 463–81.

Dalton, R. J. and Bürklin, W. (2003) 'Wahler als Wandervogel: Dealignment and the German Voter', *German Politics and Society*, 21, 1: 57–75.

Dalton, R. J., Flanagan, S. C. and Beck, P. A. (1984) *Electoral Change in Advanced Industrial Democracies* (Princeton: Princeton University Press).

Dalton, R. J. and Wattenberg, M. P. (1993) 'The Not So Simple Act of Voting', in A. Finifter (ed.), *The State of the Discipline*, 2nd edn (Washington DC: American Political Science Association): 198–210.

Denemark, D. and Bowler, S. (2002) 'Minor Parties and Protest Votes in Australia and New Zealand: Locating Populist Politics', *Electoral Studies*, 21, 1: 47–67.

Denver, D. (2000) 'Dealignment Vindicated: The 1997 General Election', *Politics Review*, 9, 4: 2–5.

Denver, D. (2007) *Elections and Voters in Britain* (Basingstoke: Palgrave Macmillan).

Deutsch, K. W. (1963) *The Nerves of Government* (New York: Free Press).

Diamond, L. (2002) 'Thinking About Hybrid Regimes', *Journal of Democracy*, 13, 2: 21–35.

Diamond, L. and Morlino, L. (2004) 'The Quality of Democracy: An Overview', *Journal of Democracy*, 15, 4: 20–31.

Diamond, L. J. and Plattner, M. F. (2006) *Electoral Systems and Democracy* (Baltimore: Johns Hopkins University Press).

Dinas, E. (2008) 'Big Expectations, Small Outcomes: The Impact of Leaders' Personal Appeal in the 2004 Greek Election', *Electoral Studies*, 27, 3: 356–90.

Doorenspleet, R. (2005) 'Electoral Systems and Democratic Quality: Do Mixed Systems Combine the Best or the Worst of Both Worlds? An Explorative Quantitative Cross-National Study', *Acta Politica*, 40: 28–49.

Dorussen, H. and Taylor, M. (2002) *Economic Voting* (London: Routledge).

Dow, J. K. (2001) 'A Comparative Spatial Analysis of Majoritarian and Proportional Elections', *Electoral Studies*, 20, 1: 109–25.

Dowding, K. (2005) 'Is it Rational to Vote? Five Types of Answer and a Suggestion', *British Journal of Politics and International Relations*, 7, 3: 442–59.

Downs, A. (1957) *An Economic Theory of Democracy* (New York: Harper & Row).

Druckman, J. N. (2003) 'The Power of Television Images: The First Kennedy–Nixon Debate Revisited', *Journal of Politics*, 65, 2: 559–71.

Druckman, J. N. and Parkin, M. (2005) 'The Impact of Media Bias: How Editorial Slant Affects Voters', *Journal of Politics*, 67, 4: 1030–49.

Duch, R. M. and Stevenson, R. T. (2008) *The Economic Vote: How Political and Economic Institutions Condition Election Results* (Cambridge: Cambridge University Press).

Dudley, R. L. and Gitelson, A. R. (2002) 'Political Literacy, Civic Education, and Civic Engagement: A Return to Political Socialization?' *Applied Developmental Science*, 6, 4: 175–82.

Dunleavy, P. and Boucek, F. (2003) 'Constructing the Number of Parties', *Party Politics*, 9, 3: 291.

Dur, R. A. J. and Swank, O. H. (1997) *On the Role of the Governmental Agreement in Breaking Political Deadlocks*, Tinbergen Institute Discussion Paper 97–23 (Rotterdam: Tinbergen Institute).

Dutch National Election Study – data and documentation: Dutch parliamentary Election Studies: http://www.dpes.nl/ (last accessed 26 March 2009).

Duverger, M. (1964 [1951]) *Political Parties: Their Organisation and Activity in the Modern State*. (Paris: Aramand Colin; English translation, 1964, London: Methuen).

Eijk, C. van der (2000) 'The Netherlands: Media and Politics between Segmented Pluralism and Market Forces', in R. Gunther and A. Mughan (eds), *Democracy and the Media: A Comparative Perspective* (Cambridge: Cambridge University Press): 303–42.

Eijk, C. van der, Brug, W. van der, Kroh, M. and Franklin, M. (2006) 'Rethinking the Dependent Variable in Voting Behavior: On the Measurement and Analysis of Electoral Utilities', *Electoral Studies*, 25, 3: 424–47.

Eijk, C. van der and van Egmond, M. (2007) 'Political Effects of Low Turnout in National and European Elections', *Electoral Studies*, 26: 561–73.

Eijk, C. van der and Franklin, M. N. (1991) 'European Community Politics and Electoral Representation: Evidence from the 1989 European Elections Study', *European Journal of Political Research*, 19, 1: 105–27.

Eijk, C. van der and Franklin, M. (eds) (1996) *Choosing Europe? The European Electorate and National Politics in the Face of Union* (Ann Arbor: University of Michigan Press).

Eijk, C. van der and Franklin, M. N. (2004) 'Potential for Contestation on European Matters at National Elections in Europe', in G. Marks and M. R. Steenbergen (eds), *European Integration and Political Conflict* (Cambridge: Cambridge University Press): 32–50.

Eijk, C. van der, Franklin, M., Mackie, T. and Valen, H. (1992) 'Cleavages, Conflict Resolution and Democracy', in M. Franklin, T. T. Mackie and H. Valen (eds), *Electoral Change: Responses to Evolving Social and Attitudinal Structures in Western Countries* (Cambridge: Cambridge University Press): 406–31.

Eijk, C. van der, Franklin, M. and Oppenhuis, E. (1996) 'The Strategic Context: Party Choice', in C. van der Eijk and M. Franklin (eds), *Choosing Europe? The European Electorate and National Politics in the Face of Union* (Ann Arbor: University of Michigan Press): 332–65.

Eijk, C. van der and Niemöller, B. (1983) *Electoral Change in the Netherlands. Empirical Results and Methods of Measurement* (Amsterdam: CT Press).

Eijk, C. van der and Niemöller, B. (1984) 'Het potentiële electoraat van de Nederlandse politieke partijen', *Beleid en Maatschappij*, 11: 192–204.

Eijk, C. van der and Niemöller, B. (1992) 'The Netherlands', in M. Franklin, T. T. Mackie and H. Valen (eds), *Electoral Change: Responses to Evolving Social and Attitudinal Structures in Western Countries* (Cambridge: Cambridge University Press): 255–83.

Eijk, C. van der and Oppenhuis, E. V. (1991) 'European Parties' Performance in Electoral Competition', *European Journal of Political Research*, 19, 1: 55–80.

Eijk, C. van der, Schmitt, H. and Binder, T. (2005) 'Left–Right Orientations and Party Choice', in J. Thomassen (ed.), *The European Voter A Comparative Study of Modern Democracies* (Oxford: Oxford University Press): 167–91.

Enyedi, Z. (2005) 'The Role of Agency in Cleavage Formation', *European Journal of Political Research*, 44, 5: 697–720.

Erikson, R. S. (1981) 'Why do People Vote? Because they are Registered', *American Politics Quarterly*, 8: 259–76.

Erikson, R. S. and Tedin, K. L. (1981) 'The 1928–1936 Partisan Realignment: The Case for the Conversion Hypothesis', *American Political Science Review*, 75: 951–62.

Erikson, R. S., MacKuen, M., Stimson, J. (2002) *The Macro Polity* (New York: Cambridge University Press).

Esaisson, P. and Holmberg, S. (1996) *Representation from Above* (Aldershot: Dartmouth).

European Election Studies (1989–2004) www.europeanelectionstudies.net.

Evans, G. (1999) *The End of Class Politics? Class Voting in Comparative Perspective* (Oxford: Oxford University Press).

Evans, G. (2000) 'The Continued Significance of Class Voting', *Annual Reviews in Political Science*, 3, 1: 401–17.

Evans, G. and Andersen, R. (2004) 'Do Issues Decide? Partisan Conditioning and Perceptions of Party Issue Positions across the Electoral Cycle', *Journal of Elections, Public Opinion and Parties*, 14, 1, 18–39.

Evans, G. and Norris, P. (1999) *Critical Elections: British Parties and Voters in Long-Term Perspective* (London: Sage).

Evans, J. (2004) *Voters and Voting: An Introduction* (London: Sage).

Farrell, D. M. (2001) *Electoral Systems: A Comparative Introduction* (Basingstoke: Palgrave MacMillan).

Fiorina, M. P. (1981) *Retrospective Voting in American National Elections* (New Haven: Yale University Press).

Fiorina, M. P. (1977, 1989) *Congress: Keystone of the Washington Establishment* (New Haven: Yale University Press).

Fiorina, M. P. (1992) *Divided Government* (New York: Macmillan).

Fisher, S. D. and Curtice, J. (2006) 'Tactical Unwind? Changes in Party Preference Structure and Tactical Voting in Britain between 2001 and 2005', *Journal of Elections, Public Opinion and Parties*, 16, 1: 55–76.

Foweraker, J. and Landman, T. (2002) 'Constitutional Design and Democratic Performance', *Democratization*, 9, 2: 43–66.

Fowler, J. H. (2006) 'Habitual Voting and Behavioral Turnout', *Journal of Politics*, 68, 2: 335–44.

Franklin, C. H. (1992) 'Measurement and the Dynamics of Party Identification', *Political Behavior*, 14, 3: 297–309.

Franklin, C. H. and Jackson, J. E. (1983) 'The Dynamics of Party Identification', *American Political Science Review*, 77: 957–73.

Franklin, M. (1985a) *The Decline of Class Voting in Britain: Changes in the Basis of Electoral Choice, 1964–1983* (Oxford: Clarendon Press).

Franklin, M. (1985b) 'Assessing the Rise of Issue Voting in British Elections since 1964', *Electoral Studies*, 4: 37–56.

Franklin, M. (1989) 'The Resurgence of Conservatism in British Elections Since 1974', in B. Cooper, A. Kornberg and W. Mishler (eds), *The Resurgence of Conservatism in Anglo-American Democracies* (Durham, NC: Duke University Press): 304–31.

Franklin, M. (1992) 'The Decline of Cleavage Politics', in M. Franklin, T. T. Mackie and H. Valen (eds), *Electoral Change: Responses to Evolving Social and Attitudinal Structures in Western Countries* (Cambridge: Cambridge University Press): 383–405.

Franklin, M. (1996) 'Electoral Participation', in L. LeDuc, R. Niemi and P. Norris (eds), *Comparing Democracies, Elections and Voting in Global Perspective* (London: Sage).

Franklin, M. (1999) 'Understanding Cross-National Turnout Differences: What Role for Compulsory Voting?', *British Journal of Political Science*, 29: 205–16.

Franklin, M. (2001) 'How Structural Factors Cause Turnout Variations at European Parliament Elections', *European Election Politics*, 2: 309–28.

Franklin, M. (2002a) 'The Dynamics of Electoral Participation', in L. LeDuc, R. Niemi and P. Norris (eds), *Elections and Voting in Global Perspective 2* (Thousand Oaks, CA: Sage).

Franklin, M. (2002b) 'Learning from the Danish Case: A Comment on Palle Svensson's Critique of the "Franklin Thesis"', *European Journal of Political Research*, 41: 751–57.

Franklin, M. (2004) *Voter Turnout and the Dynamics of Electoral Competition in Established Democracies since 1945* (New York: Cambridge University Press).

Franklin, M. (2007) 'Effects of Space and Time on Turnout in European Parliament Elections', in W. van der Brug and C. van der Eijk (eds), *European Elections and Domestic Politics: Lessons from the Past and Scenarios for the Future* (Notre Dame, IN: University of Notre Dame Press): 13–31.

Franklin, M. N. (2009) 'Epilogue', in M. N. Franklin, T. T. Mackie and H. Valen (eds), *Electoral Change: Responses to Evolving Social and Attitudinal Structures in Western Countries* (Colchester: ECPR Press).

Franklin, M. and Curtice, J. (1996) 'Britain: Opening Pandora's Box', in C. van der Eijk and M. Franklin (eds), *Choosing Europe? The European Electorate and National Politics in the Face of Union* (Ann Arbor: University of Michigan Press): 78–96.

Franklin, M., Eijk, C. van der and Oppenhuis, E. V. (1996) 'The Institutional Context: Turnout', in C. van der Eijk and M. Franklin (eds), *Choosing Europe? The European Electorate and National Politics in the Face of Union* (Ann Arbor: University of Michigan Press): 306–31.

Franklin, M. and Hughes, C. (1999) 'Dynamic Representation in Britain', in P. Norris and G. Evans (eds), *A Critical Election? British Voters and Parties in Long-Term Perspective* (Thousand Oaks, CA: Sage): 240–58.

Franklin, M. and Ladner, M. (1995) 'The Undoing of Winston Churchill: Mobilization and Conversion in the 1945 Realignment of British Voters', *British Journal of Political Science*, 25: 429–52.

Franklin, M., Lyons, P. and Marsh, M. (2004) 'Generational Basis of Turnout Decline in Established Democracies', *Acta Politica*, 39: 115–51.

Franklin, M. and Mackie, T. T. (1983) 'Familiarity and Inertia in the Formation of Governing Coalitions in Parliamentary Democracies', *British Journal of Political Science*, 13: 275–98.

Franklin, M., Mackie, T. T. and Valen, H. (1992) *Electoral Change: Responses to Evolving Social and Attitudinal Structures in Western Countries* (New York: Cambridge University Press).

Franklin, M., Niemi, R. and Whitten, G. (1994) 'The Two Faces of Tactical Voting', *British Journal of Political Science*, 24, 4: 549–57.

Franklin, M. and Weber, T. (2009) 'American Electoral Practices in Comparative Perspective', in J. Leighley (ed.), *Oxford Handbook of American Elections* (Oxford: Oxford University Press).

Franklin, M. and Wlezien, C. (1997) 'The Responsive Public: Issue Salience, Policy Change, and Preferences for European Unification', *Journal of Theoretical Politics*, 9: 347–63.

Freire, A. (2006) 'Bringing Social Identities Back In: The Social Anchors of Left–Right Orientation in Western Europe', *International Political Science Review/ Revue internationale de science politique*, 27, 4: 359–78.

Fuchs, D. and Klingemann, H. D. (1990) 'The Left–Right Scheme: Theoretical Framework', in K. M. Jennings and J. W. van Deth (eds), *Continuities in Political Action: A Longitudinal Study of Political Orientations in Three Western Democracies* (Berlin: De Gruyter): 203–34.

Gabel, M. J. and Huber, J. D. (2000) 'Putting Parties in Their Place: Inferring Party Left–Right Ideological Positions from Party Manifestos Data', *American Journal of Political Science*, 44, 1: 94–103.

Gaines, B. J. (1997) 'Where to Count Parties', *Electoral Studies*, 16, 1: 49–58.

Gallagher, M., Laver, M. and Mair, P. (2005) *Representative Government in Modern Europe: Institutions, Parties, and Governments*, 4th edn (New York: McGraw Hill).

Gallagher, M. and Marsh, M. (2002) *Days of Blue Loyalty: The Politics of Membership of the Fine Gael Party* (Dublin: PSAI Press).

Gallagher, M. and Uleri, P. V. (eds) (1996) *The Referendum Experience in Europe* (London: Macmillan).

Gamson, W. A. (1992) *Talking Politics* (New York: Cambridge University Press).

Garry, J. (2007) 'Making Party Identification More Versatile: Operationalising the Concept for the Multi-party Setting', *Electoral Studies*, 26, 2: 346–58.

Gerber, A. S., Green, D. P. and Shachar, R. (2003) 'Voting May Be Habit-Forming: Evidence from a Randomized Field Experiment', *American Journal of Political Science*, 47, 3: 540–50.

Gerring, J. and Thacker, S. C. (2008) *A Centripetal Theory of Democratic Governance* (New York: Cambridge University Press).

Gerring, J., Thacker, S. C. and Moreno, C. (2005) 'Centripetal Democratic Governance: A Theory and Global Inquiry', *American Political Science Review*, 99: 567–81.

Geys, B. (2006a) '"Rational" Theories of Voter Turnout: A Review', *Political Studies Review*, 4, 1: 16–35.

Geys, B. (2006b) 'Explaining Voter Turnout: A Review of Aggregate-level Research', *Electoral Studies*, 25, 4: 637–63.

Gibson, R., Römmele, A. and Ward, S. (2003) 'German Parties and Internet Campaigning in the 2002 Federal Election', *German Politics*, 12, 1: 79–108.

Ginsberg, B. (1982) *The Consequences of Consent: Elections, Citizen Control, and Popular Acquiescence* (Reading, MA: Addison-Wesley).

Ginsberg, B. and Stone, A. (1996) *Do Elections Matter?* (Armonk, NY: ME Sharpe).

Ginsberg, B. and Weissberg, R. (1978) 'Elections and the Mobilization of Popular Support', *American Journal of Political Science*, 22, 1: 31–55.

Glazer, A. and Robbins, M. (1985) 'How Elections Matter: A Study of US Senators', *Public Choice*, 46, 2: 163–72.

Glenn, N. D. (1977) *Cohort Analysis* (Beverly Hills, CA: Sage).

Glenn, N. D. (2003) 'Distinguishing Age, Period, and Cohort Effects', in J. T. Mortimer and M. J. Shanahan (eds), *Handbook of the Life Course* (New York: Kluwer).

Golder, S. N. (2005) 'Pre-Electoral Coalitions in Comparative Perspective: A Test of Existing Hypotheses', *Electoral Studies*, 24, 4: 643–63.

Golder, S. N. (2006) 'Pre-Electoral Coalition Formation in Parliamentary Democracies', *British Journal of Political Science*, 36, 2: 193–212.

Goodwin-Gill, G. S. (2006) *Free and Fair Elections: International Law and Practice* (Geneva: Inter-Parliamentary Union).

Goren, P. (2005) 'Party Identification and Core Political Values', *American Journal of Political Science*, 49, 4: 881–96.

Granberg, C. and Holmberg, S. (1988) *The Political System Matters: Social Psychology and Voting Behavior in Sweden and the United States* (Cambridge: Cambridge University Press).

Gray, M. and Caul, M. (2000) 'Declining Voter Turnout in Advanced Industrial Democracies, 1950 to 1997: The Effects of Declining Group Mobilization', *Comparative Political Studies*, 33, 9: 1091.

Green, D. P. and Shachar, R. O. N. (2000) 'Habit Formation and Political Behaviour: Evidence of Consuetude in Voter Turnout', *British Journal of Political Science*, 30, 4: 561–73.

Greene, S. (2004) 'Social Identity Theory and Party Identification', *Social Science Quarterly*, 85, 1: 136–53.

Green-Pedersen, C. (2001) 'Minority Governments and Party Politics: The Political and Institutional Background to the "Danish Miracle"', *Journal of Public Policy*, 21, 1: 53–70.

Griffin, J. D. and Newman, B. (2005) 'Are Voters Better Represented?', *Journal of Politics*, 67, 4: 1206–27.

Grofman, B. (1993) 'Is Turnout the Paradox That Ate Rational Choice Theory?', in B. Grofman (ed.), *Information, Participation, and Choice: An Economic Theory of Democracy in Perspective* (Ann Arbor: University of Michigan Press): 93–103.

Grofman, B. (2004) 'Downs and Two-Party Convergence', *Annual Review of Political Science*, 7: 25–46.

Grofman, B., Merrill, S., Brunell, T. L. and Koetzle, W. (1999) 'The Potential Electoral Disadvantages of a Catch-All Party: Ideological Variance among Republicans and Democrats in the 50 US States', *Party Politics*, 5, 2: 199–210.

Grofman, B., Wayman, F. and Barreto, M. (2008) 'Rethinking Partisanship: Some Thoughts on a Unified Theory', in J. Bartle and P. Bellucci (eds), *Political Parties and Partisanship: Social Identity and Individual Attitudes* (London: Routledge).

Grönlund, K. and Milner, H. (2006) 'The Determinants of Political Knowledge in Comparative Perspective', *Scandanavian Political Studies*, 29, 4: 286–406.

Grynaviski, J. D. (2006) 'A Bayesian Learning Model with Applications to Party Identification', *Journal of Theoretical Politics*, 18, 3, 323–46.

Gunther, R., Montero, J. R. and Linz, J. J. (2002) *Political Parties: Old Concepts and New Challenges* (Oxford: Oxford University Press).

Gunther, R. and Mughan, A. (eds) (2000) *Democracy and the Media. A Comparative Perspective* (Cambridge: Cambridge University Press).

Hansen, K. M. (2007) 'The Sophisticated Public: The Effect of Competing Frames on Public Opinion', *Scandinavian Political Studies*, 30, 3: 377–96.

Hayes, D. (2005) 'Candidate Qualities through a Partisan Lens: A Theory of Trait Ownership', *American Journal of Political Science*, 49, 4: 908–23.

Heath, A. and Evans, G. (1994) 'Tactical Voting: Concepts, Measurement and Findings', *British Journal of Political Science*, 24, 4: 557–61.

Heath, A. and Pierce, R. (1992) 'It was Party Identification All Along: Question Order Effects on Reports of Party Identification in Britain', *Electoral Studies*, 11, 2: 93–105.

Herrera, R. and Taylor, M. K. (1994) 'The Structure of Opinion in American Political Parties', *Political Studies*, 42, 4: 676–89.

Herrmann, M. and Pappi, F. U. (2007) 'Strategic Voting in German Constituencies', *Electoral Studies*, 27, 2: 228–44.

Herron, E. S. and Nishikawa, M. (2001) 'Contamination Effects and the Number of Parties in Mixed-Superposition Electoral Systems', *Electoral Studies*, 20, 1: 63–86.

Hess, R. D. (2005) *The Development of Political Attitudes in Children* (Chicago: Aldine).

Hill, J. L. and Kriesi, H. (2005) 'An Extension and Test of Converse's "Black-and-White" Model of Response Stability', *American Political Science Review*, 95, 2: 397–413.

Hillebrand, R. and Irwin, G. A. (1999) 'Changing Strategies: The Dilemma of the Dutch Labour Party', in W. C. Müller and K. Strøm (eds), *Policy, Office, or Votes? How Political Parties in Western Europe Make Hard Decisions* (Cambridge: Cambridge University Press).

Hillygus, D. and Jackman, S. (2003) 'Voter Decision Making in Election 2000: Campaign Effects, Partisan Activation and the Clinton Legacy', *American Journal of Political Science*, 47: 583–96.

Hix, S. (2001) 'Legislative Behaviour and Party Competition in the European Parliament: An Application of Nominate to the EU', *Journal of Common Market Studies*, 39, 4: 663–88.

Hix, S., Noury, A. and Roland, G. (2006) 'Dimensions of Politics in the European Parliament', *American Journal of Political Science*, 50, 2: 494–520.

Hobolt, S. B. and Klemmensen, R. (2008) 'Government Responsiveness and Political Competition in Comparative Perspective', *Comparative Political Studies*, 41, 3: 309–37.

Holmberg, S. (2007) 'Partisanship Reconsidered', in R. J. Dalton and H. D. Klingemann (eds), *The Oxford Handbook of Political Behaviour* (Oxford: Oxford University Press).

Horowitz, D. L. and Goals, S. (2003) 'Electoral Systems', *Journal of Democracy*, 14: 115–27.

Huber, J. and Inglehart, R. (1995) 'Expert Interpretations of Party Space and Party Locations in 42 Societies', *Party Politics*, 1, 1: 73.

Huddy, L. and Capelos, T. (2002) 'Gender Stereotyping and Candidate Evaluation', in V. C. Ottati, R. S. Tindale, J. Edwards *et al.* (eds), *The Social Psychology of Politics* (New York: Kluwer Academic Publishers).

Ikeda, K., Liu, J. H., Aida, M. and Wilson, M. (2005) 'Dynamics of Interpersonal Political Environment and Party Identification: Longitudinal Studies of Voting in Japan and New Zealand', *Political Psychology*, 26, 4: 517–42.

Inglehart, R. (1971) 'The Silent Revolution in Europe: Intergenerational Change in Post-Industrial Societies', *American Political Science Review*, 65: 991–1017.

Inglehart, R. (1977) *The Silent Revolution: Changing Values and Political Styles Among Western Publics* (Princeton: Princeton University Press).

Inglehart, R. (1984) 'Changing Cleavage Alignments in Western Democracies', in R. J. Dalton, S. C. Flanagan and P. A. Beck (eds), *Electoral Change in Advanced Industrial Democracies* (Princeton, NJ: Princeton University Press): 25–69.

Inglehart, R. (1990) *Culture Shift in Advanced Industrial Society* (Princeton, NJ: Princeton University Press).

Inglehart, R. (1997) *Modernization and Postmodernization* (Princeton: Princeton University Press).

Inglehart, R. and Abramson, P. R. (1994) 'Economic Security and Value Change', *American Political Science Association Review*, 88: 336–54.

Irwin, G. A. (1974) 'Compulsory Voting Legislation: Impact on Voter Turnout in the Netherlands', *Comparative Political Studies*, 7, 3: 292–315.

Jackman, R. W. and Miller, R. A. (1995) 'Voter Turnout in the Industrial Democracies during the 1980s', *Comparative Political Studies*, 27, 4, 467–92.

Jackman, S. (2001) 'Multidimensional Analysis of Roll Call Data via Bayesian Simulation: Identification, Estimation, Inference and Model Checking', *Political Analysis*, 9, 3: 227–41.

Jacoby, W. G. (1995) 'The Structure of Ideological Thinking in the American Electorate', *American Journal of Political Science*, 39: 314–35.

Jennings, M. K. and Markus, G. B. (1984) 'Partisan Orientations over the Long Haul: Results from the Three-Wave Political Socialization Panel Study', *American Political Science Review*, 78, 4: 1000–18.

Johns, R. and Shephard, M. (2007) 'Gender, Candidate Image and Electoral Preference', *British Journal of Politics and International Relations*, 9, 3: 434–60.

Johnston, R. (1992) 'Party Identification Measures in the Anglo-American Democracies: A National Survey Experiment', *American Journal of Political Science*, 36, 2: 542–59.

Johnston, R. (1999) 'Business Cycles, Political Cycles and the Popularity of Canadian

Governments, 1974–1998', *Canadian Journal of Political Science/Revue canadienne de science politique*, 32, 3: 499–520.

Kanazawa, S. (1998) 'A Possible Solution to the Paradox of Voter Turnout', *Journal of Politics*, 60: 974–95.

Kang, W. (2004) 'Protest Voting and Abstention under Plurality Rule Elections: An Alternative Public Choice Approach', *Journal of Theoretical Politics*, 16: 79–102.

Kato, J. and Laver, M. (2003) 'Policy and Party Competition in Japan after the Election of 2000', *Japanese Journal of Political Science*, 4, 1: 121–33.

Katz, R. S. (1997) *Democracy and Elections* (New York, NY: Oxford University Press).

Katz, R. S. and Crotty, W. J. (2006) *Handbook of Party Politics* (London: Sage).

Katz, R. S. and Mair, P. (1995) 'Changing Models of Party Organization and Party Democracy: The Emergence of the Cartel Party', *Party Politics*: 5–28.

Kaufmann, K. M. (2002) 'Culture Wars, Secular Realignment, and the Gender Gap in Party Identification', *Political Behavior*, 24, 3: 283–307.

Kennedy, F., Lyons, P. and Fitzgerald, P. (2006) 'Pragmatists, Ideologues and the General Law of Curvilinear Disparity: The Case of the Irish Labour Party', *Political Studies*, 54, 4: 786–805.

Key, V. O. (1955) 'A Theory of Critical Elections', *Journal of Politics*, 17: 3–18.

Key, V. O. (1959) 'Secular Realignment and the Party System', *Journal of Politics*, 21, 2: 198–210.

Kim, H. and Fording, R. C. (1998) 'Voter Ideology in Western Democracies, 1946–1989', *European Journal of Political Research*, 33, 1: 73–97.

Kim, S. H., Scheufele, D. A. and Shanahan, J. (2005) 'Who Cares About the Issues? Issue Voting and the Role of News Media During the 2000 US Presidential Election', *Journal of Communication*, 55, 1: 103–21.

Kinder, D. R. (2003) 'Belief Systems After Converse', in M. B. MacKuen and G. Rabinowitz (eds), *Electoral Democracy* (Ann Arbor: University of Michigan Press): 13–47.

Kinder, D. R. (2006) 'Belief Systems Today', *Critical Review*, 18, 1: 197–216.

Kirchheimer, O. (1966) 'The Transformation of the Western European Party Systems', in J. LaPalombara and M. Weiner (eds), *Political Parties and Political Development* (Princeton: Princeton University Press): 177–200.

Kitschelt, H. (1989) 'The Internal Politics of Parties: The Law of Curvilinear Disparity Revisited', *Political Studies*, 37, 3: 400–21.

Kleinnijenhuis, J. A. N. and Ridder, J. de (1998) 'A Comparative Analysis of Media Effects during the 1994 Election Campaigns in Germany and the Netherlands', *European Journal of Political Research*, 33, 3: 413–37.

Klingemann, H. D., Hofferbert, R. and Budge, I. (1994) *Parties, Policies and Democracy* (Boulder, CO: Westview Press).

Klingemann, H. D. and Inglehart, R. (1976) 'Party Identification, Ideological Preference and the Left–Right Dimension Among Western Mass Public', in I. Budge, I. Crewe and D. Farlie (eds), *Party Identification and Beyond: Representations of Voting and Party Competition* (London: Wiley).

Knutsen, O. (1995) 'Value Orientations, Political Conflicts and Left–Right Identification: A Comparative Study', *European Journal of Political Research*, 28, 1: 63–93.

Knutsen, O. (2004) 'Religious Denomination and Party Choice in Western Europe: A Comparative Longitudinal Study from Eight Countries, 1970–97', *International Political Science Review/ Revue internationale de science politique*, 25, 1: 97–128.

Knutsen, O. (2006) *Class Voting in Western Europe: A Comparative Longitudinal Study* (Lanham: Lexington Books).

Kroh, M. (2003) 'Parties, Politicians and Policies: Orientations of Vote Choice Across Voters and Contexts', PhD thesis (Amsterdam, University of Amsterdam).

Kroh, M., Brug, W. van der and Eijk, C. van der (2007) 'Prospects for Electoral Change', in W. van der Brug and C. van der Eijk (eds), *European Elections and Domestic Politics: Lessons from the Past and Scenarios for the Future* (Notre Dame: University of Notre Dame Press): 209–25.

Krosnick, J. A. and Berent, M. K. (1993) 'Comparisons of Party Identification and Policy Preferences: The Impact of Survey Question Format', *American Journal of Political Science*, 37, 3: 941–64.

Laakso, M. and Taagepera, R. (1979) 'Effective Number of Parties: A Measure with Application to West Europe', *Comparative Political Studies*, 12: 3–27.

Laver, M. (1998) 'Models of Government Formation', *Annual Reviews in Political Science*, 1, 1: 1–25.

Laver, M. (2001) *Estimating the Policy Position of Political Actors* (New York: Routledge).

Laver, M., Benoit, K. and Garry, J. (2003) 'Extracting Policy Positions from Political Texts Using Words as Data', *American Political Science Review*, 97, 2: 311–31.

Laver, M., Benoit, K. and Sauger, N. (2006) 'Policy Competition in the 2002 French Legislative and Presidential Elections', *European Journal of Political Research*, 45, 4: 667–97.

Laver, M. and Mair, P. (1999) 'Party Policy and Cabinet Portfolios in the Netherlands, 1998: Results from an Expert Survey', *Acta Politica*, 34: 49–66.

Laver, M. and Schofield, N. (1990) *Multiparty Government: The Politics of Coalition in Europe* (Oxford: Oxford University Press).

Laver, M. and Schofield, N. (1998) *Multiparty Government: The Politics of Coalition in Europe*, 2nd edn (Ann Arbor: University of Michigan Press).

Laver, M. and Shepsle, K. A. (1996) *Making and Breaking Governments: Cabinets and Legislatures in Parliamentary Democracies* (Cambridge: Cambridge University Press).

Lavine, H. and Gschwend, T. (2006) 'Issues, Party and Character: The Moderating Role of Ideological Thinking on Candidate Evaluation', *British Journal of Political Science*, 37, 1: 139–63.

Lazarsfeld, P. F., Berelson, B. and Gaudet, H. (1944) *The People's Choice* (New York: Columbia University Press).

LeDuc, L. (2002) 'Opinion Change and Voting Behaviour in Referendums', *European Journal of Political Research*, 41, 6: 711–32.

LeDuc, L. (2003) *The Politics of Direct Democracy: Referendums in Global Perspective* (Toronto: Broadview Press).

LeDuc, L., Niemi, R. G. and Norris, P. (2002) *Comparing Democracies 2: New Challenges in the Study of Elections and Voting* (London: Sage).

Lehoucq, F. (2003) 'Electoral Fraud: Causes, Types, and Consequences', *Annual Reviews in Political Science*, 6, 1: 233–56.

Levitsky, S. and Way, L. (2002) 'The Rise of Competitive Authoritarianism', *Journal of Democracy*, 13: 51–65.

Lewis-Beck, M. S. (2000) *How France Votes* (New York: Chatham House Publishers).

Lewis-Beck, M. S., Norpoth, H., Jacoby, W. G., Weisberg, H. F. and Converse, P. E. (2008) *The American Voter Revisited* (Ann Arbor: University of Michigan Press).

Lewis-Beck, M. S. and Paldam, M. (2000) 'Economic Voting: An Introduction', *Electoral Studies*, 19, 2–3: 113–21.

Lijphart, A. (1968) *The Politics of Accommodation: Pluralism and Democracy in the Netherlands* (Berkeley: University of California Press).

Lijphart, A. (1990) 'The Political Consequences of Electoral Laws, 1945–85', *American Political Science Review*, 84, 2: 481–96.

Lijphart, A. (1991) 'Constitutional Choices for New Democracies', *Journal of Democracy*, 2, 1: 72–84.

Lijphart, A. (1995) *Electoral Systems and Party Systems: A Study of Twenty-Seven Democracies, 1945–1990* (Oxford: Oxford University Press).

Lijphart, A. (1997) 'Unequal Participation: Democracy's Unresolved Dilemma', *American Political Science Review*, 91, 1: 1–14.

Lijphart, A. (1999) *Patterns of Democracy: Government Forms and Performance in Thirty-Six Countries* (New Haven: Yale University Press).

Lijphart, A. (2004) 'Constitutional Design for Divided Societies', *Journal of Democracy*, 15, 2: 96–109.

Lijphart, A. and Grofman, B. (eds) (1984) *Choosing an Electoral System: Issues and Alternatives* (New York: Praeger).

Lijphart, A. and Waisman, C. H. (eds) (1996) *Institutional Design in New Democracies: Eastern Europe and Latin America* (Boulder, CO: Westview Press).

Linz, J. (1975) *Authoritarian Regimes* (São Paulo, Brazil: Departamento de Ciências Sociais, IFCH, Unicamp).

Lipset, S. M. and Rokkan, S. (1967) *Cleavage Structures, Party Systems and Voter Alignments: Cross-national Perspectives* (New York: Free Press).

Lodge, M., Steenbergen, M. R. and Brau, S. (1995) 'The Responsive Voter: Campaign Information and the Dynamics of Candidate Evaluation', *American Political Science Review*, 89, 2: 309–32.

Lubell, S. (1952) *The Future of American Politics* (New York: Harper & Brothers).

Luebbert, G. M. (1991) *Liberalism, Fascism, or Social Democracy: Social Classes and the Political Origins of Regimes in Interwar Europe* (Oxford: Oxford University Press).

Lupia, A. and McCubbins, M. D. (1998) *The Democratic Dilemma* (Cambridge: Cambridge University Press).

Lutz, D. S. (2006) *Principles of Constitutional Design* (Cambridge: Cambridge University Press).

Lyons, W. and Alexander, R. (2000) 'A Tale of Two Electorates: Generational Replacement and the Decline of Voting in Presidential Elections', *Journal of Politics*, 62, 4: 1014–34.

MacKuen, M. B., Erikson, R. S., Stimson, J. A. and Knight, K. (2003) 'Of Ideological Representation', in M. B. MacKuen and G. Rabinowitz (eds), *Electoral Democracy* (Ann Arbor: University of Michigan Press): 1–37.

Mair, P. (1997) *Party System Change: Approaches and Interpretations* (Oxford: Clarendon Press).

Mair, P. (2006) 'Party System Change', in R. S. Katz and W. J. Crotty (eds), *Handbook of Party Politics* (London: Sage): 63–73.

Maravall, J. (2008) 'The Political Consequences of Internal Party Democracy', in J. Maravall and I. Sanchez-Cuenca (eds), *Controlling Governments – Voters, Institutions and Accountability* (Cambridge: Cambridge University Press): 157–201.

Marks, G., Hooghe, L., Steenbergen, M. and Bakker, R. (2007) 'Crossvalidating Data on Party Positioning on European Integration: A Comparison of Manifesto and Expert Data', *Electoral Studies*, 26: 23–38.

Marks, G., Hooghe, L. and Wilson, C. (2002) 'Does Left/Right Structure Party Positions on European Integration?', *Comparative Political Studies*, 35: 965–89.

Marks, G. and Wilson, C. J. (2001) 'The Past in the Present: A Cleavage Theory of Party Response to European Integration', *British Journal of Political Science*, 30, 3: 433–59.

Marsh, M. (1998) 'Testing the Second-Order Election Model after Four European Elections', *British Journal of Political Science*, 28, 4: 591–607.

Marsh, M. (2000) 'Second-Order Elections', in R. Rose (ed.), *International Encyclopedia of Elections* (London: Macmillan).

Marsh, M. (2005) 'The Results of the 2004 European Parliament Elections and the Second-Order Model', *Die Europawahl 2004*.

Marsh, M. (2006a) 'Party Identification in Ireland: An Insecure Anchor for a Floating Party System', *Electoral Studies*, 25, 3: 489–508.

Marsh, M. (2006b) 'Stability and Change in Structure of Electoral Competition 1989–2002', in D. Payne, J. Garry and N. Hardiman (eds), *Irish Social and Political Attitudes* (Liverpool: Liverpool University Press): 94–111.

Marsh, M. (2007) 'Candidates or Parties? Objects of Electoral Choice in Ireland', *Party Politics*, 13, 4: 501–28.

Marsh, M. and Lutz, G. (2007) 'Introduction: Consequences of Low Turnout', *Electoral Studies*, 26, 3: 539–47.

Marsh, M. and Mikhaylov, S. (2009) 'European Parliament Elections as Second Order National Elections: A Review of the Evidence', *Living Reviews*. Forthcoming at http://europeangovernance.livingreviews.org

Marsh, M., Sinnott, R., Garry, J. and Kennedy, F. (2008) *The Irish Voter: The Nature of Electoral Competition in the Republic of Ireland* (Manchester: Manchester University Press).

Martin, L. W. and Stevenson, R. T. (2001) 'Government Formation in Parliamentary Democracies', *American Journal of Political Science*, 45, 1: 33–50.

Maslow, A. H. (1943) 'A Theory of Human Motivation', *Psychological Review*, 50, 1943: 370–96.

Mason, W. M. and Fienberg, S. E. (eds) (1985) *Cohort Analysis in Social Research: Beyond the Identification Problem* (New York: Springer-Verlag).

Massicotte, L. and Blais, A. (1999) 'Mixed Electoral Systems: A Conceptual and Empirical Survey', *Electoral Studies*, 18, 3: 341–66.

May, J. D. (1973) 'Opinion Structure of Political Parties: The Special Law of Curvilinear Disparity', *Political Studies*, 21: 135–51.

Mayhew, D. R. (2004) *Electoral Realignments: A Critique of an American Genre* (New Haven: Yale University Press).

Mayhew, D. R. (2005) *Divided We Govern: Party Control, Lawmaking and Investigations, 1946–2002* (New Haven, CT: Yale University Press).

McAllister, I. and Wattenberg, M. P. (1995) 'Measuring Levels of Party Identification: Does Question Order Matter?', *Public Opinion Quarterly*, 59, 2: 259–68.

McCombs, M. (2004) *Setting the Agenda: The Mass Media and Public Opinion* (Cambridge: Polity).

McDonald, M. P. and Popkin, S. L. (2002) 'The Myth of the Vanishing Voter', *American Political Science Review*, 95, 4: 963–74.

McElroy, G. and Benoit, K. (2007) 'Party Groups and Policy Positions in the European Parliament', *Party Politics*, 13, 1: 5–28.

McGraw, K. M., Hasecke, E. and Conger, K. (2003) 'Ambivalence, Uncertainty, and Processes of Candidate Evaluation', *Political Psychology*, 24, 3: 421–48.

Meguid, B. M. (2005) 'Competition Between Unequals: The Role of Mainstream Party Strategy in Niche Party Success', *American Political Science Review*, 99, 3: 347–59.

Meny, Y. and Surel, Y. (2002) *Democracies and the Populist Challenge* (London: Palgrave).

Mesquita, B.B. de (1979) 'Coalition Payoffs and Electoral Performance in European Democracies', *Comparative Political Studies*, 72: 61–81.

Merrill III, S. and Grofman, B. (1999) *A Unified Theory of Voting: Directional and Proximity Spatial Models* (Cambridge: Cambridge University Press).

Middendorp, C. P. (1989) 'Models for Predicting the Dutch Vote along the Left–Right and the Libertarianism–Authoritarianism Dimensions', *International Political Science Review/ Revue internationale de science politique*, 10, 4: 279–308.

Miller, W. (1976) 'The Cross-National Use of Party Identification as a Stimulus to Political Inquiry', in I. Budge, I. Crewe and D. Farlie (eds), *Party Identification and Beyond: Representations of Voting and Party Competition* (London: John Wiley & Sons): 21–32.

Miller, W. E. and Shanks, J. M. (1996) *The New American Voter* (Cambridge, MA: Harvard University Press).

Milner, H. (2002) *Civic Literacy: How Informed Citizens Make Democracy Work* (Hanover, NH: University Press of New England).

Morrison, H. (1954) *Government and Parliament: A Survey from the Inside* (Oxford: Oxford University Press).

Morton, R. B. and Williams, K. C. (2001) *Learning by Voting: Sequential Choices in Presidential Primaries and Other Elections* (Ann Arbor: University of Michigan Press).

Moser, R. G. (1999) 'Electoral Systems and the Number of Parties in Postcommunist States', *World Politics*, 51: 359–84.

Mulé, R. (1997) 'Developments Explaining the Party-Policy Link: Established Approaches and Theoretical Development', *Party Politics*, 3: 493–512.

Müller, W. C. and Strøm, K. (eds) (1999) *Policy, Office, or Votes? How Political Parties in Western Europe Make Hard Choices* (Cambridge: Cambridge University Press): 319.

Munck, G. L. and Verkuilen, J. (2002) 'Conceptualizing and Measuring Democracy: Evaluating Alternative Indices', *Comparative Political Studies*, 35, 1: 5–34.

Nadeau, R. and Blais, A. (1993) 'Accepting the Election Outcome: The Effect of Participation on Losers' Consent', *British Journal of Political Science*, 23, 4: 553–63.

Nannestad, P. and Paldam, M. (1994) 'The VP-function: A Survey of the Literature on Vote and Popularity Functions after 25 years', *Public Choice*, 79, 3: 213–45.

Nannestad, P. and Paldam, M. (1997) 'From the Pocketbook of the Welfare Man. A Pooled Cross-section Study of Economic Voting in Denmark, 1986–92', *British Journal of Political Science*, 27: 119–36.

Nannestad, P. and Paldam, M. (2002) 'The Cost of Ruling. A Foundation Stone for Two Theories', in H. Dorussen and M. Taylor (eds), *Economic Voting* (London: Routledge/EPR Studies in European Political Science): 17–44.

Narud, H. M. and Skare, A. (1999) 'Are Party Activists the Party Extremists? The Patterns of Opinion in Political Parties', *Scandinavian Political Studies*, 22, 1: 45–65.

Nevitte, N., Blais, A., Gidengil, E. and Nadeau, R. (2000) *Unsteady State: The 1997 Canadian Federal Election* (Oxford: Oxford University Press).

Newton, K. (1999) 'Mass Media Effects: Mobilization or Media Malaise?' *British Journal of Political Science*, 29, 4: 577–99.

Nie, N. H., Verba, S. and Petrocik, J. R. (1979) *The Changing American Voter*, 2nd edn (Cambridge, MA: Harvard University Press).

Niemi, R., Wright, S. and Powell, L. (1987) ' Multiple Party Identifiers and the Measurement of Party Identification' *Journal of Politics*, 49, 4: 1093–103.

Niemi, R., Whitten, G. and Franklin, M. (1992) 'Constituency Characteristics, Individual Characteristics and Tactical Voting in the 1987 British General Election', *British Journal of Political Science*, 22: 229–54.

Nieuwbeerta, P. and Graaf, N. D. de (1999) 'Traditional Class Voting in Twenty Postwar Societies', in G. Evans (ed.), *The End of Class Politics? Class Voting in Comparative Context* (Oxford: Oxford University Press): 23–58.

Norpoth, H. (1984) 'Economics, Politics, and the Cycle of Presidential Popularity', *Political Behavior*, 6, 3: 253–73.

Norris, P. (1995) 'May's Law of Curvilinear Disparity Revisited: Leaders, Officers, Members and Voters in British Political Parties', *Party Politics*, 1, 1: 29–47.

Norris, P. (1997) 'Choosing Electoral Systems: Proportional, Majoritarian and Mixed Systems', *International Political Science Review*, 18: 297–312.

Norris, P. (1999) 'Institutional Explanations for Political Support', in P. Norris (ed.), *Critical Citizens: Global Support for Democratic Government* (Oxford: Oxford University Press): 217–35.

Norris, P. (2000) *A Virtuous Circle: Political Communications in Postindustrial Societies* (Cambridge: Cambridge University Press).

Norris, P. (2004) *Electoral Engineering: Voting Rules and Political Behavior* (New York: Cambridge University Press).

Norris, P., Curtice, J., Sanders, D., Scammell, M. and Semetko, H. A. (1999) *On Message – Communicating the Campaign* (London: Sage).

Norris, P. and Franklin, M. (1997) 'Social Representation', *European Journal of Political Research*, 32, 2: 185–210.

Norris, P. and Inglehart, R. (2003) *Rising Tide: Gender Equality and Cultural Change Around the World* (New York: Cambridge University Press).

Norris, P. and Sanders, D. (2003) 'Message or Medium? Campaign Learning During the 2001 British General Election', *Political Communication*, 20, 3: 233–62.

Oppenhuis, E. V. (1995) 'Voting Behavior in Europe', PhD thesis (Amsterdam: Het Spinhuis).

Oppenhuis, E. V., Eijk, C. van der and Franklin, M. (1996) 'The Party Context: Outcomes', in C. van der Eijk and M. Franklin (eds), *Choosing Europe? The European Electorate and National Politics in the Face of Union* (Ann Arbor: University of Michigan Press): 287–305.

Ordeshook, P. C. and Zeng, L. (1997) 'Rational Voters and Strategic Voting: Evidence from the 1968, 1980 and 1992 Elections', *Journal of Theoretical Politics*, 9, 2: 167–87.

Ottati, V. C. and Deiger, M. (2002) 'Visual Cues and the Candidate Evaluation Process', in R. Ottati, S. Tindale, J. Edwards *et al.* (eds), *The Social Psychology of Politics* (New York: Kluwer Academic Publishers).

Patterson, T. (1989) 'The Press and Candidate Images', *International Journal of Public Opinion Research*, 1: 123–35.

Patterson, T. E. (2002) *The Vanishing Voter: Public Involvement in an Age of Uncertainty* (New York: Alfred A. Knopf).

Pennings, P. and Lane, J. E. (eds) (1998) *Comparing Party System Change* (London: Routledge).

Peter, J. (2007) 'Media Effects on Attitudes toward European Integration', in W. van der Brug and C. van der Eijk (eds), *European Elections and Domestic Politics* (Notre Dame, IN: University of Notre Dame Press): 131–44.

Phelps, E. (2004) 'Young Citizens and Changing Electoral Turnout, 1964–2001', *Political Quarterly*, 75, 3: 238–48.

Phelps, E. (2005) 'Young Voters at the 2005 British General Election', *Political Quarterly*, 76, 4: 482–87.

Piven, F. F. and Cloward, R. A. (2000) *Why Americans Still Don't Vote and Why Politicians Want it that Way* (Boston MA: Beacon Press).

Plutzer, E. (2002) 'Becoming a Habitual Voter: Inertia, Resources, and Growth in Young Adulthood', *American Political Science Review*, 96, 1: 41–56.

Poole, K. T. and Rosenthal, H. (1997) *Congress: A Political-Economic History of Roll Call Voting* (New York: Oxford University Press).

Powell, G. B. (1986) 'American Voter Turnout in Comparative Perspective', *American Political Science Review*, 80: 17–43.

Powell, G. B. (2000) *Elections as Instruments of Democracy* (New Haven, CT: Yale University Press).

Price, S. and Sanders, D. (1994) 'Economic Competence, Rational Expectations and Government Popularity in Post-War Britain', *The Manchester School*, 62: 296–312.

Proksch, S. O. and Slapin, J. B. (2006) 'Institutions and Coalition Formation: The German Election of 2005', *West European Politics*, 29, 3: 540–59.

Rabinowitz, G. and Macdonald, S. (1989) 'A Directional Theory of Issue Voting', *American Political Science Review*, 83, 93–121.

Rae, D. W. (1967) *The Political Consequences of Electoral Laws* (New Haven: Yale University Press).

Rahat, G. and Hazan, R. Y. (2005) 'Israel: the Politics of an Extreme Electoral System', in M. Gallagher and P. Mitchell (eds), *The Politics of Electoral Systems* (Oxford: Oxford University Press): 333–51.

Rahn, W. M., Brehm, J. and Carlson, N. (1999) 'National Elections as Institutions for Generating Social Capital', in T. Skocpol and M. P. Fiorina (eds), *Civic Engagement in American Democracy* (Washington, DC: Brookings Institution Press): 111–60.

Rallings, C. and Thrasher, M. (2007) *British Electoral Facts, 1832–2006* (Aldershot: Ashgate Publishing Limited).

Rasinski, K. A. (1987) 'What's Fair Is Fair – Or Is It? Value Differences Underlying Public Views about Social Justice', *Journal of Personality and Social Psychology*, 53: 201–11.

Reif, K. (1985) 'Ten Second-Order Elections', in K. Reif (ed.), *Ten European Elections* (Aldershot: Gower): 10–44.

Reif, K. and Schmitt, H. (1980) 'Nine National Second-Order Elections: A Conceptual Framework for the Analysis of European Election Results', *European Journal of Political Research*, 8: 3–44.

Reynolds, A. (2002) *The Architecture of Democracy: Constitutional Design, Conflict Management, and Democracy* (Oxford: Oxford University Press).

Reynolds, A., Reilly, B., Ellis, A. and Cheibub, J. A. (2005) *Electoral System Design: The New International IDEA Handbook* (Stockholm: International Institute for Democracy and Electoral Assistance).

Riker, W. H. (1962) *The Theory of Political Coalitions* (New Haven: Yale University Press).

Riker, W. H. and Ordeshook, P. (1968) 'A Theory of the Calculus of Voting ', *American Political Science Review*, 62, 1: 25–42.

Rokkan, S. (1970) *Citizens, Elections, Parties: Approaches to the Comparative Study of the Processes of Development* (Oslo: Universitetsforlaget).

Roller, E. (2001) 'The March 2000 General Election in Spain', *Government and Opposition*, 36, 2: 209–29.

Rose, R. (1974) *Electoral Behavior: A Comparative Handbook* (New York: Free Press).

Rose, R. (ed.) (1980) *Electoral Participation: A Comparative Analysis* (London and Beverly Hills: Sage Publications).

Rose, R. and Munro, N. (2002) *Elections without Order: Russia's Challenge to Vladimir Putin* (New York: Cambridge University Press).

Rose, R. and Urwin, D. W. (1969) 'Social Cohesion, Political Parties and Strains in Regimes', *Comparative Political Studies*, 2: 7–67.

Rose, R. and Urwin, D. W. (1970) 'Persistence and Change in Western Party Systems since 1945', *Political Studies*, 18: 287–319.

Rosema, M. (2006) 'Partisanship, Candidate Evaluations, and Prospective Voting', *Electoral Studies*, 25, 3: 467–88.

Rosenof, T. (2003) *Realignment: The Theory That Changed the Way We Think About American Politics* (Lanham, MD: Rowman & Littlefield Publishers).

Rubenson, D., Blais, A., Fournier, P., Gidengil, E. and Nevitte, N. (2004) 'Accounting for the Age Gap in Turnout', *Acta Politica*, 39: 407–21.

Rule, W. and Zimmerman, J. F. (1994) *Electoral Systems in Comparative Perspective: Their Impact on Women and Minorities* (Westport: Greenwood Press).

Sanders, D. (2003) 'Party Identification, Economic Perceptions, and Voting in British General Elections, 1974–97', *Electoral Studies*, 22, 2: 239–63.

Sapiro, V. (2004) 'Not Your Parents' Political Socialization: Introduction for a New Generation', *Annual Review of Political Science*, 7, 1: 1–23.

Saris, W. E. and Sniderman, P. M. (2004) *Studies in Public Opinion: Attitudes, Nonattitudes, Measurement Error, and Change* (Princeton, NJ: Princeton University Press).

Särlvik, B. and Crewe, I. (1983) *Decade of Dealignment: The Conservative Victory of 1979 and Electoral Trends in the 1970s* (Cambridge: Cambridge University Press).

Sartori, G. (1994) *Comparative Constitutional Engineering: An Inquiry into Structures, Incentives, and Outcomes* (New York: New York University Press).

Sartori, G. (1997) *Comparative Constitutional Engineering: An Inquiry into Structures, Incentives, and Outcomes*, 2nd edn (New York: New York University Press).

Sartori, G. (2005 [1976]) *Parties and Party Systems. A Framework for Analysis* (Thousand Oaks, CA: Sage).

Scappini, E. (2006) 'The Estimable Functions of Age, Period and Generation Effects: A Political Application', *Quality and Quantity*, 40, 5: 759–81.

Scarrow, S. E. (2006) 'Party Subsidies and the Freezing of Party Competition: Do Cartel Mechanisms Work?', *West European Politics*, 29: 619–39.

Schattschneider, E. E. (1960) *The Semi-Sovereign People: A Realist's View of Democracy in America* (New York: Holt Rinehart & Winston).

Schedler, A. (2006) *Electoral Authoritarianism: The Dynamics of Unfree Competition* (Boulder: Lynne Rienner Publishers).

Schmitt, H. (1996) 'Germany. A Bored Electorate', in C. van der Eijk and M. Franklin (eds), *Choosing Europe? The European Electorate and National Politics in the Face of Union* (Ann Arbor: Michigan University Press): 137–56.

Schmitt, H. (2000) 'Multiple Party Identifications', XVIIIth World Congress of Political Science, Quebec City.

Schmitt, H. and Thomassen, J. J. A. (eds) (1999) *Political Representation and Legitimacy in the European Union* (Oxford: Oxford University Press).

Schoen, H. (2005) 'Candidate Orientations in Election Campaign: An Analysis of the German Federal Election Campaigns from 1980 to 1998', *World Political Science Review*, 1, 1: Article 2.

Schoen, H. (2007) 'Campaigns, Candidate Evaluations, and Vote Choice: Evidence from German Federal Election Campaigns, 1980–2002', *Electoral Studies*, 26, 2: 324–37.

Schofield, N., Martin, A. D., Quinn, K. M. and Whitford, A. B. (1998) 'Multiparty Electoral Competition in the Netherlands and Germany: A Model based on Multinomial Probit', *Public Choice*, 97, 3: 257–93.

Schofield, N., Miller, G. and Martin, A. (2003) 'Critical Elections and Political Realignments in the USA: 1960–2000', *Political Studies*, 51: 217–40.

Schuessler, A. (2000) 'Expressive Voting', *Rationality and Society*, 12: 87–119.

Schumpeter, J. A. (1942) *Capitalism, Socialism and Democracy* (New York: Harper & Row).

Sears, D. O. (1975) 'Political Socialization', in F. I. Greenstein and N. W. Polsby (eds),

Handbook of Political Science: Volume 2 Micropolitical Theory (Reading, MA: Addison Wesley): 93–153.

Shachar, R. (2003) 'Party Loyalty as Habit Formation', *Journal of Applied Econometrics*, 18, 3: 251–69.

Shafer, B. E. (1991) *The End of Realignment? Interpreting American Electoral Eras* (Wisconsin: University of Wisconsin Press).

Shamir, B. (1994) 'Ideological Position, Leaders' Charisma, and Voting Preferences: Personal vs. Partisan Elections', *Political Behavior*, 16, 2: 265–87.

Shamir, M. and Arian, A. (1999) 'Collective Identity and Electoral Competition in Israel', *American Political Science Review*, 93: 265–78.

Shaw, D. R. (1999) 'The Impact of News Media Favorability and Candidate Events in Presidential Campaigns', *Political Communication*, 16, 2: 183–202.

Shephard, M. and Johns, R. (2008) 'Candidate Image and Electoral Preference in Britain', *British Politics*, 3, 3: 324–49.

Silverman, L. (1985) 'The Ideological Mediation of Party-political Responses to Social Change', *European Journal of Political Research*, 13, 1: 69–93.

Sitter, N. (2002) 'Cleavages, Party Strategy and Party System Change in Europe, East and West', *Perspectives on European Politics and Society*, 3, 3: 425–51.

Siune, K. and Svensson, P. (1993) 'The Danes and the Maastricht Treaty: The Danish EC Referendum of June 1992', *Electoral Studies*, 12, 2: 99–111.

Sniderman, P. M. (1993) 'The New Look in Public Opinion Research', in A. Finifter (ed.), *Political Science: The State of the Discipline II* (Washington: American Political Science Association): 219–43.

Soroka, S. N. (2002) 'Issue Attributes and Agenda-Setting by Media, the Public, and Policymakers in Canada', *International Journal of Public Opinion Research*, 14, 3: 264–85.

Soroka, S. N. and Wlezien, C. (2009) *Degrees of Democracy: Politics, Public Opinion and Policy* (Cambridge: Cambridge University Press).

Southwell, P. L. and Everest, M. J. (1998) 'The Electoral Consequences of Alienation: Nonvoting and Protest Voting in the 1992 Presidential Race', *Social Science Journal*, 35, 1: 43–51.

Spanje, J. van (2009) 'Pariah Parties – on the Origins and Electoral Consequences of the Ostracism of Political Parties in Established Democracies', PhD thesis (European University Institute, Florence).

Steenbergen, M. R. and Lodge, M. (2003) 'Process Matters: Cognitive Models of Candidate Evaluation', in M. B. MacKuen and G. Rabinowitz (eds), *Electoral Democracy* (Ann Arbor: University of Michigan Press).

Steenbergen, M. R. and Scott, D. J. (2004) 'Contesting Europe? The Salience of European Integration as a Party Issue', in G. Marks and M. R. Steenbergen (eds), *European Integration and Political Conflict* (Cambridge: Cambridge University Press).

Stevenson, R. T. (2002) 'The Economy as Context: Indirect Links between the Economy and Voters', in H. Dorussen and M. Taylor (eds), *Economic Voting* (London: Routledge): 45–65.

Stimson, J. A. (1999) *Public Opinion in America: Moods, Cycles and Swings*, 2nd edn (Boulder, CO: Westview Press).

Stokes, D. E. (1963) 'Spatial Models of Party Competition', *American Political Science Review*, 57: 368–77.

Stokes, D. E. (1966) 'Some Dynamic Elements of Contests for the Presidency', *American Political Science Review*, 60: 19–38.

Stonecash, J. M. (2006) *Political Parties Matter: Realignment and the Return of Partisan Voting* (Boulder, CO: Lynne Rienner).

Strøm, K. (1990) *Minority Government and Majority Rule* (Cambridge, UK/New York: Cambridge University Press).

Strøm, K. (2000) 'Delegation and Accountability in Parliamentary Democracies', *European Journal of Political Research*, 37: 261–89.

Stroud, L. R., Glaser, J. and Salovey, P. (2005) 'The Effects of Partisanship and Candidate Emotionality on Voter Preference', *Imagination, Cognition and Personality*, 25, 1: 25–44.

Sundquist, J. L. (1983) *Dynamics of the Party System: Alignment and Realignment of Political Parties in the United States* (Washington: Brookings Institution Press).

Svensson, P. (2002) ' Five Danish referendums on the European Community and European Union: A Critical Assessment of the Franklin Thesis', *European Journal of Political Research*, 41: 733–50.

Swaan, A. de (1973) *Coalition Theory and Cabinet Formations* (Amsterdam: Elsevier).

Taagepera, R. (1997) 'Effective Number of Parties for Incomplete Data', *Electoral Studies*, 16, 2: 145–51.

Taagepera, R. (1998) 'How Electoral Systems Matter for Democratization', *Democratization*, 5, 3: 68–91.

Taagepera, R. (1999) 'Supplementing the Effective Number of Parties', *Electoral Studies*, 18, 4: 497–504.

Taagepera, R. (2002) 'Implications of the Effective Number of Parties for Cabinet Formation', *Party Politics*, 8, 2: 227–36.

Tavits, M. (2006) 'Party System Change: Testing a Model of New Party Entry', *Party Politics*, 12, 1: 99.

Thomassen, J. (2000) 'From Comparable to Comparative Electoral Research', in J. van Deth, H. Rattinger and E. Roller (eds), *Die Republik auf dem Weg zur Normalität?* (Opladen: Leske en Budrich).

Thomassen, J. (ed.) (2005) *The European Voter* (Oxford: Oxford University Press).

Thomassen, J. (ed.) (2009) *The Legitimacy of the European Union after Enlargement* (Oxford: Oxford University Press).

Thomassen, J. J. A., Aarts, K. and Kolk, H. van der (eds) (2000) *Politieke Veranderingen in Nederland 1971–1998: Kiezers en de smalle marges van de politiek* (Den Haag: Sdu).

Thompson, D. F. (2004) *Just Elections: Creating a Fair Electoral Process in the United States* (Chicago: University of Chicago Press).

Thomson, R. (1999) 'The Party Mandate – Election Pledges and Government Actions in the Netherlands, 1986–1998', PhD thesis (Groningen: Rijksuniversiteit Groningen).

Tilley, J. (2006) 'Party Identification in Britain: Does Length of Time in the Electorate Affect Strength of Partisanship?', *British Journal of Political Science*, 33: 332–44.

Tillie, J. (1995) *Party Utility and Voting Behaviour* (Amsterdam: Het Spinhuis).

Tingsten, H. L. G. (1963 [1937]) *Political Behavior: Studies in Election Statistics* (Totowa, NJ: Bedminster Press).

Tuckel, P. S. and Tejera, F. (1983) 'Changing Patterns in American Voting Behaviour, 1914–1980', *Public Opinion Quarterly*, 47: 143–202.

Tufte, E. R. (1975) 'Determinants of the Outcomes of Midterm Congressional Elections', *American Political Science Review*, 69, 3: 812–26.

Urquizu-Sancho, I. (2008) 'Economic Openness and Accountability: Who is Responsible?', Paper presented at American Political Science Association 2008, Boston.

Veiga, G. and Fonseca, L. R. (1998) 'Popularity Functions for the Portuguese Prime Minister, Government, Parliament and President', *European Journal of Political Research*, 33, 3: 347–61.

Verba, S., Nie, N. H. and Kim, J. (1987) *Participation and Political Equality: A Seven-Nation Comparison* (Chicago: University of Chicago Press).

Volkens, A. (2001) 'Manifesto Research since 1979', in M. Laver (ed.), *Estimating the Policy Position of Political Actors* (London and New York: Routledge): 33–49.

Voogt, R. J. J. and Saris, W. E. (2003) 'To Participate or Not to Participate: The Link Between Survey Participation, Electoral Participation, and Political Interest ', *Political Analysis*, 11, 2: 164–79.

Vreese, C. H. de, Banducci, S. A., Semetko, H. A. and Boomgaarden, H. G. (2006) 'The News Coverage of the 2004 European Parliamentary Election Campaign in 25 Countries', *European Union Politics*, 7, 4: 477–504.

Vreese, C. H. de and Semetko, H. A. (2004) *Political Campaigning in Referendums: Framing the Referendum Issue* (London: Routledge).

Walle, N. van der (2002) 'Elections without Democracy: Africa's Range of Regimes', *Journal of Democracy*, 13: 66–79.

Ware, A. (1992) 'Activist-Leader Relations and the Structure of Political Parties: "Exchange" Models and Vote-Seeking Behaviour in Parties', *British Journal of Political Science*, 22, 1: 71–92.

Wass, H. (2007) 'The Effects of Age, Generation and Period on Turnout in Finland 1975–2003', *Electoral Studies*, 26, 3: 648–59.

Wattenberg, M. P. (1998) 'Turnout Decline in the US and other Advanced Industrial Democracies', Paper 98-08, Center for the Study of Democracy (http://repositories.cdlib.org/csd/98-08).

Wayman, F. (1996) 'Staying the Course: A Five-Wave Panel Study of Realignment, 1974–1984', Annual Meeting of the American Political Science Association, San Francisco.

Webb, P. (2002) 'Parties and Party Systems: More Continuity than Change', *Parliamentary Affairs*, 55: 363–76.

Webb, P., Farrell, D. M. and Holliday, I. (eds) (2002) *Political Parties in Advanced Industrial Democracies* (Oxford: Oxford University Press).

Weisberg, H. F. (1980) 'A Multidimensional Conceptualization of Party Identification', *Political Behavior*, 2, 1: 33–60.

Weisberg, H. F. (1988) 'Measuring Change in Party Identification in an Election Campaign', *American Journal of Political Science*, 32: 996–1017.

Weisberg, H. F. and Greene, S. (2003) 'The Political Psychology of Party Identification', in M. B. MacKuen and G. Rabinowitz (eds), *Electoral Democracy* (Ann Arbor: University of Michigan Press): 83–124.

Weldon, S. (2008) 'Failure to Converge: Dominant Factions and Party Behaviour', Midwest Political Science Association Annual National Conference, Chicago.

Wessels, B. and Schmitt, H. (2008) 'Meaningful Choices, Political Supply and Institutional Effectiveness', *Electoral Studies*, 27: 19–30.

Whiteley, P. (1995) 'Rational Choice and Political Participation – Evaluating the Debate', *Political Research Quarterly*, 48, 1: 211–33.

Whiteley, P., Stewart, M. C., Sanders, D. and Clarke, H. D. (2005) 'The Issue Agenda and Voting in 2005', *Parliamentary Affairs*, 58, 4: 802–17.

Widfeldt, A. (2007) 'The Swedish Parliamentary Election of 2006', *Electoral Studies*, 26, 4: 820–3.

Wilson, A. (2005) *Virtual Politics: Faking Democracy in the Post-Soviet World* (New Haven: Yale University Press).

Wittman, D. (1983) 'Candidate Motivation: A Synthesis of Alternative Theories', *American Political Science Review*, 77, 1: 142–57.

Wlezien, C. (1995) 'The Public as Thermostat: Dynamics of Preferences for Spending', *American Journal of Political Science*, 39: 981–1000.

Wlezien, C. (1996) 'Dynamics of Representation: The Case of US Spending on Defence', *British Journal of Political Science*, 26: 1–24.

Woldendorp, J. Keman, H. and Budge, I. (2000) *Party Government in 48 Democracies (1945–1998): Composition–Duration–Personnel* (Dordrecht: Kluwer).

Wolinetz, S. B. (1988) 'The Netherlands: Continuity and Change in a Fragmented Party System', in S. B. Wolinetz (ed.), *Parties and Party Systems in Liberal Democracies* (London: Routledge): 130–58.

Wood, W., Quinn, J. M. and Kashy, D. A. (2002) 'Habits in Everyday Life: Thought, Emotion, and Action', *Journal of Personality and Social Psychology*, 83, 6: 1281–97.

Wood, W., Tam, L. and Witt, M. G. (2005) 'Changing Circumstances, Disrupting Habits', *Journal of Personality and Social Psychology*, 88, 6: 918.

Zakaria, F. (2003) *The Future of Democracy: Illiberal Democracy at Home and Abroad* (New York: WW Norton).

Zaller, J. (2002) 'The Statistical Power of Election Studies to Detect Media Exposure Effects in Political Campaigns', *Electoral Studies*, 21, 2: 297–329.

Zaslavsky, V. and Brym, R. J. (1978) 'The Functions of Elections in the USSR', *Soviet Studies*, 30, 3: 362–71.

Zielonka-Goei, M. L. (1992) 'Members Marginalising Themselves? Intra-party Participation in the Netherlands', *West European Politics*, 15, 2: 93–106.

Author Index

Subject Index